PERL
by
E x a m p l e
Second Edition

Ellie Quigley

To join a Prentice Hall PTR Internet
mailing list, point to:
http://www.prenhall.com/mail_lists/

Prentice Hall PTR
Upper Saddle River, NJ 07458

ISBN 0-13-655689-2

90000

9 780136 556893

Library of Congress Cataloging-in-Publication Data

Quigley, Ellie.
    Perl by Example / by Ellie Quigley.

      p.   cm.

    Includes index.
    ISBN 0-13-655689-2 (pbk. : alk. paper)
    1. Perl (Computer program language)   I. Title.

  QA76.73.P47Q54   1997
  005.13'3--dc21

                            97-30316
                               CIP

Editorial/production supervision: *Patti Guerrieri*
Cover design director: *Jerry Votta*
Cover designer: *TommyBoy Graphics*
Manufacturing manager: *Alexis R. Heydt*
Marketing manager: *Dan Rush*
Acquisitions editor: *Mark L. Taub*
Editorial assistant: *Tara Ruggiero*

 ©1998 by Prentice Hall PTR
Prentice-Hall Inc.
A Simon & Schuster Company
Upper Saddle River, NJ 07458

Prentice Hall books are widely used by corporations and government agencies
for training, marketing, and resale.

The publisher offers discounts on this book when ordered in bulk quantities.
For more information, contact: Corporate Sales Department, Phone: 800-382-3419;
Fax: 201-236-7141; E-mail: corpsales@prenhall.com; or write: Prentice Hall PTR,
Corp. Sales Dept., One Lake Street, Upper Saddle River, NJ 07458.

UNIX is a registered trademark of UNIX System Laboratories, Inc. SunOs is a registered trademark of Sun
Microsystems, Inc. All other products or services mentioned in this book are the trademarks or service marks
of their respective companies or organizations.

Printed in the United States of America
10 9 8 7 6

ISBN 0-13-655689-2

Prentice-Hall International (UK) Limited, *London*
Prentice-Hall of Australia Pty. Limited, *Sydney*
Prentice-Hall Canada Inc., *Toronto*
Prentice-Hall Hispanoamericana, S.A., *Mexico*
Prentice-Hall of India Private Limited, *New Delhi*
Prentice-Hall of Japan, Inc., *Tokyo*
Simon & Schuster Asia Pte. Ltd., *Singapore*
Editora Prentice-Hall do Brasil, Ltda., *Rio de Janeiro*

Dedication

*This book is dedicated to Guy Sterling Quigley,
my late husband, best friend, and business partner,
who initiated the Perl book contract with Prentice Hall,
and gave me the confidence in myself to tackle this project.*

*He was behind me every page of the way
and continues to stand by me
even after his untimely departure
from this world on Christmas Eve, 1993.*

Table of Contents

Preface

A picture is worth a th~~ousand words, and so is~~ a good example. *Perl by Example* is organized to
te~~ach~~ ... P ... :omplete succinct programs. Each line of a script
_____ ghlighted. The output of the program is then dis-
_____ numbers. Following the output is a separate expla-
_____ ɔles are small and to the point for the topic at hand.
_____ student guide to Perl, the topics are modularized.
_____ ninimum of forward referencing and a logical pro-

_____ de, but a complete guide to Perl. It covers many
_____ ion handling, to formatting reports, to interprocess
_____ , in the process, a lot about UNIX. Although some
_____ arning path, it is not assumed that you are a guru.
_____ l programs can greatly profit from this text. Topics
_____ are designed to save the time it takes to figure out
_____ d, and the correct syntax, etc. Now, in this second
_____ added, and since Perl is the standard for writing
_____ ɔ get you started writing your own dynamic Web

_____ g strings, arrays, the system interface, networking,
_____ ictions work, background information concerning
_____ ore demonstrating sample programs that function.
_____ nual pages and other UNIX books to understand
_____ what the function actually does.
_____ inctions and definitions, command line switches,
_____ lators and sample scripts, including a fully func-
~~tional, annotated Perl program using lamperr~~ and interfacing with a database application.

I have been teaching now for the past 30 years and am committed to understanding how people
learn. Having taught Perl now for over a year, I find that many new Perlers get frustrated when trying to teach themselves how to program in Perl. I, too, experienced frustration when first tackling
Perl. So I wrote a book to help myself learn and to help my students, and now to help you. In my
book you will not only learn Perl, you will also save yourself a great deal of time.

Acknowledgments

I would like to send a special appreciation to Mark Houser, a system administration instructor for Remedy Corporation. Mark, with an MS in computer science, enjoys "extending his systems beyond the ordinary" with tools like Perl. He has always been there to answer questions, and he donated his taintperl database application in Appendix B. Mark's email address is mark.houser@EBay.Sun.COM.

I also owe a great deal to Deac Lancaster, a true scholar, co-worker, and good friend. While working for Sun Education, Deac spent many an evening after a long teaching day to guide me patiently through the workings of sockets, message queues, and semaphores. He loaned me his demo C programs, and together we re-wrote them in Perl for this book. Deac is now teaching at Remedy Corporation. Thanks, Deac!

John Nouveaux, from Nouveaux Consulting, Santa Rosa, California, has also contributed a number of his Perl programs for the Appendix B in this book. John, an expert network programmer and system administrator, is a consultant and a dynamic teacher, specializing in connectivity issues using tcp/ip and the Internet.

Thanks also to Steve Hanson for his system administration work and to George Williams for compiling the CD-ROM and setting up the Web server.

Richard Evans, from Sun Microsystems, volunteered his time to test the examples in this book and offered helpful suggestions on how to improve them. Thank you, Richard.

Of course, appreciation to my editors, Mark Taub and Patti Guerrieri, for teaching me about the book business and patiently awaiting overdue chapters and correction pages. And to Roberta Harvey, from RAH Consulting, for her technical review and valuable criticism.

Thanks to Perl pioneers Larry Wall and Randal L. Schwartz, authors of the following books: *Learning Perl* by Randal L. Schwartz and *Perl Programming* by Larry Wall and Randal L. Schwartz.

And last, but not least, a huge thanks to all of my students out there who helped me learn Perl and kept it fun.

About the Author

Ellie Quigley is president of Learning Enterprises, LE, a small training/consulting company specializing in teaching UNIX related subjects and writing customized classes for on-site training. The original version of *Perl by Example* was designed as a Perl Programming class for the University of California, Extension, Santa Cruz, complete with training guide and exercises. Due to the success of the class, this book evolved. She has also authored *UNIX Shells by Example*, published by Prentice Hall in 1995. Any comments or questions can be forwarded to Ellie Quigley at Learning Enterprises by e-mail: shellieq@netcom.com.

1

The Practical Extraction
Report Language

1.1   What Is Perl?

Perl officially stands for "The Practical Extraction Report Language," but according to Larry Wall, the creator of Perl, those who love it refer to Perl as the "Pathologically Eclectic Rubbish Lister." Perl is really much more than a practical reporting language or eclectic rubbish lister. It's practically everything really likeable about the *Shells*, *awk*, *sed*, *grep*, and *C* combined.

Perl, a GNU product (i.e., it's free!!), is an interpreted language. It is used primarily as a scripting language and runs on a number of platforms. Although designed for the UNIX® operating system, Perl is renowned for its portability and also runs on DOS, Windows NT™, Macintosh, etc. The examples in this book were created on a UNIX system, running SunOs® 4.1.2, SunOs 5.5.1, and Linux.

Perl scripts are functionally similar to Unix *awk*, *sed*, *Shell* scripts, and *C* programs. *Shell* scripts consist primarily of Unix commands; Perl scripts do not.   Whereas *sed* and *awk* are used to edit and report on files, Perl does not require a file in order to function. Whereas *C* has none of the pattern matching and wild-card metacharacters of the *shells*, *sed,* and *awk*, Perl has an extended set. Perl was originally written to manipulate text in files, extract data from files, and write reports, but through continued development, it can also manipulate files, processes, and perform many networking tasks.

1.2   Who Uses Perl?

Because Perl has built-in functions for easy manipulation of processes and files, and because Perl is portable (i.e., can run on a number of different platforms), it is especially popular with system administrators who often oversee one or more systems. Due to the phenomenal growth of the World Wide Web and the ability for anyone to create WEB pages, Perl has become the most popular language for writing scripts (called CGI scripts) to generate dynamic pages for processing forms. Perl is also drawing the attention of programmers, database administrators, and simply curious users who like to keep up with the times.

Anyone can use Perl, but it is easier to learn if you are already experienced in writing Shell scripts or C programs. For these people, the migration to Perl will be relatively easy. For those who do not program in C or any of the Shells, the path may be a little steeper, but after learning Perl, there may be no reason to ever use anything else. If you understand Perl, the Unix shells and the C language will probably be a lot easier for you to learn.

If you are familiar with the UNIX utilities such as *grep*, *awk*, *sed*, and *tr*, you know that they don't share the same syntax; the options and arguments are handled differently, and the rules change from one utility to the other. If you are a Shell programmer, you usually go through the grueling task of learning a variety of utilities, shell metacharacters, regular expression metacharacters, quotes, and more quotes, etc. But Shell programs are limited and slow. To perform more complex mathematical tasks, interprocess communication, and handle binary data, for example, you may have to turn to a higher level language such as C. If you know C, you also know that searching for patterns in files, and interfacing with the operating system to process files and execute commands, are not always easy tasks.

Perl integrates the best features of Shell programming, C, and the UNIX utilities, *awk*, *grep*, *sed*, and *tr*. Because it is fast and not limited to arbitrary sized chunks of data, many system administrators and database administrators are switching from the traditional Shell scripting to Perl. C++ programmers can enjoy the object-oriented features added in Perl 5, including the ability to create reusable, extensible modules. Now Perl can be generated in other languages and other languages can be embedded in Perl.

You don't have to know everything about Perl to start writing scripts. This book will help you get a good jump-start on Perl, and you will see quickly some of its many capabilities and advantages. Then you can decide how far you want to go with Perl. But if nothing else, I think you'll find that Perl is fun!

1.3   Which Perl?

Perl has been through a number of revisions. There are two distinct versions of Perl: Perl 4 and Perl 5. The last version of Perl 4 was Perl 4, patchlevel 36 (Perl 4.036).[1] Perl 5.000, introduced in the fall of 1994, was a complete re-write of the Perl source code which optimized the language and introduced objects and many other features, but is highly compatible with the previous releases. Examples in this book have been tested using both versions, and where there are differences, they will be noted. The current version of Perl (as of this writing) is 5.004.

---

1. I tested the examples in this book using Perl 4 and Perl 5 with a number of different patch levels. There are some slight differences in how the programs run using different versions and patch levels.

1.4   Where to Get Perl

Perl is available from a number of sources, including the Internet, E-mail, UUCP, and UUNET. There are a number of Web sites and ftp sites. The primary source for Perl distribution is CPAN, the Comprehensive Perl Archive Network. (Simply search for CPAN in your browser for full details.) Although the master CPAN site is at FUNET, the Finnish University NETwork, the largest U.S. repository for Perl information is at the University of Florida at *ftp.cis.ufl.edu* in a directory called */pub/perl*. If you have access to USENET, the *comp.lang.perl.misc* newsgroup, a newsgroup exclusively devoted to Perl, has published a five-part article entitled *perl-faq*, maintained by Tom Christiansen and Stephen Potter, which is archived on *ftp.cis.ufl.edu* [128.227.100.198] in */pub/perl/doc/FAQ*. Parts 1, 2, and 3 consist of general information, where to get Perl and programming tips, and parts 4 and 5 contain more technical answers to specific programming questions.

If you are looking for information about Perl on the World Wide Web, there are two excellent URLs you can start with: *http://www.metronet.com/perlinfo/perl5.html* and *http://www.perl.com*. These sites will link you to other sites ad infinitum. There is so much material about Perl out there, it's impossible to see it all.

1.4.1   What Version Do I Have?

To obtain your Perl version and patch information and some copyright information, type the following line (the dollar sign is the Shell prompt):

E x a m p l e   1 . 1

```
$ perl –v
This is perl, version 5.003 with EMBED
    built under solaris at Sep 16 1996 15:33:37
    + suidperl security patch

Copyright 1987-1996, Larry Wall

Perl may be copied only under the terms of either the Artistic License or the
GNU General Public License, which may be found in the Perl 5.0 source kit
```

1 This is perl, version 5.003 with EMBED
       built under solaris at Sep 16 1996 15:33:37
       + suidperl security patch

2 Copyright 1987-1996, Larry Wall

3 Perl may be copied only under the terms of either the Artistic License or the GNU General Public License, which may be found in the Perl 5.0 source kit.

Explanation

1 This version of Perl is 5.003.
2 Larry Wall, the author of Perl, owns the copyright.
3 Perl may be copied under the terms specified by the Artistic License or GNU.
   Perl is distributed under GNU, the Free Software Foundation, meaning that Perl is free.

2

Perl Scripts

2.1   Perl at the Command Line

Although most of your work with Perl will be done in scripts, Perl can also be executed at the command line for simple tasks such as testing a simple function, a print statement, or simply testing Perl syntax. Perl has a number of command line switches, also called command line options, to control or modify its behavior. The switches listed below are not a complete list (see Appendix A), but will demonstrate a little about Perl syntax at the command line.

2.1.1   The –e Switch

The **–e switch** allows Perl to execute Perl statements at the command line instead of from a script.

Example 2.1

```
1 $ perl –e 'print "hello dolly\n";'
  hello dolly
```

Explanation

1   Perl prints the string "hello dolly" to the screen followed by a new line (\n). The dollar sign ($) is the *shell* prompt.

5

2.1.2   The –n Switch

If you need to print the contents of a file or search for a line if it contains a particular pattern, the *–n* switch is used to implicitly loop through the file one line at a time. Like *sed* and *awk*, Perl uses powerful pattern-matching techniques for finding patterns in text. Only specified lines from the file are printed when Perl is invoked with the *–n* switch.

E x a m p l e   2 . 2

(The text file)
1 **$ cat emp.first**
   Igor Chevsky:6/23/83:W:59870:25:35500:2005.50
   Nancy Conrad:6/18/88:SE:23556:5:15000:2500
   Jon DeLoar:3/28/85:SW:39673:13:22500:12345.75
   Archie Main:7/25/90:SW:39673:21:34500:34500.50
   Betty Bumble:11/3/89:NE:04530:17:18200:1200.75

2 **$ perl –ne 'print' emp.first**
   Igor Chevsky:6/23/83:W:59870:25:35500:2005.50
   Nancy Conrad:6/18/88:SE:23556:5:15000:2500
   Jon DeLoar:3/28/85:SW:39673:13:22500:12345.75
   Archie Main:7/25/90:SW:39673:21:34500:34500.50
   Betty Bumble:11/3/89:NE:04530:17:18200:1200.75

3 **$ perl –ne 'print if /^Igor/' emp.first**
   Igor Chevsky:6/23/83:W:59870:25:35500:2005.50

E x p l a n a t i o n

1 The text file *emp.first* is printed to the screen. Perl uses this filename as a command line argument.
2 Perl prints all the lines in the file *emp.first* by implicitly looping through the file one line at a time.
3 Perl uses *regular expression* metacharacters to specify what patterns will be matched. The pattern, *Igor*, is placed within forward slashes and preceded by a caret (^). The caret is called a beginning of line anchor. Perl prints only lines beginning with the pattern *Igor*.

Since Perl is just another program, the output of commands can be piped to Perl. Perl will use what comes from the pipe as input, rather than a file. The *–n* switch is needed so that Perl can loop through the input coming in from the pipe.

Example 2.3

1   **$ date | perl −ne 'print "Today is $_"'**
2   *Today is Fri Apr 23 12:59:48 PDT 1993*

Explanation

1   The output of the UNIX *date* command is piped to Perl and stored in the $_ variable. The quoted string "Today is" and the contents of the $_ variable will be printed to the screen followed by a newline.
2   Output illustrates that today's date was stored in the $_ variable.

Perl can take its input from a file and send its output to a file using UNIX standard i/o redirection.

Example 2.4

1   **$ perl −ne 'print' < emp.first**
    Igor Chevsky:6/23/83:W:59870:25:35500:2005.50
    Nancy Conrad:6/18/88:SE:23556:5:15000:2500
    Jon DeLoar:3/28/85:SW:39673:13:22500:12345.75
    Archie Main:7/25/90:SW:39673:21:34500:34500.50
    Betty Bumble:11/3/89:NE:04530:17:18200:1200.75

2   **$ perl −ne 'print' < emp.first > emp.temp**

Explanation

1   Perl's input is taken from a file called *emp.first*. The output is sent to the screen.
2   Perl's input is taken from a file called *emp.first*, and its output is sent to the file *emp.temp*.

2.1.3   The −c Switch

The *−c* switch is used to check the Perl syntax without really executing the Perl commands. If the syntax is correct, Perl will tell you so.

E x a m p l e   2 . 5

1 **$ perl −ce 'print if /Igor' emp.first**
   Search pattern not terminated in file /tmp/perl−ea00380 at line 1, next char ^?
   /tmp/perl−ea00380 had compilation errors.

2 **$ perl −ce 'print if /Igor/' emp.first**
   /tmp/perl-ea01474 syntax OK

E x p l a n a t i o n

1 The pattern *Igor* is supposed to be enclosed in forward slashes. One of the forward slashes is missing. With the −c switch, Perl will complain if it finds syntax errors while compiling.
2 After correcting the previous problem, Perl lets you know that the syntax is correct.

2.2   Script Setup

Perl scripts are similar to *Shell, sed,* and *awk* scripts in appearance. They consist of a list of
Perl statements and declarations. Statements are terminated with a semicolon. Since only
subroutines and report formats require declarations, they will be discussed when those topics are presented. Variables can be created anywhere in the script and, if not initialized,
automatically get a value of 0 or "null," depending on their context.

Unlike *awk* and *sed,* where a sequence of commands is executed for each line of input,
Perl executes each command just once. Therefore, when working with input files, you must
either use an explicit loop in the script to iterate over the file, or use the −*n* switch to implicitly loop over the file.

2.3   The Script

2.3.1   Startup and The #! Line

If the first line of the script contains the **#!** symbol, followed by the full pathname of the
directory where your version of Perl resides, this tells the kernel what program is interpret-
ing the script. An example of the startup line might be:

```
#!/usr/bin/perl
```

It is extremely important that the path to the interpreter is entered correctly after the
pound sign-bang (#!). Perl may be installed in different directories on different systems.
Most Web servers will look for this line when invoking CGI scripts written in Perl. Any
inconsistency will cause a fatal error.

Another way to run a Perl script is to pass the scriptname as an argument to the Perl interpreter at the command line:

```
perl scriptname
```

In older versions systems that do not provide the #! symbol for startup, the following line can be used:

```
eval 'exec /usr/bin/perl -S{1+"$@"}'¹
    'f 0;
```

2.3.2   Comments

Comments are statements that allow you to insert documentation in your Perl script with no effect on the execution of the program. They are used to help you and other programmers maintain and debug scripts. Perl does not understand the C Language comments /* and */.

Example 2.6

```
1  # This is a comment
2  print "hello";  # And this is a comment
```

Explanation

1 Comments, as in *Shell*, *sed*, and *awk* scripts, are lines preceded with the pound sign (#) and can continue to the end of the line.
2 Comments can be anywhere on the line. Here the comment follows a valid Perl print statement.

2.3.3   Perl Statements

Perl executable statements make up most of the Perl script. Like *C*, the statement is an expression, or series of expressions, terminated with a semicolon (;). Perl statements can be simple or compound and there are a variety of operators, modifiers, expressions, and functions that make up a statement.

2.3.4   Executing the Script

The Perl script can be executed at the command line directly if the #! startup line is included in the script file and the script has execute permission. (See Example 2.7.) If the #! is not the first line of the script, you can execute a script by passing the script as an argument to

---

1. Larry Wall, Tom Christianson, and Randal L. Schwartz, *Programming Perl* (Sebastopol, CA: O'Reilly), p. 12, second edition, 1996.

the Perl program. Perl will then compile your script in its own internal form. If you have syntax errors, Perl will let you know.

2.3.5 Sample Script

The following example illustrates the four parts of a Perl script:

1. The startup line.
2. Comments.
3. The executable statements in the body of the script.
4. The execution of the script.

E x a m p l e   2 . 7

```
    $ cat first.perl
1   #!/usr/bin/perl
2   # My first Perl script
3   print "Hello to you and yours!\n";

4   $ perl –c first.perl
    first.perl syntax OK

5   $ chmod +x first.perl

6   $ first.perl
7   Hello to you and yours!
```

E x p l a n a t i o n

1   The startup line tells the Shell where Perl is located.[2]
2   A comment describes information the programmer wants to convey about the script.
3   An executable statement includes the *print* function.
4   The –c switch is used to check for syntax errors.
5   The *chmod* command turns on execute permission.
6   The script is executed.
7   The string "Hello to you and yours!" is printed on the screen.

---

2. If you are not using UNIX, see Example 2.8 on page 11.

Example 2.8

$ cat first.perl
1 # Missing startup line; This is a comment.
2 # My first Perl script
3 print "Hello to you and yours!\n";

4 **$ perl first.perl**
5 *Hello to you and yours*

Explanation   *(by line number)*

1 The startup line with #! is absent.
2 This is a descriptive line; a comment explains that the startup line is missing.
3 An executable statement includes the *print* function.
4 The Perl program takes the script name as an argument and executes the script. The script's output is printed.

3

Getting a Handle on Printing

3.1   The Filehandle

By convention, whenever your program starts execution, the UNIX shell opens three pre-defined streams called *stdin*, *stdout,* and *stderr.* All three of these streams are connected to your terminal by default.

stdin is the place where input comes from, the terminal keyboard; *stdout* is where output normally goes, the screen; and *stderr* is where errors from your program are printed, also the screen.

Perl inherits *stdin*, *stdout*, and *stderr* from the Shell. Perl does not access these streams directly, but gives them names called filehandles. Perl accesses the streams via the filehandle. The filehandle for *stdin* is called STDIN; the filehandle for *stdout* is called STDOUT; and the filehandle for *stderr* is called STDERR. Later we'll see how you can create your own filehandles, but for now we'll stick with the defaults.

The *print* and *printf* functions send their output by default to the STDOUT filehandle.

3.2   Words

When printing out a list of words to STDOUT, it is helpful to understand how Perl views a word. Any unquoted word must start with an alphanumeric character. It can consist of other alphanumeric characters and an underscore. Perl words are case sensitive. If a word is unquoted, it could conflict with words used to identify filehandles, labels, and other reserved words. If the word has no special meaning to Perl, it will be treated as if surrounded by single quotes.

3.2.1 Quotes

Quoting rules affect almost everything you do in Perl, especially when printing a string of words. Strings are normally delimited by either a matched pair of double or single quotes. When a string is enclosed in single quotes, all characters are treated as literals. When a string is enclosed in double quotes, however, *almost* all characters are treated as literals with the exception of those characters that are used for variable substitution and special escape sequences. We will look at the special escape sequences in this chapter and discuss quoting and variables in Chapter 4.

Perl uses some characters for special purposes, such as the dollar sign ($), the at sign (@), and the percent sign (%). If these special characters are to be treated as literal characters, they may be preceded by a backslash or enclosed within single quotes. The backslash is used to quote a single character rather than a string of characters.

3.2.2 Literals

When assigning literal values[1] to variables or printing literals, the literals can be represented numerically as integers in decimal, octal, hexadecimal, or as floats in floating point or scientific notation.

Strings enclosed in *double quotes* may contain string literals, such as "\n" for the newline character, "\t" for a tab character, or "\033" for an escape character. String literals are alphanumeric (*and only alphanumeric*) characters preceded by a backslash.[2] They may be represented in decimal, octal, hexadecimal, or as control characters.

Perl also supports special literals for representing the current script name, the line number of the current script, and the logical end of the current script.

Since you will be using literals with the *print* and *printf* functions, let's see what these literals look like.

Numeric Literals.   Literal numbers can be represented as positive or negative integers in decimal, octal, or hexadecimal (see Table 3.1). Floats can be represented in floating point notation or scientific notation. Octal numbers contain a leading 0 (zero), hex numbers a leading 0x (zero and x), and numbers represented in scientific notation contain a trailing 'E' followed by a negative or positive number representing the exponent.

TABLE 3.1   Numeric Literals

Example	Description
12345	Integer
0x456fff	Hex
0777	Octal
23.45	Float
.234E–2	Scientific notation

---

1. Literals may also be called constants, but the Perl experts prefer the term "literal," so in deference to them we'll use the term "literal."

2. UNIX utilities, such as *sed* and *grep,* allow characters other than alphanumerics after the backslash; e.g., \<, \(.

String Literals. Like Shell strings, Perl strings are normally delimited by either single or double quotes. Strings containing string literals, also called escape sequences, are delimited by double quotes for backslash interpretation (see Table 3.2).

TABLE 3.2   String Literals

Escape Sequences	Description (ASCII Name)
\t	Tab
\n	Newline
\r	Carriage return
\f	Form feed
\b	Backspace
\a	Alarm/bell
\e	Escape
\033	Octal character
\xff	Hexadecimal character
\c[	Control character
\l	Next character is converted to lower case
\u	Next character is converted to upper case
\L	Next characters are converted to lower case until \E is found
\U	Next characters are converted to upper case until \E is found
\Q	Backslash all following non-alphanumeric characters until \E is found
\E	Ends upper or lower case conversion started with \L or \U
\\	Backslash

Special Literals. Perl's special literals __LINE__ and __FILE__ are used as separate words and will *not* be interpreted if quoted. They represent the current line number of your script and the name of the script, respectively. These special literals are equivalent to the predefined special macros used in the C language.

The __END__ special literal is used in scripts to represent the logical end of the file. Any trailing text following the __END__ literal will be ignored, just as if it had been commented. The control sequences for end of input, ^D (\004) and ^Z (\032), are synonyms for __END__.

Note: There are two underscores on either side of the special literals (see Table 3.3).

TABLE 3.3   Special Literals

Literal	Description
__LINE__	Represents the current line number
__FILE__	Represents the current filename
__END__	Represents the logical end of the script; trailing garbage is ignored.

3.3   The print Function

The *print* function prints a string or a list of comma-separated words to the Perl filehandle, STDOUT. If successful, the print function returns 1; if not, it returns 0.

The string literal, "\n", adds a newline to the end of the string. It can be embedded in the string or treated as a separate string. In order to interpret backslashes, Perl, like the Shell, requires that escape sequences like "\n" are enclosed in double quotes.

Example 3.1

(The Script)
```
1  print "Hello", "world", "\n";
2  print "Hello world\n";
```

Output

1 *Helloworld*
2 *Hello world*

Explanation

1 Each string passed to the *print* function is enclosed in double quotes and separated by a comma. To print white space, the white space must be enclosed within the quotes. The "\n" escape sequence must be enclosed in double quotes for it to be interpreted as a newline character.
2 The entire string is enclosed in double quotes and printed to standard output.

Example 3.2

(The Script)
```
1  print Hello, world, "\n";
```

Output

1 *No comma allowed after filehandle at ./perl.st line 1*

Explanation

1 If the strings are not quoted, the filehandle, STDOUT, must be specified, or the print function will treat the first word it encounters as a filehandle (i.e., the word "Hello" would be treated as a filehandle). The comma is not allowed after a filehandle; it is used only to separate strings that are to be printed.

(The Script)
```
1  print STDOUT Hello, world, "\n";
```

O u t p u t

1   *Helloworld*

E x p l a n a t i o n

1   The filehandle, STDOUT, must be specified if strings are not quoted. The "\n" must be double quoted if it is to be interpreted. Note: There is <u>no</u> comma after STDOUT.

3.3.1   Printing Literals

Now that you know what the literals look like, let's see how they are used with the *print* function.

Printing Numeric Literals

E x a m p l e   3 . 3

(The Script)

```
#!/usr/bin/perl
# Program to illustrate printing literals
1  print "The price is $100.\n";
2  print "The price is \$100.\n";
3  print "The price is \$",100, ".\n";
4  print "The number is ",0777,".\n";
5  print "The number is ",0xAbcF,".\n";
6  print "The unformatted number is ", 14.56, ".\n";
```

O u t p u t

1   The price is.
2   The price is $100.
3   The price is $100.
4   The number is 511.
5   The number is 43983.
6   The unformatted number is 14.560000.

E x p l a n a t i o n

1   The string "The price is $100" is enclosed in double quotes. The dollar sign is a special Perl character. It is used to reference scalar variables (see Chapter 4), not money. Therefore, since there is no variable called $100, nothing prints. Since single quotes protect all characters from interpretation, they would have sufficed here, or the dollar sign could have been preceded with a backslash. But when surrounded by single quotes, the \n will be treated as a literal string rather than a newline character.

2   The backslash quotes the dollar sign, so it is treated as a literal.

3   To be treated as a numeric literal, rather than a string, the number 100 is a single word. The dollar sign must be escaped even if it is not followed by a variable name. The "\n" must be enclosed within double quotes if it is to be interpreted as a special string literal.

4   The number is represented as an octal value due to the leading 0 (zero). The decimal value is printed.

5   The number is represented as a hexadecimal number due to the leading 0x (zero and x). The decimal value is printed.

6   The number, represented as 14.56, is printed with six digits to the right of the decimal point, the default. The *print* function does not format output.

Printing String Literals

Example 3.4

(The Script)

```
#!/usr/bin/perl
1  print "***\tIn double quotes\t***\n";  # backslash interpretation
2  print '%%%\t\tIn single quotes\t\t%%%\n'; # All characters are printed as literals
3  print "\n"
```

Output

```
1  ***    In double quotes       ***
2  %%%\t\tIn single quotes\t\t%%%\n
```

Explanation

1   When a string is enclosed within double quotes, backslash interpretation is performed. The "\t" is a string literal and produces a tab; the "\n" produces a newline.

2   When enclosed within single quotes, the special string literals "\t" and "\n" are not interpreted. They will be printed as is.

3   A "\n" produces a newline.

Example 3.5

(The Script)

```
#!/usr/bin/perl
1  print "\a\t\tThe \Unumber\E \LIS\E ",0777,".\n";
```

Output

```
1  (BEEP)     The NUMBER is 511.
```

E x p l a n a t i o n

1   The "\a" produces an alarm or beep sound, followed by "\t\t" (two tabs). \U causes the string to be printed in upper case until \E is reached or the line terminates. The string "*number*" is printed in upper case until the "\E" is reached. The string "*is*" is to be printed in lower case, until the "\E" is reached, and the decimal value for octal 0777 is printed, followed by a period and a newline character.

Printing Special Literals

E x a m p l e   3 . 6

(The Script)
```
#!/usr/bin/perl
# Program, named literals.perl, written to test special literals
1  print "We are on line number ", __LINE__, ".\n";
2  print "The name of this file is ",__FILE__,".\n";
3  __END__
   And this stuff is just a bunch of chitter–chatter that is to be ignored by Perl.
   The __END__ literal is like ctrl–d or \004. (See –x switch for discarding leading
   garbage, Appendix A).
```

O u t p u t

1   *We are on line number 3.*
2   *The name of this file is literals.perl.*

E x p l a n a t i o n

1   The special literal __LINE__ cannot be enclosed in quotes if it is to be interpreted. It holds the current line number of the Perl script. (*Note*: There are *two* underscores on either side of the literal.)
2   The name of this script is *literals.perl*. The special literal __FILE__ holds the name of the current Perl script.
3   The special literal __END__ represents the logical end of the script. It tells Perl to ignore any characters following it.

3.3.2   The –w Switch

The *–w* switch is used to <u>w</u>arn you about the possibility of using future reserved words. Larry Wall says in the Perl 5 man pages, "Whenever you get mysterious behavior, try the –w switch! Whenever you don't get mysterious behavior, try the –w switch anyway."

E x a m p l e   3 . 7

(The Script)
```
   #!/usr/bin/perl
1  print STDOUT ellie,"\tThe price is \$100.00.\n";
```

O u t p u t

```
   $ perl –w literals
1  "ellie" may clash with future reserved word at literals.sp line 2.
2  ellie   The price is $100.00.
```

E x p l a n a t i o n

The –w switch prints warnings about ambiguous identifiers. Since the string *"ellie"* is not quoted, Perl could mistake it for a reserved word or an undefined filehandle.

3.3.3   The Strict Pragma and Words

A pragma is a special Perl module that hints to the compiler the way that a block of statements should be compiled. You can use this module as of Perl 5 to help control the way your program behaves. The first pragma we will mention is the *strict* pragma. If your program disobeys the restrictions placed on it, it won't compile. If there is a chance that you might have used "bare" words as in the example above, the *strict* pragma will catch you and your program will abort.

E x a m p l e   3 . 8

(The Script)
```
   #!/usr/bin/perl
   # Program: stricts.test
   # Script to demonstrate the strict pragma
1  use strict "subs";
2  $name = Ellie;   #Unquoted word Ellie
3  print "Hi $name.\n";
```

O u t p u t

```
   $ stricts.test
   Bareword "Ellie" not allowed while "strict subs" in use use at ./stricts.test line 5.
   Execution of stricts.test aborted due to compilation errors.
```

Explanation

1   The *use* function allows you to use modules located in the standard Perl library. When the *strict* pragma takes "subs" as an argument, it will catch any bare words found in the program while it is being internally compiled. If a bare word is found, the program will be aborted with an error message.

3.4   The printf Function

The *printf* function prints a formatted string to the selected filehandle, the default being STDOUT. It is like the *printf* function used in the *C* and *awk* languages. The return value is 1 if *printf* is successful and 0 if it fails.

The *printf* function consists of a quoted control string that may include format specifications. The quoted string is followed by a comma and a list of comma-separated arguments, which are simply expressions. The format specifiers are preceded by a % sign. For each % sign and format specifier, there must be a corresponding argument (see Tables 3.4 and 3.5).

Example 3.9

```
printf("The name is %s and the number is %d\n", "John", 50);
```

Explanation

1   The string to be printed is enclosed in double quotes. The first format specifier is %s. It has a corresponding argument, "John", positioned directly to the right of the comma after the closing quote in the control string. The 's' following the percent sign (%) is called a conversion character. The 's' means *string* conversion will take place at this spot. In this case "John" will replace the "%s" when the string is printed.
2   The %d format specifies that the decimal (integer) value 50 will be printed in its place within the string.

Placing the quoted string and expressions within parentheses is optional.

TABLE 3.4   Format Specifiers

Conversion Character	Definition
c	Character
s	String
d	Decimal number
ld	Long decimal number
u	Unsigned decimal number
lu	Long unsigned decimal number
x	Hexadecimal number
lx	Long hexidecimal number
o	Octal number
lo	Long octal number
e	Floating point number in scientific notation
f	Floating point number
g	Floating point number using either e or f conversion, whichever takes the least space

TABLE 3.5   Modifiers

Character	Definition
-	Left justification modifier
#	Integers in octal format are displayed with a leading 0; integers in hexadecimal form are displayed with a leading 0x.
+	For conversions using d, e, f, and g, integers are displayed with a numeric sign + or -.
0	The displayed value is padded with zeros instead of white space.

When an argument is printed, the place where the output is printed is called the *field,* and the *width* of the field is the number of characters contained in that the field.

E x a m p l e   3 . 1 0

(The Script)

```
    #!/usr/bin/perl
1   printf "Hello to you and yours %s!\n","Sam McGoo";
2   printf("%-15s%-20s\n", "Jack", "Sprat");
3   printf "The number in decimal is %d\n", 45;
4   printf "The formatted number is |%10d|\n", 100;
5   printf "The number printed with leading zeros is |%010d|\n", 5;
6   printf "Left justified the number is |%-10d|\n", 100;
7   printf "The number in octal is %o\n",15;
8   printf "The number in hexadecimal is %x\n", 15;
9   printf  "The formatted floating point number is |%8.2f|\n", 14.3456;
10  printf "The floating point number is |%8f|\n", 15;
11  printf  "The character is %c\n", 65;
```

O u t p u t

1   *Hello to you and yours Sam McGoo!*
2   *Jack   Sprat*
3   *The number in decimal is 45*
4   *The formatted number is | 100|*
5   *The number printed with leading zeros is |0000000005|.*
6   *Left justified the number is |100 |*
7   *The number in octal is 17*
8   *The number in hexadecimal is f*
9   *The formatted floating point number is | 14.35|*
10 *The floating point number is |15.00000|*
11 *The character is A*

E x p l a n a t i o n

1   The quoted string contains the %s format conversion specifier. The string "*Sam Magoo*" is converted to a string and replaces the %s in the printed output.
2   The string "*Jack*" has a field width of 15 characters and is left justified. The string "*Sprat*" has a field width of 20 characters and is also left justified.
3   The number 45 is printed in decimal format.
4   The number 100 has a field width of 10 and is right justified.
5   The number 5 has a field width of 10, is right justified, and is preceded by leading zeros rather than white space.
6   The number 100 has a field width of 10 and is left justified.
7   The number 15 is printed in octal.
8   The number15 is printed in hexadecimal.
9   The number 14.3456 is given a field width of eight characters. One of them is the deci- point; the fractional part is given a precision of two decimal places. The number is then rounded up.
10 The number 15 is given a field width of eight characters, right justified. The default precision is six decimal places to the right of the decimal point.
11 The character 'A' is printed.

3.4.1   Printing Without Quotes—The Here Document

The Perl *here document* is derived from the Shell here document. Like the Shell, the Perl here document is a line-oriented form of quoting, requiring the << operator followed by an initial terminating string and a semicolon. There can be no spaces after the <<. If the termi- nating string is not quoted or double quoted, variable expansion is performed. If the termi- nating string is single quoted, variable expansion is not performed. Each line of text is inserted between the first and last terminating string. The final terminating string must be on a line by itself, with no surrounding whitespace.

Here documents are used extensively in CGI scripts for enclosing large chunks of HTML tags for printing.

Perl, unlike the Shell, does not perform command substitution (back quotes) in the text of a here document. Perl, on the other hand, does allow you to execute commands in the *here* document if the terminator is enclosed in back quotes.

Example 3.11

(The Script)
```
    $price=100;
1   print <<EOF;  # no quotes around terminator EOF are same as double quotes
2   The price of $price is right. # Variables are expanded
3   EOF

4   print <<'FINIS';
5   The price of $price is right. # The variable is not expanded if terminator is
                                  # enclosed in single quotes
6   FINIS

7   print << x 4;  # prints the line 4 times
8   Christmas is coming!
                          # Blank line is necessary here
9   print <<`END`;  # If terminator is in back quotes, will execute UNIX commands
10  echo hi there
11  echo -n "The time is "
12  date
13  END
```

Output

```
2   The price of 100 is right.
5   The price of $price is right.
8   Christmas is coming!
    Christmas is coming!
    Christmas is coming!
    Christmas is coming!
10  hi there
11  The time is Mon Jan 25 11:58:35 PST 1997
```

E x p l a n a t i o n

1   Start of here document. EOF is the terminator. The block is treated as if in double
    quotes. If there is a space after the <<, then the terminator must be in double quotes,
    e.g., "EOF".
2   Line of text to be printed. Variables are interpolated.
3   End of here document marked by matching terminator, EOF.
4   Quoted terminator FINIS turns off variable interpolation.
5   Text is treated as if in single quotes.
6   Closing terminator marks the end of the here document.
7   The number x4 says that the text "Christmas is coming" will be printed four times.
8   Text in the here document to be printed.
9   The terminator is enclosed in back quotes. The shell will execute the commands be-
    tween `END` and END.
10-11-12   The shell will execute these commands.
13   The END marks the end of the here document.

4

What's in a Name?

4.1 About Perl Variables

4.1.1 Types

Variables are data items whose values may change throughout the run of the program, whereas literals or constants remain fixed. Perl variables are of three types: scalar, array, and associative array (more commonly called hashes). A scalar variable is a variable that contains a single value; an array variable contains a list of values indexed by a positive number; and an associative array contains a list of values indexed by string. (See Section 4.2 of this chapter, "Scalars, Arrays, and Associative Arrays.")

4.1.2 Scope and the Package

The scope of a variable determines where it is visible in the program. In Perl scripts, the variable is visible to the entire script (i.e., global in scope), and can be changed anywhere within the script.

   The Perl sample programs you have seen in the previous chapters are compiled internally into what is called a *package*, which provides a namespace for variables. All variables are global within that package. A global variable is known to the whole package and if changed anywhere within the package, the change will permanently affect the variable. The default package is called *main*, similar to the *main()* function in the C language. Such variables in C would be classified as *static*. At this point, you don't have to worry about naming the *main* package or the way in which it is handled during the compilation process. The only purpose in mentioning packages now is to let you know that the scope of variables in the *main* package, your script, is global. Later, when we talk about the *local* and the *my* functions in packages, you will see that it is possible to change the scope and namespace of a variable.

Package main

scalar namespace	array namespace	associative array namespace
$department	@department $department[0]	%department $department{'Ed'}

4.1.3   Naming Conventions

Like *awk* variables, Perl variables don't have to be declared before being used. They spring to life just by the mere mention of them. Variables have their own namespace in Perl. They are identified by the "funny characters" that precede them. Scalar variables are preceded by a dollar sign ($); array variables are preceded by an at sign (@); and associative array variables, called hashes, are preceded by a percent sign (%). Since the "funny characters" indicate what type of variable you are using, you can use the same name for a scalar, array, or associative array and not worry about a naming conflict. For example, *$name*, *@name*, and *%name* are all different variables; the first is a scalar, the second is an array, and the last is an associative array.[1]

Since reserved words and filehandles are not preceded by a special character, variable names will not conflict with reserved words or filehandles. Variables are <u>case sensitive</u>. The variables named *$Num*, *$num*, and *$NUM* are all different.

If a variable starts with a letter, it may consist of any number of letters (an underscore counts as a letter) and/or digits. If the variable does not start with a letter, it must consist of only one character. Perl has a set of special variables (e.g., $_, $^, $., $1, $2, etc.), that fall into this category. (See Section A.2, Special Variables.) In special cases, variables may also be preceded with a single quote, but only when *packages* are used.

An uninitialized variable will get a value of zero or null, depending on whether its context is numeric or string.

4.1.4   Assignment Statements

The assignment operator, the equal (=) sign, consists of two operands, the variable on the left-hand side which is assigned the value of the expression on the right-hand side. Any value that can be "assigned to" represents a named region of storage and is called an

---

1. Using the same name is allowed but not recommended.

lvalue.[2] Perl reports an error if the operand on the left-hand side of the assignment operator does not represent an lvalue.

When assigning a value or values to a variable, if the variable on the left-hand side of the equal sign is a scalar, Perl evaluates the expression on the right-hand side in a scalar context. If the variable on the left of the equal sign is an array, then Perl evaluates the expression on the right in an array context. (See Section 4.2, "Scalars, Arrays, and Hashes.")

A simple statement is an expression terminated with a semicolon.

Format:

```
variable=expression;
```

E x a m p l e   4 . 1

(The Script)

```
1        $salary=50000;           #Scalar assignment

2        @months=(Mar, Apr, May);  # Array assignment

3        %states= (                # Hash assignment
             'CA' => 'California',
             'ME '=> 'Maine',
             'MT' => 'Montana',
             'NM' => 'New Mexico',
               );


4        print "$salary\n";
5        print "@months\n";
6        print "$months[0], $months[1], $months[2]\n";
7        print "$states{'CA'}, $states{'NM'}\n";
8        print $x + 3, "\n";          # $x just came to life!
9        print "***$name***\n";       # $name  is born!
```

O u t p u t

```
4 50000
5 Mar Apr May
6 Mar, Apr, May
7 California, New Mexico
8 3
9 ******
```

---

2. The value on the left-hand side of the equal sign is called an lvalue, and the value on the right-hand side an rvalue.

E x p l a n a t i o n

1   The scalar variable *$salary* is assigned the numeric literal 50000. (See Section 4.2.1, "Scalar Variables.")

2   The array *@months* is assigned the comma-separated list, *Mar, Apr, May.* The list is enclosed in parentheses. (See Section 4.2.2, "Arrays.")

3   The hash (associative array), *%states*, is assigned a list consisting of a set of strings separated either by a comma or =>.[3] The string on the left is called the *key.* The string to the right is called the *value.* The *key* is associated with its *value.* (See Section 4.2.3, "Associative Arrays.")

4   The value of the scalar, *$salary*, is printed, followed by a newline.

5   The *@months* array is printed. The double quotes preserve spaces between each element.

6   The individual elements of the array, *@months*, are scalars and are thus preceded by a dollar sign ($). The array index starts at zero.

7   The *key* elements of the associative array, *%states*, are enclosed in curly braces. The associated *value* is printed. Each *value* is a single value, a scalar. The *value* is preceded by a dollar sign ($).

8   The scalar variable, *$x*, is referenced for the first time. Because the number *three* is added to *$x*, the context is numeric. *$x* has an initial value of *zero.*

9   The scalar variable, *$name*, is referenced for the first time. The context is string and the initial value is null.

4.1.5   Quoting Rules

Since quoting affects the way in which variables are interpolated, this is a good time to review Perl's quoting rules. Perl quoting rules are similar to Shell quoting rules. This may not be good news to Shell programmers, who find using quotes frustrating, to say the least. It is often difficult to determine which quotes to use, where to use them, and how to find the culprit if they are misused, i.e., a real debugging nightmare.[4] For those of you who fall into this category, Perl offers an alternate method of quoting.[5]

Perl, like the Shell, has three types of quotes and all three types have a different function. They are: *single quotes, double quotes*, and *back quotes.*

The backslash behaves like a set of single quotes but can be used only to quote a single character.

A pair of double or single quotes may delimit a string of characters. Some of the characters in the string may be special characters. The special characters may be white space, characters preceded by backslashes, or any of the "funny" characters used to reference variables. The quotes will either allow the interpretation of special characters or protect special characters from interpretation, depending on the kind of quotes you use.

---

3. The comma can be used in both Perl4 and Perl5. The => symbol was introduced in Perl 5.

4. Barry Rosenberg in his book entitled, *KornShell Programming Tutorial*, has a chapter entitled "The Quotes From Hell."

5. Larry Wall, creator of Perl, calls his alternate quoting method "syntactic sugar."

When back quotes surround a UNIX command, the command will be executed by the Shell. This is called *command substitution*. The output of the command will either be printed as part of a print statement or assigned to a variable.

Because the quotes mark the beginning and end of a string, Perl will complain about a *"multi-line runaway" "string"* or *"Execution of quotes aborted..."*, or *"Can't find string terminator anywhere before EOF..."* and fail to compile, if you forget one of the quotes.

Double Quotes.   Double quotes must be matched unless embedded within single quotes or preceded by a backslash.

When a string is enclosed in double quotes, scalar variables (preceded with a $) and arrays (preceded by the @ symbol) are interpolated (i.e., the *value* of the variable replaces the variable *name* in the string). Hashes (preceded by the % sign) are *not* interpolated within the string enclosed in double quotes.

Strings that contain string literals (e.g., \t, \n) must be enclosed in double quotes for backslash interpretation.

A single quote may be enclosed in double quotes as in "I don't care!"

Example 4.2

(The Script)
```
   #!/usr/bin/perl
1  $num=5;
2  print "The number is $num.\n";
3  print "I need \$5.00.\n";
4  print "\t\tI can't help you.\n";
```

Output

```
2  The number is 5.
3  I need $5.00.
4                          I can't help you.
```

Explanation

1 The scalar variable *$num* is assigned the value *5*.
2 The string is enclosed in double quotes. The value of the scalar variable is printed. The string literal, '\n', is interpreted.
3 The dollar sign ($) is printed as a literal dollar sign when preceded by a backslash, i.e., variable substitution is ignored.
4 The special literals '\t' and '\n' are interpreted when enclosed within double quotes.

Single Quotes.   If a string is enclosed in single quotes, it is printed literally (i.e., all characters are treated as literals).

If a single quote is needed within a string, then it can be embedded within double quotes. If double quotes are to be treated literally, they can be embedded within single quotes.

E x a m p l e   4 . 3

(The Script)
1   print 'I need $100.00.', "\n";
2   print 'The string literal, \t, is used to represent a tab.', "\n";
3   print 'She cried, "Help me!"', "\n";

O u t p u t

1   *I need $100.00.*
2   *The string literal, \t, is used to represent a tab.*
3   *She cried, "Help me!"*

E x p l a n a t i o n

1   The dollar sign is interpreted literally. In double quotes it would be interpreted as a scalar. The "\n" is in double quotes in order for backslash interpretation.
2   The string literal, *t*, is not interpreted to be a tab, but is printed literally.
3   The double quotes are protected when enclosed in single quotes (i.e., printed literally).

Back Quotes.   UNIX[6] commands placed within back quotes are executed by the Shell, and the output is returned to the Perl program. The output is usually assigned to a variable or made part of a print string. When the output of a UNIX command is assigned to a variable, the context is scalar (i.e., a single value is assigned). [7]In order for command substitution to take place, the back quotes cannot be enclosed in either double or single quotes. (Make note, Shell programmers, that double quotes do <u>not</u> allow command substitution to be performed in back quotes as they do in Shell programs.)

E x a m p l e   4 . 4

(The Script)
1   print "The date is ", **'date'**;
2   print "The date is 'date'", "./n";   # *Back quotes will be treated as literals*
3   **$dir='pwd'**;
4   print "\nThe current directory is $dir.";

---

6. If using other operating systems, such as Windows , Dos, or Macperl, the OS commands available for your system will differ. For example if using Windows in order to launch a program, you would use the Win32::Process module with the following basic format: *use Win32::Process;*

7. If output of a command is assigned to an array, the first line of output becomes the first element of the array; the second line of output becomes the next element of the array, etc.

O u t p u t

1   *The date is Sat Nov 27 17:41:59 PST 1997.*
2   *The date is 'date'.*
4   *The current directory is /home/jody/ellie/perl.*

E x p l a n a t i o n

1   The UNIX *date* command will be executed by the Shell, and the output will be returned
    to Perl's *print* string. The output of the *date* command includes the newline character.
2   Command substitution will not take place when the back quotes are enclosed in single
    or double quotes.
3   The scalar variable *$dir*, including the newline, is assigned the output of the UNIX *pwd*
    command (i.e., the present working directory).
4   The value of the scalar, *$dir,* is printed to the screen.

Perl's Alternative Quotes.   Perl provides an alternate form of quoting—the *q*, *qq*, *qx* and
qw constructs.
    The *q* represents single quotes.
    The *qq* represents double quotes.
    The *qx* represents back quotes.
    The *qw* represents a quoted list of words. (See arrays.)

E x a m p l e   4 . 5

1 q/Hello/   *is the same as*   'Hello'
2 qq/Hello/ *is the same as*   "Hello"
3 qx/date/   *is the same as*   'date'
4 @list=qw/red yellow blue/;   *is the same as*   @list=('red', 'yellow', 'blue');

    The string to be quoted is enclosed in *forward slashes*, but alternate delimiters can be
used as the delimiter for all four of the q constructs. A single character or paired characters
can be used:

        q/Hello/
        q#Hello#
        q{Hello}
        q[Hello]
        q(Hello)

E x a m p l e   4 . 6

(The Script)
```
    #!/usr/bin/perl
1   print 'She cried, "I can\'t help you!"',"\n";   # Clumsy
2   print qq/She cried, "I can't help you!"\n/; # qq for double quotes
3   print qq/I need $5.00\n/;  # Really need single quotes for a literal
                               # dollar sign to print
4   print q/I need $5.00\n/;  # What about backslash interpretation?
5   print qq/\n/, q/I need $5.00/,"\n";
6   print q!I need $5.00!,"\n";
7   print "The present working directory is ", `pwd`;
8   print qq/Today is /, qx/date/;
9   print "The hour is ", qx{date +%H};
```

O u t p u t

```
1   She cried, "I can't help you!"
2   She cried, "I can't help you!"
3   I need .00
4   I need $5.00\n

5   I need $5.00
6   I need $5.00
7   The present working directory is /home/jody/ellie/perl
8   Today is Fri Mar 19 17:05:37 PST 1997
9   The hour is 17
```

E x p l a n a t i o n

1   The string is enclosed in single quotes. This allows the conversational quotes to be print-
    ed as literals. The single quote in "can't" is quoted with a backslash so that it will also
    be printed literally. If it were not quoted, it would be matched with the first single quote.
    The ending single quote would then have no mate, alas, and the program would either
    tell you you have a "runaway quote," or search for its mate until it reached the end of file
    unexpectedly.
2   The *qq* construct replaces double quotes. The forward slashes delimit the string.
3   Because the *qq* is used, the dollar sign ($) in *$5.00* is interpreted as a scalar variable with
    a null value. The *.00* is printed. (This is not the way to handle your money!)
4   The single *q* replaces single quotes. The *$5* is treated as a literal. Unfortunately, so is the
    "\n". Backslash interpretation does not take place within single quotes.
5   The "\n" is double quoted with the *qq* construct; the string "I need $5.00" is single quot-
    ed with the *q* construct; and old-fashioned double quotes are used for the second "\n".

6   An alternative delimiter, the exclamation point (!), is used with the *q* construct (instead of the forward slash) to delimit the string.

7   The string *"The present working directory"* is enclosed in double quotes; the UNIX command *pwd* is enclosed in back quotes for command substitution.

8   The *qq* construct quotes "Today is"; the *qx* construct replaces the back quotes used for command substitution.

9   Alternative delimiters, the curly braces, are used with the *qx* construct (instead of the forward slash). The output of the UNIX *date* command is printed.

4.2   Scalars, Arrays, and Hashes

Now that we have discussed the basics of Perl variables (types, visibility, names, etc.), we can look at them in more detail and without (or should I say "with less"?) confusion about the quoting mechanism, and how quoting effects variable interpretation.

4.2.1   Scalar Variables

Scalar variables hold a single number or string and are preceded by a dollar sign ($). Perl scalars need a preceding dollar sign whenever the variable is referenced, even when the scalar is being assigned a value. If you are familiar with Shell programs, using the dollar sign when making assignments may seem a little strange at first.

Assignment.   When making an assignment, the value on the right-hand side of the equal sign is evaluated as a single value (i.e., its context is scalar). A quoted string, then, is considered a single value even if it contains a number of words.

E x a m p l e   4 . 7

```
1  $number=150;
2  $name="Jody Savage";
```

E x p l a n a t i o n

1   The numeric literal, 150, is assigned to the scalar variable *$number.*

2   The string literal, *Jody Savage*, is assigned to the scalar variable *$name* as a single string.

Curly Braces.   If a scalar variable is surrounded by curly braces, the scalar is shielded from any characters that may be appended to the variable.

E x a m p l e   4 . 8

```
1  $var=net;
2  print "${var}work\n";
```

O u t p u t

```
2  network
```

E x p l a n a t i o n

1 The value, *net*, is assigned to the scalar variable, $var.
2 The curly braces surrounding the variable insulate it from the string *work* which has been appended to it. Without the curly braces, nothing would be printed because a variable called $varwork has not been defined.

E x a m p l e   4 . 9

```
(TheScript)
    #!/usr/bin/perl
1   $num = 5;
2   $friend = "John Smith";
3   $money = 125.75;
4   $now = `date`;                        # Backquotes for command substitution
5   $month=Jan;

6   print  "$num\n";
7   print "$friend\n";
8   print "I need \$$money.\n";           # Protecting our money
9   print qq/$friend gave me \$$money.\n/;
10  print qq/The time is $now/;
11  print "The month is ${month}uary.\n"; # Curly braces shield the variable
```

O u t p u t

```
6   5
7   John Smith
8   I need $125.75.
9   John Smith gave me $125.75.
10  The time is Sat Apr 26 09:34:41 PDT 1997.
11  The month is January.
```

Explanation

1   The scalar, *$num*, is assigned the numeric literal, 5.
2   The scalar, *$friend*, is assigned the string literal, John Smith.
3   The scalar, *$money*, is assigned the numeric floating point literal, 125.75.
4   The scalar, *$now*, is assigned the output of the UNIX date command.
5   The scalar, *$month,* is assigned Jan.
6   The value of the scalar, *$num*, is printed.
7   The value of the scalar, *$friend*, is printed.
8   The quoted string is printed. The backslash allows the first dollar sign ($) to be printed literally; the value of *$money* is interpolated within double quotes, its value printed.
9   The Perl *qq* construct replaces double quotes. The string to be quoted is enclosed in forward slashes. The value of the scalar, *$friend*, is interpolated; a literal dollar sign precedes the value of the scalar interpolated variable, *$money*.
10   The quoted string is printed. The *$now* variable is interpolated.
11   As in the *Shell*, curly braces can be used to shield the variable from characters that are appended to it. *January* will be printed.

The defined Function.   If a scalar has neither a valid string nor valid numeric value, it is undefined. The *define* function allows you to check for the validity of a variable's value. It returns 1 if the variable has a value, and null if not. The function is also used to check the validity of arrays, subroutines, and null strings.

Example 4.10

```
$name="Tommy";
print "OK \n" if defined $name;
```

The undef Function.   This function *undefines* an already defined variable. It releases whatever space was allocated for the variable to memory. The function returns the undefined value. This function also releases storage associated with arrays and subroutines.

Example 4.11

```
undef $name;
```

The $_ Scalar Variable.   The $_ is a ubiquitous little character. Although it is very useful in Perl scripts, it is often not seen. It is used as the default pattern space for searches and to hold the current line. When used as a pattern space for searches, it behaves like *sed*. When used to hold the current line, it is like the $0 variable in *awk*.

Example 4 . 1 2

1 **$ perl –ne 'print' emp.names** *Steve Blenheim* *Betty Boop* *Igor Chevsky* *Norma Cord* *Jon DeLoach* *Karen Evich*	2 **$perl –ne 'print $_' emp.names** *Steve Blenheim* *Betty Boop* *Igor Chevsky* *Norma Cord* *Jon DeLoach* *Karen Evich*

Explanation

1 The *–n* switch allows you to implicitly loop through the file. Since the $_ is a default used to hold the current line of the *emp.names* file, it is not required in the print statement.
2 This example is equivalent to the first example. This time the $_ is used explicitly to hold the current line, even though it is not necessary.

4.2.2   Arrays

When you have a collection of similar data elements, it is easier to use an array than to create a separate variable for each of the elements. The array name allows you to associate a single variable name with a list of data elements. Each of the elements in the list is referenced by its name and a subscript (also called an index).

Perl, unlike C, doesn't care whether the elements of an array are of the same data type. They can be a mix of numbers and strings. To Perl, an array is a named list containing an ordered set of scalars. The name of the array starts with a @ sign. The subscript follows the array name and is enclosed in square brackets. Subscripts are simply integers and start at zero.

Assignment.   If the array is initialized, the elements are enclosed in parentheses, and each element is separated by a comma. The list is parenthesized due to the lower precedence of the comma operator over the assignment operator. Elements in an array are simply scalars.

Perl 5 introduced the *qw* construct for creating a list (similar to *qq*, *q*, and *qx*). The items in the list are treated as singly quoted words.

Example 4 . 1 3

```
1   @name=( "Guy", "Tom", "Dan",  "Ron" );
2   @list=(2..10);
3   @grades=( 100, 90, 65, 96, 40, 75 );
4   @items=($a, $b, $c);
5   @empty=();
6   $size=@items;
7   @mammals = qw/dogs cats cows/;
```

E x p l a n a t i o n

1   The array, @*name*, is initialized with a list of four string literals.
2   The array, @*list,* is assigned numbers ranging from 2 through 10. (See Section 4.15.)
3   The array, @*grades*, is initialized with a list of six numeric literals.
4   The array, @*items*, is initialized with the values of three scalar variables.
5   The array, @*empty*, is assigned a null list.
6   The array, @*items*, is assigned to the scalar variable, *$size*. The value of the scalar is the number of elements in the array (in this example, *3*).
7   The qw (quote word) construct is followed by a delimeter of your choice. Each of the words in the list is treated as a singly quoted word. The list is terminated with a closing delimiter. This example could be written: @mammals = qw('cats', 'dogs', 'cows');

Special Scalars and Array Assignment.   The special scalar variable *$#arrayname* returns the number of the last subscript in the array. Since the array subscripts start at zero, this value is one less than the array size. The $#*arrayname* variable can also be used to shorten or truncate the size of the array.

The **$[** variable is the current array base subscript, zero. Its value can be changed so that the subscript starts at 1 instead of 0, but changing this value is discouraged by Larry Wall.

E x a m p l e   4 . 1 4

```
1  $indexsize=$#grades;
2  $#grades=3;
3  $#grades=$[ – 1;
4  @grades=();
```

E x p l a n a t i o n

1   The scalar variable, *$indexsize*, is assigned the value of the last subscript in the @grades array.
2   The last subscript in the array has been shortened to 3.
3   The array base subscript, starting at zero, has been decremented by one. This will truncate the entire array to a null or empty list; this is the same as: @grades=();
4   The @*grades* array is assigned a null list creating an empty list.

The Range Operator and Array Assignment.   The .. operator, called the *range* operator, when used in an array context returns an array of values starting from the left value to the right value, counting by ones.

Example 4.15

```
1  @digits=( 0 .. 10 );
2  @letters=( 'A' .. 'Z' );
3  @alpha-( 'A' .. 'Z', 'a' .. 'z' );
4  @n = ( -5 .. 20 );
```

Explanation

1 The array, *@digits*, is assigned a list of numbers, 0, 1, 2, 3, ... 9, 10.
2 The array, *@letters*, is assigned a list of capital letters, A,B,C,D...X,Y,Z.
3 The array, *@alpha*, is assigned a list of capital letters and a list of lower case letters.
4 The array, *@n*, is assigned a list of numbers, –5, –4, –3, –2, –1, 0, 1, 2, ... 19, 20.

Accessing Elements.   To reference the individual elements in an array, each element is considered a scalar (preceded by a dollar sign) and the subscripts start at zero. The subscripts are positive whole numbers. In the array, *@names*, for example, the first element in the array is *$name[0]*, and the next element is *$name[1]*, etc.

Example 4.16

(The Script)
```
   #!/usr/bin/perl
1  @names=('John', 'Joe', 'Jake');
2  print @names, "\n";  # prints without the separator
3  print "Hi $names[0], $names[1], and $names[2]!\n";

4  $number=@names;  # The scalar is assigned the number of elements in the
                    # array
5  print "There are $number elements in the \@names array.\n";
6  print "The last element of the array is $names[$number – 1].\n";
7  print "The last element of the array is $names[$#names].\n";
   # Remember, subscript starts at zero!!
8  @fruit = qw/apples pears peaches plums/;
9  print "The first element of the \@fruit array  is $fruit[0]; the second element is
   $fruit[1].\n";
```

Output

```
2  JohnJoeJake
3  Hi John, Joe, and Jake!
5  There are 3 elements in the @names array.
6  The last element of the array is Jake.
7  The last element of the array is Jake.
9  The first element of the @fruit array is apples; the second element is pears.
```

Explanation

1   The *@names* array is initialized with three strings—*John*, *Joe*, and *Jake*.
2   The entire array is printed to STDOUT. The space between the elements is not printed.
3   Each element of the array is printed, starting with subscript number zero.
4   The scalar variable *$number* is assigned the array *@names*. The value assigned is the number of elements in the array *@names*.
5   The number of elements in the array *@names* is printed.
6   The last element of the array is printed. Since subscripts start at zero, the number of elements in the array decremented by one evaluates to the number of the last subscript.
7   The last element of the array is printed. The *$#names* value evaluates to the number of subscripts in the array. This value used as a subscript will retrieve the last element in the *$names* array.
8   The *qw* construct allows you to create an array of <u>singly</u> quoted words without enclosing the words in quotes or separating the words with commas.

Array Slices.   When the elements of one array are assigned the values from another array, the resulting array is called an *array slice*.

   If the array on the right-hand side of the assignment operator is larger than the array on the left-hand side, the unused values are discarded. If it is smaller, the values assigned are undefined. As indicated in the following example, the array indices in the slice do not have to be consecutively numbered; each element is assigned the corresponding value from the array on the right-hand side of the assignment operator.

Example 4.17

(The Script)
```
   #!/usr/bin/perl
1  @names=('Tom', 'Dick', 'Harry', 'Pete' );
2  @pal=@names[1,2,3];  # slice--@names[1..3] also O.K.
3  print "@pal\n\n";

4  ($friend[0], $friend[1], $friend[2])=@names;  # Array slice
5  print "@friend\n";
```

Output

3   *Dick Harry Pete*

5   *Tom Dick Harry*

Explanation

1   The array, @*names*, is assigned the elements, *'Tom'*, *'Dick'*, *'Harry'*, and *'Pete'*.
2   The array, @*pal*, is assigned the elements 1, 2, and 3 of the @*names* array. The elements of the @names array are sliced out and stored in the @*pal* array.
4   The @*friend* array is created by taking a slice from the @*names* array, i.e., elements 0, 1, and 2.

Example 4.18

(The Script)
```
    #!/usr/bin/perl
1   @colors=('red','green','yellow','orange');
2   ($c[0], $c[1],$c[3], $c[5])=@colors;  # The slice

3   print "**********\n";

4   print @colors,"\n";  # prints entire array, but does not separate elements
5   print "@colors,\n";  # quoted, prints the entire array with elements
                         # separated

6   print "**********\n";

7   print $c[0]."\n";    # red
8   print $c[1],"\n";    # green
9   print $c[2],"\n";    # undefined
10  print $c[3],"\n";    # yellow
11  print $c[4],"\n";    # undefined
12  print $c[5],"\n";     # orange

13  print "**********\n" ;
```

Output

```
3    **********
4    redgreenyelloworange
5    red  green yellow orange
6    **********
7    red
8    green
9
10   yellow
11
12   orange
13   **********
```

E x p l a n a t i o n

1   The array, @*colors*, is assigned the elements, '*red*', '*green*', '*yellow*', and '*orange*'.
2   An array slice is created, consisting of four scalars, $c[0], $c[1], $c[3], and $c[5].
    Note: The subscripts in the array slice are not numbered consecutively.
3   A row of stars is printed, just for clarity.
4   The elements are not separated when printed.
5   When the array is enclosed in double quotes, the white space between elements is pre-
    served.
6   Another row of stars is printed.
7   The first element of the array slice, *red*, is printed.
8   The second element of the array slice, *green*, is printed.
9   The third element of the array slice is undefined. Its value is null because it was not
    assigned a value.
10 The fourth element of the array slice, *yellow*, is printed.
11 The fifth element of the array slice is undefined.
12 The sixth element of the array slice, *orange*, is printed.
13 Another row of stars is printed.

Multidimensional Arrays—Lists of Lists   (Perl 5)
Multidimensional arrays are sometimes called tables or matrices. They consist of rows and
columns and can be represented with multiple subscripts. In a two-dimensional array, the
first subscript represents the row and the second subscript represents the column.

In Perl, each row in a two-dimensional array is enclosed in square brackets. The row is an
unnamed list. An unnamed list is called an anonymous array which contains its own elements. The arrow operator, also called an infix operator, can be used to get the individual
elements of an array. There is an implied –> between adjacent brackets. (Anonymous variables will be discussed in detail in Chapter 10.)

E x a m p l e   4 . 1 9

```
(The Script)
   #!/usr/bin/perl
   # A two–dimensional array consisting of 4 rows and 3 columns.
1  @matrix=( [ 3 , 4, 10 ],   # Each row is an unnamed list
              [ 2,  7, 12 ],
              [ 0,  3,  4 ],
              [ 6,  5,  9 ],
        );
2  print "@matrix\n";
3  print "Row 0, column 0 is $matrix[0][0].\n";
              # can also be written - $matrix[0]–>[0]
4  print "Row 1, column  0 is $matrix[1][0].\n";
              # can also be written - $matrix[1]–>[0]
```

```
5        for($i=0;$i<=4;$i++){
6        for($x=0;$x<=3;$x++){
7                print "$matrix[$i][$x] ";
         }
   print "\n";
```

Output

```
2 ARRAY(0xbf838) ARRAY(0xc7768) ARRAY(0xc77a4) ARRAY(0xc77e0)
3 Row 0, column 0 is 3.
4 Row 1, column 0 is 2.
7 3 4 10
  2 7 12
  0 3 4
  6 5 9
```

Explanation

1   The array, @*matrix*, is assigned four unnamed or anonymous arrays. Each of the arrays has three values.
2   The addresses of the four anonymous arrays are printed. To access the individual elements of an anonymous array, double subscripts or the arrow operator must be used.
3   The first element of the first anonymous array in the @*matrix* array is printed. The –> is called the arrow or infix operator. It is used to dereference array and hash references. $*matrix[0][0]* or $*matrix[0]->[0]* is the first element of the first row, where subscripts start at zero.
4   The second row, first element of the @*matrix* is printed. $*matrix[1]->[0]* is another way to say $*matrix[1][0]*.
7   Print each element in the matrix.

Example 4.20

(The Script)
```
  #!/usr/bin/perl
1 @record=( "Adams",   [2, 1, 0, 0],
2           "Edwards", [1, 0, 3, 2],
            "Howard",  [3 ,3 ,2,0 ],
   );
3 print "In the first game $record[0] batted $record[1]->[0].\n";
4 print "In the first game $record[2] batted $record[3]->[0].\n";
5 print "In the first game $record[4] batted $record[5]->[0].\n";
```

O u t p u t

3 *In the first game Adams batted 2.*
4 *In the first game Edwards batted 1.*
5 *In the first game Howard batted 3.*

E x p l a n a t i o n

1 @*record* is a 6 element array consisting of three anonymous arrays, each of which is enclosed in brackets. "Adams" is the first element of the array, [2, 1, 0, 0] is the second element of the array, etc.
2 "Edwards" is the third element of the @record array.
3 When printing the first element, the subscript is 0. When printing the value of the second array, the anonymous array in brackets, two subscripts are required. The –> operator is not necessary. It is implied if not used. In the example, the –> is used to show that it can be placed only between adjacent brackets. For example, *$record->[1]->[0]* would be incorrect. *$record[1][0]* is fine without the arrow operator.
4 The third element of the @*record* is printed. The first element of the anonymous array (fourth element of the @*record* array) is printed.
5 The fifth element of the @*record* is printed. The first element of the anonymous array (sixth element of the @*record* array) is printed.

4.2.3   Associative Arrays (Hashes)

An associative array, more commonly called a hash, consists of one or more pairs of scalars—either strings, numbers, or Booleans. The first set of scalars is associated with the second set of scalars. The first string in the pair of strings is called the *key*, and the second string is called the *value*.

Assignment.   The array must be defined before the elements can be referenced. Since an associative array consists of pairs of values, indexed by the first element of each pair, if one of the elements in a pair is missing within the array definition, the association of the keys and their respective values will be affected. When assigning keys and values, make sure that you have a key associated with its corresponding value. When indexing an associative array, curly braces are used instead of square brackets.

E x a m p l e   4 . 2 1

```
1  %seasons=('Sp', 'Spring', 'Su', 'Summer', 'F', 'Fall', 'W', 'Winter');
2  %days=('Mon', 'Monday', 'Tue', 'Tuesday' ,'Wed',);
3  $days{'Wed'}="Wednesday";
4  $days{5}="Friday";
```

Explanation

1 The hash (associative array), *%seasons*, is assigned keys and values. The string *'Sp'*, is the key with a corresponding value of *'Spring'*; the string *'Su'* is the key for its corresponding value *'Summer'*, etc.

2 The associative array, *%days*, is assigned keys and values. The third key, *Wed*, has no corresponding value. This does not produce an error; the value for that key is simply undefined.

3 Individual elements of an associative array are scalars. The key, *'Wed'*, is assigned the string value "*Wednesday*". The index is enclosed in curly braces.

4 The key, *5*, is assigned the string value "*Friday*". Note: the keys do not have any consecutive numbering order and the pairs can consist of numbers and/or strings.

Accessing Elements.   When accessing the values of a hash, the subscript consists of the key enclosed in curly braces. Perl provides a set of functions to list the keys, values, and each of the elements of the hash. (See Section 4.4, *Array Functions*.)

Due to the internal hashing techniques used to store the keys, Perl does not guarantee the order in which an entire hash is printed.

Example 4.22

```
(The Script)
     #!/usr/bin/perl
1    %department = (
2       'Eng'=> 'Engineering',      # Eng is the key, Engineering is the value
        'M' =>    'Math',
        'S'=>     'Science',
        'CS'=>    'Computer Science',
        'Ed'=>    'Education',
3    );
4    $department = $department{"M"};
5    $school = $department{"Ed"};
6    print "I work in the $department section\n" ;
7    print "Funds in the $school department are being cut.\n";
8    print qq/I'm currently enrolled in a $department{"CS"} course.\n/;
9    print qq/The department associative array looks like this:\n/;
10   print %department, "\n";   #The printout is not in the expected order due to
                                # internal hashing
```

O u t p u t

6   *I work in the Math section*
7   *Funds in the Education department are being cut.*
8   *I'm currently enrolled in a Computer Science course.*
9   *The department associative array looks like this:*
10 *SScienceCSComputer ScienceEdEducationMMathEngEngineering*

E x p l a n a t i o n

1   The hash is called *%department*. It is assigned keys and values.
2   The first *key* is the string, *Eng*, and the *value* associated with it is, *Engineering*.
3   The closing parenthesis and semicolon end the assignment.
4   The scalar, *$department*, is assigned, *Math*, the value associated with the *'M'* key.
5   The scalar, *$school*, is assigned, *Education*, the value associated with the *'Ed'* key.
6   The quoted string is printed; the scalar, *$department*, is interpolated.
7   The quoted string is printed; the scalar, *$school*, is interpolated.
8   The quoted string and the value associated with the *'CS'* key are printed.
9   The quoted string is printed.
10 The entire hash is printed with keys and values packed together and not in expected order.

Hashes of Hashes (Perl 5)

Nested Associative Arrays (Perl 5). More complex data structures can be created in Perl 5. For example, a hash can contain another hash. It is like a record that contains records. The nested hash has no name. It is an anonymous hash and can be dereferenced with the arrow operator. Each of the keys in the named hash contains a value which is itself another hash. This anonymous hash consists of its own key/value pairs. (See Chapter 10, References.)

E x a m p l e   4 . 2 3

(The Script)

```
                          key              value
                     key   value    key   value
    #!/usr/bin/perl       /    \       /    \
1   %students=(  Math => { Joe => 100, Joan => 95 },
                 Science => { Bill => 85, Dan => 76 }
    );
2   print "On the math test Joan got ";
3   print qq/$students{"Math"}->{"Joan"}.\n/;
4   print "On the science Bill got ";
5   print qq/$students{"Science"}->{"Bill"}.\n/;
```

O u t p u t

3 *On the math test Joan got 95.*
5 *On the science test Bill got 85.*

E x p l a n a t i o n

1 The associative array, *%students*, consists of two keys, *Math* and *Science*.
   The values associated with those keys are enclosed in curly braces. The value contains
   a set of nested keys and values. The value for the *Math* key contains two nested keys,
   Joe and *Joan*, with their respective values, *100* and *95*. The value for the *Science* key
   contains two nested keys, *Bill* and *Dan*, with their respective values, *85* and *76*. The nested keys and values are in an unnamed or anonymous hash.
3 The arrow (infix operator) operator, –>, allows you to access the anonymous nested hash
   value of the *%student* associative array.

Array of Hashes. (Perl 5).   An array can contain nested hashes.   It's like an array of
records. Each of the elements of the array is an anonymous hash with a set of keys and corresponding values.

E x a m p l e   4 . 2 4

```
(The Script)
    #!/usr/bin/perl
 1 @stores=( { Boss=>"Ari Goldberg",
        Employees=> 24,
         Registers => 10,
            Sales => 15000.00,
            },
 2          { Boss=>"Ben Chien",
        Employees=> 12,
          Registers => 5,
            Sales => 3500.00,
            },
    );
 3 print "The number of elements in the array: ",
 4       $#stores + 1, "\n";   # The number of the last subscript + 1

 5 for($i=0; $i< $#stores + 1; $i++){
 6          print $stores[$i]{"Boss"},"\n";   #Accessing an element of the array
            print $stores[$i]{"Employees"},"\n";
            print $stores[$i]{"Registers"},"\n";
            print $stores[$i]{"Sales"},"\n";
            print "-" x 20 ,"\n";

    }
```

O u t p u t

3   *The number of elements in the array: 2*
6   *Ari Goldberg*
    24
    10
    15000

    Ben Chien
    12
    5
    3500

E x p l a n a t i o n

1   The array *@stores* contains two hashes, one for Ari Goldberg's store and one for Ben Chien's store. Each of the elements of the array is a hash.
2   This is the second element of the *@stores* array. It is a hash.
4   *$#stores* evaluates to the number of the last subscript in the *@stores* array. Since subscripts start at *0,* by adding *1,* we get the number of elements in the array, which is *2.*
6   To access a value in one of the elements of the array, first the number of the index is specified and then the key into the hash.

4.3   **Reading from STDIN**

The three filehandles STDIN, STDOUT, and STDERR, as you may recall, are names given to three predefined streams, *stdin*, *stdout*, and *stderr*. By default, these filehandles are associated with your terminal. When printing output to the terminal screen, STDOUT is used. When printing errors, STDERR is used. When assigning user input to a variable, STDIN is used.

The Perl <> input operator encloses the STDIN filehandle so that the next line of standard input can be read from the terminal keyboard and assigned to a variable. Unlike the *Shell* and *C* operations for reading input, Perl retains the newline on the end of the string when reading a line from standard input. If you don't want the newline, then you have to explicitly remove it or "chop" it off (see the *chop* function).

4.3.1   Assigning Input to a Scalar Variable

When reading input from the filehandle STDIN, if the context is scalar, one line of input is read, including the carriage return, and assigned to a scalar variable as a single string.

E x a m p l e   4 . 2 5

```
    #!/usr/bin/perl
1   print "What is your name?  ";
2   $name = <STDIN>;
    print "What is your father's name? ";
3   $paname=<>;
    print "Hello respected one, $paname";
```

O u t p u t

```
    What is your name? Isabel
    What is your father's name? Nick
    Hello respected one, Nick
```

E x p l a n a t i o n

1 The string "What is your name?" is sent to STDOUT, the screen by default.
2 The input operator <> surrounding STDIN reads one line of input and assigns that line and its trailing newline to the scalar variable *$name*.
3 If the input operator is empty, the next line of input is read from STDIN and the behavior is identical to line 2, except input is assigned to *$paname*.

4.3.2   The chop and the chomp Functions

The *chop* function removes the last character in a scalar variable and the last character of each word in an array. It is used primarily for removing the newline from the line of input coming into your program, whether it is STDIN, a file, or the result of command substitution. When you first start learning Perl, the trailing newline can be a real pain!

The *chomp* function was introduced in Perl 5 to remove the last character in a scalar variable and the last character of each word in a array only if that character is the newline (or, to be more precise, the character that represents the input line separator, initially defined as a newline and stored in the $/ variable). Using *chomp* instead of *chop* protects you from inadvertently removing some character other than the newline.

Example 4.26

(The Script)

```
     #!/usr/bin/perl
1    print "Hello there, and what is your name? ";
2    $name = <STDIN>;
3    print "$name is a very high class name.\n";
4    chop($name);    # Removes the last character no matter what it is.
5    print "$name is a very high class name.\n\n";
6    chop($name);
7    print "$name has been chopped a little too much.\n";

8    print "What is your age?  ";
9    chomp($age=<STDIN>); # Removes the last character if it is the newline.
10   chomp($age);    # The last character is not removed unless a newline
11   print "For $age, you look so young!\n";
```

Output

1   *Hello there, and what is your name?* **Joe Smith**
3   *Joe Smith*
    is a very high class name.
5   *Joe Smith is a very high class name.*

7   *Joe Smit has been chopped a little too much.*

8   *What is your age?* **25**
11 *For 25, you look so young!*

Explanation

1   The quoted string is printed by default to the screen, STDOUT.
2   The scalar variable is assigned a single line of text typed in by the user. The <> operator (called the diamond operator) is used for read operations. In this case, it reads from STDIN, your terminal keyboard until the carriage return is entered. The newline is included in the text that is assigned to the variable, *$name*.
3   The value of *$name* is printed. Note that the newline breaks the line after *Joe Smith,* the user input.
4   The *chop* function removes the last character of the string assigned to *$name*. The character that was chopped is returned.
5   The string is printed again after the *chop* operation. The last character was removed (in this case, the newline).
6   This time *chop* will remove the last character in *Joe Smith's* name, i.e., the 'h' in *Smith*.
7   The quoted string is printed to STDOUT, indicating that the last character was removed.

9   The user input is first assigned to the variable *$age*. The trailing newline is *chomped*. The character whose value is stored in the special variable, $/, is removed. This value is by default the newline character. The number of characters chomped is returned. Because of the low precedence of the equal (=) operator, parentheses ensure that the assignment occurs before the *chomp* function "chomps."

10 The second *chomp* will have no effect. The newline has already been removed and *chomp* removes only the newline. It's safer than using *chop*.

11 The chomped variable string is printed.

The read Function. The *read* function[8] allows you to read a number of bytes into a variable from a specified file handle. If reading from standard input, the file handle is STDIN. The *read* function returns the number of bytes that were read.

Format:

```
number_of_bytes = read(FILEHANDLE,buffer,
how_many_bytes);
```

E x a m p l e   4 . 2 7

(The Script
```
#!/usr/bin/perl
# Program to demonstrate the read function
```
1   print "Describe your favorite food in 10 bytes or less.\n";
    print "If you type less than 10 characters, press Ctrl-d on a line by itself.\n";
2   **$number=read(STDIN, $favorite, 10);**
3   print "You just typed: $favorite\n";
4   print "The number of bytes read was $number.\n";

O u t p u t

1   *Describe your favorite food in 10 bytes or less.*
    If you type less than 10 characters, press Ctrl-d on a line by itself.
    apple pie and ice cream
3   *You just typed: apple pie*
4   *The number of bytes read was 10.*

---

8. Similar to the *fread* function in the C language.

Explanation

1 The user is asked for input. If he types less than 10 characters, he should press Ctrl-d to exit.
2 The *read* function takes three arguments: the first argument is STDIN, the place from where the input is coming; the second argument is the scalar, *$favorite*, where the input will be stored; and the last argument is the number of characters (bytes) that will be read.
3 The 10 characters read in are printed. The rest of the characters were discarded.
4 The number of characters (bytes) was stored in *$number* and is printed.

The getc Function.   The *getc* function gets a single character from the keyboard or from a file. At EOF, *getc* returns a null string.

Format:

```
getc(FILEHANDLE)
getc FILEHANDLE
getc
```

Example 4.28

(The Script)
```
    #!/usr/bin/perl
    print "Answer y or n   ";
1   $answer=getc;   # Gets one character from stdin
2   $restofit=<>;      # What remains in the input buffer is assigned $restofit.
3   print "$answer\n";
4   print "The characters left in the input buffer are: $restofit\n";
```

Output

1 *Answer y or n   yessirreebob <CR>*
3 *y*
4 *The characters left in the input buffer are: essirreebob*

Explanation

1 Only one character is read from the input buffer by *getc* and stored in the scalar, *$answer*.
2 The characters remaining in the input buffer are stored in *$restofit*. This clears the input buffer. Now, if you ask for input later on in the program, you will not be picking up those characters that were left hanging around in the buffer.
3 The character that was read in by *getc* is printed.
4 The characters stored in *$restofit* are displayed.

4.3.3   Assigning Input to an Array

When reading input from the filehandle, STDIN, if the context is array, then each line is read with its newline and is treated as a single list item, and the read is continued until you press ^d (Ctrl-d) for end of file. Normally, you will not assign input to an array because it could eat up a large amount of memory.

E x a m p l e   4 . 2 9

(The Script)
```
    #!/usr/bin/perl
1   print "Tell me everything about yourself.\n ";
2   @all = <STDIN>;
3   print "@all";
```

O u t p u t

```
1   Tell me everything about yourself.
2   O.K. Let's see I was born before computers.
    I grew up in the 50s.
    I was in the hippie generation.
    I'm starting to get bored with talking about myself.
    ^D (Must press ^d (Ctrl-d) to stop input)
3   O.K. Let's see I was born before computers.
    I grew up in the 50s.
    I was in the hippie generation.
    I'm starting to get bored with talking about myself.
```

E x p l a n a t i o n

1   The string "Tell me everything about yourself." is printed to STDOUT.
2   The input operator <> surrounding STDIN, reads input lines until Ctrl-d, end-of-file, is reached. Each line and its trailing newline are stored as a list element of the array @*all*.
3   The user input is printed to the screen after the user presses Ctrl-d.

4.3.4   Assigning Input to an Associative Array

E x a m p l e   4 . 3 0

```
    #!/usr/bin/perl
1   $course_number=101;
2   print "What is the name of  course 101?";
3   $course{$course_number} = <STDIN>;
```

E x p l a n a t i o n

1   The scalar variable, *$course_number*, is assigned the value *101*.
2   The string "What is the name of course 101?" is printed to STDOUT.
3   The name of the associative array is *%course*. We are assigning a *value* to one of the hash
    elements. The key is *$course_number* enclosed in curly braces.

4.4   Array Functions

Arrays can grow and shrink. The Perl array functions allow you to insert or delete elements
of the array from the front, middle, or end of the list.

4.4.1   The chop and chomp Functions (With Lists)

The *chop* function chops off the last character of a string and returns the chopped character,
usually, for removing the newline after input is assigned to a scalar variable. If a list is
chopped, *chop* will remove the last letter of each string in the list.

The *chomp* function removes the last character of each element in a list if it ends with a newline and returns the number of newlines it removed.

Format:

```
chop(LIST)

chomp(LIST)
```

E x a m p l e   4 . 3 1

(In the Script)
```
    #!/usr/bin/perl
1   @line=( "red", "green", "orange");
2   chop(@line);  # chops the last character off each string in the list
3   print "@line";
4   @line=( "red", "green", "orange");
5   chomp(@line);  # chomps the newline off each string in the list
6   print "@line";
```

O u t p u t

3   *re gree orang*
6   *red green orange*

E x p l a n a t i o n

1 The array, *@line*, is assigned list elements.
2 The array is chopped. The *chop* function chops the last character from each element of the array.
3 The chopped array is printed.
4 The array, *@line*, is assigned elements.
5 The *chomp* function will chop off the newline character from each word in the array. This is a safer function than chop.
6 Since there were no newlines on the end of the words in the array, it was not chomped.

4.4.2   The grep Function

The *grep* function evaluates the expression (EXPR) for each element of the array (LIST). The return value is another array consisting of those elements for which the expression evaluated as true. As a scalar value, the return value is the number of times the expression was true (i.e., the number of times the pattern was found).

Format:

```
grep(EXPR,LIST)
```

E x a m p l e   4 . 3 2

```
   #!/usr/bin/perl
1  @list = (tomatoes, tomorrow, potatoes, phantom, Tommy);
2  $count = grep( /tom/i, @list);
3  @items= grep( /tom/i, @list);
4  print "Found items: @items\nNumber found: $count\n";
```

O u t p u t

4 *Found items: tomatoes tomorrow phantom Tommy*
   Number found: 4

E x p l a n a t i o n

1 The array, *@list*, is assigned list elements.
2 The *grep* function searches for the regular expression, *tom*. The *i* turns off case sensitivity. When the return value is assigned to a scalar, the result is the number of times the regular expression was matched.
3 Grep searches for the regular expression, *tom*. The *i* turns off case sensitivity. When the return value is assigned to an array, the result is a list of the items that were matched.

4.4.3   The join Function

The *join* function joins the elements of an array into a single string and separates each element of the array with a given delimiter—opposite of *split*. It can be used after the *split* function has broken a string into array elements. The expression, DELIMITER, is the value of the delimiter that will separate the array elements. The LIST consists of the array elements. (See also the *pack* function.)

Format:

```
join(DELIMITER, LIST)
```

E x a m p l e   4 . 3 3

(The Script)
```
    #!/usr/bin/perl
1   $name="Joe Blow";
    $birth="11/12/86";
    $address="10 Main St.";
2   print join(":", $name, $birth, $address ), "\n";
```

O u t p u t

2   *Joe Blow:11/12/86:10 Main St.*

E x p l a n a t i o n

1   A string is assigned to a scalar.
2   The *join* function joins the three scalars using a colon delimiter and the new string is printed.

4.4.4   The pop Function

The *pop* function pops off the last element of an array and returns it. The array size is decreased by one.

Format:

```
pop(ARRAY)
pop ARRAY
```

E x a m p l e   4 . 3 4

(In Script)
```
   #!/usr/bin/perl
1  @names=("Bob", "Dan", "Tom", "Guy");
2  print "@names\n";
3  $got = pop(@names);   # pops off last element of the array
4  print "$got\n";
5  print "@names\n";
```

O u t p u t

2 *Bob Dan Tom Guy*
4 *Guy*
5 *Bob Dan Tom*

E x p l a n a t i o n

1   The @*name* array is assigned list elements.
2   The array is printed.
3   The *pop* function removes the last element of the array and returns the popped item.
4   The *$got* scalar contains the popped item, *Guy*.
5   The new array is printed.

4.4.5   The push Function

The *push* function pushes values onto the end of an array, increasing the length of the array.

Format:

```
push(ARRAY, LIST)
```

E x a m p l e   4 . 3 5

(In Script)
```
   #!/usr/bin/perl
1  @ names=("Bob", "Dan", "Tom", "Guy");
2  push(@names, Jim, Joseph, Archie);
3  print "@names \n";
```

O u t p u t

2 *Bob Dan Tom Guy Jim Joseph Archie*

E x p l a n a t i o n

1   The array, *@names*, is assigned list values.
2   The *push* function pushes three more elements onto the end of the array.
3   The new array has three more elements appended to it.

4.4.6   The shift Function

The *shift* function shifts off and returns the first element of an array, decreasing the size of the array by one element. If ARRAY is omitted, then the ARGV array is shifted, and if in a subroutine, the @_ array is shifted.

Format:

```
shift(ARRAY)
shift ARRAY
shift
```

E x a m p l e   4 . 3 6

(In Script)
```
    #!/usr/bin/perl
1   @names=("Bob", "Dan", "Tom", "Guy");
2   $ret  = shift @names;
3   print "@names\n";
4   print "The item shifted is $ret.\n";
```

O u t p u t

3   *Dan Tom Guy*
4   *The item shifted is Bob.*

E x p l a n a t i o n

1   The array, *@names*, is assigned list values.
2   The *shift* function removes the first element of the array and returns that element to the scalar, *$ret*, i.e., *Bob*.
3   The new array has been shortened by one element.

E x a m p l e   4 . 3 7

(In Script)
```
   #!/usr/bin/perl
1  @names=( Jody, Bert, Tom ) ;
2  unshift(@names, Liz, Daniel);
3  print "@names\n";
```

O u t p u t

3   *Liz Daniel Jody Bert Tom*

E x p l a n a t i o n

1   The array *@names* is assigned three values: *Jody, Bert,* and *Tom.*
2   The unshift function will prepend *Liz* and *Daniel* to the array.
3   The *@names* array is printed.

4.4.7   The splice Function

The *splice* function removes and replaces elements in an array. The OFFSET is the starting position where elements are to be removed. The LENGTH is the number of items from the OFFSET position to be removed. The LIST consists of new elements that are to replace the old ones.

Format:

```
splice(ARRAY, OFFSET, LENGTH, LIST)
splice(ARRAY, OFFSET, LENGTH)
splice(ARRAY, OFFSET)
```

E x a m p l e   4 . 3 8

(The Script)
```
   #!/usr/bin/perl
1  @colors=(red, green, purple, blue, brown);
2  print "The original array is @colors\n";
3  @newcolors=splice(@colors, 2, 3, yellow, orange);
4  print "The removed items are  @newcolors\n";
5  print "The spliced array is now @colors\n";
```

O u t p u t

2 *The original array is red green purple blue brown*
4 *The removed items are purple blue brown*
5 *The spliced array is now red green yellow orange*

E x p l a n a t i o n

1 An array of five colors is created.
2 The original array is printed.
3 The *splice* function will delete elements starting at offset 2 (offset is initially 0) and re-move the next three elements. The removed elements (*purple*, *blue*, and *brown*) are stored in @*newcolors*. The colors "*yellow*" and "*orange*" will replace the ones that were removed.

4.4.8   The split Function

The *split* function splits up a string (EXPR) by some delimiter (whitespace by default) and returns an array. The first argument is the delimiter, and the second is the string to be split. When processing files, as you would with *awk*, the Perl *split* function is used to create fields. If a string is not supplied as the expression, the $_ string is split.

The DELIMITER matches the delimiters that are used to separate the fields. If DELIM-ITER is omitted, the delimiter defaults to whitespace (spaces, tabs, or newlines). If the DELIMITER doesn't match a delimiter, *split* returns the original string. You can specify more than one delimiter using the regular expression metacharacter, [ ]. For example, [+\t:] represents zero or more spaces, or a tab, or a colon.

The LIMIT specifies the number of fields that can be split. If there are more than LIMIT fields, the remaining fields will all be part of the last one.   If the LIMIT is omitted, the *split* function has its own LIMIT, which is one more than the number of fields in EXPR. (See -a switch for auto split mode, Appendix A.)

Format:

```
split(/DELIMITER/,EXPR,LIMIT)
split(/DELIMITER/,EXPR)
split(/DELIMITER/)
split
```

Example 4.39

(The Script)
```
  #!/usr/bin/perl
1 $line="a b c d e";
2 @letter=split(' ',$line);
3 print "The first letter is $letter[0]\n";
4 print "The second letter is $letter[1]\n";
```

Output

3 *The first letter is a*
4 *The second letter is b*

Explanation

1   The scalar variable *$line* is assigned the string "a b c d e".
2   The value in *$line* (scalar) is a single string of letters. The *split* function will split the string using whitespace as a delimiter. The *@letter* array will be assigned the individual elements, 'a', 'b','c','d', 'e'. Using single quotes as the delimiter is NOT the same as using the regular expression, / /. The ' ' resembles *awk* in splitting lines on whitespace. Leading whitespace is ignored. The regular expression, / /, includes leading whitespace, creating as many null initial fields as there are whitespaces.
3   The first element of the *@letters* array is printed.
4   The second element of the *@letters* array is printed.

Example 4.40

(At the Command Line)
```
1 $ perl –ne '@str=split(/:/);print $str[0],"\n"' /etc/passwd
  nobody
  daemon
  sys
  bin
  uucp
  news
  ingres
  audit
  sync
  sysdiag
  sundiag
  ellie
```

Explanation

1   The *$_* variable holds each line of the file "*/etc/passwd*"; Each line of */etc/passwd* is assigned to *$_*. *$_* is also the default line for *split*. The *split* function splits the line using the ":" as a delimiter and returns the line to the array, *@str*. The first element of the *@str* array, *str[0]*, is printed.

Example 4.41

(Printing the contents of the "datebook" file)
$ cat datebook
Betty Boop:245–836–8357:635 Cutesy Lane, Hollywood, CA 91464:6/23/23:14500
Igor Chevsky:385–375–8395:3567 Populus Place, Caldwell, NJ 23875:6/18/68:23400
Norma Corder:397–857–2735:74 Pine Street, Dearborn, MI 23874:3/28/45:245700
Jennifer Cowan:548–834–2348:583 Laurel Ave., Kingsville, TX 83745:10/1/35:58900
Fred Fardbarkle:674 843 1385:20 Park Lane, Duluth, MN 23850:4/12/23:78000

(The Script)
```
    #!/usr/bin/perl
    # This script is called empscript.
    while(<>){
1        ($name,$phone,$address,$bd,$sal)=split(/:/);
2        print "$name\t $phone\n" ;
    }
```

Output

$ empscript datebook
2	*Betty Boop*	*245–836–8357*
	Igor Chevsky	*385–375–8395*
	Norma Corder	*397–857–2735*
	Jennifer Cowan	*548–834–2348*
	Fred Fardbarkle	*674–843–1385*

Explanation

1   Perl loops through the file one line at a time. Each line of the file is stored in the *$_* variable. The *split* function splits each line, using the colon as a delimiter.
2   The array consists of five scalars, *$name*, *$phone*, *$address*, *$bd*, and *$sal*. The values of *$name* and *$phone* are printed.

Example 4.42

(The Script)

```
   #!/usr/bin/perl
1  $string= "Joe Blow:11/12/86:10 Main St.:Boston, MA:02530";
2  @line=split(/:/, $string);        # the string delimiter is a colon
3  print @line,"\n";
4  print "The guy's name is $line[0].\n";
5  print "The birthday is $line[1].\n\n";

6  @str=split(/:/, $string, 2);
7  print $str[0],"\n"; #the first element of the array
8  print $str[1],"\n"; #the rest of the array because limit is 2
9  print $str[2],"\n"; #nothing is printed

10 @str=split(/:/, $string);  # Limit not stated will be one more than total
                                 number of fields
11 print $str[0],"\n";
12 print $str[1],"\n";
13 print $str[2],"\n";
14 print $str[3],"\n";
15 print $str[4],"\n";
16 print $str[5],"\n";

17 ( $name, $birth, $address )=split(/:/, $string); #limit is implicitly 4, one
                  # more than the number of fields specified
18 print $name , "\n";
19 print $birth,"\n";
20 print $address,"\n";
```

Output

```
3     Joe Blow11/12/8610 Main St.Boston, MA02530
4     The guy's name is Joe Blow.
5     The birthday is 11/12/86.

7     Joe Blow
8     11/12/86:10 Main St.:Boston, MA:02530
9

11    Joe Blow
12    11/12/86
13    10 Main St.
14    Boston, MA
```

15	*02530*
16	
18	*Joe Blow*
19	*11/12/86*
20	*10 Main St.*

Explanation

2   The scalar, *$string*, is split by colons.

6   The delimiter is a colon. The limit is 2.

10 Limit not stated will be one more than total number of fields.

17 Limit is implicitly 4, one more than the number of fields specified.

4.4.9   The sort Function

The *sort* function sorts and returns a sorted array. If SUBROUTINE is omitted, the sort is in string comparison order. If SUBROUTINE is specified, the first argument to *sort* is the name of the subroutine followed by a list of integers. The subroutine returns an integer less than, equal to, or greater than 0. The values are passed to the subroutine by reference and are received by the special variables, *$a* and *$b*, not the normal *@_* array.

Format:

```
sort(SUBROUTINE LIST)
sort(LIST)
sort SUBROUTINE LIST
sort LIST
```

Example 4.43

```
(In Script)
  #!/usr/bin/perl
1 @string=(4.5, x, 68,  a, B, c, 10, 1000, 1);
2 @string_sort=sort(@string);
3 print "@string_sort\n";

4 sub numeric { $a <=> $b ; }
5 @number_sort=sort numeric 1000, -22.5, 10, 55, 0;
6 print "@number_sort.\n";9
```

---

9. Larry Wall, *Programming Perl* (Sebastopol, CA: O'Reilly)

O u t p u t

3 *1 10 1000 4.5 68 B a c x*
6 *-22.5 0 10 55 1000*

E x p l a n a t i o n

1 The @*string* array will contain a list of items to be sorted.
2 The **sort** function performs a string (ASCII) sort on the items.
3 The sorted string is printed.
4 A subroutine, *numeric*, is defined. The special variables, $a and $b, replace the @_ in the subroutine and are used with the comparison operator. $a and $b receive the numeric values to be sorted.
5 The *sort* function performs a numeric sort by calling the subroutine, *numeric*, and passing a list of numbers. These values are passed call by reference.

4.4.10   The reverse Function

The *reverse* function reverses the elements in an array, so that if it was descending, now it is ascending, etc.

Format:

```
reverse(LIST)
reverse LIST
```

E x a m p l e   4 . 4 4

(In Script)
```
    #!/usr/bin/perl
1   @names=("Bob", "Dan", "Tom", "Guy");
2   print "@names \n";
3   @reversed=reverse(@names),"\n";
4   print "@reversed\n";
```

O u t p u t

2 *Bob Dan Tom Guy*
4 *Guy Tom Dan Bob*

E x p l a n a t i o n

1 The array, @*names*, is assigned list values.
2 The original array is printed.
3 The *reversed* function reverses the elements in the list.
4 The reversed array is printed.

4.4.11   The unshift Function

The *unshift* function prepends LIST to the front of the array.

Format:

```
unshift(ARRAY, LIST)
```

4.5   Associative Array Functions

4.5.1   The keys Function

The *keys* function returns, in random order, an array whose elements are the keys of an associative array (see Section 4.5.2, *values Function,* and Section 4.5.3, *each Function*).

Format:

```
keys(ASSOC_ARRAY)
keys ASSOC_ARRAY
```

E x a m p l e   4 . 4 5

```
(In Script)
   #!/usr/bin/perl
1  %weekday= (
         '1'=> 'Monday',
         '2'=>'Tuesday',
         '3'=>'Wednesday',
         '4'=>'Thursday',
         '5'=>'Friday',
         '6'=>'Saturday',
         '7'=>'Sunday',
   );
2  foreach $key ( keys(%weekday) ){print "$key ";}
   print "\n";
```

O u t p u t

1 2 3 4 5 6 7

E x p l a n a t i o n

1 The associative array, *%weekday*, is assigned keys and values.
2 For each value in the associative array, *%weekday*, call the *keys* function to get the key. Assign the key value to the scalar, *$key*, and print it.

4.5.2   The values Function

The *values* function returns, in random order, an array consisting of all the values of an associative array.

Format:

```
values(ASSOC_ARRAY)
values ASSOC_ARRAY
```

E x a m p l e   4 . 4 6

(In Script)
```
   #!/usr/bin/perl
1  %weekday= (
          '1'=> 'Monday',
          '2'=>'Tuesday',
          '3'=>'Wednesday',
          '4'=>'Thursday',
          '5'=>'Friday',
          '6'=>'Saturday',
          '7'=>'Sunday',
   );
2  foreach $value ( values(%weekday)){print "$value";}
   print "\n";
```

O u t p u t

2 *Monday Tuesday Wednesday Thursday Friday Saturday Sunday*

E x p l a n a t i o n

1 The associative array, *%weekday*, is assigned keys and values.
2 For each value in the associative array, *%weekday*, call the *values* function to get the value associated with each key. Assign that value to the scalar, *$value*, and print it to STDOUT.

4.5.3   The each Function

The *eeach* function returns, in random order, a two-element array whose elements are the *key* and the corresponding *value* of an associative array.

Format:

```
each(ASSOC_ARRAY)
```

E x a m p l e   4 . 4 7

(In Script)
```
   #!/usr/bin/perl
1  %weekday=(
         '1'=> 'Monday',
         '2'=>'Tuesday',
         '3'=>'Wednesday',
         '4'=>'Thursday',
         '5'=>'Friday',
         '6'=>'Saturday',
         '7'=>'Sunday',
   );

2  while(($key,$value)=each %weekday){
3      print "$key = $value\n";
   }
```

O u t p u t

```
3  1 = Monday
   2 = Tuesday
   3 = Wednesday
   4 = Thursday
   5 = Friday
   6 = Saturday
   7 = Sunday
```

E x p l a n a t i o n

1   The associative array, *%weekday*, is assigned keys and values.
2   The *each* function returns each key and its associated *value* of the *%weekday* associative array. They are assigned to the scalars $key and $value, respectively.
3   The keys and values are printed.

4.5.4   The delete Function

The *delete* function deletes a value from an associative array. The deleted value is returned if successful.[10]

Format:

```
delete   $ASSOC_ARRAY{KEY}
```

E x a m p l e   4 . 4 8

```
(In Script)
   #!/usr/bin/perl
1  %weekday= (
          '1', 'Monday',
          '2', 'Tuesday',
          '3', 'Wednesday',
          '4', 'Thursday',
          '5', 'Friday',
          '6', 'Saturday',
          '7', 'Sunday',
   );
2  foreach $key (keys %weekday){
3        delete $weekday{$key};
   }
```

E x p l a n a t i o n

1   The associative array, *%weekday*, is assigned keys and values.
2   The *keys* function returns each key in the *$weekday* associative array.
3   The delete function removes all elements of the associative array.

---

10. If a value in the %ENV array is deleted, the environment is changed. (See Section 4.6.2.)

4.6   **More Associative Arrays**

4.6.1   **Loading an Associative Array from a File**

E x a m p l e   4 . 4 9

(The Database)
```
    1 Steve Blenheim
    2 Betty Boop
    3 Igor Chevsky
    4 Norma Cord
    5 Jon DeLoach
    6 Karen Evich
```

(The Script)
```
    #!/usr/bin/perl
    # Loading an Associative Array from a file.
1   open(NAMES,"emp.names") || die "Can't open emp.names: $!\n";
2   while(<NAMES>){
3       ( $num, $name )= split(' ', $_);
4       $realid{$num} = $name;
    }
5   close NAMES;

6   while(1){
7       print "Number for which name? ";
8       chomp($num=<STDIN>);
9       last unless $num;
10      print $realid{$num},"\n";
    }
```

O u t p u t

```
7   Number for which name? 1
10  Steve Blenheim
    Number for which name? 4
    Norma Cord
    Number for which name? 5
    Jon DeLoach
    Number for which name? 2
    Betty Boop
    Number for which name? 6
    Karen Evich
    Number for which name? 8

    Number for which name? 3
    Igor Chevsky
    Number for which name?   ( CR )
```

E x p l a n a t i o n

1   Open a file called "emp.names" for reading via the *NAMES* filehandle.
2   Loop through the file a line at a time.
3   Assign a number to *$num* and a name to *$name*.
4   Create an associative array called *%realid*.
5   Close the filehandle.
6   Start the *while* loop.
7   Ask the user for a number to be associated with a name.
8   Read in the number and chomp the newline.
9   Exit the loop if *$num* does not have a value.
10   Print the "name" value associated with the "number" key.

4.6.2   Special Associative Arrays

The %ENV Associative Array.   The %ENV associative array contains the environment variables handed to Perl from the parent Shell. The key is the name of the environment variable, and the value is what was assigned to it. If you change this value, you will alter the environment for your Perl script and any processes spawned from it.

E x a m p l e   4 . 5 0

```
(In Script)
   #!/usr/bin/perl
1  foreach $key (keys(%ENV){
2              print "$key\n";
   }
3  print "Your login name $ENV{'LOGNAME'}\n";
4  $pwd=$ENV{'PWD'};
5  print "\n", $pwd, "\n";
   }
```

O u t p u t

```
2  OPENWINHOME
   MANPATH
   FONTPATH
   LOGNAME
   USER
   TERMCAP
   TERM
   SHELL
   PWD
   HOME
```

PATH
WINDOW_PARENT
WMGR_ENV_PLACEHOLDER

3 *Your login name is ellie*

5 */home/jody/home*

E x p l a n a t i o n

1 Iterate through the *foreach* loop to get the keys of the *%ENV* associative array.
2 Print the key value.
3 Print the value of the key 'LOGNAME' .
4 Assign the value of the key 'PWD' to *$pwd*.
5 Print the value of $pwd.

The %SIG Associative Array.   The %SIG associative array allows you to set signal handlers for signals. If, for example, you press ^C when your program is running, that is a signal, identified by the name, SIGINT. (See UNIX manual pages for a complete list of signals.) The default action of SIGINT is to interrupt your process. The signal handler is a subroutine that is automatically called when a signal is sent to the process. Normally the handler is used to perform a clean-up operation or to check some flag value before the script aborts. (All signal handlers are assumed to be set in the main package.)

The %SIG array only contains values for signals set within the Perl script.

E x a m p l e   4 . 5 1

```
(In Script)
    #!/usr/bin/perl
1   sub handler{
2        local($sig) = @_;  # first argument is signal name
3        print "Caught SIG$sig—shutting down\n";
         exit(0);
    }
4   $SIG{'INT'} = 'handler';  # Catch ^C
    print "Here I am!\n";
5   sleep(10);
6   $SIG{'INT'}='DEFAULT';
```

E x p l a n a t i o n

1   *"handler"* is the name of the subroutine. The subroutine is defined.
2   *$sig* is a local variable and will be assigned the signal name.
3   When the SIGINT signal arrives, this message will appear, and the script will exit.
4   The value assigned to the key 'INT' is the name of the subroutine, *handler*. When the signal arrives, the handler is called.
5   The *sleep* function gives you 10 seconds to press ^C to see what happens.
6   The default action is restored. The default action is to abort the process.

4.6.3   The %INC Associative Array

The %INC associative array contains the entries for each filename that has been included via the *do* or *require* functions. The key is the filename; the value is the location of the actual file found. (See Chapter 9.)

4.6.4   Context

In summary of the "funny" characters, the way that Perl evaluates variables depends on how the variables are being used, i.e., they are evaluated by context, either scalar or list.

If the value on the left-hand side of an assignment statement is a scalar, then the expression on the right-hand side is evaluated in a scalar context, whereas if the value on the left-hand side is an array, the right-hand side is evaluated in a list context.

Section 4.3 is a good review of how context is handled. You'll see examples throughout the rest of this book where context plays a major roll.

5

Where's the Operator?

5.1 About Perl Operators

An operator manipulates data objects called operands. The operands can be either strings, numbers, or a combination of both. Data objects can be manipulated in a number of ways by the large number of operators provided by Perl. Operators are symbols that produce a result based on some rules. Most of the Perl operators are borrowed from the C language, although Perl has some additional operators of its own.[1]

5.2 Mixing Data Types

If you have operands of mixed types (e.g., numbers and strings), Perl will make the appropriate conversion by testing whether the operator expects a number or a string for an operand. This is called overloading the operator.

If the operator is a numeric operator, such as an arithmetic operator, and the operand(s) is a string, Perl will convert the string to a decimal floating point value. If there are leading whitespace or trailing non-numeric characters, they will be ignored and if a string cannot be converted to a number, it will be converted to zero. Likewise, if Perl encounters a string operator and the operand(s) is numeric, Perl will treat the number as a string.

---

1. The operators can be symbols or words. Perl 5 functions can be used as operators if the parentheses are omitted.

E x a m p l e   5 . 1

(The Script)
1   $x = "   12!!" + "4\n";
2   print "$x";
3   print "\n";

4   $y = ZAP . 5.5;
5   print "$y\n";

O u t p u t

2   *16*
5   *ZAP5.5*

E x p l a n a t i o n

1   The plus sign (+) is a numeric operator. The strings "   *12!!*" and *"4\n"* are converted to numbers and addition is performed. The result is stored in the scalar, *$x*.
2   The scalar, *$x*, is printed.
3   Since the "\n" was stripped from the string "*4\n*" in order to convert it to a number, another "\n"is needed to get the newline in the print out.
4   The period (.) ,when surrounded by white space, is a string operator. It concatenates two strings. The number *5.5* is converted to a string and concatenated to the string "*ZAP*".
5   The value of the scalar, *$y*, is printed.

5.3   Precedence and Associativity

When an expression contains a number of operators and operands, and the result of the operation is potentially ambiguous, the order of precedence and associativity tells you how the compiler evaluates such an expression. Precedence refers to the way is which the operator binds to its operand. The multiplication operator binds more tightly to its operands than the addition operator, so it is of higher precedence, whereas the assignment operators are low in precedence and thus bind loosely to their operand. Parentheses are of the highest precedence and are used to control the way an expression is evaluated. When parentheses are nested, the expression contained within the innermost set of parentheses is evaluated first.

Associativity refers to the order in which an operator evaluates its operands: left to right, in no specified order, or right to left.

In the following statement, how is the expression evaluated? Is addition, multiplication, or division done first? And in what order, right to left or left to right?

E x a m p l e   5 . 2

(The Script)
1   $x = 5 + 4 * 12 / 4;
2   print "The result is $x\n";

O u t p u t

2   *The result is 17*

E x p l a n a t i o n

1   The order of associativity is from left to right. Multiplication and division are of a higher precedence than addition and subtraction, and addition and subtraction are of higher precedence than assignment. To illustrate this, we'll use parentheses to group the operands as they are handled by the compiler. In fact, if you want to force precedence, use the parentheses around the expression to group the operands in the way you want them evaluated.

```
$x = (5 + ( ( 4 * 12 ) / 4));
```

2   The expression is evaluated and the result is assigned to the scalar, *$x*. The value of *$x* is printed to STDOUT.

Table 5.1 summarizes the rules of precedence and associativity for the Perl operators. The operators on the same line are of equal precedence. The rows are in order of highest to lowest precedence.

TABLE 5.1   Precedence and Associativity

Operator	Description	Associativity
() [] { }	Function call, array subscripts	Left to right
++ --	Auto increment, decrement	None
! ~ -	Logical not, bitwise not, unary minus	Right to left
**	Exponentiation	Right to left
=~ !~	Match and not match	Left to right
* / % x	Multiply, divide, modulus, string repetition	Left to right
+ - .	Add, subtract, string concatenation	Left to right
<< >>	Bitwise left shift, right shift	Left to right
-r -w -x -o , etc. unary operators	File test operators	None
< <= > >= lt le gt ge	Numeric and string tests, e.g., less than, greater than, etc.	None
== != <=> eq ne cmp	Numeric and string tests, e.g., equal to, not equal to, etc.	None
&	Bitwise and	Left to right
| ^	Bitwise or, exclusive or	Left to right
&&	Logical and	Left to right
||	Logical or	Left to right
..	Range operator	None
? :	Ternary, conditional	Right to left
= += -= *= /= %=	Assignment	Right to left
, (comma)	Evaluate left operand, discard it, and evaluate right operand	Left to right

5.3.1 Assignment Operators

Table 5.2 illustrates assignment and shortcut assignment statements borrowed from the C language.

TABLE 5.2 Assignment Operators

Operator	Example	Meaning
=	$var = 5;	Assign 5 to *$var.*
+=	$var += 3;	Add 3 to *$var* and assign result to *$var.*
-=	$var -= 2;	Subtract 2 from *$var* and assign result to *$var.*
.=	$str.="ing";	Contatenate *"ing"* to $str and assign result to *$str.*
*=	$var *= 4;	Multiply *$var* by 4 and assign result to *$var.*
/=	$var /= 2;	Divide *$var* by 2 and assign result to *$var.*
**=	$var **= 2;	Square *$var* and assign result to $var.
%=	$var %= 2;	Divide *$var* by 2 and assign remainder to *$var.*
x=	$str x= 20;	Repeat value of *$str* 20 times and assign result to *$str.*
<<=	$var <<= 1;	Left-shift bits in *$var* one position and assign result to *$var.*
>>=	$var>>= 2;	Right-shift bits in *$var* two positions and assign result to *$var.*
&=	$var &= 1;	One is Bitwise-ANDed to *$var* and the result is assigned to *$var.*
|=	$var |= 2;	Two is Bitwise-ORed to *$var* and the result is assigned to *$var.*
^=	$var ^= 2;	Two is Bitwise-ExclusiveORed to *$var* and the result is assigned to *$var.*

E x a m p l e   5 . 3

```
(The Script)
    #!/usr/bin/perl
    $name=Dan;
    $line="*";
    $var=0;                   # assign 0 to var

1   $var+=3;                  # add 3 to $var; same as $var=$var+3
    print  "\$var+=3 is $var \n";

2   $var-=1;                  # subtract one from $var
    print "\$var-=1 is $var\n";

3   $var**=2;                 # square $var
    print "\$var squared is $var\n";

4   $var%=3;                  # modulus
    print "The remainder of \$var/3 is $var\n";

5   $var<<=2;                 # bitwise left-shift
    print "\$var shifted left by two is $var\n";
```

6   $name.="ielle";   *# concatenate string "Dan" and "ielle"*
    print "$name is the girl's version of Dan.\n";

7   ${line}x=10;   *# repetition; print 10 stars*
    print "$line\n";

8   printf "\$var is %.2f\n", $var=4.2+4.69;

O u t p u t

1   *$var+=3 is 3*
2   *$var–=1 is 2*
3   *$var squared is 4*
4   *The remainder of $var/3 is 1*
5   *$var shifted left by two is 4*
6   *Danielle is the girl's version of Dan.*
7   ************
8   *$var is 8.89*

E x p l a n a t i o n

1   The short-cut assignment operator, +=, adds three to the scalar *$var*. This is equivalent
    to: *$var = $var + 3;*
2   The short-cut assignment operator, -=, subtracts *one* from the scalar *$var*. This is equiv-
    alent to: *$var = $var - 1;*
3   The short-cut assignment operator, **, squares the scalar *$var*. This is equivalent to:
    $var = $var ** 2;
4   The short-cut assignment modulus operator, %, yields the integer amount that remains
    after the scalar *$var* is divided by three. The operator is called the modulus operator or
    remainder operator. The expression *$var%=3* is equivalent to: *$var = $var % 3;*
5   The short-cut assignment, <<, is a bitwise shift operator used at the bit level. The left-
    shift operator shifts the value of the scalar, *$var*, to the left two places. Since the binary
    value of $var is now *1*, shifting to the left by two would result in binary *100* or decimal
    4. This is equivalent to: *$var = $var << 2;*
6   The short-cut assignment operator, ., concatenates the string "ielle" to the string value of
    the scalar, *$name*. This is equivalent to: *$name = $name . "ielle"*
7   The repetition operator takes two operands. The operand on the right is the number of
    times that the string operand on the left is repeated. The value of the scalar *$line*, an as-
    terisk, is repeated ten times. The curly braces shield the variable from the repetition op-
    erator so that it is not interpreted as the letter 'x'.
8   The *printf* function is used to format and print the result of the addition of two floating
    point numbers.

5.3.2 Relational Operators

When operands are compared, relational operators are used. The result of the comparison is either true or false. Perl has two classes of relational operators, one set that compares numbers and another that compares strings.

The expression (5 > 4 > 2) will produce a syntax error because there is no associativity. (See Table 5.1.)

Numeric.   Table 5.3 contains a list of numeric relational operators.

TABLE 5.3   Relational Operators and Numeric Values

Operator	Example	Meaning
>	$x > $y	$x is greater than $y
>=	$x >= $y	$x is greater than or equal to $y
<	$x < $y	$x is less than $y
<=	$x <= $y	$x is less than or equal to $y

E x a m p l e   5 . 4

```
(The Script)
    $x = 5;
    $y = 4;
1   $result = $x > $y;
2   print "$result\n";

3   $result = $x < $y;
4   print $result;
```

O u t p u t

```
2  1
4  0
```

E x p l a n a t i o n

1 If $x is greater than $y, the value *1* (true) is returned and stored in $result; otherwise *0* (false) is returned.
2 Since the expression was true, the value of $result, *1*, is printed to STDOUT.
3 If $x is less than $y, the value *1* (true) is returned and stored in $result; otherwise *0* (false) is returned.
4 Since the expression was false, the value of $result, *0*, is printed to STDOUT.

String.   The string relational operators evaluate their operands (strings) by comparing the ASCII value of each character in the first string to the corresponding character in the second string. The comparison includes trailing whitespace.

If the first string contains a character that is of a higher or lower than ASCII value than the corresponding character in the second string, the value one is returned. Otherwise zero is returned.

Table 5.4 contains a list of relational string operators.

TABLE 5.4   Relational Operators and String Values

Operator	Example	Meaning
gt	$str1 gt $str2	$str1 is greater than $str2
ge	$str1 ge $str2	$str1 is greater than or equal to $str2
lt	$str1 lt $str2	$str1 is less than $str2
le	$str1 le $str2	$str1 is less than or equal to $str2

E x a m p l e   5 . 5

(The Script)
```
1  $fruit1 = "pear";
2  $fruit2 = "peaR";
3  $result = $fruit1 gt $fruit2;
4  print "$result\n";

5  $result = $fruit1 lt $fruit2;
6  print "$result\n";
```

O u t p u t

```
4  1
6  0
```

E x p l a n a t i o n

1   The scalar, *$fruit1*, is assigned the string value *"pear"*.
2   The scalar, *$fruit2*, is assigned the string value *"peaR"*.
3   When lexographically comparing each of the characters in *$fruit1* and *$fruit2*, all of the characters are equal until the *'r'* and *'R'* are compared. The ASCII value of the lowercase *'r'* is 114 and the ASCII value of the upper case *'R'* is 82. Since 114 is greater than 82, the result of evaluating the strings is *1* (true).
4   Since the expression was true, the value of *$result*, *1*, is printed to STDOUT.
5   This is the reverse of #3. The ASCII value of uppercase *'R'* (82) is less than the value of the lowercase *'r'* (114). The result of evaluating the two strings is *0* (false).
6   Since the expression was false, the value of *$result*, *0*, is printed to STDOUT.

5.3.3 Equality Operators

The equality operators evaluate numeric operands and string operands (see Tables 5.5 and 5.6).

Numeric.   The numeric equality operators evaluate their operands (numbers) by comparing their numeric values. If the operands are equal, one (true) is returned; if the operands are not equal, zero (false) is returned.

The numeric comparison operator evaluates its operands, returning a negative one (-1) if the first operand is less than the second operand, zero (0) if the numbers are equal, and one (1) if the first operand is greater than the second.

TABLE 5.5   Equality Operators and Numeric Values

Operator	Example	Meaning
==	$num1 == $num2	$num1 is equal to $num2
!=	$num1 != $num2	$num1 is not equal to $num2
<=>	$num1 <=> $num2	$num1 is compared to $num2 with signed return; 1 if $num1 is greater than $num2, 0 if $num1 is equal to $num2, and -1 if $num1 is less than $num2

E x a m p l e   5 . 6

(The Script)
```
    $x = 5;
    $y = 4;
1 $result = $x == $y;
2 print "$result\n";

3 $result = $x != $y;
4 print "$result\n";

5 $result = $x <=> $y;
6 print "$result\n";

7 $result = $y <=> $x;
8 print "$result\n";
```

O u t p u t

```
2 0
4 1
6 1
8 -1
```

Explanation

1. If *$x* is equal to *$y*, the value *1* (true) is returned and stored in *$result*; otherwise *0* (false) is returned.
2. Since the expression was not true, the value of *$result*, *0*, is printed to STDOUT.
3. If *$x* is not equal to *$y*, the value *1* (true) is returned and stored in *$result;* otherwise *0* (false) is returned.
4. Since the expression was true, the value of *$result*, 1, is printed to STDOUT.
5. The scalars, *$x* and *$y*, are compared. If *$x* is greater than $y, a positive *1* is returned; if *$x* is equal to *$y*, 0 is returned; if *$x* is less than *$y*, a signed *-1* is returned.
6. Since *$x* is greater than *$y*, the value of *$result*, 1, is printed to STDOUT.
7. The scalars, *$x* and *$y*, are compared. If *$y* is greater than *$x*, a positive *1* is returned; if *$x* is equal to *$y*, 0 is returned; if *$y* is less than *$x*, a signed *-1* is returned.
8. Since *$x* is less than *$y*, the value of *$result*, *-1*, is printed to STDOUT.

String. The string equality operators evaluate their operands (strings) by comparing the ASCII value of each character in the first string to the corresponding character in the second string. The comparison includes trailing whitespace.

If the first string contains a character that is of a higher ASCII value than the corresponding character in the second string, the value one is returned. Otherwise zero is returned.

The string comparison operator evaluates its operands by comparing the ASCII value of each character in the first string to the corresponding character in the second string. If the first string operand is less than the second operand, negative one (-1) is returned. If the first string is greater than the second string, one (1) is returned, and if the strings are equal, zero (0) is returned.

TABLE 5.6   Equality Operators and String Values

Operator	Example	Meaning
eq	$str1 eq $str2	$str1 is equal to $str2
ne	$str1 ne $str2	$str1 is not equal to $str2
cmp	$str1 cmp $str2	$str1 is compared to $str2, with signed return

Example 5.7

```
(The Script)
    $str1 = "A";
    $str2 = "C";
1   $result = $str1 eq $str2;
    print "$result\n";

2   $result = $str1 ne $str2;
    print "$result\n";

3   $result = $str1 cmp $str2;
    print "$result\n";
```

```
4   $result = $str2 cmp $str1;
    print "$result\n";

5   $str1 = "C";  # Now both strings are equal.
6   $result = $str1 cmp $str2;
    print "$result\n";
```

O u t p u t

1 *0*
2 *1*
3 *-1*
4 *1*
6 *0*

E x p l a n a t i o n

1 The scalar, *$str1*, is assigned the value "*A*" and scalar, *$str2*, is assigned the value "*C*". If *$str1* is equal to $str2, the value *1* (true) is returned and assigned to *$result*. The value of *$result* is printed to STDOUT.
2 If *$str1* is not equal to *$str2*, the value 0 (true) is returned and assigned to *$result*. The value of *$result* is printed to STDOUT.
3 If *$str1* is compared to *$str2* and they compare (i.e., an ASCII comparison is made on each character), and all characters are the same, the value 0 is returned and assigned to *$result*. If *$str1* is greater than *$str2*, the value *1* is returned, and if *$str1* is less than *$str2, -1* is returned. In this example, *$str1* is less than *$str2*. The value of *$result* is printed to STDOUT.
4 In this example, *$str1* is greater than *$str2*. The result is *1*. The value of *$result* is printed to STDOUT.
5 *$str1* is assigned "*C*". It has the same value as *$str2*.
6 Now *$str1* and *$str2* are equal. Since all of the characters are the same, the value *0* is returned and assigned to *$result*. The value of *$result* is printed to STDOUT.

5.3.4   Logical Operators (Short-Circuit Operators)

The short-circuit operators evaluate their operands, from left to right, testing the truth or falsity of each operand in turn. There is no further evaluation once a true or false condition is satisfied. Unlike C, the short-circuit operators do not return 0 (false) or 1 (true), but rather the <u>value</u> of the last operand evaluated. These operators are most often used in conditional statements. (See Chapter 7.)

If the expression on the left-hand side of the && evaluates to zero, the expression is false and zero is returned. If the expression on the left-hand side of the operator evaluates to true (non-zero), the right-hand side is evaluated and its value is returned.

If the expression on the left-hand side of the || operator is evaluated as true (non-zero), the value of the expression is returned. If the value on the left-hand side of the || is false, the value of the expression on the right-hand side of the operator is evaluated, and its value is returned.

A list of logical operators can be found in Table 5.7.

TABLE 5.7   Logical Operators (Short Circuit Operators)

Operator	Example	Meaning
&&	$x && $y	if $x is true, evaluate $y and return $y.
		if $x is false, evaluate $x and return $x.
||	$x || $y	if $x is true, evaluate $x and return $x.
		if $x is false, evaluate $y and return $y.
!	! $x	Not $x; true if $x is not true.

E x a m p l e   5 . 8

(The Script)
```
    #!/usr/bin/perl
    # short circuit operators
1   $num1=50;
2   $num2=100;
3   $num3=0;

4   print $num1 && $num3, "\n";        # result is 0
5   print $num3 && $num1, "\n";        # result is 0
6   print $num1 && $num2, "\n";        # result is 100
7   print $num2 && $num1, "\n\n";      # result is 50

8   print $num1 || $num3, "\n";        # result is 50
9   print $num3 || $num1, "\n";        # result is 50
10  print $num1 || $num2, "\n";        # result is 50
11  print $num2 || $num1, "\n"         # result is 100
```

O u t p u t

```
4   0
5   0
6   100
7   50
8   50
9   50
10  50
11  100
```

E x p l a n a t i o n

1   The scalar, *$num1*, is assigned the value 50.
2   The scalar, *$num2*, is assigned the value 100.
3   The scalar, *$num3*, is assigned the value 0.
4   Since the expression to the left of the && operator, *$num1*, is non-zero (true), the expression to the right of the &&, *$num3*, is returned.
5   Since the expression to the left of the && operator, *$num3*, is zero (false), the expression, *$num3*, is returned.
6   Since the expression to the left of the && operator, *$num1*, is true (true), the expression on the right-hand side of the && operator, *$num2*, is returned.
7   Since the expression to the left of the && operator, *$num2*, is true (true), the expression on the right-hand side of the && operator, *$num1*, is returned.
8   Since the expression to the left of the || operator, *$num1*, is non-zero (true), the expression, *$num1* is returned.
9   Since the expression to the left of the || operator, *$num3*, is zero (false), the expression to the right of the || operator, *$num1*, is returned.
10   Since the expression to the left of the || operator, *$num1*, is non-zero (true), the expression, *$num1,* is returned.
11   Since the expression to the left of the || operator, *$num2*, is non-zero (true), the expression, *$num2*, is returned.

5.3.5   Arithmetic Operators

Perl's arithmetic operators are listed in Table 5.8.

TABLE 5.8   Arithmetic Operators

Operator	Example	Meaning
+	$x + $y	Addition
-	$x – $y	Subtraction
*	$x * $y	Multiplication
/	$x / $y	Division
%	$x % $y	Modulus
**	$x ** $y	Exponentiation

E x a m p l e   5 . 9

(The Script)
```
1  printf "%d\n", 4 * 5 / 2;
2  printf "%d\n", 5 ** 3;
3  printf "%d\n", 5 + 4 - 2 * 10;
4  printf "%d\n", (5 + 4 - 2 ) * 10;
5  printf "%d\n", 11 % 2;
```

O u t p u t

1 *10*
2 *125*
3 *-11*
4 *70*
5 *1*

E x p l a n a t i o n

1   The *printf* function formats in decimal the result of arithmetic expression. Multiplication and division are performed. Operators are of the same precedence, left to right associativity.
2   The *printf* function formats in decimal the result of arithmetic expression. The exponentiation operator cubes its operand, *5.*
3   The *printf* function formats in decimal the result of arithmetic expression. Since the multiplication operator is of higher precedence than the addition and subtraction operators, multiplication is performed first.
4   The *printf* function formats in decimal the result of arithmetic expression. Since the parentheses are of highest precedence, the expression enclosed in parentheses is calculated first.
5   The *printf* function formats in decimal the result of arithmetic expression. The modulus operator produces the remainder after performing division on its operands. (See Section 3.4, *printf Function.*)

5.3.6   Autoincrement and Autodecrement Operators

The autoincrement operator and autodecrement operators are taken straight from the C language (see Table 5.9). The autoincrement operator adds one to the value of a variable and the autodecrement operator subtracts one from the value of a variable. When used with a single variable, these operators are just a short cut for the traditional method of adding and subtracting one. However, if used in an assignment statement or if combined with other operators, the end result depends on the placement of the operator. The placement of the operators makes a difference when an assignment is made to another variable. (See Table 5.10.)

TABLE 5.9   Autoincrement and Autodecrement Operators

Example	Description	Equivalence
++$x	Pre–increment	$x = $x + 1
$x++	Post–increment	$x = $x + 1
--$x	Pre–decrement	$x = $x - 1
$x--	Post–decrement	$x = $x - 1

TABLE 5.10   Autoincrement and Autodecrement Operators and Assignment

Example	Description	Equivalence	Result
If $y is 0 and $x is 0:			
$y=$x++;	Assign the value of $x to $y;	$y=$x;	$y is 0
	then increment $x	$x=$x + 1;	$x is 1
If $y is 0 and $x is 0:			
$y= ++$x;	Increment $x;	$x=$x+1;	$x is 1
	then assign $x to $y	$y=$x;	$y is 1
If $y is 0 and $x is 0:			
$y=$x--;	Assign the value of $x to $y;	$y=$x;	$y is 0
	then decrement $x	$x=$x − 1;	$x is −1
If $y is 0 and $x is 0:			
$y= --$x;	Decrement $x;	$x=$x−1;	$x is −1
	then assign $x to $y	$y=$x;	$y is −1

E x a m p l e   5 . 1 0

(The Script)
```
   #!/usr/bin/perl
1  $x=5; $y=0;
2  $y=++$x;  # add one to $x first; then assign to $y
3  print "Pre−increment:\n";
4  print "y is $y\n";
5  print "x is $x\n";
6  print "————————————————\n";
7  $x=5;
8  $y=0;
9  print "Post−increment:\n";
10 $y=$x++;  # assign value in $x to $y; then add one to $x
11 print "y is $y\n";
12 print "x is $x\n";
```

O u t p u t

```
3  Pre−increment:
4  y is 6
5  x is 6

   ————————————————

9  Post−increment
11 y is 5
12 x is 6
```

5.3.7   Bitwise Logical Operators

When you're ready to manipulate integer values at the bit level, the bitwise logical operators are used. The bitwise operators are binary operators and manipulate their operands in terms of the internal binary representation of those operands. A bit-by-bit comparison is made on each of the corresponding operands, producing its result as the binary value (see Tables 5.11 and 5.12).

TABLE 5.11   Bitwise Logical Operators

Operator	Example	Meaning
&	$x & $y	Bitwise AND
|	$x | $y	Bitwise OR
^	$x ^ $y	Bitwise exclusive OR
<<	$x << 1	Bitwise left shift, integer multiply by two
>>	$x >> 1	Bitwise right shift, integer divide by two

TABLE 5.12   Resulting Values of Bitwise Operators

$x	$y	$x & $y	$x | $y	$x ^ $y
0	0	0	0	0
0	1	0	1	1
1	0	0	1	1
1	1	1	1	0

Example 5.11

```
(The Script)
     $num1=5;
     $num2=4;
     $num3=0;
1    print $num1 & $num2,"\n";
2    print $num1 & $num3,"\n";
3    print $num2 & $num3,"\n";
4    print $num3 & $num2,"\n";
5    print "=" x 10, "\n";  # print 10 equal signs
6    print $num1 | $num2,"\n";
7    print $num1 | $num3,"\n";
8    print $num2 | $num3,"\n";
9    print $num3 | $num2,"\n";
     print "=" x 10, "\n";  # print 10 equal signs
10   print $num1 ^ $num2,"\n";
11   print $num1 ^ $num3,"\n";
12   print $num2 ^ $num3,"\n";
13   print $num3 ^ $num2,"\n";
```

O u t p u t

```
1    4
2    0
3    0
4    0
5    ==========
6.   5
7    5
8    4
9    4
     ==========
10   1
11   5
12   4
13   4
```

E x p l a n a t i o n

1   The scalar, *$num1*, is assigned the value 5. The scalar, *$num2*, is assigned the value 4. The scalar, *$num3*, is assigned the value *0*. The value of *$num1* is decimal *5*, which is represented internally as binary *101*. The value of *$num2* is decimal *4*, which is represented internally as binary *100*. *$num1* BitwiseANDed to *$num2* results in *100* binary, *4* decimal.

2   *$num1* BitwiseANDed to *$num3* results in *000* binary, *0* decimal.

3   *$num*1 BitwiseANDed to *$num3* results in *000* binary, *0* decimal.

4   *$num2* BitwiseANDed to *$num3* results in *000* binary, 0 decimal.

5   The *x* operator tells the print function to print 10 equal signs.

6   *$num1* BitwiseORed to *$num2* results in *101* binary, *5* decimal.

7   *$num1* BitwiseORed to *$num3* results in *101* binary, *5* decimal.

8   *$num2* BitwiseORed to *$num3* results in *100* binary, *4* decimal.

9   *$num3* BitwiseORed to *$num2* results in *101* binary, *5* decimal.

10 *$num1* BitwiseExclusivlyORed to *$num2* results in *001* binary, *1* decimal.

11 *$num1* BitwiseExclusivlyORed to *$num3* results in *101* binary, *5* decimal.

12 *$num2* BitwiseExclusivlyORed to *$num3* results in *100* binary, *4* decimal.

13 *$num3* BitwiseExclusivlyORed to *$num2* results in *100* binary, *4* decimal.

Example 5.12

(The Script)

```perl
   #!/usr/bin/perl
   # Convert a number to binary
1  while (1) {
2       $mask = 0x80000000;   # 32 bit machine
3       printf("Enter a number: ");
4       chomp($num=<STDIN>);
5       printf("Binary of %x is: ", $num);
6       for ($j = 0; $j < 32; $j++) {
7            $bit = ($mask & $num) ? 1 : 0;
8            printf("%d", $bit);
9            if ($j == 15)){
10                printf("--");
11                $mask /=2;   # $mask >>= 1;   not portable
             }
        printf("\n");
     }
```

Output

Enter a number: 5
Binary of 5 is: 0000000000000000--0000000000000101

Explanation

1   This little program introduces some constructs that have not yet been discussed. It is presented here as an example of using bitwise operations to perform a real task (in this case, to convert a number to binary and print it). The first line starts a loop that will continue until the user presses Ctrl-c.

2   The scalar is set to the hexadecimal value representing 32 zero's. This program works on a machine with a 32 bit word.

3   The user is asked to type in an integer.

4   The number is assigned and the newline is chomped.

5   The *printf* will print the value of the number in hexadecimal notation.

6   The for loop will iterate 32 times, once for each bit.

7   The value of *$mask* is bitwise *ANDed* to *$num*. If the result is 1, 1 will be assigned to $bit; otherwise, 0 is assigned. (See next section on conditional operators.)

8   The value of *$bit* is printed.

9   If the value of *$j* is 15 (the loop has iterated 16 times) a double underscore is printed.

11 The value of *$mask* is divided by 2. This has the same effect as shifting the bits to the right once, but will not try to shift the sign bit if there is one.

5.3.8 Conditional Operator

The conditional operator is another taken from the C language. It requires three operands, thus it is often called a ternary operator. It is used as a short-cut for the if/else construct.

Format:

```
conditional expression?expression:expression
```

E x a m p l e   5 . 1 3

```
$x ? $y : $z
```

E x p l a n a t i o n

If *$x* is true, *$y* becomes the value of the expression. If $x is false, $z becomes the value of the expression.

E x a m p l e   5 . 1 4

```
(The Script)
1  print "What is your age? ";
2  chomp($age=<STDIN>);

3  $price=($age > 60 ) ? 0 : 5.55;
4  printf "You will pay \$%.2f.\n", $price;
```

O u t p u t

```
1  What is your age? 44
4  You will pay $5.55.
```

O u t p u t

```
1  What is your age? 77
4  You will pay $0.00.
```

E x p l a n a t i o n

1 The string "What is your age?" is printed to STDOUT.
2 The input is read from the terminal and stored in the scalar, *$age*. The newline is chomped.
3 The scalar, *$price*, is assigned the result of the conditional operator; if the age is greater than 60, the price is assigned the value to the right of the question mark (?). Otherwise, the value after the colon (:) is assigned to the scalar, *$price*.
4 The *printf* function prints the formatted string to STDOUT.

E x a m p l e   5 . 1 5

(The Script)
1 print "What was your grade? ";
2 $grade = <STDIN>;
3 **print $grade > 60 ? "Passed.\n" : "Failed.\n";**
   # or
   # $grade > 60 ? print "Passed.\n" : print "Failed.\n";

O u t p u t

1 *What was your grade? 76*
3 *Passed.*

O u t p u t

1 *What was your grade? 34*
3 *Failed.*

E x p l a n a t i o n

1 The user is asked for input.
2 The input is assigned to the scalar *$grade.*
3 The *print* function takes as its argument the result of the conditional expression. If the grade is greater than 60, "Passed.\n" is printed; otherwise, "Failed.\n" is printed.

5.3.9   Range Operator

The range operator is used in both scalar and array context. In a scalar context the value returned is a Boolean, 1 or 0. In an array context, it returns a list of items starting on the left side of the operator and counting by one until the value on the right-hand side is reached.

E x a m p l e   5 . 1 6

1 $ perl -ne 'if (**1 .. 3**){print}' emp.names
   Steve Blenheim
   Betty Boop
   Igor Chevsky

2 $ perl –e 'print **0..10**,"\n";'
   1 2 3 4 5 6 7 8 9 10

3 $ perl –e '@alpha=(**'A' .. 'Z'**) ; print "@alpha";'
   A B C D E F G H I J K L M N O P Q R S T U V W X Y Z

4   perl −e '@a=('a'..'z', 'A'..'Z') ; print "@a\n";'
    a b c d e f g h i j k l m n o p q r s t u v w x y z A B C D E F G H I J K L M N O P Q R S T U V W X Y Z

5   perl −e '@n=(−5 .. 20) ; print "@n\n";'
    −5 −4 −3 −2 −1 0 1 2 3 4 5 6 7 8 9 10 11 12 13 14 15 16 17 18 19 20

Explanation

1   The first three lines of the file *emp.names* are printed. As long as the expression evaluates true, the lines are printed. The context is scalar and Boolean.
2   Print the numbers zero to ten to STDOUT.
3   Create an array called *@alpha* and store all upper case letters in the array. The context is array. Print array.
4   Create an array called *@alpha* and store all lower case letters in one list and all uppercase letters in another list. Print array.
5   Create an array called *@n* and store all numbers in the range between -5 and 20. Print array.

5.3.10   Special String Operators and Functions

There are a number of operations that can be performed on strings. For example, the concatenation operator joins two strings together, and the string repetition operator concatenates as many copies of its operand as specified.

Perl also supports some special functions for manipulating strings. The *substr* function returns a substring found within an original string, starting at a byte offset in the original string and ending with the number of character positions to the right of that offset. The *index* function returns the byte offset of the first character of a substring found within the original string. The *length* function returns the number of characters in a given expression.

TABLE 5.13   String Operations

Example	Meaning
$str1 . $str2	Concatenate strings $str1 and $str2
$str1 x $num	Concatenate $str1, $num times
substr ($str1, $offset, $len)	Substring of $str1 at $offset for $len bytes
index ($str1, $str2)	Byte offset of string $str2 in string $str1
length (EXPR)	Returns the length in characters of expression, EXPR
rindex($str, $substr, POSITION)	Returns the position of the last occurrence of $substr in $str. If the POSITION is specified, start looking there. If POSITION is not specified, start at the end of the string.
chr(NUMBER)	Returns the character represented by that NUMBER in the ASCII character set. For example, *chr(65)* is 'A'.
lc($str)	Returns a lowercase string.
uc($str)	Returns an uppercase string.

E x a m p l e   5 . 1 7

(The Script)

```
   #!/usr/bin/perl
1  $x="kid";
2  $y="nap";
3  $z="*";
4  print $z x 10, "\n";      # print 10 stars
5  print $x . $y, "\n";      # concatenate "kid" and "nap"
6  print $z x 10, "\n";      # print 10 stars
7  print (($x . $y ." ") x 5 );  # concatenate "kid" and "nap" and print 5 times
8  print "\n";
9  print uc($x . $y), "\n";  #convert string to uppercase
```

O u t p u t

```
4  **********

5  kidnap
6  **********
7  kidnap kidnap kidnap kidnap kidnap
9  KIDNAP
```

E x p l a n a t i o n

1 The scalar, *$x*, is assigned "*kid*".

2 The scalar, *$y*, is assigned "*nap*".

3 The scalar, *$z*, is assigned "***".

4 The string "***" is concatenated ten times and printed to STDOUT.

5 The value of *$x*, string "*kid*", and the value of *$y*, string "*nap*", are concatenated and printed to STDOUT.

6 The value of *$x*, string "***" is concatenated *ten* times and printed to STDOUT.

7 The strings "*kid*" and "*nap*" are concatenated *five* times and printed to STDOUT.

8 Print a newline to STDOUT.

9 The *uc* function converts and returns the string in uppercase. The *ul* function will convert a string to lowercase.

E x a m p l e   5 . 1 8

(The Script)

```
1  $line="Happy New Year";
2  print substr($line, 6, 3),"\n";  # offset starts at zero
3  print index($line, "Year"),"\n";
4  print substr($line, index($line, "Year")),"\n";
5  substr($line, 0, 0)="Fred, ";
6  print $line,"\n";
```

```
7    substr($line, 0, 1)="Ethel";
8    print $line,"\n";
9    substr($line, −1, 1)="r to you!";
10   print $line,"\n";
11   $string="I'll eat a tomato tomorrow.\n";
12   print rindex($string, tom), "\n";
```

Output

```
2    New
3    10
4    Year
5    Fred, Happy New Year
7    Ethelred, Happy New Year
8    Ethelred, Happy New Year to you!
9    18
```

Explanation

1   The scalar, *$line*, is assigned *"Happy New Year"*.

2   The substring, *"New"* of the original string *"Happy New Year"* is printed to STDOUT. The offset starts at byte zero. The beginning of the substring is position 6, the *"N"*, and the end of the substring is three characters to the right of *"N"*. The substring, *"New"*, is returned.

3   The *index* function returns the first position in the string where the substring is found. The substring *"Year"* starts at position 10. Remember, the byte offset starts at 0.

4   The *substr* and *index* functions are used together. The *index* function returns the starting position of the substring, "Year". The *substr* function uses the return value from the *index* function as the starting position for the *substring*. The *substring* returned is *"Year"*.

5   The substring, *"Fred,"* is inserted at starting position, byte 0, and at ending position byte 0 of the scalar *$line*.

6   The new value of *$line*, *"Fred, Happy New Year"* is printed to STDOUT.

7   The substring, *"Ethel"*, is inserted at starting position, byte 0, and at ending position byte1 of the scalar *$line*.

8   The new value of *$line, "Ethelred, Happy New Year"* is printed to STDOUT.

9   The substring, "r to you!" is appended to the scalar, $line, starting the end (-1) of the substring, over one character.

10 The new value of $line, *"Ethelred, Happy New Year to you!"* is printed to STDOUT.

11 The $string scalar is assigned.

12 The *rindex* function will start looking from the <u>end of the string</u> for the position where it first finds the substring, *tom*, and return the position where it found the substring. The position, 18, is the number of characters starting at the zeroith position from the beginning of the string; i.e., the position where "item" begins in the substring "tomorrow".

6

Regular Expressions— They're Back!

6.1 What Is a Regular Expression?

If you are familiar with UNIX utilities such as *vi, sed, grep*, and *awk*, you have met face-to-face with the infamous regular expressions and metacharacters used in delimiting search patterns. Well, with Perl, they're back!

What is a regular expression, anyway?

A regular expression is really just a sequence or pattern of characters that is matched against a string of text when performing searches and replacements. A simple regular expression consists of a character or set of characters that matches itself. The regular expression is normally delimited by forward slashes.[1] The special scalar, $_, is the default search space where Perl does its pattern matching. Sometimes you'll see $_; sometimes you won't. Don't worry; all this will become clear as you read through this chapter.

E x a m p l e   6 . 1

```
1  /abc/
2  ?abc?
```

E x p l a n a t i o n

1 The pattern *abc* is enclosed in forward slashes. If searching for this pattern, for example, in a string or text file, any string that matched the pattern *abc* would be matched.
2 The pattern *abc* is enclosed in question marks. If searching for this pattern, only the first occurrence of the string is matched. (See Appendix A: the reset function.)

---

1. Actually, any character can be used as a delimiter. See pattern matching operators in Section 6.3.1.

6.2   Expression Modifiers and Simple Statements

A simple statement is an expression terminated with a semicolon. Perl supports a set of modifiers that allow you to further evaluate an expression based on some condition. A simple statement may contain an expression *ending* with a single modifier. The modifier and its expression are always terminated with a semicolon. These modifiers are very useful when evaluating regular expressions.

The modifiers are:

> *if*
> *unless*
> *while*
> *until*

6.2.1   Conditional Modifiers

The if Modifier.   The *if* modifier is used to control a simple statement consisting of two expressions. If *Expression1* is true, *Expression2* is executed.

Format:

```
Expression2 if Expression1;
```

E x a m p l e   6 . 2

```
1  $ perl -e '$x = 5; print $x  if $x == 5;'
   5

2  $ perl -e '$_ ="xabcy"; print "Yes\n" if /abc/;
   Yes
```

E x p l a n a t i o n

1 The *if* modifier controls the print statement. If the expression, $x == 5, is <u>true</u>, then the value of $x is printed.
2 The $_ variable is assigned the string "xabcy". "Yes" is printed if the regular expression, abc, is matched anywhere in the $_ variable. Since $_ is the default space for pattern matching, Perl knows to do pattern matching on $_ in the conditional expression *if /abc/* ; the expression could have been written: if $_ =~ /abc/. The =~ match operator will be discussed at the end of this chapter.

E x a m p l e   6 . 3

(In Script)
1 **$_ = "I lost my gloves in the clover.";**
2 print "Found love in gloves!\n" **if /love/;**

O u t p u t

Found love in gloves!

E x p l a n a t i o n

1 The *$_* is assigned the string "I lost my gloves in the clover."
2 The regular expression, love, is matched in the *$_* variable and the string "Found love in gloves!" is printed; otherwise, nothing will be printed. The regular expression love is found in both *gloves* and *clover*, but the search starts at the left hand side of the string, so that matching love in gloves will produce the true condition before clover is reached.

E x a m p l e   6 . 4

1 **$ cat emp.names**
   Steve Blenheim
   Betty Boop
   Igor Chevsky
   Norma Cord
   Jon DeLoach
   Karen Evich

2 $ perl –ne '**print if /Norma/;**' emp.names
   Norma Cord

3 $ perl –ne '**if /Norma/ print;**' emp.names
   syntax error in file /tmp/perl–ea01985 at line 1, next 2 tokens "if /Norma/"
   Execution of /tmp/perl–ea01985 aborted due to compilation errors.

E x p l a n a t i o n

1 The contents of the file *emp.names* is printed.
2 Lines from the file *emp.names* are printed only if they contain the regular expression, *Norma*. The -n switch tells Perl to loop through the filename given at the command line, *emp.names*.
3 The modifier must be at the end of the expression, or a syntax error results.

E x a m p l e   6 . 5

(In a Script)
```
    #/bin/perl
    # Scriptname: finder
    # looping through a file. The file, "emp.names," is passed in from the command line.
1   while(<>){
2       print if /Norma/;
3   }
```

(At the command line)
```
4   $ chmod +x finder
5   $ finder emp.names
Norma Cord
```

E x p l a n a t i o n

1 The *while* loop will be discussed in detail in Chapter 7. It is used here to demonstrate another way to process a file. This time, instead of using the *-n* switch at the command line, the file is processed in a script. The <> (empty angle brackets) allow the program to read from a file a line at a time. Each line is stored in the $_ variable. The file being processed is named at the command line. In this example, each line from the *emp.names* file is processed and stored in $_ each time the loop iterates.

2 If the regular expression *Norma* is matched in the $_ variable, the line (contents of $_) is printed.

3 The closing curly brace marks the end of the while loop.

4 The execute permission is turned on for the Perl script.

5 The script takes one argument, the name of the file to be processed.

The unless Modifier.   The unless modifier is used to control a simple statement consisting of two expressions. If *Expression1* is false, *Expression2* is executed.

Format:

```
        Expression2 unless Expression1;
```

E x a m p l e   6 . 6

```
1   $ perl -e '$x=5; print $x  unless $x == 6;'
    5
```

E x p l a n a t i o n

1 The *unless* modifier controls the print statement. If the expression, *$x == 5*, is <u>false</u>, then the value of *$x* is printed.

E x a m p l e   6 . 7

1 **$ perl –ne 'print; ' emp.names**
  Steve Blenheim
  Betty Boop
  Igor Chevsky
  Norma Cord
  Jon DeLoach
  Karen Evich

2 **$ perl –ne 'print unless /Norma/;' emp.names**
  Steve Blenheim
  Betty Boop
  Igor Chevsky
  Jon DeLoach
  Karen Evich

E x p l a n a t i o n

1 The contents of the file *emp.names* are printed.
2 Lines from the file *emp.names* are printed only if they do *not* contain the regular expression, *Norma* (i.e., Perl prints the line *unless* it contains Norma).

6.2.2   Looping Modifiers

The while Modifier.   The *while* modifier repeatedly executes the second expression as long as the first expression is <u>true</u>.

Format:

```
Expression2   while Expression1;
```

E x a m p l e   6 . 8

(The Command Line)
1 $ perl –e '$x=1; print $x++,"\n" **while $x != 5'**
  1
  2
  3
  4

Explanation

1 Perl prints the value of *$x* while *$x* is not 5.

The until Modifier.   The *until* modifier repeatedly executes the second expression as long as the first expression is <u>false</u>.

Format:

```
Expression2   until Expression1;
```

Example 6.9

(The Command Line)
1   $ perl −e '$x=1; print $x++,"\n" **until $x == 5**'
       1
       2
       3
       4

Explanation

1 Perl prints the value of *$x* until *$x* is equal to 5. The variable *$x* is set to one (see scalar variables) and then incremented. Be careful that you don't get yourself into an infinite loop.

6.3   Regular Expression Operators

The regular expression operators are used for matching patterns in searches and for replacements in substitution operations. The *m//* operator is used for matching patterns and the *s///* operator is used when substituting one pattern for another.

6.3.1   The m Operator

The *m* operator is used for matching patterns. The *m* operator is optional if the delimiter is the forward slash (the forward slash is the default), but required if you change the delimiter. You may want to change the delimiter if the regular expression contains forward slashes (e.g., when searching for birthdays [*3/15/93*] or pathnames [*/usr/var/adm*]).

Format:

```
m/Regular Expression/
```

TABLE 6.1 Modifiers

Modifier	Meaning
i	Turn off case sensitivity
m	Treat a string as multiple lines[2]
o	Only compile pattern onces. Used to optimize the search
s	Treat string as single line when newline is embedded[2]
x	Use extended regular expressions[2]
g	Match globally, i.e., find all occurrences. Returns a list if an array context, and true or false if a scalar context

E x a m p l e   6 . 1 0

```
1  m/Good morning/
2  /Good evening/
3  /\usr\/var\/adm/
4  m#/usr/var/adm#
```

E x p l a n a t i o n

1 The *m* operator is not needed in this example since forward slashes delimit the regular expression.

2 The forward slash is the delimiter; therefore, the *m* operator is optional.

3 Each of the forward slashes in the search path is quoted with a backslash so that it will not be confused with the forward slash used for the pattern delimiter—a messy approach.

4 The *m* operator is required because the pound sign(#) is used as an alternative to the forward slash. The pound sign delimiter clarifies and simplifies the previous example.

E x a m p l e   6 . 1 1

(The Text File)
```
1  $ cat emp.names
   Steve Blenheim
   Betty Boop
   Igor Chevsky
   Norma Cord
   Jon DeLoach
   Karen Evich
```

---

2. The m, s, and x options are defined only for Perl 5.

(The Command Line)
2 $ perl -ne **'print if /Betty/'** emp.names
   Betty Boop

3 $ perl -ne **'print unless /Evich/'** emp.names
   Steve Blenheim
   Betty Boop
   Igor Chevsky
   Norma Cord
   Jon DeLoach

4 $ perl -ne **'print if m#Jon#'** emp.names
   Jon DeLoach

Explanation

1 The text file is printed.
2 Perl will implicitly loop through the file and print only those lines containing the regular expression, *Betty*. Remember, the $_ holds the current line for each iteration of the loop.
3 Perl will implicitly loop through the file and print those lines that <u>do not</u> contain the regular expression, *Evich*.
4 The *m* operator is necessary because the delimiter has been changed from the default to a pound sign (#).

Example 6.12

(In a Script)
```
#!/usr/bin/perl
1  $_ = "I lost my gloves in the clover, Love.";
2  @list=/love/g;
3  print "@list.\n";

4  $_ = "I lost my gloves in the clover, Love.";
5  @list=/love/gi;
6  print "@list.\n";
```

Output

3 *love love.*
6 *love love Love.*

E x p l a n a t i o n

1   The $_ scalar variable is assigned the string.
2   If the search is done with the *g* modifier, in an array context, each match is stored in the @list array. The regular expression, *love*, was found in the string twice, once in *gloves* and once in *clover.*
3   The list of matched items is printed.
4   The $_ scalar variable is assigned the string.
5   This time the *i* modifier is used to turn off the case sensitiviy. Both *love* and *Love* will be found.
6   The pattern is found three times. The list is printed.

6.3.2   The s Operator

The *s///* operator is used for substitutions. The substitution operator replaces the first regular expression pattern with the second. The delimiter can also be changed. The *g* stands for global change on a line. Without it, only the first occurrence of the pattern is affected by the substitution.

↗ The special built-in variable, *$&*, gets the value of whatever was found in the search string.

Format:

```
s/old/new/
s/old/new/g
s+old+new+g
s/old/expression to be evaluated/e
```

TABLE 6.2   Modifiers

Modifier	Meaning
e	Evaluate the replacement side as an expression.
i	Turn off case sensitivity.
m	Treat a string as multiple lines.[3]
o	Only compile pattern once. Used to optimize the search.
s	Treat string as single line when newline is embedded.[3]
x	Use extended regular expressions.[3]
g	Replace globally, i.e., find all occurrences.

---

3.   The m, s, and x options are defined only for Perl 5.

E x a m p l e   6 . 1 3

```
s/Igor/Boris/
s/Igor/Boris/g
s/norma/Jane/i
s!Jon!Susan!
s/$sal/$sal*1.1/e
```

E x a m p l e   6 . 1 4

(The Text File)
  $cat emp.names
  Steve Blenheim
  Betty Boop
  Igor Chevsky
  Norma Cord
  Jon DeLoach
  Karen Evich

(The Command Line)
1 $ perl –ne **'s/Norma/Jane/;** print;' emp.names
  Steve Blenheim
  Betty Boop
  Igor Chevsky
  Jane Cord
  Jon DeLoach
  Karen Evich

2 $ perl –ne **'print if s/Igor/Ivan/;'** emp.names
  Ivan Chevsky

3 $ perl –ne **'s#Igor#Boris#;** print' emp.names
  Steve Blenheim
  Betty Boop
  Boris Chevsky
  Norma Cord
  Jon DeLoach
  Karen Evich

Explanation

1 All lines are printed. The regular expression *Norma* is replaced with the string *Jane*.
2 The *if* modifier controls the print statement. If the regular expression, *Igor*, is matched, it will be replaced with *Ivan* and printed.
3 The delimiter following the *s* operator has been changed to a pound sign (#). This is fine as long as all the delimiters following the first # are the same. The regular expression *Igor* is replaced with *Boris*.

The i Modifier—Case Insensitivity.   Perl is sensitive to whether or not characters are upper or lower case when performing matches. If you want to turn off case sensitivity, an *i* *(insensitive)* is appended to the last delimiter of the match or substitution operator.

Format:

```
m/pattorn/i
s/old/new/i
```

Example 6.15

(The Text File)
   Steve Blenheim
   Betty Boop
   Igor Chevsky
   Norma Cord
   Jon DeLoach
   Karen Evich

(At the Command Line)
1 $ perl -ne 'print **if /norma cord/i**' emp.names
   Norma Cord

2 $ perl -ne 'print **if s/igor/Daniel/i**' emp.names
   Daniel Chevsky

Explanation

1 The regular expression */ norma cord/* would not be matched because all the letters are lower case. The *i* option turns off the case sensitivity.
2 The regular expression in the substitution is also case-insensitive, due to the *i* option.

The e Modifier--Evaluating an Expression.   On the replacement side of a substitution operation, it is possible to evaluate an expression. The special variable, *$&*, holds the string that was matched.

Example 6.16

```
1  $_=5000;
2  s/$_/$& * 2/e;
3  print "The new value is $_\.n";
```

Output

The new value is 10000.

Explanation

1 The *$_* variable is assigned *5000.*
2 The search string, 5000, is stored in the $& variable. In the replacement side the expression is evaluated, i.e., the value of *$&* is multiplied by 2. The new value is substituted for the original value. *$_* is assigned the new value.

6.3.3   Pattern Binding Operators

The *pattern binding* operators are used to bind a matched pattern, substitution, or translation (see tr) to another scalar expression. In the previous examples, pattern searches were done implicitly (or explicitly) on the $_ variable, the default pattern space. For example, each line was stored in the $_ variable when looping through a file. In the previous example, the $_ was assigned a value and used as the search string for the substitution. But what if you store a value in some other variable than $_? Instead of :

        $_ = 5000;
You say:
        $salary = 5000;

If you have a string that is not stored in the $_ variable and need to perform matches or substitutions on that string, then the pattern binding operators are used.They are also used with the *tr* function for string translations. (See Section 6.4.1.)

The pattern matching operators are listed in Table 6.3.

Format:

```
        Variable  =~ /Expression/
        Variable  !~ /Expression/
        Variable  =~ s/old/new/
```

TABLE 6.3   Pattern Matching Operator

Example	Meaning
$name =~ /John/	True if $name contains pattern.
	Returns 1 for true, null for false.
$name !~ /John/	True if $name does not contain pattern.
$name =~ s/John/Sam/	Replace first occurrence of *John* with *Sam*.
$name =~ s/John/Sam/g	Replace all occurrences of *John* with *Sam*.
$name =~ tr/a–z/A–Z/	Translate all lower case letters to upper case.
$name =~ /$pal/	A variable can be used in the search string.

Example 6.17

(The Script)
```perl
   #!/usr/bin/perl
1  $salary=5000;
2  $salary=~s/$salary/$& * 2/e;
3  print "The salary is \$$salary.\n";
```

Output

The salary is $10000.

Explanation

1 The scalar *$salary* is assigned *5000*.
2 The substitution is performed on *$salary*. The replacement side evalutes the expression. The special variable *$&* holds the value found on the search side. To really change the value in *$salary* after the substitution, the pattern matching operator =~ is used. This binds the result of the substitution to the scalar *$salary*.

Example 6.18

(The Script)
```perl
   #!/usr/bin/perl
1  while(<>){
2      print if /Igor/;    # Using the default $_
   }
```

(The Script)
```perl
   #!/usr/bin/perl
3  while(<>){
4      ($name, $phone, $address) = split(/:/, $_);
5      print $name  if $phone =~ /408-/    # Using the pattern matching operator
   }
```

Output

5 Igor Chevsky

Explanation

1   The *while* loop is used to explicitly loop through the file named at the command line. The example reads: get a line from the file and store it in the *$_* variable.

2   If the regular expression */Igor/* is matched in the *$_* variable, the *print* function will print the value of *$_*, the line containing the pattern.

3   When this *while* loop in entered, each line from the file will be split by colons and the value returned stored in an anonymous list consisting of three scalars: *$name*, *$phone*, and *$address*.

4   The pattern */408-/* is matched against the *$phone* variable. If that pattern is matched in *$phone*, the value of *$name* is printed.

5   Prints *Igor*'s name because his phone is in the *408* area code.

Example 6.19

(The Script)
```
   #!/usr/bin/perl
1  $name="Tommy Tuttle";
2  print "Hello Tommy\n" if $name =~ /Tom/;  #prints Hello Tommy,  if true
3  print "$name\n" if $name !~ /Tom/;   #prints  nothing  if  false

4  $name =~ s/T/M/;       #substitute first 'T' with an 'M'
5  print "$name.\n";

   $name="Tommy Tuttle";
6  print "$name\n" if $name =~ s/T/M/g;  #substitute all 'T's' with 'M's'
7  print "What is Tommy's last name? ";
8  print "You got it!\n" if <STDIN> =~ /Tuttle/;
```

Output

2 *Hello Tommy*
5 *Mommy Tuttle.*
6 *Mommy Muttle*
7 *What is Tommy's last name? Tuttle*
8 *You got it!*

Explanation

1 The scalar, $name, is assigned Tommy Tuttle.
2 The string, *$name*, is printed if *$name* contains the pattern *Tom*.
3 The string *$name* is not printed if *$name* does <u>not</u> contain the pattern *Tom*.
4 The first occurrence of the letter ’*T*’ in *$name* is replaced with the letter ’*M*’.
5 *$name* is printed, reflecting the substitution.
6 <u>All</u> occurrences of the letter ’*T*’ in *$name* are replaced with the letter ’*M*’. The ’*g*’ at ̇ end of the substitution expression causes a global replacement across the line.
7 User input is requested.
8 The user input (<STDIN>) is matched against the regular expression, *Tuttle*, and if there is a match, the print statement is executed.

6.4   Regular Expression Metacharacters

Regular expression metacharacters do not represent themselves. They allow you to control the search pattern in some way (e.g., find the pattern only at the beginning of line, or at the end of the line, or if it starts with an upper or lower case letter, etc.).

Example 6.20

```
/^a...c/
```

Explanation

This regular expression contains metacharacters. (See Table 6.4.) The first one is a caret (^). The caret metacharacter matches for a string only if it is at the beginning of the line.   The period (.) is used to match for a single character, any character, including a whitespace. This expression contains three periods, representing any three characters. To find a literal period or any other character that does not represent itself, the character must be preceded by a backslash to prevent interpretation.

The expression reads: Search at the beginning of the line for an ’*a*’, followed by any three single characters, followed by a ’*c*’. It will match, for example: *abbbc, a123c, a   c, aAx3c*, etc., only if those patterns were at the beginning of the line. (See Table 6.4.)

le

.cters

	What It Matches	**Character Class**
		Single Characters and Digits
	Matches any character except newline	
	Matches any single character in set	
	Matches any single character not in set	
	Matches one digit	
	Matches a non–digit, same [^0–9]	
	Matches an alphanumeric (word) character	
	Matches a non–alphanumeric (non–word) character	
		Whitespace Characters
	Matches whitespace character, spaces, tabs, and newlines	
	Matches non–whitespace character	
\n	Matches a newline	
\r	Matches a return	
\t	Matches a tab	
\f	Matches a formfeed	
\b	Matches a backspace	
\0	Matches a null character	
\12	Matches that octal value	
\x811	Matches that hex value	
\cX	Matches that control character	
\[	Matches that metacharacter	
		Anchored Characters
\b	Matches a word boundary (When not inside [ ])	
\B	Matches a non–word boundary	
^	Matches to beginning of line	
$	Matches to end of line	
\A	Matches the beginning of the string	
\Z	Matches the end of the string	
\G	Matches where previous m//g left off	
		Repeated Characters
x?	Matches 0 or 1 x	
x*	Matches 0 or more x's	
x+	Matches 1 or more x's	
x{m,n}	Matches at least m, x's and no more than n x's.	
abc	Matches all of a, b, and c, respectively	
was|were|will	Matches one of *was, were,* or *will*	
		Remembered Characters
(string)	Used for backreferencing (see example)	
\1 or $1	Matches first set of parentheses[4]	
\2 or $2	Matches second set of parentheses	
\3 or $3	Matches third set of parentheses	

---

4. \1 and $1 are called backreferences. They differ in that the \1 backreference is valid within a pattern whereas the $1 notation is valid within the enclosing block or until another successful search .

Metacharacters for Single Characters and Digits.

E x a m p l e   6 . 2 1

(The Text File)
 Steve Blenheim 101
 Betty Boop 201
 Igor Chevsky 301
 Norma Cord 401
 Jonathan DeLoach 501
 Karen Evich 601

1 $ **perl –ne 'print "Found Norma!\n" if /N..ma/' emp.names**
 Found Norma!

2 $ **perl -ne 'print if /[A-Z][a-z]eve/' emp.names**
 Steve Blenheim 101

3 $ **perl -ne 'print if /[^123]0/' emp.names**
 Norma Cord 401
 Jonathan DeLoach 501

4 $ **perl -ne 'print if /2\d\d/' emp.names**
 Betty Boop 201

5 $ **perl -ne 'print if /[ABC]\D/' emp.names**
 Steve Blenheim 101
 Betty Boop 201
 Igor Chevsky 301
 Norma Cord 401

E x p l a n a t i o n

1 The regular expression contains the period metacharacter, often called the *dot*, representing any single character. The expression reads: Find an *'N'*, followed by any two single characters, followed by *'m'*, then *'a'*.

2 The regular expression contains the square bracket metacharacter, representing one character from the set of characters enclosed in the square brackets. The expression reads: Find an upper case letter in the range from *'A'* through *'Z'*, followed by a lower case letter in the range of *'a'* to *'z'* followed by the letters, *'eve'*.

3 The regular expression contains bracket metacharacters. The caret (^) is a *not* operator when enclosed within the brackets. The expression reads: Find a pattern <u>not</u> containing an upper case *'1'*, *'2'*, or *'3'*, followed by a *'0'*.

4 The regular expression contains the \d metacharacter, representing one digit. The expression reads: Find a *'2'* followed by exactly two digits.

5 The regular expression contains the \D metacharacter, representing one non-digit. Its expression reads: Find an *'A'*, *'B'*, or *'C'*, followed by one non-digit.

Whitespace Metacharacters.

E x a m p l e   6 . 2 2

(The Text File)
Steve Blenheim 101
Betty Boop 201
Igor Chevsky 301
Norma Cord 401
Jonathan DeLoach 501
Karen Evich 601

1 **$ perl -ne 'print if s/\s/*/g' emp.names**
Steve Blenheim*101* Betty *Boop* 201*Igor*Chevsky *301*Normal
*Cord*401* Jonathan DeLoach* 501*Karen*Evich* 601

2 **$ perl -ne 'print if s/\S/*/g' emp.names**
```
***** ********* ***

***** **** ***

**** ******* ***

***** **** ***

******** ******* ***

***** ****** ***
```

3 **$ perl -ne 'print if s/\n/**\n/' emp.names**
Steve Blenheim 101**
Betty Boop 201**
Igor Chevsky 301**
Norma Cord 401**
Jonathan DeLoach 501**
Karen Evich 601**

E x p l a n a t i o n

1 The regular expression contains the \s metacharacter, representing a single whitespace character. The expression reads: Replace each space with a literal asterisk (*).
2 The regular expression contains the \S metacharacter, representing a single non-whitespace character. The expression reads: Replace each non-whitespace with a literal asterisk (*).
3 The regular expression contains the \n character, representing the newline. It reads: Replace each newline with two asterisks (*) and a new line.

Metacharacters to Repeat Pattern Matches.

E x a m p l e   6 . 2 3

(The Text File)
    Steve Blenheim 1.10
    Betty Boop .5
    Igor Chevsky 555.100
    Norma Cord 4.01
    Jonathan DeLoach .501
    Karen Evich 601

1 **$ perl -ne 'print if / [0-9]\.?/' emp.names**
    Steve Blenheim 1.10
    Igor Chevsky 555.100
    Norma Cord 4.01
    Karen Evich 601

2 **$perl -ne 'print if /5+/' emp.names**
    Betty Boop .5
    Igor Chevsky 555.100
    Jonathan DeLoach .501

3 **$perl -ne 'print if /10*/' emp.names**
    Steve Blenheim 1.10
    Igor Chevsky 555.100
    Norma Cord 4.01
    Jonathan DeLoach .501
    Karen Evich 601

4 **$ perl –ne 'print if /5{1,3}/;' emp.names**
    Betty Boop .5
    Igor Chevsky 555.100
    Jonathan DeLoach .501

5 **$ perl -ne 'print if /5{3}/; ' emp.names**
    Igor Chevsky 555.100

6 **$ perl -ne 'print if /5{1,}/;' emp.names**
    Betty Boop .5
    Igor Chevsky 555.100
    Jonathan DeLoach .501

Explanation

1 The regular expression contains the ? metacharacter, representing zero or one of the preceding characters. The expression reads: Find a space, followed by a number between 0 and 9, followed by either one literal period or no literal period.

2 The regular expression contains the + metacharacter, representing one or more of the preceding characters. The expression reads: Find one or more 5's.

3 The regular expression contains the * metacharacter, representing zero or more of the preceding characters. The expression reads: Find a '1' followed by zero or more 0's.

4 The regular expression contains the curly brace { } metacharacters, representing the number of times the preceding expression will be repeated. The expression reads: Find at least one occurrence of the pattern '5' and not more than three.

5 The expression reads: Find exactly three consecutive 5's.

6 The expression reads: Find at least one or more consecutive 5's.

Anchoring Metacharacters.

Example 6.24

(The Text File)
Steve Blenheim 1.10
Betty Boop .5
Igor Chevsky 555.10
Norma Cord 4.01
Jonathan DeLoach .501
Karen Evich 601.100

1 **$ perl -ne 'print if /^[JK]/' emp.names**
Jonathan DeLoach .501
Karen Evich 601.100

2 **$ perl -ne 'print if /10$/' emp.names**
Steve Blenheim 1.10
Igor Chevsky 555.10

3 **$ perl -ne /\bJon/' emp.names**
Jonathan DeLoach .501

4 **$ perl -ne /\bJon\b/' emp.names**

Explanation

1 The regular expression contains the caret (^) metacharacter, representing the beginning of line anchor when it is the first character in the pattern. The expression reads: Find a 'J' or 'K' at the beginning of the line.

2 The regular expression contains the dollar sign ($) metacharacter, representing the end of line anchor when it is the last character in the pattern. The expression reads: Find a '1' and a '0' followed by a newline.

3 The regular expression contains the \b metacharacter, representing a word boundary. The expression reads: Find a word beginning with the pattern *Jon*.

4 The regular expression also contains the \b metacharacter, representing a word boundary. The expression reads: Find a word beginning and ending with *Jon*. Nothing is found.

Metacharacters That Remember Patterns.

E x a m p l e   6 . 2 5

(The Text File)
Steve Blenheim
Betty Boop
Igor Chevsky
Norma Cord
Jon DeLoach
Karen Evich

1 **$ perl –ne 's/([Jj]on)/$1athan/;print' emp.names**
Steve Blenheim
Betty Boop
Igor Chevsky
Norma Cord
Jonathan DeLoach
Karen Evich

2 **$ perl –ne 's/(Steve) (Blenheim)/$2 $1/;print' emp.names**
Blenheim Steve
Betty Boop
Igor Chevsky
Norma Cord
Jon DeLoach
Karen Evich

3 **$ perl –ne 's/([A–Z][a–z]+) ([A–Z][a–z]+)/$2 $1/; print' emp.names**
Blenheim Steve
Boop Betty
Chevsky Igor
Cord Norma
De JonLoach   *# Whoops!*
Evich Karen

Explanation

1   The regular expression contains a pattern enclosed in parentheses. This pattern is tagged as pattern number 1 and stored in Perl's memory, so that it can be *remembered*. If a second pattern is enclosed in parentheses, it will be tagged pattern number 2, etc. The numbers are represented on the replacement side as $1, $2, $3, etc. The expression reads: Find *Jon* or *jon* and replace it with *Jonathan* or *jonathan*.

2   The regular expression contains two patterns enclosed in parentheses. The first pattern is tagged as pattern number 1 and the second pattern is pattern number 2. On the replacement side, since pattern 2 is referenced first, *Blenheim* is printed first, followed by pattern number 1, *Steve* (i.e., the effect is to reverse *Steve* and *Blenheim*).

3   This regular expression also contains two patterns enclosed in parentheses. In this example, the metacharacters are used in the pattern-matching process. The first pattern reads: Find an upper case letter followed by one or more lower case letters. A space follows the remembered pattern. The second pattern reads: Find an upper case letter followed by one or more lower case letters. The patterns are reversed on the replacement side. Note the problem that arises with the last name *DeLoach*. The pattern should be:

$ perl −ne 's/([A-Z][a-z]+) ([A-Z][A-Za-z]+)/$2 $1/; print' emp.names

Example 6.26

```
(The Text file)
$ cat emp.names
Steve Blenheim
Betty Boop
Igor Chevsky
Norma Cord
Jon DeLoach
Betty Boop
-----------------------------------
(The Script)
#!/bin/perl
# Scriptname: lastfirst
1  while(<>){
2  ($first, $last)=/(\S+) (\S+)/;
3  print "$last, $first\n";
}
-----------------------------------
(The Command Line)
$ chmod +x lastfirst
$ lastfirst emp.names
Blenheim, Steve
Boop, Betty
```

Chevsky, Igor
Cord, Norma
DeLoach, Jon
Boop, Betty

Explanation

1   The *while* loop is entered. The name of the file being processed is passed in from the command line. Each line of the file is stored in the *$_* variable.
2   The regular expression contains two patterns enclosed in parentheses. The \$+ represents one or more non-white space characters (a word). The regular expression consists of two parenthesized patterns called backreferences. The return value is an array of all the backreferences. Each word is assigned to *$first* and *$last*, respectively.
3   The values of the variables are printed for each line of the file.

Example 6.27

(The Script)
```
    #!/usr/bin/perl
1   $string="ABCdefghiCxyzwerC YOU!";
2   $string=~s/.*C/ZAP/;
3   print "$string", "\n";
```

Output

3   *ZAP YOU!*

Explanation

1   The scalar, *$string*, is assigned a string containing a number of 'C's.
2   The search side of the substitution, /.*C/, reads, "find the largest pattern that contains any number of characters ending in C". The search is "greedy". It will search from left to right until it reaches the last C. The string ZAP will replace what was found in *$string*.
3   The new string is printed showing the result of the substitution.

Example 6.28

(The Script)
```
    #!/usr/bin/perl
1   $string="ABCdefghiCxyzwerC YOU!";
2   $string=~s/(.*C)(.*)/ZAP/;
3   print $1, "\n";
4   print $2, "\n";
5   print "$string", "\n";
```

O u t p u t

3 *ABCdefghiCxyzwerC*
4 *YOU!*
5 *ZAP*

E x p l a n a t i o n

1 The scalar, *$string*, is assigned the string.
2 The */*.C/* regular expression is enclosed in parentheses. The pattern found will be stored in the *$1* special variable. Whatever is left will be stored in *$2*.
3 The largest possible pattern was stored in *$1*. It is printed.
4 The remainder of the string was stored in *$2*. It is printed.
5 The entire line was replaced with *ZAP*.

E x a m p l e   6 . 2 9

(The Script)
1 $fruit="apples pears peaches plums";
2 **$fruit=~/(.*) (.*) (.*)/;**   *# There is a single space between each set of parens*
3 print "$1\n";
4 print "$2\n";
5 print "$3\n";

O u t p u t

3 *apples pears*
4 *peaches*
5 *plums*

E x p l a n a t i o n

1 The scalar, *$fruit*, is assigned the string.
2 The string is divided into three remembered substrings, each substring enclosed within parentheses. The .* metacharacter sequence reads zero or more of any character. The .* always matches for the largest possible pattern (it's greedy). The largest possible pattern would be the whole string. However, there are two white spaces, outside of the parentheses that must also be matched in the string. What is the largest possible pattern that can be saved in $1 and still have two spaces left in the string? The answer is: "apples pears".
3 The value of $1 is printed.
4 The first substring was stored in $1. *"peaches plums"* is what remains of the original string. What is the largest possible pattern (.*) that can be matched and still have one white space remaining? The answer is *"peaches"*. *"peaches"* will be assigned to $2. The value of $2 is printed.
5 The third substring is printed. *"plums"* is all that is left for $3.

Miscellaneous Pattern Matching Operators. There are a number of options, as we have seen, that are used with search patterns. The ones listed below are difficult to understand just by reading the definition and better understood with examples.

The s Option.
The s option is used so that the dot metacharacter can match a newline character.

E x a m p l e   6 . 3 0

```
(The Script)
    #!/usr/bin/perl
1   $string="ABC                    # There's a new line in the string.
    DEF";

2   $string=~s/^ABC.*/ZAP/;         # Without the s option
3   print "$string";
4   print "\n--------\n";

5   $string="ABC                    # There's a newline in the string.
    DEF";
6   $string=~s/^ABC.*/ZAP/s;        # The s option added
7   print "$string";
8   print "\n--------\n";
```

O u t p u t

```
3   ZAP
    DEF
4   --------
7   ZAP
8   --------
```

E x p l a n a t i o n

1 The scalar $string is assigned a string with an embedded newline character.
2 The search string starts the match at the beginning of the line (caret) and if the string *ABC* is found, followed by zero or more of any character, with the exception of the newline, that string will be replaced with the string *ZAP*. Since the dot doesn't match on the newline, *ABC* will be replaced with *ZAP* and the rest of the string left alone.
3 The string is printed after the substitution.
4 A row of dashes is printed to visually separate the two examples in the program.
5 The scalar *$string* is assigned the same string as on line1.

6   This time the **s** option is included in the substitution statement. The **s** option tells Perl
    to treat the string as one single line. The newline is treated as any other single character
    when using the dot metacharacter in the search string. Normally the dot metacharacter
    cannot match on a newline. Everything is replaced with *ZAP*.

The m Option.

The *m* option is used to control the behavior of the $ and ^ anchor metacharacters. A string
containing newlines will be treated as multiple lines.

E x a m p l e   6 . 3 1

(The Script)
```
#!/usr/bin/perl
1    $string="ABC                                   \nDEF";

2    $string=~s/^.*$/ZAP/;                 # Without the m option
3    print "$string";
4    print "\n--------\n";

5    $string="ABC\nDEF";                   ";# There's a newline in the string.
6    $string=~s/^.*$/ZAP/m;                 # The m option added
7    print "$string";
8    print "\n--------\n";

9    $string="ABC\nDEF";
10   $string=~s/^.*$/ZAP/gm;              #The g is added for global change
11   print "$string";
12   print "\n--------\n";


13   $string="ABC\nDEF\nABC";
14   $string=~s/^.*$/ZAP/gms;             # Both the m and s options are applied
15   print "$string";                     # ABC in one line; DEF is another line
16   print "\n--------\n"
```

O u t p u t

```
3    ABC
     DEF
4    --------
7    ZAP
     DEF
8    --------
```

11 *ZAP*
    ZAP
12 --------
15 *ZAP*
16 --------

E x p l a n a t i o n

1   The scalar *$string* is assigned a string with an embedded newline character.
2   The search string starts the match at the beginning of the line (caret) to the end of the line ($). Nothing is matched because the newline, embedded in the line, is not recognized by the dot metacharacter as a character that can be matched.
3   The string is printed. Since a match never was made, the string was unchanged.
4   A row of dashes is printed to separate visually the examples in the program.
5   The scalar *$string* is assigned the same string as on line1.
6   This time the **m** option is included in the substitution statement. The **m** option tells Perl that the caret or the dollar sign is not limited to a specific line but to any string ending in a newline. There is a newline embedded in the first line. Perl will start matching from the beginning of the line ending at the first newline. *ABC* will be replaced with *ZAP.* The rest of the line, DEF, is left as is.
7   The new value of $*string* is printed.
8   A row of dashes is printed to separate visually the examples in the program.
9    $*string* is assigned a new string including two embedded newlines.
10   This time the g modifier is added to make the change global. Perl will start matching from the beginning of the line to the first newline, make the substitution, and then go to to the next line up until the last newline.
11   The new value of *$string* is printed, demonstrating that both lines were changed.
12   A row of dashes is printed to separate visually the examples in the program.
13   The scalar *$string* is assigned the same string as on line1.
14   This time both the *m* and the *s* modifiers are used. The *m* allows the $ to match to the end of any line. The *s* allows the dot metacharacter to match on a newline. Everything will be replaced with ZAP up until the end of the entire line.

6.4.1   The tr or y Function

The *tr* function translates characters, on a one-on-one correspondence, from the characters in the search string to the characters in the replacement string. It returns the number of characters replaced. This is similar to the UNIX *tr* utility. The tr function does not recognize regular expression metacharacters other than the dash to represent a range of characters. The letter y is used as a synonym for *tr*, emulating the UNIX *sed* utility. If the replacement string is shorter than the search string, the last character in the replacement string is replaced wherever necessary.

The *c* option <u>c</u>omplements the search string.

The *s* option is called the "<u>s</u>queeze" option. Multiple occurrences of characters found in the search string are replaced by a single occurrence of that character (e.g., you may want to replace multiple tabs with single tabs). See Table 6.5 for a list of modifiers.

Format:

```
tr/search/replacement/
tr/search/replacement/d
tr/search/replacement/c
tr/search/replacement/s

y/search/replacement/  (same as tr; uses same modifiers)
```

TABLE 6.5   tr Modifiers

Modifier	Meaning
d	Delete characters
c	Complement the search list
s	Squeeze out multiple characters to single character

(The Text File)
$cat emp.names
Steve Blenheim 101
Betty Boop 201
Igor Chevsky 301
Norma Cord 401
Jon DeLoach 501
Karen Evich 601

(At the Command Line)
1 $ **perl –ne 'tr/a–z/A–Z/;print' emp.names**
STEVE BLENHEIM 101
BETTY BOOP 201
IGOR CHEVSKY 301
NORMA CORD 401
JON DELOACH 501
KAREN EVICH 601

2 $ **perl -ne 'tr/0-9/:/; print' emp.names**
Steve Blenheim :::
Betty Boop :::
Igor Chevsky :::
Norma Cord :::
Jon DeLoach :::
Karen Evich :::

3 **$ perl –ne 'tr/A–Z/a–c/;print' emp.names**
   cteve blenheim 101
   betty boop 201
   cgor chevsky 301
   corma cord 401
   con cecoach 501
   caren cvich 601

4 **$ perl –ne 'tr/ /#/; print' emp.names**
   Steve#Blenheim#101
   Betty#Boop#201
   Igor#Chevsky#301
   Norma#Cord#401
   Jon#DeLoach#501
   Karen#Evich#601

5 **$ perl –ne 'y/A–Z/a–z/;print' emp.names**
   steve blenheim 101
   betty boop 201
   igor chevsky 301
   norma cord 401
   jon deloach 501
   karen evich 601

Explanation

1 The *tr* function makes a one-on-one correspondence between each character in the search string with each character in the replacement string. Each lower case letter will be translated to its corresponding upper case letter.
2 Each number will be translated to a colon.
3 The translation is messy here. Since the search side represents more characters than the replacement side, all letters from D to Z will be replaced with a 'c'.
4 Each space will be replaced with pound signs (#).
5 The *y* is a synonym for *tr*. Each upper case letter is translated to its corresponding lower case letter.

The tr Delete Option.   The **d** (delete) **option** removes all characters in the search string not found in the replacement string.

Example 6.32

1 **$ perl –ne 'tr/ //; print;' emp.names**
   1 Steve Blenheim
   2 Betty Boop

```
3 Igor Chevsky
4 Norma Cord
5 Jon DeLoach
6 Karen Evich
```

2 $ **perl –ne 'tr/ //d;print;' emp.names**
```
1SteveBlenheim
2BettyBoop
3IgorChevsky
4NormaCord
5JonDeLoach
6KarenEvich
```

Explanation

1 In this example, the translation does not take place as it would if you were using *sed* or *vi*.
2 The d option is required to delete each space when using the *tr* function.

The tr Complement Option. The **c** (complement) **option** complements the search string; that is, it translates each character not listed in this string to its corresponding character in the replacement string.

Example 6.33

1 $ **perl –ne 'tr/0–9/*/;print' emp.names**
```
* Steve Blenheim
* Betty Boop
* Igor Chevsky
* Norma Cord
* Jon DeLoach
* Karen Evich
```

2 $ **perl –ne 'tr/0–9/*/c;print' emp.names**
```
1***************2*************3*************4************5*************6************
```

Explanation

1 Without the *c* option, *tr* translates each number to an asterisk (*).
2 With the *c* option, *tr* translates each character that is not a number to an asterisk (*); this includes the newline character.

The tr Squeeze Option.   The **s** (squeeze) **option** translates all characters that are repeated to a single character.

Example 6.34

(The Text File)
```
$ cat file.colons
1:::Steve Blenheim
2::Betty Boop
3:Igor Chevsky
4:Norma Cord
5:::::Jon DeLoach
6:::Karen Evich
```

(The Command Line)
```
1  $ perl -ne 'tr/:/:/s;print' file.colons
   1:Steve Blenheim
   2:Betty Boop
   3:Igor Chevsky
   4:Norma Cord
   5:Jon DeLoach
   6:Karen Evich
```

Explanation

1   Multiple colons are (squeezed) translated to single colons.

7

If Only, Unconditionally, Forever...

7.1 Control Structures, Blocks, and Compound Statements

So far, we have seen script examples that are linear in structure, i.e., simple statements are executed one after the other. Control structures, such as branching and looping statements, allow the flow of the program's control to change depending on some conditional expression.

The decision-making constructs (*if, if/else, if/elsif/else, unless,* etc.) contain a control expression that determines whether or not a block of statements will be executed. The looping constructs (*while, for, foreach*) allow the program to repetitively execute a statement block until some condition is satisfied.

A compound statement or block consists of a group of statements surrounded by curly braces. The block is syntactically equivalent to a single statement and usually follows an *if, else, while,* or *for* construct. But unlike *C*, where curly braces are not always required, Perl requires them even with one statement when that statement comes after the *if, else, while,* etc. The conditional modifiers, discussed in Chapter 6, can be used when a condition is evaluated within a *single* statement.

7.2 Decision Making—Conditional Constructs

7.2.1 if and unless Statements

The *if* and *unless* modifiers discussed in Chapter 6 are used only to modify simple statements. They are always placed at the end of the statement and cannot be nested. When a

129

block structure is used, the statement or statements are enclosed in curly braces following the test expression. Then the *if* or *unless* keywords are placed <u>before</u> the test expression.

An *if* statement is a conditional statement. It allows you to test an expression and, based on the results of the test, make a decision. The expression is enclosed in parentheses, and Perl, unlike *C*, evaluates the expression in a *string* context. If the string is non-null, the expression is true; if null, the expression is false. If the expression is a numeric value, it will be converted to a string and tested. If the expression is evaluated to be true (non-null), the next statement block is executed; if the condition is false (null), Perl will ignore the block associated with the expression and go onto the next executable statement within the script.

The *unless* statement is constructed exactly the same as the *if* statement; the results of the test are simply reversed. If the expression is evaluated to be false, the next statement block is executed; if the expression is evaluated to be true, Perl will ignore the block of statements controlled by the expression.

Format:

```
if ( Expression ) { Block}
if ( Expression ) { Block} else { Block}
if ( Expression ) { Block } elsif ( Expression )
     { Block }... else { Block}
```

The if Construct.   The *if* statement consists of the keyword, *if,* followed by a conditional expression, followed by a block of one or more statements enclosed in curly braces. Each statement within the block is terminated with a semicolon. The block of statements collectively is often called a compound statement.

E x a m p l e   7 . 1

```
(The Script)
1  $num1=1;
2  $num2=0;

3  $str1="hello";
4  $str2="";              # Null string

5  if ( $num1 ) {print "TRUE!\n"; $x++;}   # $x and $y were initially assigned zero
6  if ( $num2 ) {print "FALSE! \n";$y++;}  # never execute this block
7  if ( $str1 ) {print "TRUE AGAIN!\n";}
8  if ( $str2 ) {print "FALSE AGAIN!\n";}
9  print "Not Equal!\n" if $x != $y;
```

O u t p u t

5   *TRUE!*
7   *TRUE AGAIN!*
9   *Not Equal!*

E x p l a n a t i o n

1   The scalar, *$num1*, is assigned the number 1, which will be converted to "1".
2   The scalar, *$num2*, is assigned the number 0, which will be converted to "0".
3   The scalar, *$str1*, is assigned the string "hello".
4   The scalar, *$str2*, is assigned the null string.
5   Since the value of *$num1* is not a null string, true, the block statement(s) is executed; $x is incremented.
6   Since the value of *$num2* is the null string, false, the block statement(s) is not executed.
7   Since the value of *$str1* is not a null string, the block statement(s) is executed
8   Since the value of *$str2* is an empty string, the block statement(s) is not executed.
9   The *if* construct is used as a statement modifier when a simple expression is being tested.

The if/else Construct.   Another form of the *if* statement is the *if/else* construct. This construct allows a two-way decision. If the first conditional expression following the *if* keyword is true, the block of statements following the *if* are executed. Otherwise, if the conditional expression following the *if* keyword is false, control branches to the *else* and the block of statements following the *else* are executed. The *else* statement is never an independent statement. It must follow an *if* statement. When the *if* statements are nested within other *if* statements, the *else* statement is associated with the closest previous *if* statement.

Format:

```
if ( Expression )
      { Block }
else
      { Block }
```

E x a m p l e   7 . 2

(The Script)
1   print "What version of the operating system are you using? ";
2   chomp($os=<STDIN>);

3   if ($os > 2.2) { print "Most of the bugs have been worked out!\n;}
4   else { print "Expect some problems.\n";}

Output

1 *What version of the operating system are you using ? 2.4*
2 Most of the bugs have been worked out!

Output

1 *What version of the operating system are you using ? 2.0*
4 *Expect some problems.*

Explanation

1 The user is asked for input.
2 The newline is removed.
3 If the value of $os is greater than 2.2, the block enclosed in curly braces is executed.
4 If the $os is not greater than 2.2, this block is executed.

The if/elsif/else Construct.   Yet another form of the *if* statement is the *if/else/elsif* construct. This construct allows a multiway decision structure. If the first conditional expression following the *if* keyword is true, the block of statements following the *if* is executed. Otherwise, the first *elsif* statement is tested. If the conditional expression following the first *elsif* is false, the next *elsif* is tested, etc. If all of the conditional expressions following the *elsif's* are false, the block after the *else* is executed; this is the default action.

Format:

```
if ( Expression1 )
        { Block }
elsif ( Expression2 )
        { Block }
elsif ( Expression3 )
        { Block }
else
        { Block }
```

Example 7.3

(The Script)
1 $hour=`date +%H`;
2 if ($hour >= 0 && $hour < 12){print "Good–morning!\n";}
3 elsif ($hour == 12){print "Lunch time.\n";}
4 elsif ($hour > 12 && $hour < 17) {print "Siesta time.\n";}
5 else {print "Goodnight. Sweet dreams.\n";}

Output

4 *Siesta time*

Explanation

1 The scalar, *$hour*, is set to the current hour. Command substitution is performed within the backquotes.

2 The *if* statement tests whether the value of *$hour* is greater than or equal to *0* and less than *12*. The result of the evaluation is true, and the block following the control expression is executed (i.e., the *print* statement is executed).

3 If the first *if* test is false, this expression is tested. If the value of *$hour* is equal to *12*, the *print* statement is executed.

4 If the previous *elsif* test failed, and this *elsif* expression evaluates to true, the *print* statement will be executed.

5 If none of the above statements is true, the *else* statement, the default action, is executed.

7.2.2 The unless Construct

The *unless* statement is similar to the *if* statement, except that the control expression after the *unless* is tested for the reverse condition; that is, if the conditional expression following the *unless* is false, the statement block is executed.

The *unless/else* and *unless/elsif* behave in the same way as the *if/else* and *if /elsif* statements with the same reversed test as stated above.

Format:

```
unless ( Expression ) {Block}
unless ( Expression ) {Block} else { Block}
unless ( Expression ) {Block} elsif ( Expression )
    { Block }... else {Block}
```

Example 7.4

```
(The Script)
1  $num1=1;
2  $num2=0;

3  $str1="hello";
4  $str2="";               # Null string

5  unless ( $num1 ) {print "TRUE!\n"; $x++;} # never execute this block
6  unless( $num2 ) {print "FALSE! \n"; $y++;}
```

```
7  unless ( $str1 ) {print "TRUE AGAIN!\n";}
8  unless( $str2 ) {print "FALSE AGAIN!\n";}
9  print "Not Equal!\n" unless  $x == $y;     #unless modifier and simple statement
```

Output

```
6  FALSE!
8  FALSE AGAIN!
9  Not Equal!
```

Explanation

1   The scalar, *$num1*, is assigned the number 1, which will be converted to "1".
2   The scalar, *$num2*, is assigned the number 0, which will be converted to "0".
3   The scalar, *$str1*, is assigned the string "hello".
4   The scalar, *$str2*, is assigned the null string.
5   Since the value of *$num1* is <u>not</u> an empty string, i.e., true, the block statement(s) *is not* executed.
6   Since the value of *$num2* is an empty string, i.e. false, the block statement(s) *is* executed; $y is incremented.
7   Since the value of *$str1* is not an empty string, the block statement(s) *is not* executed.
8   Since the value of *$str2* is an empty string, i.e., false, the block statement(s) *is* executed.
9   The *unless* construct is used as a statement modifier when a simple expression is being tested.

Example 7.5

```
(The Script)
   #!/bin/perl
   # Scriptname: excluder
1  while(<>){
2  ($name, $phone)=split(/:/);
3  unless($name eq barbara){
      $record="$name\t$phone";
4      print "$record";
   }
}
5 print "\$name has moved from this district.\n";
```

O u t p u t

$ excluder names

igor chevsky	*408-123-4533*
paco gutierrez	*510-453-2776*
ephram hardy	*916-235-4455*
james ikeda	*415-449-0066*
barbara kerz	*207-398-6755*
jose santiago	*408-876-5899*
tommy savage	*408-876-1725*
lizzy stachelin	*415-555-1234*

barbara has moved from this district.

E x p l a n a t i o n

1 The *while* loop is entered. It will read one line at a time from whatever filename is given as a command line argument to this script. The argument file is called "names".
2 Each line is split by a colon delimiter. The first field is assigned to $*name* and the second field to $*phone*.
3 The *unless* statement is executed. It reads: unless $*name* evaluates to *barbara*, enter the block, i.e., anyone except *barbara* is o.k.
4 All names and phones are printed with the exception of *barbara*.
5 When the loop exits, this line is printed.

7.3 Loops

Loops are used to execute a segment of code repeatedly. Perl's basic looping constructs are:

> *while*
> *until*
> *for*
> *foreach*

Each loop is followed by a block of statements enclosed in curly braces.

7.3.1 The while Loop

The *while* statement executes the block as long as the control expression after the *while* is true. An expression is true if it evaluates to non–zero (non-null); *while(1)* is always true and loops forever. An expression is false if it evaluates to zero (null); *while(0)* is false and never loops.

Often the *while* statement is used to loop through a file. (See "Reading from the Filehandle" and "The Null Filehandle" in Chapter 8.)

Format:

```
while ( Expression ) {Block}
```

E x a m p l e   7 . 6

(The Script)
```
    #!/usr/bin/perl
1   $num=0;  #initialize $num
2   while($num < 10 ){   # test expression;
    # loop quits when expression is false or 0
3       print "$num ";
4       $num++;   # update the loop variable $num; increment $num
5   }
6   print "\nOut of the loop.\n";
```

O u t p u t

```
3  0 1 2 3 4 5 6 7 8 9
6  Out of the loop.
```

E x p l a n a t i o n

1 The scalar, *$num*, is initialized. The initialization takes place before entering the loop.
2 The test expression is evaluated. If the result is true, the block of statements in curly braces is executed.
4 The scalar, *$num*, is incremented. If not, the test expression would always yield a true value, and the loop would never end.

E x a m p l e   7 . 7

(The Script)
```
    #!/usr/bin/perl
1   $count=1;  #Initialize variables
    $beers=10;
    $remain=$beers;
    $where="on the shelf";
2   while($count <= $beers) {
        if($remain == 1){print "$remain bottle of beer $where $where " ;}
        else{ print "$remain bottles of beer $where $where";}
        print " Take one down and pass it all around.\n";
        print "Now ", $beers - $count , " bottles of beer $where!\n";
```

```
3          $count++;
4          $remain––;
5          if ( $count > 10 ){print "Party's over. \n";}
     }
   print "\n";
```

Output

10 bottles on the shelf on the shelf Take one down and pass it all around.
Now 9 bottles of beer on the shelf!
9 bottles on the shelf on the shelf Take one down and pass it all around.
Now 8 bottles of beer on the shelf!
8 bottles on the shelf on the shelf Take one down and pass it all around.
Now 7 bottles of beer on the shelf!
7 bottles on the shelf on the shelf Take one down and pass it all around.
Now 6 bottles of beer on the shelf!
6 bottles on the shelf on the shelf Take one down and pass it all around.
Now 5 bottles of beer on the shelf!
5 bottles on the shelf on the shelf Take one down and pass it all around.
Now 4 bottles of beer on the shelf!
4 bottles on the shelf on the shelf Take one down and pass it all around.
Now 3 bottles of beer on the shelf!
3 bottles on the shelf on the shelf Take one down and pass it all around.
Now 2 bottles of beer on the shelf!
2 bottles on the shelf on the shelf Take one down and pass it all around.
Now 1 bottle of beer on the shelf!
1 bottle of beer on the shelf on the shelf Take one down and pass it all around.
Now 0 bottles of beer on the shelf!
Party's over.

Explanation

1   The scalars, *$count, $beers, $remain*, and *$where* are initialized.
2   The *while* loop is entered; the control expression is tested and evaluated.
3   The scalar, *$count*, is incremented.
4   The scalar, *$remain*, is decremented.
5   When the value of *$count* is greater than 10, this line is printed.

7.3.2   The until Loop

The *until* statement executes the block as long as the control expression after the *until* is false or zero. When the expression evaluates to true (non-zero), the loop exits.

Format:

```
until ( Expression ) {Block}
```

E x a m p l e   7 . 8

(The Script)
```
   #!/usr/bin/perl
1  $num=0;  #initialize
2  until ($num == 10 ){  # test expression; loop quits when expression is true or 1
3      print "$num ";
4      $num++;   # update the loop variable $num;  increment $num
5  }
6  print "\nOut of the loop.\n";
```

O u t p u t

```
3  0 1 2 3 4 5 6 7 8 9
6  Out of the loop.
```

E x p l a n a t i o n

1 The scalar, *$num*, is initialized. The initialization takes place before entering the loop.
2 The test expression is evaluated. If the result is *false*, the block of statements in curly braces is executed. When $num is equal to 10, the loop exits.
4 The scalar, *$num*, is incremented. If not, the test expression would always yield a false value, and the loop would never end.

The do/while and do/until Loops.   The *do/while* or *do/until* loops evaluate the conditional expression for true and false just as in the *while* and *until* loop statements. However, the expression is not evaluated until after the block is executed at least once.

Format:

```
do { Block } while Expression;
do { Block } until Expression;
```

E x a m p l e   7 . 9

(The Script)
```perl
   #!/usr/bin/perl
1  $x = 1;
2  do {
3       print "$x ";
4       $x++; } while ($x <= 10);
   print "\n";
5  $y = 1;
6  do {
7       print "$y " ;
8       $y++; } until ( $y >= 10 );
```

O u t p u t

```
3  1 2 3 4 5 6 7 8 9 10
7  1 2 3 4 5 6 7 8 9 10
```

E x p l a n a t i o n

1   The scalar, *$x*, is assigned the value, *1*.
2   The *do/while* loop statement starts.
3   The block of statements is executed.
4   The scalar, *$x,* is incremented once; the conditional expression following the *while* is evaluated. If true, the block of statements is executed again, etc.
5   The scalar, *$y*, is assigned the value, *1*.
6   The *do/until* loop statement starts.
7   The block of statements is executed.
8   The scalar, *$y,* is incremented once; the conditional expression following the *until* is evaluated. If false, the block of statements is executed again, etc.

7.3.3   The for Loop

The *for* statement is like the C *for* loop. The *for* keyword is followed by three expressions separated by semicolons and enclosed within parentheses. Any or all of the expressions can be omitted, but the two semicolons cannot.[1] The first expression is used to set the initial value of variables; the second expression is used to test whether the loop should continue or stop; and the third expression updates the loop variables.

Format:

```
        for(Expression1;Expression2;Expression3){Block}
```

---

1. The infinite loop can be written as: for(;;)

The above format is equivalent to the following *while* statement:

```
Expression1;
while( Expression2 )
      { Block; Expression3};
```

Example 7.10

(The Script)
```
  #!/usr/bin/perl
1 for($i=0;$i<10;$i++){      # initialize, test, and increment $i
2         print "$i ";
  }
3 print "\nOut of the loop.\n";
```

Output

2 *0 1 2 3 4 5 6 7 8 9*
3 *Out of the loop.*

Explanation

1 The *for* loop contains three expressions. In the first expression, the scalar, *$i*, is assigned the value *0*. This statement is executed just once. The second expression tests whether *$i* is less than 10, and if so, the block statements are executed (i.e., the value of *$i* is printed). The last expression increments the value of *$i* by one. The second expression is again tested, and the block is executed, *$i* is incremented, etc., etc., until the test evaluates to false.
2 The value of *$i* is printed.

Example 7.11

(The Script)
```
  #!/usr/bin/perl
  # Initialization, test, and increment, decrement of counters is done in one step.
1 for($count=1, $beers=10, $remain=$beers, $where="on the shelf"; $count
  <= $beers; $count++, $remain--){
2 if($remain == 1){print "$remain bottle of beer $where $where " ;}
  else{ print "$remain bottles of beer $where $where";}
  print " Take one down and pass it all around.\n";
  print "Now ", $beers – $count , " bottles of beer $where!\n";
3 if ( $count == 10 ){print "Party's over.\n";}
  }
```

Output

> *10 bottles of beer on the shelf on the shelf Take one down and pass it all around.*
> *Now 9 bottles of beer on the shelf!*
> 9 bottles of beer on the shelf on the shelf Take one down and pass it all around.
> Now 8 bottles of beer on the shelf!
> 8 bottles of beer on the shelf on the shelf Take one down and pass it all around.
> Now 7 bottles of beer on the shelf!
> < continue >
> 2 bottles of beer on the shelf on the shelf Take one down and pass it all around.
> Now 1 bottle of beer on the shelf!
> 1 bottle of beer on the shelf on the shelf Take one down and pass it all around.
> Now 0 bottles of beer on the shelf!
> Party's over.

Explanation

1 The initialization of all scalars is done in the first expression of the *for* loop. Each initialization is separated by a comma, and the expression is terminated with a semicolon. The first expression is executed only once, when the loop starts. The second expression is the test. If it evaluates to true, the statements in the block are executed. After the last statement in the block is executed, the third expression is evaluated. The control is then passed to the second expression in the *for* loop, etc., etc.

2 The block is executed if the second expression in the *for* loop is evaluated as true.

3 This statement will be tested and, if the condition is true, the statement will be executed and control will go to the third expression within the *for* loop, incrementing *$count* for the last time.

7.3.4 The foreach Loop

If you are familiar with *C Shell* programming, the Perl *foreach* loop is similar in appearance and behavior to the C Shell *foreach* loop, but appearances can be deceiving and there are some obvious differences between the two constructs. So, read on.

The *foreach* loop iterates over each element in the parenthesized list, an array, assigning each element of the array to a scalar variable, one after the other, until the list is empty.

Format:

```
foreach VARIABLE ( ARRAY )
        { BLOCK }
```

The *VARIABLE* is local to the *foreach* block. It will regain its former value when the loop is exited. Any changes made when assigning values to *VARIABLE* will, in turn, affect the individual elements of the Array. If *VARIABLE* is not present, the $_ special scalar variable is implicitly used.

E x a m p l e   7 . 1 2

(The Script)

```
  #!/usr/bin/perl
1 foreach $pal ( Tom, Dick, Harry, Pete ) {
2     print "Hi $pal!\n";
  }
```

O u t p u t

```
2 Hi Tom!
  Hi Dick!
  Hi Harry!
  Hi Pete!
```

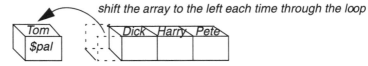

The foreach loop

E x p l a n a t i o n

1 The *foreach* is followed by the scalar $pal and a list of names. Each name will be assigned, in turn, to the scalar $pal. The list is shifted to the left each time the loop iterates. The loop ends when all names have been shifted off.

2 Each time through the loop, the value of $pal is printed.

E x a m p l e   7 . 1 3

(The Script)

```
1 foreach $hour ( 1 .. 24 )  # The range operator is used here
  {
2     if ( $hour > 0 && $hour < 12){ print "Good–morning.\n"; }
3     elsif ( $hour == 12){ print "Happy Lunch.\n";}
4     elsif ( $hour > 12 && $hour < 17) { print "Good afternoon.\n" ; }
5     else { print "Good–night.\n" ; }
  }
```

Output

2 *Good--morning.*
  Good--morning.
  Good--morning.
  Good--morning.
  Good--morning.
  Good--morning.
  Good--morning.
  Good--morning.
  Good--morning.
  Good--morning.
  Good--morning.
3 *Happy Lunch.*
4 *Good afternoon.*
  Good afternoon.
  Good afternoon.
  Good afternoon.
5 *Good--night.*
  Good--night.
  Good--night.
  Good--night.
  Good--night.
  Good--night.
  Good--night.
  Good--night.

Explanation

1 The list 1..24 is a range of list items starting with *1* and ending with *24*. Each of those values is assigned in turn to the scalar, *$hour*, the block is executed, and the next item in the list is assigned to *$hour*, etc.

2 The scalar, *$hour*, is tested and if the value is greater than 0 and less than 12, the print statement is executed.

3 If the previous *elsif* statement is false, this statement is tested. If the scalar, *$hour*, is equal to 12, the print statement is executed.

4 If the previous *elsif* statement is false, this statement is tested. If the scalar, *$hour*, is greater than *12* and less than *17*, the print statement is executed.

5 If all of the previous statements are false, the *else* or default statement, is executed.

Example 7.14

(The Script)
```perl
     #!/usr/bin/perl
1    $str="hello";
2    @numbers = ( 1, 3, 5, 7, 9 );
3    print "The scalar \$str is initially $str.\n";
4    print "The array \@numbers is initially @numbers.\n";

5    foreach $str ( @numbers ){
6         $str+=5;
7         print "$str\n";
8    }
9    print "Out of the loop--\$str is $str.\n";
10   print "Out of the loop--The array \@numbers is now @numbers.\n";
```

Output

```
3    The scalar $str is initially hello.
4    The array @numbers is initially 1 3 5 7 9.
7    6
     8
     10
     12
     14
9    Out of the loop--$str is hello.
10   Out of the loop--The array @numbers is now 6 8 10 12 14.
```

Explanation

1 The scalar, *$str*, is assigned the string *"hello"*.
2 The array, *@numbers*, is assigned the list of numbers—1,3,5,7,9.
3 The *print* function prints the initial value of *$str* to STDOUT.
4 The *print* function prints the initial value of *@numbers* to STDOUT.
5 The *foreach* statement assigns, in turn, each element in the list to *$str*. The variable, *$str*, is local to the loop. When the loop exits, it will regain its former value.
6 Each time through the loop, the value assigned to *$str* is incremented by *5*.
7 The *print* function prints the new value of *$str* to STDOUT.
8 After exiting the loop, the original value of *$str* is printed to STDOUT.
9 After exiting the loop, the new and modified values of the *@number* array are printed to STDOUT.

E x a m p l e   7 . 1 5

(The Script)
```
   #!/usr/bin/perl
1  @colors=(red, green, blue, brown);
2  foreach ( @colors ) {
3      print "$_ ";
4      $_="YUCKY";
   }
5  print "\n@colors\n";
```

O u t p u t

3 *red green blue brown*
5 *YUCKY YUCKY YUCKY YUCKY*

E x p l a n a t i o n

1   The array, *@colors*, is initialized.
2   The *foreach* loop does not have a variable, but it does have a list. Since the variable is missing, the $_ special scalar is used implicitly.
3   As each item of the list, *@colors*, is assigned to the $_ variable, the value is printed to STDOUT.
4   The $_ variable is assigned the string, "YUCKY", while within the *foreach* loop. It is local to the *foreach* loop. Each original element in the array, *@colors*, will be replaced permanently by the value, "YUCKY", in turn.
5   The *@color* array has really been changed. The $_ variable is null, its value before entering the loop.

7.3.5   Loop Control

To interrupt the normal flow on control within a loop, Perl provides labels and simple control statements. These statements are used for controlling a loop when some condition is reached; that is, the control is transferred directly to either the bottom or the top of the loop, skipping any statements that follow the control statement condition.

Labels.   Labels are optional but can be used to control the flow of a loop. By themselves, labels do nothing. They are used with the loop control modifiers, listed below. A block by itself, whether or not with a label, is equivalent to a loop that executes only <u>once</u>. If labels are capitalized, they will not be confused with reserved words.

Format:

```
LABEL: while ( Expression ){ Block}
LABEL: while ( Expression) { Block} continue{ Block}
LABEL: for ( Expression; Expression; Expression )
    { BLOCK}
LABEL: foreach Variable ( Array){ Block}
LABEL: { Block} continue { Block }
```

To control the flow of loops, the following simple statements may be used within the block:

```
nextn
next LABEL
last
last LABEL
redo
redo LABEL
goto LABEL
```

The *next* statement restarts the next iteration of the loop, skipping over the rest of the statements in the loop and re-evaluating the loop expression, like a *C, Awk,* or *Shell continue* statement.

The last statement leaves or breaks out of a block and is like the *break* statement in *C, awk,* and *Shell.*

The *redo* statement restarts the block without evaluating the loop expression again.

The *continue block* is executed just before the conditional expression is about to be evaluated again.

The *goto* statement, although frowned upon by most programmers, is allowed in Perl programs. It takes a label as its argument and jumps back to the label when the goto statement is executed. The label can be anywhere in your script but does not work when inside a *do* statement or within a subroutine.

A Labeled Block without a Loop. A block is like a loop that executes once. A block can be labeled.

The *redo* statement causes control to start at the top of the innermost or labeled block without reevaluating the loop expression if there is one (similar to a goto).

E x a m p l e   7 . 1 6

(The Script)
```
    #!//usr/bin/perl
    # Program that uses a label without a loop and the redo statement
1   ATTEMPT: {
2       print "Are you a great person? ";
        chomp($answer = <STDIN> );
3       redo ATTEMPT unless "$answer" =~ /[Yy].*/;
    }
```

O u t p u t

2 Are you a great person? *Nope*
2 Are you a great person? *Sometimes*
2 Are you a great person? *Yes*

E x p l a n a t i o n

1 The label is user defined. It precedes a block. It is as though you had named the block
   ATTEMPT.
2 The user is asked for input.
3 The *redo* statement restarts the block similar to a *goto* statement unless the $answer eval-
   uates to *yes* or *Yes* or *ya* or *yup*, etc.

E x a m p l e   7 . 1 7

(The Script)
```
   #!/usr/bin/perl
1  whlle(1){   # start an infinite loop

2       print "What was your grade? ";
        $grade = <STDIN>;

3       if ( $grade < 0 || $grade > 100 ) {
                print "Illegal choice\n";
4               next; }  # start control at the beginning of the innermost loop
5       if ( $grade  > 89 && $grade < 101){print "A\n";}
        if ( $grade > 79 && $grade < 90 ) { print "B\n";}
        if ( $grade > 69 && $grade < 80 ) { print "C\n";}
        if ( $grade > 59 && $grade < 70 ) { print "D\n";}
        if ( $grade >= 0 && $grade < 60 ) { print "You Failed."};
6       print "Wanna enter another grade? (y/n)? ";
        $choice = <STDIN>;
7       last if $choice !~ /[Yy].*/;  # break out of the innermost loop if the condition
                is true
   }
```

O u t p u t

2 *What was your grade? 94*
   A
6 *Wanna enter another grade (y/n)? y*
2 *What was your grade? 66*
   D
6 *Wanna enter another grade (y/n)? n*

Explanation

1 Start an infinite loop.
2 Ask for user input.
3 Logical test. If the value of *$grade* is less than 0 or greater than 100.
4 If the test yields false, control starts again at the beginning of the while loop.
5 Test each of the if conditional statements.
6 Ask for user input.
7 Break out of the innermost loop if the conditional modifier tests true.

Example 7.18

(The Script)

```
1 ATTEMPT:{
2       print "What is the course number? ";
        chop($number = <STDIN>);
        print "\What is the course name? ";
        chop($course = <STDIN>);

3       $department{$number} = $course;

        print "\nReady to quit? ";
        chop($answer = <STDIN>);
4       last if "$answer" =~ /[Yy].*/;
5       redo ATTEMPT;
  }
6 print "Course 101 is $department{#number}\n"; if $number==101;
```

Output

```
What is the number of the class? 101
What is the course name?  CIS342
Ready to quit? n
What is the number of the class? 201
What is the course name? BIO211
Ready to quit? n
What is the number of the class? 301
What is the course name? ENG120
Ready to quit? y
Course 101 is CIS342
```

Explanation

1   The label ATTEMPT prepends the block. A block without a looping construct is like a loop that executes only once.
2   The script gets user input in order to fill an associative array. Both the key and value are provided by the user.
3   The associative array, *%department*, is assigned a value.
4   If the user is ready to quit, the last statement sends the control out of the block
5   The *redo* statement returns control to the top of the labeled block. Each of the statements is executed again.
6   If the value of $number is 101, this line is printed.

Nested Loops and Labels.   A loop within a loop is a nested loop. The outside loop is initialized and tested; the inside loop then iterates completely through all of its cycles; and the outside loop starts again where it left off. The inside loop moves faster than the outside loop. Loops can be nested as deeply as you wish, but there are times when it is necessary to terminate the loop due to some condition. Normally, if you use loop-control statements such as next and last, the control is directed to the innermost loop. There are times when it may be necessary to switch control to some outer loop. This is accomplished by using labels.

By prefixing a loop with a label, you can control the flow of the program with *last, next,* and *redo* statements. Labeling a loop is like giving the loop its own name.

Example 7.19

```
(A Demo Script)
1  OUT: while(1){
2         < Program continues here >
3         MID: while(1){
4                 if ( <expression is true> ) { last OUT;}
                  < Program continues here >
5                 INNER: while(1){
6                         if ( <expression is true> ){ next OUT;}
                          <Program continues here>
                  }
          }
   }
7  print "Out of all loops.\n";
```

Explanation

1   The OUT label is used to control this infinite *while* loop, if necessary. The label is followed by a colon and the loop statement.
2   The program code continues here.
3   The MID label is used to control this inner *while* loop, if necessary.
4   If the expression being evaluated is true, the *last* loop-control statement is executed, breaking from this labeled loop all the way out to line 7. It breaks out of the loop labeled OUT.
5   The innermost *while* loop is labeled INNER.
6   This time the *next* statement with the OUT label causes loop control to branch back to line 1.
7   This statement is outside all of the loops and is where the *last* statement branches, if given the OUT label.

Example 7.20

(The Script)
```
1  for ( $rows=5; $rows>=1; $rows-- ){
2       for ( $columns=1; $columns<=$rows; $columns++ ){
3            printf "*";
4       }
5  print "\n";
6  }
```

Output

```
3  *****
   ****
   ***
   **
   *
```

Explanation

1   The first expression in the outside loop initializes the scalar, *$rows*, to 5. The variable is tested. Since it is greater or equal to 1, the inner loop starts.
2   The first expression in the inner loop initializes the scalar, *$columns*, to *1*. The scalar *$columns* is tested. The inner loop will iterate through all of its cycles. When the inner loop has completed, the outer loop will pick up where it left off; that is, *$rows* will be decremented, then tested, and if true, the block will be executed again, etc.
3   This statement belongs to the inner *for* loop and will be executed for each iteration of the loop.
4   This curly brace closes the inner *for* loop.
5   The *print* statement is executed for each iteration of the outer *for* loop.
6   This curly brace closes the outer *for* loop.

When a label is omitted, the loop control statements, *next, last*, and *redo*, reference the innermost loop. When branching out of a nested loop to an outer loop, labels may precede the loop statement.

E x a m p l e   7 . 2 1

(The Script)

```
     # This script prints the average salary of employees earning over $50,000
       annually
     # There are 5 employees.  If the salary falls below $50,000 it is not included in
       the tally.
```

```
1    EMPLOYEE: for ( $emp=1; $emp <= 5; $emp++ ){
2        do {  printf "What is the monthly rate for employee #$emp? ";
                printf "(Type q to quit)";
3                chop($monthly=<STDIN>);
4                last EMPLOYEE if $monthly eq 'q';
5                next EMPLOYEE if (( $year=$monthly * 12.00 ) <= 50000);
6                $number++;
7                $total_sal+=$year;
8                next EMPLOYEE;
            } while ( $monthly ne 'q' );
        }
        unless ( $number eq "" ) {
            $average = $total_sal / $number;
9            printf "$number employees earn over \$50,000 annually.\n";
10           printf "Their average salary is \$%.2f\.n", $average;
        }
```

O u t p u t

```
2    What is the monthly rate for employee #1? (Type q to quit)  10000
2    What is the monthly rate for employee #2? (Type q to quit)  12500
2    What is the monthly rate for employee #3? (Type q to quit)  400
2    What is the monthly rate for employee #4? (Type q to quit)  500
2    What is the monthly rate for employee #5? (Type q to quit)  3500
9    2 employees earn over $50,000 annually.
10   Their average salary is $135000.00.
```

E x p l a n a t i o n

1 The label *EMPLOYEE* precedes the outer loop. This loop keeps track of five employees.
2 The *do/while* loop is entered.
3 The script gets user input for the monthly salary.
4 If the user types '*q*', the *last* control statement is executed. Branching goes to the bottom of the outer loop due to the EMPLOYEE label, if the condition is true.
5 The *next* control statement transfers execution to the top of the outer *for* loop due to the *EMPLOYEE* label, if the condition is true.
6 The scalar, *$number*, is incremented.
7 The value of the scalar, *$total_sal*, is calculated.
8 The *next* control statement transfers execution to the top of the outermost *for* loop due to the label, *EMPLOYEE*.

The continue Block.   The *continue* block with a *while* loop preserves the correct semantics as a *for* loop, even when the *next* statement is used.

E x a m p l e   7 . 2 2

```
(The Script)
1   for($i=1; $i<=10 ; $i++) {
2         if($i==5){
                  print "half mark";
3                 next;  # go to the top of the loop and increment $i
                  }
            print "$i ";
    }
    print "\n"; print '=' x 35; print "\n";

    $i=1;
    while($i <= 10 ){
          if($i == 5 ){
                print "half mark";
4               $i++;  # increment $i
5               next;
          }
          print "$i ";
6         $i++;  # increment $i; $i is incremented twice
    }
    print "\n"; print '=' x 35; print "\n";
```

```
    $i=1;
    while($i <= 10 ){
        if($i == 5 ){
        print "half mark";
        next;
        }
    print "$i ";
7  } continue {$i++;}  # $i is incremented once
```

Output

1 2 3 4   half mark 6 7 8 9 10

=====================================

1 2 3 4   half mark 6 7 8 9 10

=====================================

1 2 3 4   half mark 6 7 8 9 10

Explanation

1 The *for* loop is entered and will loop ten times.
2 When the value of $i is 5, "half mark" is printed.
3 The *next* statement returns control back to the *for* loop. When control is returned to the *for* loop, the third expression is always evaluated before the second expression is tested. *Before* the second expression is tested, $i is incremented.
4 If the *$i* is not incremented here, it will never be incremented; it will be in an infinite loop.
5 After *$i* is incremented, go back to the top of the *while* loop and test the expression.
6 If *$i* is not equal to *5*, the value of *$i* must be incremented here. $i must be incremented twice in the *while* loop, but only once in the *for* loop.
7 The *continue* block is executed at the end of the *while* loop block, before the *next* statement returns control to the top of the loop or, if *next* is not executed, after the last statement in the loop block.

7.3.6   The Phoney Switch statement

Perl does not have an official switch statement. A block (labeled or not) is equivalent to a loop that executes once, and loop control statements, such as *last, next* and *redo*, can be used within this block to emulate the C's *switch/case* construct.

The *do block* executes the sequence of commands in the block and returns the value of the last expression evaluated in the block.

E x a m p l e   7 . 2 3

```
(The Script)
#! /usr/bin/perl
1   $hour=0;
2   while($hour < 24) {
3       SWITCH: {      # SWITCH is just a user–defined label
4           $hour =~ /^[0–9]$|^1[0–1]$/  &&do { print "Good–morning!\n";
5                                               last SWITCH;};

6           $hour == 12          && do {   print "Lunch!\n";
                                           last SWITCH;};

7           $hour =~ /1[3–7]/     && do {   print "Siesta time!\n";
                                           last SWITCH;};

8           $hour > 17           && do {   print "Good night.\n";
                                           last SWITCH;};
        }  # End of block labeled SWITCH

9       $hour++;
    }   # End of loop block
```

O u t p u t

Good–morning!
Good–morning!
Good–morning!
  <Output continues>
Good–morning!
Good–morning!
Good–morning!
Lunch!
Siesta time!
Siesta time!
Siesta time!
Siesta time!
Siesta time!
Good night.
Good night.
Good night.
Good night.
Good night.

Explanation

1   The *$hour* scalar is assigned an initial value of 0 before entering the loop.
2   The *while* loop expression is evaluated.
3   The label SWITCH labels the block. It is simply a label, nothing more.
4   After entering the block, the expression is evaluated. The expression reads: *if $hour contains a number between 0 and 9 or 10 or 11...* If true, the expression on the right of the && is evaluated. This is a *do* block. Each of the statements within this block is executed in sequence. The value of the last statement evaluated is returned.
5   The last statement causes control to branch to the end of this block labeled SWITCH to line 8.
6   This statement is evaluated if the expression in the previous statement evaluates to false. The expression reads: *if $hour is equal to 12 ...*
7   This statement is evaluated if the expression in the previous statement evaluates to false. The expression reads: *if $hour contains a number between 13 and 17...*
8   If this statement is true, the *do* block is executed. The express reads: *if $hour is greater than 17...*
9   The *$hour* scalar is incremented once each time after going through the loop.

8

Getting a Handle on Files

8.1 The User-Defined Filehandle

A filehandle is a name for a file, device, pipe, or socket. In Chapter 3, we discussed the three default filehandles, STDIN, STDOUT, and STDERR. Perl allows you to create your own filehandles for input and output operations on files, devices, pipes, or sockets. A filehandle allows you to associate the filehandle name with a UNIX file and to use that filehandle to access the file.

8.1.1 Opening Files—the open Function

The *open* function lets you name a filehandle and the file you want to attach to that handle. The file can be opened for reading, writing, or appending and the file can be opened to pipe data to or from a process. The *open* function returns non-zero if successful, and an undefined value if it fails. Like scalars, arrays, and labels, filehandles have their own name space. So that they will not be confused with reserved words, the Perl wizards recommend that filehandle names be spelled in all upper case letters. (See *open* function, Appendix A.)

8.1.2 open for Reading

Format:

```
1  open(FILEHANDLE, FILENAME);
2  open(FILEHANDLE);
3  open FILEHANDLE;
```

E x a m p l e   8 . 1

```
1  open(MYHANDLE, "myfile");
2  open(MYHANDLE);
3  open MYHANDLE;
```

E x p l a n a t i o n

1 The *open* function will create the filehandle, *MYHANDLE*, and attach it to the real file, *myfile*. The file will be opened for reading. Since a full pathname is not specified for *my-file*, it must be in the current working directory and you must have read permission to open it for reading.

2 If *FILENAME* is omitted, the name of the filehandle is the same name as a scalar variable previously defined. The scalar variable has been assigned the name of the real file. In the example, the filename could have been defined:

> $MYHANDLE="myfile";
> open(MYHANDLE);

The *open* function will create the filehandle, *MYHANDLE*, and attach it to the value of the variable, *$MYHANDLE*. The effect will be the same as in the first example.

3 This example is the same as the previous example. The parentheses are optional.

8.1.3   Closing the Filehandle

The *close* function closes the file, pipe, or socket or device attached to FILEHANDLE. Once FILEHANDLE is opened, it stays open until the script ends or you call the *open* function again. (The next call to open closes FILEHANDLE before reopening it.) If you don't explicitly close the file, when you so reopen it, the line counter variable, $., will not be reset. Closing a pipe causes the process to wait until the pipe is complete and reports the status in the $? variable. It's a good idea to explicitly close files and handles after you are finished using them.

Format:

```
close (FILEHANDLE);
close FILEHANDLE;
```

E x a m p l e   8 . 2

```
1  close(INPIPE);
```

E x p l a n a t i o n

1 The user defined filehandle, INPIPE, will be closed.

"Do or Die"—The die Function.   In the following examples the *die* function is used if a call to the *open* function fails. If Perl cannot open the file, the *die* function is used to exit the Perl script and print a message to STDERR, usually the screen.

If you were to go to your Shell prompt and type:

> $ cat junk

and if *junk* is a non-existent file, the following system error would appear on your screen:

> *cat: junk: No such file or directory*

The Perl special $! variable holds the value of the system error (see Section 9.4, "Error Handling," in Chapter 9) that occurs when you are unable to successfully open a file or execute a system utility. When used with the *die* function, this is very useful for detecting a problem with the filehandle before continuing with the execution of the script.

Example 8.3

(Line from Script)
```
1  open(MYHANDLE, "/etc/password") || die "Can't open: $!\n";
```

Output

1 *Can't open: No such file or directory*

(Line from Script)
```
2  open(MYHANDLE, "/etc/password") || die "Can't open: ";
```

Output

2 *Can't open: No such file or directory at ./handle line 3.*

Explanation

1 When trying to open the file */etc/password*, the *open* fails (it should be */etc/passwd*). The short-circuit operator causes its right operand to execute if the left operand fails. The *die* operator is executed. The string, "*Can't open:*", is printed, followed by the system error, "*No such file or directory*". The '\n' suppresses any further output from the *die* function. All of *die's* output is sent to STDERR after the program exits.
2 This is exactly like the first example, except that the '\n' has been removed from the string "*Can't open:* ". Omitting the '\n' causes the *die* function to append a string to the output indicating the line number in the script where the system error occurred.

Reading from the Filehandle.

Example 8.4

(The Text File)
```
$ cat datebook
Steve Blenheim
Betty Boop
Lori Gortz
Sir Lancelot
Norma Cord
Jon DeLoach
Karen Evich
```

(In the Script)
```
  #!/usr/bin/perl
  # open a file with a filehandle
1 open(FILE, "datebook") II die "Can't open datebook: $!\n";
2 print "Hello to you and yours!\n";
3 while(<FILE>) {
4       print "HI Lori\n" if  /^Lori/;
5       print "HI Sir Lancelot\n" if $_ =~ /Sir Lancelot/;
  }
```

Output

```
2  Hello to you and yours!
4  HI Lori
5  HI Sir Lancelot
```

Explanation

1 The *open* function will create a filehandle called *FILE* and attach the UNIX file *datebook* to it. If the open fails because the file *datebook* does not exist, the *die* operator will print to the screen, *Can't open datebook: No such file or directory.*
2 The *print* function sends the string, *Hello to you and yours!*, to STDOUT, the screen.
3 The expression in the *while* loop is the filehandle, *FILE,* enclosed in angle brackets. The angle brackets are the operators used for reading input. They are not part of the filehandle name. When the loop starts, the first line from the filehandle, *FILE,* will be stored in the $_ scalar variable. (Remember the $_ variable holds each line of input from the file.) If it has not reached end of file, the loop will continue to take a line of input from the file, execute statements *4* and *5*, and continue until end of file is reached.

4 The default input variable, $_, is implicitly used to hold the current line of input read from the filehandle. If that line contains the regular expression *Lori* where *Lori* is at the beginning of the line, the string "*Hi Lori*" is printed to STDOUT. For each loop iteration, the next line read is stored in $_ and tested.

5 The default input variable, $_, is used explicitly. It holds the current line of input. If that line contains the regular expression *Sir Lancelot,* the string "*Hi Sir Lancelot*" is printed to STDOUT. For each loop iteration, the next line read is stored in $_ and tested.

8.1.4 open for Writing

To open a file for writing, the file will be created if it does not exist, and if it already exists, it must have write permission. If the file exists, its contents will be overwritten. The filehandle is used to access the UNIX file.

Format:

```
1   open(FILEHANDLE,  ">FILENAME");
```

E x a m p l e   8 . 5

```
1  open(MYOUTPUT, ">temp");
```

E x p l a n a t i o n

1 The user-defined filehandle, *MYOUTPUT*, will be used to send output to the file called *temp*. As with the Shell, the redirection symbol directs the output from the default filehandle, STDOUT, to the *temp* file.

E x a m p l e   8 . 6

```
(The Script)
   #!/usr/bin/perl
   # Write to a file with a filehandle. Scriptname: file.handle
1  $file="/home/jody/ellie/perl/newfile";
2  open(HANDOUT, ">$file") || die "Can't open newfile: $!\n";

3  print HANDOUT "hello world.\n";
4  print HANDOUT "hello world again.\n";

(At the Command Line)
   $ file.handle
5  $ cat newfile
   hello world.
   hello world, again.
```

Explanation

1 The scalar variable *$file* is set to the full pathname of a UNIX file called *newfile*. The scalar will be used to represent the name of the UNIX file to which output will be directed via the filehandle.

2 The user-defined filehandle, *HANDOUT*, will change the default place where output normally goes, *STDOUT*, to the file that it represents, *newfile*. The ">" symbol indicates that *newfile* will be created if it does not exist and opened for writing. If it does exist, it will be opened and any text in it will be overwritten.

3 The *print* function will send its output to the filehandle, *HANDOUT*, instead of to the screen. The string *hello world.* will be written into *newfile* via the *HANDOUT* filehandle. The file, *newfile*, will remain opened unless it is explicitly closed or the Perl script ends (see Section 8.1.3, "Closing the Filehandle").

4 The *print* function will send its output to the filehandle, *HANDOUT*, instead of to the screen. The string *hello world again.* will be written into *newfile* via the *HANDOUT* filehandle. The operating system keeps track of where the last write occurred and will send its next line of output to the location immediately following the last byte written to the file.

5 The contents of the file, *newfile*, are printed.

8.1.5   open for Appending

To open a file for appending, the file will be created if it does not exist, and if it already exists, it must have write permission. If the file exists, its contents will be left intact, and the output will be appended to the end of the file. Again, the filehandle is used to access the file rather than accessing it by its real name.

Format:

```
1 open(FILEHANDLE, ">> FILENAME");
```

Example 8.7

```
1 open(APPEND, ">> temp");
```

Explanation

1 The user-defined filehandle, *APPEND*, will be used to append output to the file called *temp*. As with the Shell, the redirection symbol directs the output from the default, standard out filehandle, *STDOUT*, to the *temp* file.

E x a m p l e   8 . 8

(The Text File)
   $ cat newfile
   hello world.
   hello world, again.

(In the Script)
   #!/usr/bin/perl
1 **open(HANDLE, ">> newfile") || die print "Can't open newfile: $!\n";**
2 print HANDLE "Just appended \"hello world\" to the end of newfile.\n";

O u t p u t

   $ cat newfile
   hello world.
   hollo world, again.
   Just appended "hello world" to the end of newfile.

E x p l a n a t i o n

1 The user-defined filehandle, *HANDLE*, will be used to send and append output to the file
   called *newfile*. As with the Shell, the redirection symbol directs the output from the default, standard out filehandle, *STDOUT*, and appends the output to the file *newfile*. If the
   file cannot be opened because, for example, the write permissions are turned off, the *die*
   operator will print the error message, *"Can't open newfile: Permission denied."*, and the
   script will exit.
2 The *print* function will send its output to the filehandle, *HANDLE*, instead of to the
   screen. The string, *Just appended "hello world" to the end of newfile,* will be written to
   end of *newfile* via the *HANDLE* filehandle.

8.1.6   The select Function

The *select* function sets the default output to the specified FILEHANDLE and returns the
previously selected filehandle.

Example 8.9

(The Script)
```perl
#! /usr/bin/perl
1  open (FILEOUT,">newfile") || die "Can't open newfile: $!\n";
2  $oldfilehandle = select(FILEOUT) ;    # select the new filehandle for output
3  open (DB, "datebook") || die "Can't open datebook: $!\n";
   while(<DB>) {
4       print ;                # Output goes to FILEOUT, i.e. newfile
   }
5  select($oldfilehandle);  # select STDOUT, the filehandle returned by the first
                            # select; Could have just been written: select STDOUT
   print "Good-bye.\n";      # Output goes to the screen
```

Explanation

1 *"newfile"* is opened for writing and assigned to the filehandle FILEOUT.
2 The *select* function assigns FILEOUT as the current default filehandle for output. The return value is the name of the current filehandle, STDOUT, the one opened before FILEOUT is selected, i.e., the most previously selected filehandle.
3 The DB filehandle is opened for reading.
4 As each line is read into the $_ variable from DB, it is then printed to the currently selected filehandle, FILEOUT. Notice that you don't have to name the filehandle.
5 By selecting *$oldfilehandle*, the rest of the program's output will go to STDOUT. "Good-bye" will be printed to the screen.

8.1.7   File Locking with flock

To prevent two programs from writing to a file at the same time, you can lock the file so that you have exclusive access to it and then unlock it when you're finished using it. The *flock* function takes two arguments, a filehandle and a filelocking operation. The operations are listed in Table 8.1.

TABLE 8.1   File Locking Operations

Name	Operation	What It Does
lock_sh	1	Creates A Shared Lock
lock_ex	2	Creates An Exclusive Lock
lock_nb	4	Creates A Non-blocking Lock
lock_un	8	Unlocks An Existing Lock

Read permission is required on a file to obtain a shared lock, and write permission is required to obtain an exclusive lock. With operations 1 and 2, normally the caller requesting the file will block (wait) until the file is unlocked. If using a non-blocking lock on a filehandle, an error is produced immediately if a request is made to get the locked file.[1]

---

1. *flock* may not work if the file is being accessed from a networked system.

Example 8.10

```
#!/bin/perl
# Program that uses filelocking
1 $LOCK_EX = 2;
2 $LOCK_UN = 8;

3 print "Adding an entry to the datafile.\n";
  print "Enter the name: ";
  chomp($name=<STDIN>);
  print "Enter the address: ";
  chomp($address=<STDIN>);

4 open(DB, ">>datafile") || die "Can't open: $!\n";

5 flock(DB, $LOCK_EX) || die ;  # Lock the file

6 print DB "$name:$address\n";

7 flock(DB, $LOCK_UN) || die;   # Unlock the file
```

Explanation

1 The scalar is assigned the value of the operation that will be used by the *flock* function to lock the file. This operation is to block (wait) until an exclusive lock can be created.
2 This operation will tell *flock* when to unlock the file so that others can write to it.
3 The user is asked for the information to update the file. This information will be appended to the file.
4 The filehandle is opened for appending.
5 The *flock* function locks the file exclusively.
6 The data is appended to the file.
7 Once the data has been appended, the file is unlocked so that others can access it.

8.1.8 open for Pipes

When using a pipe (also called a filter) , a connection is made from one program to another. The program on the left-hand side of a pipe sends its output into a temporary kernel buffer. This program writes into the pipe. On the other side of the pipe is a program that is a reader. It gets its input from the buffer. Here is an example of a typical UNIX pipe:

who | wc -l

The output of the *who* command is sent to the *wc* command. The *who* command sends its output to the pipe; it writes to the pipe. The *wc* command gets its input from the pipe; it reads from the pipe. (If the *wc* command were not a reader, it would ignore what is in the pipe.) The output is sent to the STDOUT, the terminal screen. The number of people logged on is printed.

UNIX Pipe Example

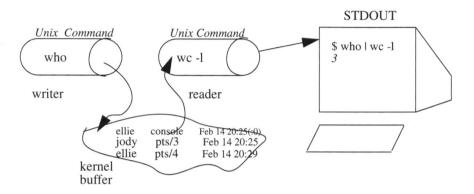

The Output Filter.   When creating a filehandle with the *open* function, you can open a filter so that output is piped to a *UNIX* command. The command is preceded by a pipe symbol and replaces the filename argument in the previous examples. The output will be piped to the command and sent to *STDOUT.*

Format:

```
1 open(FILEHANDLE,|COMMAND);
```

E x a m p l e   8 . 1 1

(The Script)
```
    #!/bin/perl
    # Scriptname: outfilter
1   open(MYPIPE, "| wc -l");
2   print MYPIPE "apples\npears\npeaches\n";
3   close(MYPIPE);
```

O u t p u t

3

E x p l a n a t i o n

1   The user-defined filehandle, *MYPIPE*, will be used to pipe output from your Perl script
    to the UNIX command, *wc -l*, which counts the number of lines in the string.
2   The print function sends the string *apples\npears\npeaches* to the output filter filehan-
    dle, *MYPIPE*; the string is piped to the *wc* command. Since there are three newlines in
    the string, the output '*3*' will be sent to the screen.
3   After you have finished using the filehandle, use the *close* function to close it. This guar-
    antees that the command will complete before the script exits. If you don't close the file-
    handle, the output may not be flushed properly.

Perl Output Filter

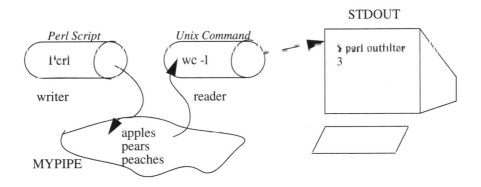

E x a m p l e   8 . 1 2

(The Script)
1   **open(FOO, "| tr '[a–z]' '[A–Z]'");**
2   print FOO "hello there\n";
3   close FOO; *# if you don't close FOO, the output is delayed.*

O u t p u t

2 *HELLO THERE*

E x p l a n a t i o n

1   The user-defined filehandle, *FOO*, will be used to send output from your Perl script to
    the UNIX command *tr* which will translate lower case letters to upper case.
2   The *print* function sends the string *hello there* to the output filter filehandle, *FOO*; that
    is, the string is piped to the *tr* command. The string, after being filtered, will be sent to
    the screen with all the characters translated to upper case.

Example 8.13

(The Text File)
$cat emp.names
1 Steve Blenheim
2 Betty Boop
3 Igor Chevsky
4 Norma Cord
5 Jon DeLoach
6 Karen Evich

(The Script)
```
   #!/usr/bin/perl
1  open(FOO, "| sort +1| tr '[a–z]' '[A–Z]'");  # open the output filter
2  open(DB, "emp.names");        # open DB for reading
3  while(<DB>){ print FOO ; }
4  close FOO;
```

Output

```
2  BETTY BOOP
3  IGOR CHEVSKY
5  JON DELOACH
6  KAREN EVICH
4  NORMA CORD
1  STEVE BLENHEIM
```

Explanation

1 The user-defined filehandle, *FOO*, will be used to pipe output to the UNIX command *sort* and the output of *sort* will be piped to the *tr* command.
2 The *open* function creates the filehandle, *DB*, and attaches it to the UNIX file, *emp.names*.
3 The expression in the *while* loop contains the filehandle, *DB*, enclosed in angle brackets, indicating a read operation. The loop will read the first line from the *emp.names* file and store it in the $_ scalar variable. The input line will be sent through the output filter, *FOO*, and printed to the screen. The loop will iterate until end of file is reached.
4 The *close* function closes the filehandle, *FOO*.

Sending the Output of a Filter to a File.
In the previous example, what if you had wanted to send the output of the filter to a file intead of to STDOUT? You can't send output to a filter and a filehandle at the same time, but you can redirect STDOUT to a filehandle. Since, later in the program, you may want

STDOUT to be redirected back to the screen, you can first save it or simply reopen STD-OUT to the terminal device, e.g.:

```
open(STDOUT, ">/dev/tty");
```

E x a m p l e   8 . 1 4

```
#!/usr/bin/perl
# Program to redirect STDOUT from filter to a file
1    $| = 1;  # Flush buffers
2    $tmpfile = "temp";
3    open(DB, "data") || die qq/Can't open "data": $!\n/;  # Open DB for reading
4    open(SAVED, ">&STDOUT") || die "$!\n";   # Save stdout
5    open(STDOUT, ">$tmpfile" ) || die "Can't open: $!\n";
6    open(SORT, "| sort +1") || die;      # Open output filter
7    while(<DB>){
8        print SORT;   # Output is first sorted and then sent to temp.
9    }
10       close SORT;
11   open(STDOUT, ">&SAVED") || die "Can't open";
12   print "Here we are printing to the screen again.\n";
                        # This output will go to the screen
```

E x p l a n a t i o n

1   The $| variable guarantees an automatic flush of the output buffer after each *print* statement is executed. (See *autoflush* module in Appendix A.)
2   The scalar, *$empfile*, is assigned "temp" to be used later as an output file.
3   The UNIX "data" file is opened for reading and attached to the DB filehandle.
4   STDOUT is being copied and saved in another filehandle called SAVED. Behind the scenes, the file descriptors are being manipulated.
5   The "temp" file is being opened now for writing and is assigned to the file descriptor normally reserved for STDOUT, the screen. The file descriptor for STDOUT has been closed and reopened for *temp*.
6   The output filter will be assigned to SORT. Perl's output will be sent to the UNIX *sort* utility.
7   The DB filehandle is opened for reading.
8   The output filehandle will be sent to the *temp* file after being sorted.
9   Close the loop.
10   Close the output filter.
11   Open the standard output filehandle so that output is redirected back to the screen.
12   This line prints to the screen because STDOUT has been reassigned there.

Input Filter

When creating a filehandle with the *open* function, you can also open a filter so that input is piped <u>into</u> Perl. The command ends with a pipe symbol.

Format:

```
1  open(FILEHANDLE, COMMAND|);
```

E x a m p l e   8 . 1 5

```
   #!/bin/perl
   # Scriptname: infilter
1  open(INPIPE, "date |");
2  $today = <INPIPE> ;
3  close(INPIPE);
```

E x p l a n a t i o n

1   The user-defined filehandle, *INPIPE*, will be used to pipe the output from the filter as input to Perl. The output of a UNIX *date* command will be used as input by your Perl script via the *INPIPE* filehandle.
2   The scalar, *$today*, will receive its input from the *INPIPE* filehandle, i.e., Perl reads from *INPIPE*.
3   After you have finished using the filehandle, use the *close* function to close it. This guarantees that the command will complete before the script exits. If you don't close the filehandle, the output may not be flushed properly.

Perl Input Filter

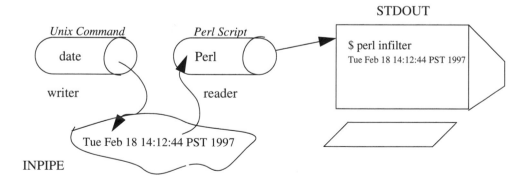

E x a m p l e   8 . 1 6

(The Script)
```
1  open(FINDIT, "find . –name 'perl*' –print |") || die;
2  while( $filename = <FINDIT> ){
3      print $filename;
   }
```

O u t p u t

```
3  ./perl2
   ./perl3
   ./perl.man
   ./perl4
   ./perl5
   ./perl6
   ./perl7
   ./perlsub
   ./perl.arg
```

E x p l a n a t i o n

1   The output of the UNIX *find* command will be piped to the input filehandle, *FINDIT*.
    When enclosed in angle brackets, the standard input will come from *FINDIT* instead of
    STDIN. If the open fails, the *die* operator will cause the script to exit.
2   The output from the UNIX *find* command has been piped into the filehandle, *FINDIT*.
    For each iteration of the *while* loop, one line from the FINDIT filehandle will be as-
    signed to the scalar variable, *$filename*.
3   The *print* function prints the value of the variable *$filename* to the screen.

8.1.9   The seek and tell Functions

The seek Function. Seek allows you to randomly access a file. The *seek* function is the
same as the *fseek* standard i/o function in C. Rather than closing the file and then reopening
it, the *seek* function allows you to move to some byte (not line) position within the file. The
seek function returns 1 if successful, 0 otherwise.

Format:

```
seek(FILEHANDLE, BYTEOFFSET, FILEPOSITION);
```

Seek sets a position in a file, where the first byte is 0. Positions are:

> 0 = Beginning of the file
> 1 = Current position in the file
> 2 = End of the file

The offset is the number of bytes from the file position. A positive offset moves the position forward in the file; a negative offset moves the position backward in the file for position 1 or 2.

Example 8.17

```
#!/usr/bin/perl
# Example using the seek function
1 open(PASSWD,"/etc/passwd") || die "Can't open: $!\n";
2 while($line=<PASSWD>){    # loop through the whole file
3     if ($line =~ /daemon/) { print "—$line—\n";}
  }
4 seek(PASSWD,0,0);    # Start at the beginning of the file
5 while(<PASSWD>) {
6     print if /root/;
  }
```

Explanation

1 The "/etc/passwd" file is assigned to the PASSWD filehandle and opened for reading.
2 Each line of the file is assigned to the scalar, *$line*, in turn while looping through the file.
3 If *$line* contains *daemon*, the *print* statement is executed.
4 The *seek* function causes the file pointer to be positioned at the top of the file at byte 0, the first character.
5 Loop through the "/etc/passwd" file starting at the top at byte 0.
6 Each line is stored in the $_ variable as it is read. If the pattern *root* is found, the line will be printed.

The tell Function. The *tell* function returns the current byte position in the file and is used with the *seek* function to move to that position in the file. If FILEHANDLE is omitted, *tell* returns the position of the file last read.

Format:

```
tell(FILEHANDLE);
tell;
```

E x a m p l e   8 . 1 8

```
    #! /usr/bin/perl
    # Example using the tell function
1   open(PASSWD,"/etc/passwd") || die "Can't open: $!\n";
2   while ($line=<PASSWD>) {    # loop through the whole file
3       chomp($line);
4       if ($line =~ /adm/) {
5           $currentpos=tell;
6           print "—$line—\n";
        }
    }
7   print "The current byte postion is ", $currentpos,"\n";
8   seek(PASSWD,$currentpos,0);    # Start at the beginning of the file
9   while(<PASSWD>) {
10      print;
    }
```

E x p l a n a t i o n

1 The "/etc/passwd" file is assigned to the PASSWD filehandle and opened for reading.
2 Each line of the file is assigned to the scalar, *$line*, in turn while looping through the file.
3 The newline is chomped off.
4 If the scalar *$line* contains the regular expression *adm*, the *if* block is entered.
5 The *tell* function is called and returns the current byte position (starting at byte 0) in the file.
6 The value of *$line* is printed.
7 The value in bytes is stored in *$currentpos*. It is printed.
8 The *seek* function will position the file pointer for PASSWD at the byte offset, *$currentpos*, starting from the beginning of the file. Without *seek*, the filehandle would have to be closed in order to start reading from the top of the file.

E x a m p l e   8 . 1 9

(The Script)
```
    #!/usr/bin/perl
    # Seek with read/write
    print "\n\n";
1   open(FH, "+>joker") || die;   # joker is opened for reading and writing
2   print FH "This line is written to joker.\n";
3   seek(FH,0,0);   # Goto the beginning of the file
4   while(<FH>) {
5       print;   # reads from joker; the line is in $_
    }
```

Output

5 This line is written to joker.

Explanation

1 The filehandle FH is opened for reading and writing.
2 The output is sent to "joker" via the FH filehandle.
3 The *seek* function moves the filepointer to the beginning of the file.
4 The filehandle FH is now being read from one line at a time and stored in $_.
5 The value of $_ is printed.

8.2   Passing Arguments

8.2.1   The ARGV Array

How does Perl pass command line arguments to a Perl script? If you are coming from a *C, awk*, or *C Shell* background, at first glance you might think, "Oh, I already know this! Beware! There are some subtle differences. So again, read on.

Perl does store arguments in a special array called *ARGV*. The subscript starts at zero and, unlike *C* and *awk*, ARGV[0] does <u>not</u> represent the name of the program; it represents the name of the first word after the script name. Like the *Shell* languages, the *$0* special variable is used to hold the name of the Perl script. Unlike the *C Shell*, the *$#ARGV* variable contains the number of the last subscript in the array, <u>not </u>the number of elements in the array. The number of arguments is *$#ARGV + 1*. *$#ARGV* initially has value of -1.

When *ARGV*, the filehandle, is enclosed in angle brackets, <ARGV>, the command line argument is treated as a filename. The filename is assigned to *ARGV* and the *@ARGV* array is shifted immediately to the left by one, thereby shortening the *@ARGV* array.

The value that is shifted off the *@ARGV* array is assigned to *$ARGV. $ARGV* contains the name of the currently selected filehandle.

The Many Faces of ARGV

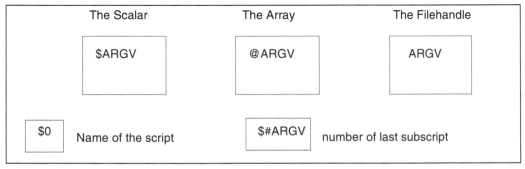

The Scalar	The Array	The Filehandle
$ARGV	@ARGV	ARGV

$0 Name of the script

$#ARGV number of last subscript

E x a m p l e   8 . 2 0

(The Script)
```
  $!/usr/bin/perl
1 die "$0 requires an argument.\n" if $#ARGV < 0;  #must have at least one
     argument
2 print "@ARGV\n";  # print all arguments
3 print "$ARGV[0]\n"; #print first argument
4 print "$ARGV[1]\n"; #print second argument
5 print "There are ", $#ARGV + 1," arguments.\n";  # $#ARGV is the last subscript
6 print "$ARGV[$#ARGV] is the last one.\n"; #print last arg
```

(The Command Line)
  $ perl.arg
2 *perl.arg requires an argument.*

  $ perl.arg t1 t2 t3 t4 t5
2 *f1 f2 f3 f4 f5*
3 *f1*
4 *f2*
5 *There are 5 arguments.*
6 *f5 is the last one.*

E x p l a n a t i o n

1 If there are no command line arguments, the *die* function is executed and the script is terminated. The $0 special variable holds the name of the Perl script, *perl.arg*.
2 The contents of the *ARGV* array are printed.
3 The first argument, not the script name, is printed.
4 The second argument is printed.
5 The *$#ARGV* variable contains the number value of the last subscript. Since the subscript starts at zero, *$#ARGV + 1* is the total number of arguments, not counting the script name.
6 Since the *$#ARGV* contains the value of the last subscript, *$ARGV[$#ARGV]* is the value of the last element of the *ARGV* array.

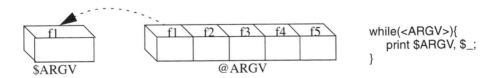

8.2.2   ARGV and the Null Filehandle

When used in loop expressions and enclosed in the input angle brackets (<>), each element of the *ARGV* array is treated as a *special filehandle*. Perl shifts through the array, storing each element of the array in a variable *$ARGV*. A set of empty angle brackets is called the *null filehandle* and Perl implicitly uses each element of the *ARGV* array as a filehandle. When using the input operators <>, either with or without the keyword, *ARGV*, Perl shifts through its arguments one at a time, allowing you to process each argument in turn. Once the *ARGV* filehandle has been opened, the arguments are shifted off one at a time, so that if they are to be used later, they must be saved in another array.

E x a m p l e   8 . 2 1

(The Text Files)
```
$ cat f1
Hello there. Nice day.
$ cat f2
Are you sure about that?
$ cat f3
This  is it.
This is the end.
```

(In Script)
```
1  while( <ARGV> ) {print ;}
2  print "The value of ARGV[0] is $ARGV[0].\n";
```

(The Command Line)
```
$ argv.test f1 f2 f3
Hello there. Nice day.
Are you sure about that?
This is it.
This is the end.
The value of ARGV[0] is .
```

E x p l a n a t i o n

1   Will print the contents of all the files named at the command line. Once used, the argument is shifted off. The contents of *f1, f2,* and *f3* are read and then printed, respectively.
2   Since the arguments were all shifted off, *ARGV[0]* has no value and nothing is printed.

E x a m p l e   8 . 2 2

(The Text File emp.names)
   Steve Blenheim
   Betty Boop
   Igor Chevsky
   Norma Cord
   Jon DeLoach
   Karen Evich

(The Script)
```
   #!/usr/bin/perl
   #Scriptname: argv.p
1  if ( ($#ARGV + 1) < 1 ) {die "$0 requires an argument.\n";}
2  print "Who are you looking for? ";
   chop($person=<STDIN>);
3  while(<>){
       ( $num, $name ) = split(' ', $_);
       print "Entry $num: $name\n" if /$person/ ;}
   }
```

O u t p u t

   $ argv.p
1 *argv.p requires an argument.*

   $ argv.p emp.names
2 *Who are you looking for?* Igor
   Entry 3: Igor

   $ argv.p emp.names
1 *Who are you looking for?* Betty
2 *Entry 2: Betty*

E x p l a n a t i o n

1 If there are no command line arguments, the *die* function is executed.
2 The user is asked for input.
3 The *while* loop uses the null filehandle to loop through any arguments passed in from the command line. The file is opened for reading and each line is stored in the $_ variable, split on whitespace, and then printed to STDOUT, the screen.

E x a m p l e   8 . 2 3

(The Script)

```
    # the checkon program
    # Illustrates the use of FILEHANDLES  and ARGV
1   unless ( $#ARGV == 0 ){ die "Usage: $0 <argument>: $!"; }
2   open(PASSWD, "/etc/passwd") || die "Can't open: $!";
3       while( $pwline = <PASSWD>){
4           if ( $pwline =~ /^ARGV[0]:/){ $found=1; last;}
        }
5   die "$ARGV[0] is not a user here.\n" if ! $found;
    close PASSWD;
6   open(LOGGEDON, "who |" ) || die "Can't open: $!" ;
    while($logged = <LOGGEDON> ){
7       if ( $logged =~ /^$ARGV[0]\b/){ $logged_on = 1; last; }
    }
    die print "$ARGV[0] is not logged on.\n" if ! $logged_on;
    print "$ARGV[0] is logged on and running these processes.\n";
    close LOGGEDON;
8   open(PROC, "ps –aux | ") || die "Can't open: $! ";
        while($line=<PROC>){
            print "$line" if  $line =~ /^$ARGV[0]:/;
        }
    close PROC;
    print '*' x 80; "\n";
    print "So long.\n";
```

(The Command Line)

```
    $ checkon
1   Usage: checkon <argument>:  at checkon line 6.
    $ checkon joe
5   Joe is not a user here.
    $ checkon ellie
8   ellie is logged on and running these processes:
    ellie    3825  6.4  4.5  212  464 p5 R    12:18  0:00 ps –aux
    ellie    1383  0.8  8.4  360  876 p4 S    Dec 26 11:34 /usr/local/OW3/bin/xview
    ellie     173  0.8 13.4 1932 1392 co S    Dec 20389:19 /usr/local/OW3/bin/xnews
    ellie     164  0.0  0.0  100    0 co IW   Dec 20 0:00 –c
            < some of the output was cut to save space >
    ellie    3822  0.0  0.0    0    0 p5 Z    Dec 20 0:00 <defunct>
    ellie    3823  0.0  1.1   28  112 p5 S    12:18  0:00 sh –c ps –aux | grep '^'
    ellie    3821  0.0  5.6  144  580 p5 S    12:18  0:00 /bin/perl checkon ellie
    ellie    3824  0.0  1.8   32  192 p5 S    12:18  0:00 grep ^ellie
    ellie    3815  0.0  1.9   24  196 p4 S    12:18  0:00 script checkon.tsc
    **********************************************************************
```

E x p l a n a t i o n

This script calls for only one argument.

1 If *ARGV* is empty (i.e., no arguments are passed at the command line), the *die* function is executed and the script exits with an error message. (Remember: *$#ARGV* is the number of the last subscript in the *ARGV* array and ARGV[0] is the first argument, not counting the name of the script, which is $0.) If more than one argument is passed, the script will also exit with the error message.

2 The */etc/passwd* file is opened for reading via the *PASSWD* filehandle.

3 Each time the while loop is entered, a line of the */etc/passwd* file is read via the PASSWD filehandle.

4 The =~ is used to test if the first argument passed matches the name of a user in */etc/passwd*. If a match is found, the *$found* scalar is set to one, and the loop is exited.

5 If the scalar, *$found*, was not set, the user is not in the */etc/passwd file*. The script will terminate with the error message.

6 The filehandle, *LOGGEDON*, is opened as an input filter. Output from the UNIX *who* command will be piped to the filehandle.

7 Each line of the input filter is tested. If the user is logged on, the scalar, *$logged_on,* is set to one, and the loop is exited.

8 The filehandle, *PROC*, is opened as an input filter. Output from the UNIX *ps* command will be piped to the filehandle. Each line from the filter is read in turn and placed in the scalar, *$line*. If *$line* contains a match for the user, that line will be printed to STDOUT, the screen.

8.2.3 The eof Function

The *eof* function can be used to test if end of file has been reached. It returns 1 if either the next read operation on a FILEHANDLE is at the end of the file or if the file was not opened. Without an argument, the *eof* function returns the *eof* status of the last file read. The *eof* function with parentheses can be used in a loop block to test the end of file when the last filehandle has been read. Without parentheses, each file opened can be tested for end of file.

Format:

```
eof(FILEHANDLE)
eof()
eof
```

E x a m p l e   8 . 2 4

(The Text File emp.names)
  Steve Blenheim
  Betty Boop
  Igor Chevsky
  Norma Cord
  Jon DeLoach
  Karen Evich

(In Script)
```
1   open ( DB, "emp.names") || die "Can't open emp.names: $!";
2   while(<DB>){
3       print if /Norma/ .. eof();      # .. is the range operator
    }
```

O u t p u t

  Norma Cord
  Jonathan DeLoach
  Karen Evitch

E x p l a n a t i o n

1 The file, *emp.names*, is opened via the *DB* filehandle.
2 The *while* loop reads a line at a time from the filehandle, *DB*.
3 When the line containing the regular expression *Norma* is reached, that line and all lines in the range from it until *eof* (the end of file) are printed.

E x a m p l e   8 . 2 5

(The Text Files)
  $ cat file1
  abc
  def
  ghi

  $ cat file2
  1234
  5678
  9101112

(The Script)

```
    #!/usr/bin/perl
    # eof.p script
1   while(<>){
2       print "$.\t$_";
3       if (eof){
            print "-" x 30, "\n";
4           close(ARGV);
        }


    }
```

(The Command Line)

$ eof.p file1 file2

1 abc
2 def
3 ghi

----

1 1234
2 5678
3 9101112

Explanation

1 The first argument stored in the ARGV array is *file1*. The null filehandle is used in the *while* expression. The file, *file1*, is opened for reading.
2 The $. variable is a special variable containing the line number of the currently opened filehandle. It is printed, followed by a tab, and then the line itself.
3 If end of file is reached, print a row of 30 dashes.
4 Close the filehandle in order to reset the $. value back to 1 when the next file is opened. When file1 reaches end of file, the next argument, *file2*, is processed.

8.2.4   The -i Switch—Editing Files in Place

The -i option is used to edit files in place. The files are named at the command line and stored in the ARGV array. Perl will automatically rename the output file to the same name as the input file. The output file will be the selected default file for printing. To ensure that you keep a backup of the original file, you can specify an extension to the -i flag, such as -i.bak. The original file will be renamed *filename.bak*. The file must be assigned to the ARGV filehandle when it is being read from. Multiple files can be passed in from the command line and each one in turn will be edited in place.

1 (The Original Text File)
   $ more names
   igor chevsky
   norma corder
   jennifer cowan
   john deloach
   fred fardbarkle
   lori gortz
   paco gutierrez
   ephram hardy
   james ikeda

   (The Script)
2 **#!/usr/bin/perl –i.bak**
   # Scriptname: inplace

3 **while(<ARGV>){**   *# Open ARGV for reading*
4   tr/a-z/A-Z/;
5   **print;**   *# Output goes to the file currently being read in-place*
6   close ARGV if eof;
   }

7 (At the command line)
   $ inplace names
   $ more **names**
   IGOR CHEVSKY
   NORMA CORDER
   JENNIFER COWAN
   JOHN DELOACH
   FRED FARDBARKLE
   LORI GORTZ
   PACO GUTIERREZ
   EPHRAM HARDY
   JAMES IKEDA

8 $ more **names.bak**
   igor chevsky
   norma corder
   jennifer cowan
   john deloach
   fred fardbarkle
   lori gortz
   paco gutierrez
   ephram hardy
   james ikeda

Explanation

1 The contents of the original text file, called *names*, is printed.
2 The *-i*, in-place switch, is used with an extension. The *names* file will be edited in place and the original file will be saved in *names.bak*.
3 The *while* loop is entered. The ARGV filehandle will be opened for reading.
4 All lowercase letters are translated to uppercase letters in the file being processed (*tr* function).
5 The *print* function sends its output to the file being processed in place.
6 The ARGV filehandle will be closed when the end of file is reached. This makes it possible to reset line numbering for each file when processing multiple files or to mark the end of files when appending.
7 The *names* file has been changed, illustrating the file was modified in place.
8 The *names.bak* file was created as a backup file for the original file. The original file has been changed.

8.3 File Testing

Like the Shells, Perl provides a number of file test operators (see Table 8.2) to check for the various attributes of a file, such as existence, access permissions, directories, files, etc. Most of the operators return 1 for true and "" (null) for false.

A single underscore can be used to represent the name of the file if the same file is tested more than once. The *stat* structure of the previous file test is used.

TABLE 8.2 File Testing Operators[2]

Operator	Meaning
–r $file	True if $file is a readable file.
–w $file	True if $file is a writeable file.
–x $file	True if $file is an executable file.
–o $file	True if $file is owned by effective uid.
–e $file	True if file exists.
–z $file	True if file is zero in size.
–s $file	True if $file has non–zero size. Returns the size of the file in bytes.
–f $file	True if $file is a plain file.
–d $file	True if $file is a directory file.
–l $file	True if $file is a symbolic link.
–p $file	True if $file is a named pipe or FIFO.
–S $file	True if $file is a socket.
–b $file	True if $file is a block special file.
–c $file	True if $file is a character special file.
–u $file	True if $file has a setuid bit set.
–g $file	True if $file has a setgid bit set.
–k $file	True if $file has a sticky bit set.
–t $file	True if filehandle is opened to a tty.
–T $file	True if $file is a text file.
–B $file	True if file is a binary file.
–M $file	Age of the file in days since modified.
–A $file	Age of the file in days since last accessed.
–C $file	Age of the file in days since the inode changed.

2. If a filename is not provided, $_ is the default.

E x a m p l e   8 . 2 6

(At the Command Line)
1 **$ ls –l perl.test**
   –rwxr–xr–x 1 ellie   417 Apr 23 13:40 perl.test
2 **$ ls –l afile**
   –rws—x—x 1 ellie   0 Apr 23 14:07 afile

(In Script)
   #!/usr/bin/perl
   $file=perl.test;

3 print "File is readable\n" if –r $file;
   print "File is writeable\n" if –w $file;
   print "File is executable\n" if –x $file;
   print "File is a regular file\n" if –f $file;
   print "File is a directory\n" if –d $file;
   print "File is text file\n" if –T $file;
   printf "File was last modified %f days ago.\n", –M $file;
4 print "File has read, write, and execute set.\n" if –r $file && –w _ && –x _;
5 **stat("afile")**; # stat another file
   print "File is a set user id program.\n" if –u _; #underscore evaluates to last file
                                                        #stat'ed
   print "File is zero size.\n" if –z _;

O u t p u t

3 *File is readable*
   File is writeable
   File is executable
   File is a regular file
   *** No print out here because the file is not a directory ***
   File is text file
   File was last modified 0.000035 days ago.
   File has read, write, and execute set.
   File is a set user id program.
   File is zero size.

Explanation

1   The permissions, ownership, file size, etc., on *perl.test* are shown.
2   The permissions, ownership, file size, etc., on *afile* are shown.
3   The print statement is executed if the file is readable, writeable, executable, etc.
4   Since the same file is checked for more than one attribute, an underscore is appended to the file test flag. The underscore references the *stat*[3] structure, an array that holds information about the file.
5   The *stat* function returns a 13-element array containing the statistics about a file. The statistics for *afile* are used in the tests that follow, as long as the underscore is appended to the file test flag.

---

3. See stat structure, "Interfacing with the System," Section 12.2.6.

9

Modularize It, Package It, and Send It to the Library!

9.1 Subroutine Definition

In addition to the large number of Perl functions already available, you can create your own functions or subroutines[1] to break the program into one or more component parts, commonly called modules.

A subroutine declaration consists of one or more statements that are not executed until the function is called. Subroutines are global and can be anywhere in the script, even in another file. When coming from another file they are loaded into the script with either the do, require, or use keywords. All variables created within the subroutine or accessed by it are global within the script unless specifically made local.

Format:

```
Subroutine definition:
        sub subroutine_name { Block }
Subroutine call:
        do subroutine_name;
        &subroutine_name;
        subroutine_name();
        subroutine_name;
```

---

1. The terms subroutine and function are interchangeable in Perl.

<u>Subroutine call with parameters:</u>
```
        &subroutine_name(parameter1, parameter2, ... )
        subroutine_name(parameter1, parameter2, ... )
```

<u>Forward reference:</u>
```
sub subroutine_name;  # Forward reference
subroutine_name;   #Ampersand not required.
```

The subroutine is called either by prefixing the subroutine name with an ampersand, by prefixing the subroutine with the *do* function,[2] or by appending parentheses to the subroutine name. If a forward reference is used, neither an ampersand nor parentheses is needed to call the subroutine.

Arguments, whether scalar values or arrays, are passed into the subroutine and stored in @_ array. The @_ array is a local array whose values are implicit references to the actual parameters. If you modify the @_ array, you will modify the actual parameters. However, if you shift or pop off elements of the @_ array, you merely lose your reference to the actual parameters. (See Section 9.3 and the *local* and *my* functions.)

If a nonexistent subroutine is called, the program quits with an error message: "Undefined subroutine in "main::prog" ...". If you want to check whether or not the subroutine has been defined, you can do so with the *defined* function.

The return value of a subroutine is the value of the last expression evaluated (either a scalar or an array). The *return* function can be used explicitly or to return a value or to exit from the subroutine early due to the result of testing some condition.

If the call to the subroutine is made part of an expression, the returned value can be assigned to a variable, thus emulating a function call.

Recursion is performed when a subroutine calls itself. Perl supports recursion.

E x a m p l e   9 . 1

```
(The Script)
    #!/bin/perl
    # Variables used in subroutines are global by default.
1   sub bye {
         print "Bye $name\n";
         $name=Tom;
      } # subroutine definition
2   $name="Ellie";
    print "Hello to you and yours!\n";
3   if ( defined &bye ){
4        &bye;     # call the bye subroutine;
    }
5   print "Out of the subroutine. Hello $name.\n";  #name is now Tom
```

---

2. The primary use of the *do* function was to include Perl subroutines from the Perl4 library (e.g., do 'pwd.pl').

Output

Hello to you and yours!
1   *Bye Ellie*
5   *Out of the subroutine. Hello Tom.*

Explanation

1   The subroutine, *bye*, is defined. The variable, *$name*, is assigned the value *Tom* in the subroutine block. Its scope is global.
2   The variable, *$name*, is assigned the value *Ellie* outside of the subroutine. This variable is global to the script until it is redefined.
3   The *defined* function checks to see if the subroutine has been defined. A fatal error occurs if it has not been defined.
4   A call is made to the subroutine, *bye*. The subroutine statement is invoked by preceding its name with an ampersand. Parentheses after the subroutine name are not necessary unless arguments are passed or the ampersand is omitted.
5   The value of *$name* was changed in the function. Since variables are global to the program, changing the variable, *$name*, in the subroutine changes it for the whole program.

9.2   Passing Arguments

9.2.1   Call by Reference

The special variable @_ is a special array that handles arguments passed to the subroutine. It is local to the subroutine and its values refer to the *actual* scalar parameters. These values can be modified.

In Perl, the default is *call by reference* when arrays or scalars are passed to a function or subroutine. The @_ is a special local array used for referencing the names of the formal arguments. Its values can be changed, thus changing the value of the actual parameters. The elements of the @_ array are $_[0], $_[1], $_[2], etc. If a scalar variable is passed, its value is the first element of the @_ array, $_[0]. Perl doesn't care if you don't use all the parameters passed, or if you have an insufficient number of parameters. If you shift or pop the @_ array you merely lose your reference to the actual arguments. If you want to modify the global copy rather than the local @_ array, then you can use either typeglob or hard references. Hard references are discussed in Chapter 10.

E x a m p l e   9 . 2

(The Script)
```
   #!/bin/perl
   # This script is called sub.greet
   $first="Steve";
   $last="Blenheim";
1  while(<>){
2      &greeting ( $first, $last ) if /[Ss]teve/;
   }

3  sub greeting{
4      print "Welcome to the club, $_[0] $_[1]\n";
   }
```

@_ array

(The Command Line)
$ cat datafile
Betty Boop
Steve Blenheim
Norma Cord
Jon DeLoach
Karen Evich
Igor Chevsky

O u t p u t

(The Script)
   $ sub.greet datafile
4 *Welcome to the club, Steve Blenheim*

E x p l a n a t i o n

1 The *while* loop starts using the null filehandle to read a line at a time from the file named at the command line, *datafile*.
2 After entering the loop, the *greeting* subroutine is called with two parameters, if the $_ variable matches the regular expression, *Steve*.
3 The subroutine is defined.
4 The parameters are stored in the @_ array, and the first two elements of that array are printed when the subroutine is called. The individual elements are represented as scalars, $_[0] and $_[1].

E x a m p l e   9 . 3

(The Script)
```
     #!/bin/perl
     # Program to demonstrate how @_ references values.
1  sub params{
2        print 'The values in the @_ array are ', "@_\n";
3        print "The first value is $_[0]\n";
4        print "The last value is ", pop(@_),"\n";
5        foreach $value ( @_ ) {
6             $value+=5;
              print "The value is $value", "\n";
        }
     }

     print "Give me 5 numbers : ";
7  @n=split(' ',<STDIN>);
8  &params(@n);
     print "Back in main\n";
9  print "The new values are @n \n";
```

O u t p u t

```
      Give me 5 numbers: 1 2 3 4 5
2     The values in the @_ array are 1 2 3 4 5
3     The first value is 1
4     The last value is 5
      The value is 6
      The value is 7
      The value is 8
      The value is 9
9     Back in main
10    The new values are 6 7 8 9 5   <--- Look here.
```

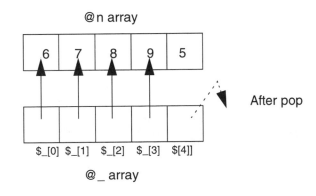

@n array

After pop

$_[0] $_[1] $_[2] $_[3] $[4]]

@_ array

E x p l a n a t i o n

1 The subroutine, *params*, is defined.
2 The value of @_, the actual parameter list, is printed.
3 The first value of the @_ array is printed.
4 The last element of the array is removed with the *pop* function and then printed.
5 The *foreach* loop assigns to scalar, *$value*, in turn, each element of the @_ array.
6 Each element of the array is incremented by 5 and stored in the scalar, *$value*.
7 After the user has typed five numbers, the *split* function returns an array consisting of each of the numbers read from STDIN.
8 The subroutine is called passing the array as a parameter.
9 The values printed illustrate that those values changed in the function were really changed. The only value that wasn't changed is the last element of the original array. It was dereferenced in line 4 of the program by the *pop* function.

9.2.2   Passing by Value

When an argument is passed *call by value*, a copy of the value of the argument is sent to the subroutine. If the copy is modified, the original value is untouched.

The local Function.   The *local* function is used to turn on *call-by-value*, and it can be used in both Perl4 and Perl5. Perl5 has introduced another function, called *my*, which further ensures the privacy of variables within a block.

The *local* function creates local variables from its list. Any variable declared by *local* is said to be dynamically scoped; i.e., it is visible to any functions called from within this block or any blocks (or subroutines) nested within the block where it is defined. A local variable may even have the same name as a global variable. After the last statement in the subroutine is executed, the local variable is discarded and the global one is restored. It is recommended that all local variables be set at the beginning of the subroutine block.

E x a m p l e   9 . 4

(The Script)
```
1 $first=Tom;
  $last=Jones;
2 &greeting ( $first, $last ) ; # Call the greeting subroutine
3 print "——$fname——\n" if defined $fname;  # $fname is local to sub greeting.

  # Subroutine defined
  sub greeting{
4     local ($fname, $lname) = @_ ;
5     print "Welcome $fname!!\n";
  }
```

Output

5 *Welcome Tom!!*

Explanation

1 The scalar variables are assigned values.
2 A call is made to the *greeting* subroutine. Two arguments are passed.
3 The *print* statement is not executed because *$fname* is not defined here. It was defined as a local variable in the subroutine. It is local to the *greeting* subroutine.
4 The *local* function takes a list of arguments from the @_ array and creates two local variables, *$fname* and *$lname*, from that list. The values in the local variables are copies of the values that were passed.
5 The print statement is executed. The contents of the local variable, *$fname*, are printed, a copy of what is in *$first*.

The my Function.   The *my* function is used to turn on *call-by-value* and is said to be lexically scoped. This means that variables declared as *my* variables are visible from the point of declaration to the end of the innermost enclosing block. That block could be a simple block enclosed in curly braces, a subroutine, eval, or file. Unlike the variables declared with the *local* function, any variables declared as *my* variables are visible only within the subroutine in which they are declared, not in any subroutines called from this subroutine. If more than one variable is listed, the list must be enclosed in parentheses. The previous subroutine (Example 9.4) could have been written:

```
sub greeting{
        my ($fname, $lname) = @_ ;
        print "Welcome $fname!!\n";
}
```

Example 9.5

(The Script)
```
    #!/bin/perl
1 $friend = Louise;          # global variables
2 $pal = Danny;
3 print "$friend and $pal are global.\n";

4 sub guests {
5        my $friend=Pat;
6        local $pal=Chris;
7        print "$friend and $pal are welcome guests.\n";
8        &who_is_it;  # call subroutine
    }
```

```
9    sub who_is_it {
10        print "You still have your global friend, $friend, here.\n";
11        print "But your pal is now $pal .\n";
     }

12   &guests;   # call subroutine
```

Output

```
3    Louise and Danny are global.
7    Pat and Chris are welcome guests.
10   You still have your global friend,Louise, here.
11   But your pal is now Chris .
```

Explanation:

1 The variable, *$friend*, is assigned a value, *Louise*. All variables are global within *main*.
2 The variable *$pal* is assigned a value, *Danny*. It is also global.
3 The values of the variables are printed.
4 The subroutine *guests* is defined.
5 The *my* function localizes the scalar *$friend* to this subroutine.
6 The *local* function localizes the variable *$pal* to this and all subroutines called from here.
7 The *$friend* and the *$pal* variables are printed in the *guests* subroutine.
8 The subroutine *who_is_it* is called.
9 The subroutine, *who_is_it* is defined.
10 In the subroutine *who_is_it*, the global variable *$friend(Louise)* is visible. The *$friend* variable *(Pat)* declared as a *my* variable in the calling subroutine, *guests,* is not visible in this subroutine.
11 The *local* scalar variable, *$pal (Chris),* on the other hand, was assigned in the *guests* subroutine and is still visible in this subroutine, *who_is_it.*
12 The *guests* subroutine is called.

9.2.3 Return Value

The subroutine can act like a function if it is included in an assignment statement and its returned value is assigned to a variable, either scalar or array. The value returned is really the value of the last expression evaluated within the subroutine (similar to Shell function return values).

The *return* function returns a specified value, but is not recommended. If used outside a subroutine, it causes a fatal error.

E x a m p l e   9 . 6

(The Script)
```
   #!/bin/perl
   sub MAX {
1          local($max) = shift(@_);
2          foreach $foo ( @_ ){
3                  $max = $foo if $max < $foo;
                   print $max,"\n";
          }
      print "------------------------------\n";
4  $max;
   }
   sub MIN {
          local($min) = pop( @_ );
          foreach $foo ( @_ ) {
                  $min = $foo if $min > $foo;
                  print $min,"\n";
          }
      print "------------------------------\n";
   return $min;
   }

5  $biggest = &MAX ( 2, 3, 4, 10, 100, 1 );
6  $smallest= &MIN ( 200, 2, 12, 40, 2, 20 );
   print "The biggest is  $biggest and the smallest is $smallest.\n";
7  print $foo, $min, $max;  #nothing prints - local variables
```

O u t p u t

```
   3
   4
   10
   100
   100
   _____
   200
   2
   2
   2
   2
   _____
```

The biggest is 100 and the smallest is 2.

Explanation

1   The scalar, *$max*, is assigned the value of the first element in the array, @_. The local function makes *$max* local to this subroutine. If *$max* is modified, the original copy is not affected.

2   For each element in the list, the loop will assign, in turn, an element of the list to scalar, *$foo*.

3   If *$max* is less than *$foo*, *$max* gets *$foo*.

4   Since the last statement executed in subroutine MAX is *$max*,the value of *$max* is returned and assigned to *$biggest* at line 5.

5   The scalar, *$biggest*, is assigned the value of the last expression in the MAX subroutine.

6   The scalar, *$smallest*, is assigned the return value from function *MIN*. The return function is explicitly used in subroutine *MIN*.

7   Variables were local in the subroutines and within the *foreach* loop. Nothing prints.

9.2.4   Aliases and Typeglob

Definition.

A typeglob is an alias for a variable. An alias is just another name for a variable. It is called a symbolic reference and is analogous to a soft link in the UNIX filesystem. It is another name for all identifiers on the symbol table with the same name. Aliases were used predominantly in Perl4 programs as a mechanism to pass parameters by reference and are still used in Perl5 programs, although with the advent of hard references (Chapter 10), the practice of using typeglob and aliases is not as widespread.

Passing Arrays by Reference.

Aliases can be passed to functions to assure true call by reference so that you can modify the global copy of the variable rather than the local copy stored in the @_ array. If you are passing an array or multiple arrays to a subroutine, rather than copying the entire array into the subroutine, you can pass the name of the array(s). To create an alias for a variable, an asterisk is prepended to the alias name.

*alias=*variable;

The asterisk represents all of the funny characters that prefix variables, including subroutines, filehandles, and formats. Typeglob produces a scalar value that represents all objects with the same name. It "globs" onto all the symbols in the symbol table that have that name.[3] It is your job to determine what symbol you want the alias to reference. This is done by prepending the correct "funny" character to the alias name when you want to access its underlying value.

---

3.   This is not the same as the globbing done for filename substitution as in <p*>.

For example:

> Given: *alias = *var
> Then:

> > $alias refers to the scalar $var
> > @alias refers to the array @var
> > $alias{string} refers to an element of a hash %var

If a filehandle is passed to a subroutine, typeglob can be used to make the filehandle local.

Perl5 improved the alias mechanism so that the alias can now represent one "funny charac-ter" rather than all of them and introduced an even more convenient method for passing by reference, the hard reference or what you may recognize as a C/Pascal like pointer.

E x a m p l e 9 . 7

(The Script)

```
    #!/usr/bin/perl
1   $colors="rainbow";
2   @colors=("red", "green", "yellow" );
3   &printit(*colors);                 #Which color is this?
4   sub printit{
5       local(*whichone)=@_;           # Must use local, not my with globs
6       print *whichone, "\n";         # The package is main
7       $whichone="Prism of Light";    # Alias for the scalar
8       $whichone[0]="PURPLE";         # Alias for the array
    }
9   print "Out of subroutine.\n";
10  print "\$colors is $colors.\n";
11  print "\@colors is @colors.\n";
```

O u t p u t

6   *main::colors
10   Out of subroutine.
11   $colors is Prism of Light.
12   @colors is PURPLE green yellow.

Explanation

1   The scalar, *$colors*, is assigned "rainbow".
2   The array, *@colors*, is assigned three values, "red", "green", and "yellow".
3   The *printit* subroutine is called. An alias for all symbols named "colors" is passed as a parameter. The asterisk creates the alias also called a typeglob.
4   The *printit* subroutine is defined.
5   The @_ array contains the alias that was passed. Its value is assigned to the local alias, a **whichone*. **whichone* is now an alias for any *colors* symbol .
6   Attempting to print the value of the alias itself only tells you that it is in the *main* package and is a symbol for all variables, subroutines, and filehandles called *colors*.
7   The scalar represented by the alias is assigned a new value.
8   The array represented by the alias, the first element of the array, is assigned a new value.
9   Out of the subroutine.
10   Out of the subroutine the scalar *$colors* has been changed.
11   Out of the subroutine the array *@colors* has also been changed.

Example 9.8

```
     #!/bin/perl
     # Revisiting Example 9.3 -- Now using typeglob
1    print "Give me 5 numbers: ";
2    @n = split(' ', <STDIN>);
3    &params(*n);

4    sub params{
5        local(*arr)=@_;
6        print 'The values of the @arr array are ', @arr, "\n";
7        print "The first value is $arr[0]\n";
8        print "the last value is ", pop(@arr), "\n";
9        foreach $value(@arr){
10               $value+=5;
11               print "The value is $value.\n";
         }
     }
     print "Back in main\n";
12   print "The new values are @n.\n";
```

O u t p u t

1   *Give me 5 numbers:* 1 2 3 4 5
6   *The values in the @ arr array are 12345*
7   *The first value is 1*
8   *The last value is 5*
11 *The value is 6*
    The value is 7
    The value is 8
    The value is 9
    Back in main
12 **The new values are 6 7 8 9   <--- Look here. Got popped this time!**

E x p l a n a t i o n

1   The user is asked for input.
2   The user input is split on whitespace and returned to the @*n* array.
3   The subroutine *params* is called. An alias for any *n* in the symbol table is passed as a parameter.
4   The *params* subroutine is defined.
5   In the subroutine, the alias was passed to the @_ array. This value is assigned to a local typeglob, **arr*.
6   The values in the @*arr* array are printed. Remember, @*arr* is just an alias for the array @n. It refers to the values in the @*n* array.
7   The first element in the array is printed.
8   The last element of the array is popped, not just the reference to it.
9   The *foreach* loop assigns to scalar $*value*, in turn, each element of the @*arr* array.
10 Each element of the array is incremented by 5 and stored in the scalar, $*value*.
11 The new values are printed.
12 The values printed illustrate that those values changed in the function by the alias changed the values in the @*n* array. See Example 9.3.

Passing Filehandles by Reference.

One of the only ways to pass a filehandle directly to a subroutine is by reference. You can use typeglob to create an alias for the filehandle. You can also use a hard reference discussed in Chapter 10.

E x a m p l e   9 . 9

(The Script)
```
   #!/bin/perl
1  open(READMEFILE, "f1") || die;
2  &readit(*READMEFILE);    # Passing a filehandle to a subroutine
   sub readit{
3      local(*myfile)=@_;     # myfile is an alias for READMEFILE
4      while(<myfile>){
           print;
       }
   }
```

E x p l a n a t i o n

1 The *open* function opens the UNIX file *f1* for reading and attaches it to the README-
   FILE handle.
2 The *readit* subroutine is called. The filehandle is aliased with typeglob and passed as a
   parameter to the subroutine.
3 The local alias *myfile* is assigned the value of @_, i.e., the alias that was passed into the
   subroutine.
4 The alias is another name for READMEFILE. It is enclosed in angle brackets, and each
   line from the filehandle will be read and then printed as it goes through the while loop.

Perl5 Aliases and the backslash operator.

Perl5 references allow you to alias a particular variable rather than all variable types
with the same name; e.g.:

```
*array=\@array;
*scalar=\$scalar;
*hash=\%assoc_array
*func=\&subroutine
```

E x a m p l e   9 . 1 0

(The Script)
```
   #! /bin/perl
   # References And Type Glob
1  @list=(1, 2, 3, 4, 5);
2  $list="grocery";
3  *arr = \@list;   # *arr is a reference only to the array @list
4  print @arr, "\n";
5  print "$arr\n";     # not a scalar reference
```

```
    sub alias {
6       local (*a) = @_;   # Must use local, not my
7       $a[0] = 7;
8       pop @a;
    }
9  &alias(*arr);   # Call the subroutine
10 print "@list\n";
11  $num=5;
12 *scalar=\$num;   # *scalar is a reference to the scalar $num
13 print "$scalar\n";
```

Output

```
4    1 2 3 4 5
5
10 7 2 3 4
13 5
```

Explanation

1   The *@list* array is assigned a list of values.
2   The *$list* scalar is assigned a value.
3   The **arr* alias is another name for the array *@list*. It is not an alias for any other type.
4   The alias **arr* is used to refer to the array, *@list*.
5   The alias **arr* does not reference a scalar. Nothing prints.
6   In the subroutine, the local alias **a* receives the value of the alias passed in as a parameter and assigned to the *@_* array.
7   The array is assigned new value via the alias.
8   The last value of the array is popped off via the alias.
9   The subroutine is called passing the alias, **arr*, as a parameter.
10 The *@list* values are printed reflecting the changes made in the subroutine.
11 The scalar, *$num,* is assigned a value.
12 A new alias is created. **scalar* refers only to the scalar, *$num*.
13 The alias is just another name for the scalar, *$num*. Its value is printed.

9.2.5 Autoloading

The Perl5 *autoload* function lets you check to see if a subroutine has been defined. The *AUTOLOAD* subroutine is called whenever Perl is told to call a subroutine and the subroutine can't be found. The special variable *$AUTOLOAD* is assigned the name of the undefined subroutine.

The *AUTOLOAD* function can also be used with objects to provide an implementation for calling unnamed methods. (A method is an object oriented name for a subroutine.)

Example 9.11

```
(The Script)
#!/bin/perl
1 sub AUTOLOAD {
2       my(@arguments)=@_;
3       $args=join(', ', @arguments);
4       print "$AUTOLOAD was never defined.\n";
5 print "The arguments passed were $args.\n";
   }


6 $driver="Jody";
  $miles=50;
  $gallons=5;


7 &mileage($driver, $miles, $gallons);   # Call to an undefined subroutine
```

Output

4 *main::mileage was never defined.*
5 *The arguments passed were Jody, 50, 5.*

Explanation

1 The subroutine *AUTOLOAD* is defined.
2 The *AUTOLOAD* subroutine is called with the same arguments as would have been passed to the original subroutine called on line 7.
3 The arguments are joined by a comma and stored in the scalar *$args*.
4 The name of the package and the subroutine that was originally called are stored in the *$AUTOLOAD* scalar. (For this example, *main* is the default package.)
5 The arguments are printed.
6 The scalar variables are assigned values.
7 The *mileage* subroutine is called with three arguments. Perl calls the *AUTOLOAD* function if there is a call to an undefined function, passing the same arguments as would have been passed in this example to the *mileage* subroutine.

E x a m p l e   9 . 1 2

```
#!/bin/perl
# Program to call a subroutine without defining it.
1 sub AUTOLOAD {
2       my(@arguments) = @_;
3       my($package, $command)=split("::",$AUTOLOAD, 2);
4       return `$command @arguments`;   # Command substitution

  }

5 $day=date("+%D");     # date is an undefined subroutine
6 print "Today is $day.\n";
7 print cal(3,1997);      # cal is an undefined subroutine
```

O u t p u t

Today is 03/19/97.

```
   March 1997
S M  Tu  W  Th  F  S
                    1
 2  3  4  5  6  7  8
 9 10 11 12 13 14 15
16 17 18 19 20 21 22
23 24 25 26 27 28 29
30 31
```

E x p l a n a t i o n

1 The subroutine *AUTOLOAD* is defined.
2 The *AUTOLOAD* subroutine is called with the same arguments as would have been passed to the original subroutine on lines 5 and 7.
3 The *$AUTOLOAD* variable is *split* into two parts by a double colon delimiter. The array returned consists of the package name and the name of the subroutine that was called.
4 The value returned is the name of the function called, which in the first case happens to be a UNIX command and its arguments. The backquotes cause the enclosed string to be executed as a UNIX command. Tricky!
5 The *date* function has never been defined. *AUTOLOAD* will pick its name and assign it to *$AUTOLOAD* in the *AUTOLOAD* function. The *date* function will pass an argument. The argument, *+%D*, is also an argument to the UNIX *date* command. It returns today's date.
6 The returned value is printed.

7 The *cal* function has never been defined. It takes two arguments. *AUTOLOAD* will assign *cal* to $*AUTOLOAD*. The arguments are 3 and 1997. They will be passed to the
   AUTOLOAD function and used in line 4. After variable substitution, the backquotes
   cause the string to be executed. The UNIX command "cal 3 1997" is executed and the
   result returned to the *print* fucntion.

9.2.6   BEGIN and END Subroutines (Startup and Finish)

The BEGIN and END subroutines may remind UNIX programmers of the special BEGIN
and END patterns used in the Awk programming language. For C++ programmers the
BEGIN has been likened to a constructor and the END, a destructor. The BEGIN and END
subroutines are similar to both in functionality.

A BEGIN subroutine is executed immediately, i.e., before the rest of the file is even
parsed. If you have multiple BEGINs, they will be executed in the order they were defined.

The END subroutine is executed when all is done; that is, when the program is exiting,
even if the *die* function caused the termination. Multiple END blocks are executed in
reverse order.

The keyword *sub* is not necessary when using these special subroutines.

Example 9.13

```
#!/bin/perl
# Program to demonstrate BEGIN and END subroutines
1  chdir("/poop") || die "Can't cd: $!\n";
2  BEGIN{ print "Welcome to my Program.\n"};
3  END{ print "Bailing out somewhere near line ",__LINE__, " So long.\n"};
```


Output

```
Welcome to my Program.
Can't cd: No such file or directory
Bailing out somewhere near line 5. So long.
```


Explanation

1 An effort is make to change directories to */poop*. The chdir fails and the *die* is executed.
   Normally the program would exit immediately, but this program has defined an END
   subroutine. The END subroutine will be executed before the program dies.
2 The BEGIN subroutine is executed as soon as possible, i.e., as soon as it has been defined. This subroutine is executed before anything else in the program happens.
3 The END subroutine is always executed when the program is about to exit, even if a *die*
   is called. The line printed is there just for you awk programmers.

9.2.7 The subs Function

The subs function allows you to predeclare subroutine names. Its arguments are a list of subroutines. This allows you to call a subroutine without the ampersand or parentheses and to override built-in Perl functions.

Example 9.14

```
#!/bin/perl
# The subs module
1 use subs qw(fun1 fun2 );

2 fun1;
3 fun2;

4 oub fun1{
   print "In fun1\n";
   }

5 sub fun2{
   print "In fun2\n";
   }
```

Output

```
In fun1
In fun2
```

Explanation

1 The *subs* module is loaded (see *use*, Section 9.4.3) into your program and given a list of subroutines.
2 *fun1* is called with neither an ampersand nor parentheses because it was in the subs list. The function is not defined until later.
3 *fun2* is also called before it is defined.

9.3   Packages and Modules

9.3.1   Definition

The bundling of data and functions into a separate namespace is termed encapsulation (to C++ programmers, this is called a class and to object oriented Perl programmers it can also be called a class). The separate namespace is termed a package. A separate namespace means that Perl has a separate symbol table for all the variables in a named package. By default the current package is called package "main". All the example scripts up to this point are in package main. All variables are global within the package. The package mechanism allows you to switch namespaces, so that variables and subroutines in the package are private, even if they have the same name somewhere outside of the package.

The scope of the package is from the declaration of the package to the end of the innermost enclosing block or until another package is declared. To reference a package variable in another package, the package name is prefixed by the funny symbol representing the data type of the variable and followed by two colons and the variable name. In Perl4, an apostrophe is used instead of the colon.[4] (The double colons are reminiscent of the C++ scope resolution operator.) When referring to the main package, the name of the package can be eliminated.

Perl5 extends the notion of packages to that of modules. A module is a package that is usually defined in a library and is reusable. Modules are more complex than simple packages. They have the ability to export symbols to other packages and to work with classes and methods (Chapter 11). Modules are packages stored in a file where the basename of the file is given the package name appended with a *.pm* extension. The *use* function takes the module name as its argument and loads the module into your script.

9.3.2   The Symbol Table

To compile a program, the compiler must keep track of all the names for variables, filehandles, directory handles, formats, and subroutines that are used. Perl stores the names of these symbols as keys in a hash table for each package. The values associated with the keys are the corresponding typeglob values. The name of the hash is the same name as the package. Any time you use the package declaration, you switch to the symbol table for that package.

In the following example, you will notice that the main package not only stores symbols that are provided by the program, but also other symbols such as *STDIN, STDOUT, STDERR, ARGV, ARGVOUT, ENV,* and *SIG*. These symbols and special variables such as $_ and $! are forced into package main. Other packages refer to these symbols unless qualified. (See signals.)

---

4. The apostrophe is still acceptable in Perl 5 scripts as of 5.003.

E x a m p l e   9 . 1 5

```
#!/bin/perl
# Package main
```
1 `$name=Tom;`
2 `@name=qw(Joe Jeff Jan );`

3 **while(($key, $value) = each (%main::)){**   *# Look at main's symbol table*
4   **print "$key:\t$value\n";**
```
}
print "-" x 25, "\n";
```
5 **local *alias = *name;**
6 `print "*alias is ", *alias, "\n";`
7 ***PI=\3.14159265358979;*   *# A constant*
8 `# $PI=55;` *After testing this, it is commented so the program can continue*
9 my $pal = Linda;   *# Not in the symbol table*
10   **local $dude = Ernle;**

11 **package friends;**
12 **print "Hello $main::dude, dude.\n";**
13 **print "My pal is $main::pal.\n";**

O u t p u t

4	*FileHandle:::*	**main::FileHandle*
	@:	**main::@*
	name	***main::name**
	dude:	***main::dude**
	stdin:	**main::stdin*
	STDIN:	**main::STDIN*
	":	**main::"*
	stdout:	**main::stdout*
	STDOUT:	**main::STDOUT*
	$:	**main::$*
	_<perlmain.c:	**main::_<perlmain.c*
	key:	***main::key**
	ENV:	**main::ENV*
	alias:	***main::alias**
	_<package.dump:*	*main::_<package.dump*
	/:	**main::/*
	ARG	**main::ARGV*
	0:	**main::0*
	STDER	**main::STDERR*
	stderr:	**main::stderr*

:	*main::
DynaLoader:::	*main::DynaLoader
:	*main::
PI:	***main::PI***
main:::	*main::main
DATA:	*main::DATA
DB:::	*main::DB
INC:	*main::INC
value	***main::value***
_:	*main::_

    ----

6 *alias is *main::name
8 Modification of a read-only value attempted at package.dump line 15.
12 Hello Ernie, dude.
13 My pal is .

Explanation

1   The scalar *$name* is assigned a value.

2   The array *@name* is assigned a value. Both appear on the symbol table as a key/value pair where the key is the name of the symbol and the value is the typeglob associated with the symbol.

3   The *each* function returns the key/value pair for main's symbol table.

4   The keys and values from the main symbol table are printed. The key is the name of the identifier and the value is the corresponding typeglob value.

5   The local glob *alias* is assigned a typeglob. Any type having the symbol, *name*, can be referenced via the alias. The typeglob also appears on the symbol table.

6   The printout of **alias* shows that it is in package main and an alias for an identifier, *name*.

7   The scalar *$PI* is assigned a reference to a value that cannot be changed. This is a way to create a constant in Perl.

8   An attempt to assign a value to a constant produces an error message.

9   Variables created with the *my* function are not stored on the symbol table and are therefore inaccessible from other packages.

10 The *local* variable, *$dude,* shows up on the symbol table, which makes it accessible from another package.

11 A new package, *friends*, is declared.

12 The *local* value is qualified with the *main* package name. It is still within scope and accessible from the main symbol table.

13 The *my* variable is not accessed here. It was not put in the main symbol table.

9.3.3 Using Packages

Format:
(Assuming variable is a scalar in this example)

```
package name;

$package'variable
$package::variable

$main::variable
$::variable
```

E x a m p l e   9 . 1 6

```perl
#!/bin/perl
# Default package is main
1    @town = ( Boston, Chico, Tampa );
2    $friend=Mary;

3    print "In main: \$friend is $friend\n";

4    package boy;  # package declaration
5    $name=Steve;
6    print "In boy \$name is $name.\n";
7    $main::friend=Patricia;
8    print "In boy \@town is @::town\n";


9    package main;  # package declaration
10   print "In main: \$name is $name\n";
11   print "In main: \$name is $boy::name\n";
12   print "In main: \$friend is $friend.\n";
```

O u t p u t

```
3    In main: $friend is Mary
6    In boy $name is Steve.
8    In boy @town is Boston Chico Tampa
10   In main: $name is
11   In main: $name is Steve
12   In main: $friend is Patricia
```

Explanation

1   The default package is called main. In the main package an array, @*town*, is assigned values. @*town* is in main's symbol table.

2   In package main, the scalar, *$friend,* is assigned *Mary. $friend* is in main's symbol table.

3   The value of *$friend* is printed.

4   The package *boy* is declared. We now switch from the *main* package to the *boy* package. This package has its own symbol table. From this point on until the program ends or another package is declared, the *boy* package is in scope. Variables created in this package are global within this package, but not part of the main package.

5   The scalar, *$name*, is assigned Steve.

6   The value in *$name* is printed.

7   To access the variable *$friend* in package main, first the dollar sign is prepended to the package name to indicate that the type of the variable is a scalar, followed by the name of the package, *main*, two colons, and the variable name, *friend*. This allows you to switch name spaces from within this package. *Patricia* is assigned to main's variable *$friend*.

8   Since main is the default package, it is not necessary to use its name when switching namespaces. @*::town* tells Perl to switch namespaces back to the array @*town* in the *main* package.

9   Package *main* is declared. We will now switch back into the *main* package.

10   In the *main* package *$name* is not defined.

11   The value of the variable *$name* from the *boy* package is printed.

12   The *$friend* scalar was changed in package *boy* because it was fully qualified with main's package main, meaning that the program was temporarily switched to package *main* when this variable was assigned. Its value is printed.

Example 9.17

(The Script)

```
   #!/bin/perl
   # Package declarations
1  $name="Suzanne";   # These variables are in package main
2  $num=100;
3  package friend;     # package declaration
4  sub welcome {
       print "Who is your pal? ";
5      chomp($name=<STDIN>);
6      print "Welcome $name!\n";
7      print "\$num is $num.\n";    #unknown to this package.\n";
8      print "Where is $main::name?\n\n";
   }

9  package main;      # package declaration; back in main
```

10   **&friend::welcome;** *# Call subroutine*
11   print "Back in main package \$name is $name\n";
12   print "Switch to friend package, Bye ",**$friend::name**,"\n";
13   print "Bye $name\n\n";

14   **package birthday;**   *# package declaration*

15   **$name=Beatrice;**
16   print "Happy Birthday, $name.\n";
17   print "No, **$::name** and **$friend::name**, it is not your birthday!\n";

O u t p u t

4   *Who is your pal? Tommy*
6   *Welcome Tommy!*
7   *$num is .*
8   *Where is Suzanne?*

11   *Back in main package $name is Suzanne*
12   *Switch to friend package, Bye Tommy*
13   *Bye Suzanne*

16   *Happy Birthday, Beatrice!!*
17   *No, Suzanne and Tommy, it is not your birthday!*

E x p l a n a t i o n

1   Scalar, *$name*, is assigned Suzanne for the default package, *main*.
2   Scalar, *$num*, is assigned 100.
3   Package *friend* is declared. It is in scope until line 9.
4   The subroutine *welcome* is defined within the *friend* package.
5   *$name* is assigned a value in package *friend*.
6   The value of *$name* is printed.
7   The scalar, *$num*, was local to the main package; it is not defined here.
8   To access the *$name* variable from the *main* package, the name of the package, *main*, is followed by two colons and the variable name. Note that the $ precedes the package name, not the variable.
9   Out of the subroutine, the package *main* is declared.
10   The subroutine *welcome* cannot be called unless qualified by its package name.
11   *$name* is *Suzanne* in package main.
12   To access a variable from the package *friend*, the package has to precede the variable name. This causes a switch in namespaces.
13   *$name* is Suzanne in package main.
14   A new package called *birthday* is declared. It remains in effect until the block ends—in this case, when the script ends.

15 The *$name* variable for package *birthday* is assigned.
16 *$name* is *Beatrice* in package birthday.
17 In order to access variables from the previous packages with the same name, the package name and a double colon must precede the variable.

package main	package friend	package birthday
$name=Suzanne	$name=Tommy	$name=Beatrice

9.4   The Standard Perl Library

The Perl distribution comes with a number of standard Perl library functions and packages. The Perl4 library routines ended in the *.pl* extension. The Perl5 modules end in the *.pm* extension. In Perl5 the notion of packages has been extended to that of modules. It's now possible to load selected modules into your program rather than a complete file. This is done by using the Exporter module and the @EXPORTER array.

Here is a sample listing from the standard Perl5 library:[5]

$ ls /opt/pks/perl/lib

AnyDBM_File.pm	IPC	Text	find.pl	pod
AutoLoader.pm	Math	Tie	finddepth.pl	pwd.pl
AutoSplit.pm	NDBM_File.pm	Time	flush.pl	shellwords.pm
Benchmark.pm	Net	abbrev.pl	ftp.pl	sigtrap.pm
Carp.pm	ODBM_File.pm	assert.pl	getcwd.pl	site_perl
Cwd.pm	POSIX.pm	auto	getopt.pl	splain
Devel	POSIX.pod	bigfloat.pl	getopts.pl	stat.pl
DirHandle.pm	Pod	bigint.pl	hostname.pl	strict.pm
DynaLoader.pm	SDBM_File.pm	bigrat.pl	i86pc-solaris	subs.pm
English.pm	Safe.pm	cacheout.pl	mportenv.pl	sun4-solaris
Env.pm	Search	chat2.inter	integer.pm	sun4-sunos
Exporter.pm	SelectSaver.pm	chat2.pl	less.pm	syslog.pl
ExtUtils	SelfLoader.pm	complete.pl	lib.pm	tainted.pl
Fcntl.pm	Shell.pm	ctime.pl	look.pl	termcap.pl
File	Socket.pm	diagnostics.pm	newgetopt.pl	timelocal.pl
FileCache.pm	Symbol.pm	dotsh.pl	open2.pl	validate.pl
FileHandle.pm	Sys	dumpvar.pl	open3.pl	vars.pm
Getopt	Term	exceptions.pl	overload.pm	
I18N	Test	fastcwd.pl	perl5db.pl	

5. The pathname to the standard Perl library is determined at the time Perl is installed. This can be assigned either a default value or a pathname designated by the person installing Perl.

9.4.1   The @INC Array

The special array **@INC**, contains the directory path to where the library subroutines are located. To include directories not in the @INC array, you can use the -I switch[6] at the command line, or set the *PERL5LIB* environment variable to the full pathname. Normally, this variable is set in one of your shell initialization files, either *.login* or *.profile*.

```
$ perl -e 'print "@INC\n"'
/opt/pkgs/perl/lib
/opt/pkgs/perl/lib/usr/dist/pkgs/perl,v5.003/lib/sun4-solaris/5.003
/usr/dist/pkgs/perl,v5.003/lib /usr/dist/pkgs/perl,v5.003
/lib/site_perl/sun4-solaris /usr/dist/pkgs/perl,v5.003/lib/site_perl .
```

To give your own library routines precedence over those in listed in the @INC array, you can use:

```
unshift(@INC,".");
```

Unshift causes the "." to be prepended to the @INC array, making your present working directory the first element in the search path. If your library is in a different directory, use its full pathname, rather than the dot.

9.4.2   Packages and .pl Files

Most of the library routines found in the Standard Perl library ending in *.pl* were written in the Perl4 days. They consisted of subroutines contained within a package. The library files are still available and widely used.

The require Function. In order to include and execute routines from the Perl standard library[7] or Perl code from any other file, the *require* function is used, similar to the C *#include* statement. The *require* function checks to see if the library has already been included, unlike the *eval* and the *do* functions, which are older methods for including files. Without an argument, the value of $_ is included. If the @INC array does not have the correct path to the library, the require will fail with a message like this:

Can't locate pwd.pl in @INC at package line 3.

The *require* function loads files into the program during run time. The @INC array is also updated at run time.

---

6. See Appendix A for a description of the -I switch.
7. To include UNIX system calls from the Standard C library, see Chapter 10, "The syscall Function."

Format:

```
require (Expr)
require Expr
require
```

Including Standard Library Routines.

To find out how to use a routine in Perl's library or to see what it consists of, an excerpt from the *pwd.pl* routine (written by Larry Wall) is shown below. The *pwd* package consists of two subroutines which update the PWD environment variable after the *chdir* function has been executed. The value of $ENV{PWD} is the present working directory.

Notice that in the following Perl library function, the package 'pwd' is declared before the subroutines are defined, thus placing the rest of the file within the 'pwd' package. All variables belong to the package. The *names* of the subroutines are explicitly switched to package 'main'. They may be called from your package 'main', but the variables remain local to package 'pwd'. (The apostrophe is used here to switch namespaces instead of two colons. The apostrophe is the Perl4 symbol for switching name spaces.)

Sample .pl Routine from Perl's Standard Library

E x a m p l e   9 . 1 8

```
(The pwd package)
    #
1 # Usage:
2 #      require "pwd.pl";
    #      &initpwd;
    #      ...
    #      &chdir($newdir);
3 package pwd;
4 sub main'initpwd {
  if ($ENV{'PWD'}) {
    local($dd,$di) = stat('.');
    local($pd,$pi) = stat($ENV{'PWD'});
    return if $di == $pi && $dd == $pd;
  }
  chop($ENV{'PWD'} = 'pwd');
  }
5 sub main'chdir {
      local($newdir) = shift;
      if (chdir $newdir) {
          if ($newdir =~ m#^/#) {
              $ENV{'PWD'} = $newdir;
          }
          else {
```

```
                local(@curdir) = split(m#/#,$ENV{'PWD'});
                @curdir = " unless @curdir;
                foreach $component (split(m#/#, $newdir)) {
                    next if $component eq '.';
                    pop(@curdir),next if $component eq '..';
                }
                $ENV{'PWD'} = join('/',@curdir) || '/';
            }
        }
        else {
            0;
        }              # return value
    }
6  1;   <--- Looky here!
```

Explanation

1 The usage message tells you how you're supposed to use this package.
2 In the usage message, you are being told to be sure to require the file, *pwd.pl*. The two subroutines that will be called are *initpwd* and *chdir*. The *chdir* function requires an argument which is a directory name.
3 The package *pwd* is declared. This is the only package in the file.
4 The subroutine *initpwd* is defined. Notice that its name is qualified as a symbol for the *main* package. This means that when you call *initpwd* from your main package, you won't have to mention the package *pwd* at all.
5 The *chdir* subroutine is defined.
6 The 1 is required at the end of this package for the *require* function. If the last expression evaluated in this file is not true, the *require* function will not load the file into your program.

Using Library Routines in a Script

Example 9.19

```
(The Script)
    #!/bin/perl
1  require  "ctime.pl";
2  require "pwd.pl";
3  &initpid;   # Call the subroutine
4  printf "The present working directory is %s\n", $ENV{PWD};
5  &chdir "../..";
6  printf "The present working directory is %s\n", $ENV{PWD};
7  $today=&ctime(time);
8  print "$today";
```

O u t p u t

4 *The present working directory is /home/jody/ellie/perl*
6 *The present working directory is /home/jody*
8 *Wed Mar 12 11:51:59 1997*

E x p l a n a t i o n

1 The *ctime.pl* Perl standard library function is included here.
2 The *pwd.pl* Perl standard library function is included.
3 The *initpwd* subroutine is called for the *pwd.pl* function. It initializes the value of PWD.
4 The present value of the environment variable, PWD, is printed.
5 A call to *chdir* changes the present working directory.
6 The present value of the environment variable, PWD, is printed.
7 Today's date is set in a human readable format by the subroutine *ctime*, a Perl library function.
8 Today's date is printed in its new format.

Using Perl to Include Your Own Library

The following example shows you how to create your own library functions and include them with the require function into a Perl script. When including user defined routines, or adding routines to a library, make sure to include as the last line of the routine: 1;

E x a m p l e   9 . 2 0

```
$ cat midterms
    #!/bin/perl
    # Program name: midterms
    # This program will call a subroutine from another file
1   unshift(@INC, "/home/jody/ellie/perl/mylib");
2   require "average.pl";
    print "Enter your midterm scores.\n";
    @scores=split(' ', <STDIN>);
3   printf "The average is %.1f.\n", $average=&ave(@scores);
    # The ave subroutine is found in a file called average.pl
```

4   $ **cd mylib**   # *Directory where library is located*

(The Script)
5   $ **cat average.pl**   # *File where subroutine is defined*
    # *Average a list of grades*

```
6  sub ave {
7          my(@grades)=@_;
           my($num_of_grades)=$#grades + 1;
           foreach $grade ( @grades ){
                $total=$total + $grade;
           }
8          $total/$num_of_grades;   # What gets returned
   }
9          1;   # Make sure the file returns true or require will not succeed!
```

Explanation

1 The *unshift* function prepends the @INC array with the pathname to your personal directory, *mylib*.

2 The *require* function first checks the @INC array to get a listing of all directories it will search for the .pl file. The *require* function includes the Perl function *average.pl*.

3 The *ave* function is called and returns a value to be stored in the scalar *$average*.

4 We will change directories to *mylib* from the command line. The dollar sign is the Shell prompt.

5 Now we look at the contents of the file *average.pl*.

6 The subroutine *ave* is defined.

7 It will accept a list of grades as parameters. The list is made local with the *my* function.

8 The expression is evaluated and returned.

9 This statement evaluates to true and is located at the end of the file. The *require* function needs it in order to load in this file when asked.

9.4.3   Modules and .pm Files

When using one of the modules (those file ending in .pm) provided in the standard Perl library, you must first make sure the @INC array contains the full pathname to your library distribution and that you include the *use* function with the module name.

The use Function (Modules and Pragmas)

The *use* function allows the correct importation of Perl modules and pragmas into your program at compile time. The *use* function will not import a module if the module's filename does not have the .pm extension. The *require* function does the same thing, but does not do imports, and loads the module at run time.

A module is a file in a library that behaves according to certain set of conventions. The modules in the standard Perl library are suffixed with the *.pm* extension. They can also be found in subdirectories. For example, the module *Bigfloat.pm* is found in a subdirectory called *Math*. To use a module found in a subdirectory, the directory name is followed by two colons and the name of the module; e.g., *Math::Bigfloat.pm*.

A pragma, spelled in lowercase letters, is a warning to the compiler that your program should behave in a certain way and if it doesn't, the program will abort. Some common pragmas are: *lib, strict, subs*, and *diagnostics*.

For a complete list of modules and pragmas, see Appendix A. In object-oriented terminology, subroutines are called methods.   If you receive diagnostics using the term
"method", for now, just think of them as glorified subroutines. Many of the modules in the
library use object-oriented Perl. The modules discussed in this chapter do not require any
understanding of objects. For a complete discussion on how to use the object-oriented type
modules, see Chapter 11.

Format:
```
use Module;
use Module ( list );
use Directory::Module;
no Module;
use pragma ( list );
```

The Exporter Module

The *Exporter.pm* module found in the standard Perl library supplies the necessary
semantics for other modules to be able to import methods (subroutines). The names listed
in the @EXPORT array are by default switched into the namespace of the program using
the module and the names on the @EXPORT_OK array are added to the user's namespace
only if requested. If the module is imported with *use* and parentheses are added to the module name, as in *use Module()*, none of the symbols is imported.

TABLE 9.1   Exporting Symbols

The Exporting Module	The Importing Module

package Testmodule;
use Exporter;
@ISA = qw(Exporter) ;
@EXPORT = qw(fun1, a, b);
@EXPORT_OK = qw(fun2, b, c);
	use Testmodule;
	use Testmodule qw(fun2);
	use Testmodule();

Using a Perl5 module from the Standard Perl Library

The following module, *English.pm*, provides aliases for built-in variables such as $_ and $/.
For any variables that are also part of the *awk* programming language, there are both long
and short English names for the variable. For example, the number of the current record is
represented and $. in Perl and NR in awk. The English names are either $RS (awk) or
$INPUT_RECORD_SEPARATOR (Perl).

E x a m p l e   9 . 2 1

(The Script)
```
   #!/usr/bin/perl
1  use English;   # Use English words to replace special Perl variables
2  print "The pid is $PROCESS_ID.\n";
3  print "The pid is $PID.\n";
4  print "The real uid $REAL_USER_ID.\n";
5  print "This version of perl is  $PERL_VERSION.\n";
```

O u t p u t

```
2  The pid is 948.
3  The pid is 948.
4  The real uid 9496.
5  5.004
```

E x p l a n a t i o n

1 The *English.pm* module is loaded in at compile time with the *use* directive.
2 The process id number of this process is printed.
3 The $PID variable is the same as $PROCESS.ID.
4 The real user id for the user of this program is printed.
5 The version of Perl is 5.004.

Sample .pm file from Perl's Standard Library

E x a m p l e   9 . 2 2

(A Module from the Standard Perl Library)
```
1  package Carp;
   # This package implements handy routines for modules that wish to throw
   # exceptions outside of the current package.
2  require Exporter;
3  @ISA = Exporter;
4  @EXPORT = qw(confess croak carp);
5  sub longmess {
6      my $error = shift;
       my $mess = "";
       my $i = 2;
    my ($pack,$file,$line,$sub);
    while (($pack,$file,$line,$sub) = caller($i++)) {
        $mess .= "\t$sub " if $error eq "called";
        $mess .= "$error at $file line $line\n";
```

```
        $error = "called";
    }
    $mess || $error;
    }
    sub shortmess {
    my $error = shift;
    my ($curpack) = caller(1);
    my $i = 2;
    my ($pack,$file,$line,$sub);
    while (($pack,$file,$line,$sub) = caller($i++)) {
        return "$error at $file line $line\n" if $pack ne $curpack;
    }
    longmess $error;
    }
7  sub confess { die longmess @_; }
8  sub croak { die shortmess @_; }
9  sub carp { warn shortmess @_; }
```

Explanation

1 This is the package declaration. The package is named after the file it resides in, *Carp.pm*. The functions *carp, croak,* and *confess* generate error messages such as *die* and *warn*. The difference is that with *carp* and *croak*, the error is reported at the line in the calling routine where the error was invoked and *confess* prints out stack backtrace showing the chain of subroutines that was involved in generating the error. It prints its message at the line where it was invoked.

2 The *Exporter* module is required so that subroutines and variables can be made available to other programs.

3 The @ISA array contains the names of packages this module will use. Perl implements inheritance by listing other modules this package will use in the @ISA array.

4 The @EXPORT array lists the subroutines from this module that will be exported by default to any program using this module. The subroutines *confess, croak,* and *carp,* are now available to you if you want to use this module. Since *longmess* and *shortmess* are not on the list to be exported, you cannot directly use these subroutines.

5 This is a subroutine definition for this module.

6 The error message provided as an argument to *confess* is passed here and shifted into the *$error* scalar.

7 The definition for subroutine *confess* is to call *die* with the return value of *longmess*.

8 The definition for subroutine *croak* is to call *die* with the return value of *shortmess*.

9 The definition for subroutine *carp* is to call *warn* with the return value of *shortmess*.

Example 9.23

(Using a Module from the Standard Perl Library in a Script)
```
    #!/bin/perl
1   use Carp qw(croak);

2   print "Give me a grade: ";
    $grade = <STDIN>;
3   try($grade);  # Call subroutine

4   sub try{
5       my($number)=@_;
6       croak "Illegal value: " if $number < 0 || $number > 100;
    }
```

Output

2 *Give me a grade:* **200**
6 *Illegal value: at expire line 13*
        main::try called at expire line 8

Explanation

1 The *Carp* module is imported into the current package, main. Only the subroutine *croak* will be allowed in this program. Using either *confess* or *carp* will produce an error message.
2 The user is asked for input.
3 The subroutine *try* is called and passed the scalar, *$grade*.
4 If subroutine try is defined.
5 The argument passed in is assigned to *$number*.
6 The *croak* function is called with an error message. The program will die if the value of *$number* is not in the range between 0 and 100. The error message reports the line where the program died as well as the name of the package, subroutine name, and the number of the line where the subroutine was invoked.

Using Perl to Create Your Own Module

The following example illustrates how to create a module in a separate *.pm* file and use the module in another program. Although this module itself looks like any other package, it must additionally include the *Exporter* module, the @ISA array, and the @EXPORT array in order for it to really behave as a module. The ability to export specific functions to other programs and to import other modules is what differentiates a module from a *.pl* file.

E x a m p l e   9 . 2 4

(From the Command Line Display the Script)

```
1  $ cat Module/Me.pm
2  package Me;
3  require 5.003;   # Make sure we're using some version above Perl5.002
4  require Exporter;  # Exporter.pm allows routines to be imported by others
5  @Me::ISA=qw(Exporter); # ISA is a list of packages needed by this package
6  @Me::EXPORT=qw(hello goodbye );  # list of your subroutines to export


7  sub hello { my($name)=shift;
       print "Hi there, $name.\n" };
8  sub goodbye { my($name)=shift;
       print "Good bye $name.\n";}
9  sub do_nothing { print "Didn't print anything. Not in EXPORT list\n";}
```

```
   #!/usr/bin/perl
   # Program name: main.perl
10  use lib ("/home/ellie/Module");   # a pragma to update @INC.
   # If use lib doesn't work, try:
   #      BEGIN{ unshift(@INC, "/home/ellie/Module");
   # or at Shell prompt: export PERL5LIB "/home/ellie/Module"
11  use Me;  # Import package
12  &hello (Daniel);
13  &goodbye (Steve);
14  &do_nothing;        # This was not on the Export list in Me.pm so cannot be
                        # imported
```

O u t p u t

```
12   Hi there, Daniel.
13   Good–bye Steve.
14   Undefined subroutine &main::do_nothing
```

Explanation

1   The file is called *Me.pm*. It contains a package of the same name without the extension.

2   The *Me* package is declared.

3   The *require* is used to make sure that the Perl version being used is not less than 5.003. If it is, the script will abort.

4   The *Exporter* module is a special Perl module that allows the *use* function to import subroutines (called methods) from a particular module.

5   The @ISA array lists any packages containing subroutines (methods) that will be used by this package but are found somewhere else. This is how Perl implements inheritance from one module to another. (Chapter 11)

6   The @EXPORT array lists all subroutines (methods) that can be exported by default. Those subroutines on the export list are *hello* and *goodbye,* defined below.

7   The subroutine *hello* is defined.

8   The subroutine *goodbye* is defined.

9   The subroutine *do_nothing* is defined. Note: this subroutine is not on the export list; i.e., not in the @EXPORT array.

10   The *lib* pragma tells the compiler to update the @INC array at compile time. It is the same as saying: *BEGIN{ require "/home/ellie/Module"; import Module;}*

11   The *use* function causes Perl to include the *Me.pm* module into this package.

12   The subroutine *hello* is called with an argument. This subroutine was imported.

13   The subroutine *goodbye* is called with an argument. It was also imported.

14   This subroutine was not imported. It was not on the export list (@EXPORT) in *Me.pm*. An error message is printed indicating that package main does not recognize this subroutine.

10

Does This Job Require a Reference?

10.1 What Is a Reference?

10.1.1 Symbolic vs. Hard References

A reference is a variable that <u>refers</u> to another one. A symbolic reference is a variable that <u>names</u> another variable. A typeglob is a type of symbolic reference, just another name or alias for a variable. A hard reference is a scalar variable that holds the address of another type of data. It is similar to pointers found in C and Pascal. In fact, the terms reference and pointer are interchangeable in Perl. This chapter will focus on hard references.

Larry Wall describes the difference between a hard reference and a symbolic reference as follows:

"...a Perl variable lives in a symbol table and holds one hard reference to its underlying thingy (which may be a simple thingy like a number or a complex thingy like an array or hash, but there's still only one reference from the variable to the value). There may be other hard references to the same thingy, but if so, the variable doesn't know (or care) about them. A symbolic reference names another variable, so there's always a named location involved, but a hard reference just points to a thingy...[1]

Let's take a look at how these "thingys" work.

---

1. *Programming Perl* by Larry Wall, p. 244, 1996.

E x a m p l e   1 0 . 1

```
#!/bin/perl
# Program using symbolic references
#use strict "refs";
```

1 **$language="english"**; *# hard reference*
2 **$english="Brooklyn"**;
3 print "Your native tongue is **$language**. \n";

4 print "But you speak with a **${$language}** accent.\n"; *# symbolic reference*
   print "-------------------------\n";

5 print qq/What's wrong with a **$english** accent.\n/;

6 **eval "\$$language=British ;"**; *# symbolic reference*

7 print "Why don't you try a **$english** accent? \n";

O u t p u t

3 *Your native tongue is english.*
4 *But you speak with a Brooklyn accent.*
   ----
5 *What's wrong with a Brooklyn accent.*
7 *Why don't you try a British accent?*

E x p l a n a t i o n

1 The scalar *$language* is assigned the value string "english". The name language is stored on the symbol table and a hard reference to its value *english*.
2 The scalar *$english* is assigned the string *Brooklyn*.
3 The value of *$language* is printed.
4 The variable *${$language}* is evaluated to *Brooklyn*. This is a symbolic reference. *$language*, one variable, is evaluated to *english*. The second dollar sign causes another variable, *$english*, to be evaluated to its underlying value *Brooklyn*. One variable has referenced another.
5 The value of the *$english* scalar is printed.
6 The *eval* function evaluates the statement as if in a separate little Perl program. The first dollar sign is escaped. *$language* will be evaluated to its value *english*. The literal dollar sign, prepended to the result of the evaluation, leaves *$english=British* as the statement.
7 After the *eval*, the value of *$english* is *British*. It is printed.

The strict Pragma. (Perl5) To protect yourself from inadvertently using symbolic references in a program, use the *strict* pragma with the refs argument This causes Perl to check that only hard references are used in the program. The previous example is re-executed using the *strict* pragma.

E x a m p l e   1 0 . 2

```
#!/bin/perl
# Program using symbolic references
1  use strict "refs";

   $language="english";  # hard reference
   $english="Brooklyn";

2  print "Your native tongue is $language. \n";

3  print "But you speak with a ${$language} accent.\n"; # symbolic reference
   print "------------------------\n";

   print qq/What's wrong with a  $english accent.\n/;


4  eval "\$$language=British ;";  # symbolic reference

   print "Why don't you try an $english accent? \n";
```

O u t p u t

```
2  Your native tongue is english.
3  Can't use string ("english") as a SCALAR ref while "strict refs" in use at symfile
   line 10
```

E x p l a n a t i o n

1 The *strict pragma* ensures that the program uses only hard references and if it doesn't, will abort during compilation and print an error message as shown in the output of this script.
3 This is line number 10 in the script. The program died at this point because of the first use of a symbolic reference, *${$language}*.
4 This line also includes a symbolic reference, but is never reached because the program had already aborted due to the use of the *strict* pragma.

Hard References

A hard reference is a scalar that holds the address of another data type. A variable that is assigned an address can also be called a pointer because it "points" to some other address or to another reference This type of reference can point to a scalar, array, associative array, or a subroutine. The pointer was introduced to Perl5 to give you the ability to create complex data types such as arrays of arrays, arrays of hashes, hashes of hashes, etc. In all of the examples where typeglobs were used, we can now opt for pointers instead. So this is yet another way to pass parameters to subroutines by reference.

The Backslash Operator. The backslash unary operator is used to create a hard reference similar to the & used in C to get the "address of". In the following example, *$p* is the reference. It is assigned the address of the scalar, $x.

$$p = \backslash \$x;$$

An example of hard references from the Perl man page *perlref*:

```
$scalarref = \$foo;        # reference to scalar $foo
$arrayref  = \@ARGV;       # reference to array @ARGV
$hashref   = \%ENV;        # reference to hash %ENV
$coderef   = \&handler;    # reference to subroutine handler
$globref   = \*STDOUT;     # reference to typeglob STDOUT
$reftoref  = \$scalarref;  # reference to another reference
                             (pointer to pointer, ugh)
```

Dereferencing the Pointer. If you print the value of the reference, you will see an address. If you want to go to that address and get the value stored there; i.e., dereference the pointer, the pointer must be prefaced by two "funny" symbols, one the dollar sign because the pointer itself is a scalar, and preceding that, the "funny" symbol representing the type of data it points to. When using more complex types, the arrow (infix) operator can be used.

Example 10.3

(The Script)
```
    #!/bin/perl
1   $num=5;
2   $p = \$num;
3   print 'The address assigned $p is ', $p, "\n";
4   print "The value stored at that address is $$p\n";
```

Output

```
3   The address assigned $p is SCALAR(0xb057c)
4   The value stored at that address is 5
```

Explanation

1   The scalar, *$num*, is assigned the value 5.
2   The scalar, *$p,* is assigned the address of *$num.* This is the function of the backslash operator. *$p* is called either a reference or a pointer. The terms are interchangeable.
3   The address stored in *$p* is printed. Perl also tells you the data type is SCALAR.
4   To dereference *$p,* another dollar sign is prepended to *$p.* This dollar sign tells Perl that you are looking for the value of the scalar that *$p* references, i.e. ,*$num.*

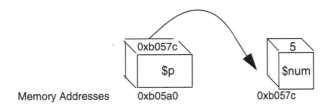

Memory Addresses   0xb05a0   0xb057c

Example 10.4

```
#!/bin/perl
1   @toys = ( Buzzlightyear, Woody, Thomas, Barney );
2   $num = @toys;
3   $ref1 = \$num;
4   $ref2 = \@toys;
5   print "There are $$ref1 toys.\n"; # dereference pointers
6   print "They are: @$ref2.\n";
7   print "His favorite toy is $$ref2[0].\n";
```

Output

5   *There are 4 toys.*
6   *They are: Buzzlightyear Woody Thomas Barney.*
7   *His favorite toy is Buzzlightyear.*

Explanation

1   The array, *@toys*, is assigned a list.
2   The array, @toys, is assigned to the scalar variable, *$num*, returning the number of elements in the array.
3   The reference, *$ref1*, is a scalar. It is assigned the address of the scalar *$num*. The backslash operator allows you to create the reference.
4   The reference, *$ref2*, is a scalar. It is assigned the address of the array *@toys.*
5   The reference is dereferenced, meaning: go to the address that *$ref1* is pointing to and print the value of the scalar stored there.
6   The reference is again dereferenced, meaning: go to the address that *$ref2* is pointing to, get the array, and print it.
7   Dereference the reference and get the first element of the array that it points to.

10.1.2 Passing Arrays by Reference

In the last chapter, the typeglob mechanism was used to pass parameters by reference. With Perl5, you can use hard references to do the same thing. Using references allows you to just pass an address rather that the whole array, which obviously saves space, if that's what you need to do.

E x a m p l e   1 0 . 5

(The Script)
```
    #!/bin/perl
    # Program passes the address of an array instead of the whole array.
1   print "Give me 5 numbers: ";
2   @n = split(' ', <STDIN>);
3   &params(\@n);   # Pass a reference
4   sub params{
5       my($arref) = shift;
6       print 'The values of the @arref array are', @$arref, "\n";
7       print "The first value is $$arref[0]\n";
8       print "The last value is ", pop(@$arref), "\n";
9       foreach $value(@$arref){
10          $value+=5;
11          print "The value is $value.\n";
        }
    }
    print "Back in main\n";
12  print "The new values are @n.\n";
```

O u t p u t

```
Give me 5 numbers: 1 2 3 4 5
The values of the @arref array are12345
The first value is 1
The last value is 5
The value is 6.
The value is 7.
The value is 8.
The value is 9.
Back in main
The new values are 6 7 8 9.
```

E x p l a n a t i o n

1   The user is asked for input.

2   The user input is split on whitespace and returned to the @*n* array.

3   The subroutine *params* is called. A reference for the @*n* array is passed as a parameter.

4   The *params* subroutine is defined.

5   In the subroutine, the @_ array is shifted once to the left. The shifted value is assigned to a local reference, *$arref*.

6   The reference is dereferenced, i.e., the values in the array are printed. The @ tells Perl that the reference is to an array.

7   The first element in the array is printed by dereferencing the *$arref* reference.

8   The last element of the array is popped via the reference.

9   The *foreach* loop assigns to scalar *$value*, in turn, each element of the pointed to by the *$arref* reference.

10 Each element of the array is incremented by 5 and stored in the scalar, *$value*.

11 The new values are printed.

12 The values printed illustrate that those values changed in the function by the reference changed the values in the @*n* array.

10.1.3   References and Anonymous Variables

It is not necessary to name a variable to create a reference to it. If a variable or subroutine has no name, it is called anonymous. If an anonymous variable (or subroutine) is assigned to a scalar, then the scalar is a reference to that variable (subroutine).

The **arrow operator** (->), also called the infix operator, is used to dereference the anonymous arrays, hashes, and subroutines. It is not really necessary but makes the program a lot more readable.

Anonymous Arrays

The anonymous array elements are enclosed in square brackets. These square brackets are not to be confused with the square brackets used to subscript an array. Here they are used as an expression to be assigned to a scalar. The brackets will not be interpolated if enclosed within quotes. The arrow (infix) operator is used to get the individual elements of the array.

E x a m p l e   1 0 . 6

(The Script)

```perl
#!/bin/perl
1  $arrayref = [ 'Woody', 'Buzz', 'Bo', 'Mr. Potato Head' ];
2  print "$arrayref->[3]", "\n";
3  print $$arrayref[3], "\n";        # All of these examples dereference $arrayref
4  print ${$arrayref}[3], "\n";
```

O u t p u t

2 *Mr. Potato Head*
3 *Mr. Potato Head*
4 *Mr. Potato Head*

E x p l a n a t i o n

1 The anonymous array elements are assigned to the array reference, *$arrayref*.
2 The fourth element of the array is printed. The arrow operator is not really needed here. Instead, the element could have been accessed by the last two methods in lines 3 and 4.

E x a m p l e   1 0 . 7

```
#!/bin/perl
# Program to demonstrate a reference to a list of lists.
1  $arrays = [ '1', '2', '3', [ 'red', 'blue', 'green' ]];
2  for($i=0;$i<3;$i++){
3       print $arrays->[$i],"\n";
   }

4  for($i=0;$i<3;$i++){
        print $arrays->[3]->[$i],"\n";
   }
```

O u t p u t

1
2
3
red
blue
green

E x p l a n a t i o n

1 *$arrays* is a reference to an four-element array that contains another anonymous three-element array whose elements are 'red', 'blue', and 'green'.
2 The *for* loop is used to get the values of the first array, consisting of elements 1, 2, and 3.
3 The arrow operator is used here to dereference *$arrays*.
4 The second *for* loop is used to iterate through the nested anonymous array. Since this array is the fourth element of the first array, starting at subscript 0, the first index is 3 and the second index references each of its elements.

E x a m p l e   1 0 . 8

(The Script)
```
   #!/bin/perl
   # Program to demonstrate a reference to a two-dimensional array.
1 $matrix = [ [ 0, 2, 4],
                 [ 4, 1, 32 ],
                 [12, 15, 17 ] ] ;

2 print "Row 3 column 2 is $matrix->[2][1].\n"
3 for($x=0;$x<3;$x++){
4        for($y=0;$y<3;$y++){
5              print "$matrix->[$x]->[$y] ";
         }
         print "\n";
  }
    print "\n";
6 $p=\$$matrix;          # Reference to a reference
7 print $$p->[1][2] "\n";
```

O u t p u t

```
5  Row 3 column 2 is 15.
   0 2 4
   4 1 32
   12 15 17

7  32
```

E x p l a n a t i o n

1 The reference *$matrix* is assigned an anonymous array of three anonymous arrays, i.e., a two-dimensional array.
2 The arrow operator is used to access the first element of the array. An arrow is implied between adjacent subscript brackets and is not needed. It could have been written as *$matrix->[2]->[1]*.
3 The outer *for* loop is entered. This will iterate through the rows of the array.
4 The inner *for* loop is entered. This loop iterates through the columns of the array.
5 Each of the elements of the two-dimensional array is printed via the reference.
6 *$p* is a reference assigned another reference, *$matrix*. This is like a pointer to a pointer.
7 If you want to access the array elements, that is dereference *$p*, an additional dollar sign is needed, one for *p* and one for *matrix*.

Anonymous Hashes

An anonymous hash is created by using curly braces. You can mix array and hash compos-
ers to produce complex data types. These braces are not the same braces that are used when
subscripting a hash. The anonymous hash is assigned to a scalar reference.

E x a m p l e   1 0 . 9

(The Script)
```
    #!/bin/perl
1   $hashref = { Name=>"Woody", Type=>"Cowboy" };
2   print $hashref->{Name}, "\n\n";
3   print keys %$hashref, "\n";
4   print values %$hashref, "\n";
```

O u t p u t

2 Woody

3 NameType
4 WoodyCowboy

E x p l a n a t i o n

1   The anonymous hash contains a set of key/value pairs enclosed in curly braces. The
    anonymous hash is assigned to the scalar *$hashref* reference.
2   The hash reference, *$hashref,* uses the arrow operator to dereference the hash. The key,
    Name, is associated with the value *,Woody.*
3   The *keys* function returns all the keys in the anonymous hash via the reference.
4   The *values* function returns all the values in the anonymous hash via the reference.

E x a m p l e   1 0 . 1 0

```
    #!/bin/perl
    # Program to demonstrate a hash containing anonymous hashes.
1   %students=(
2           Math=>{
                        Anna => 100,
                        Hao => 95,
                        Rita => 85,
            },
```

```
3               Science => {
                       Sam => 78,
                       Lou => 100,
                       Vijay =>98,
                },
        );
```

4 $hashref=\%students;   *# Reference to a hash*

5 print "Anna got **$hashref->{Math}->{Anna}** on the Math test.\n";
6 $hashref->{Science}{Lou}=90;

7 print "Lou's grade was changed to $hashref->{Science}{Lou}.\n";

O u t p u t

5 *Anna got 100 on the Math test.*
7 *Lou's grade was changed to 90*

E x p l a n a t i o n

1 The *%students* hash is defined. It consists of two hash keys, *Math*, and *Science*, whose values are themselves a hash (key/value pair).
2 *Math* is the key for its value, a nested hash.
3 *Science* is the key for its value, also a nested hash.
4 *$hashref* is assigned the address of the hash, *%students*. Note that the backslash operator is used to create the reference.
5 To access Anna's grade, first the key *Math* is dereferenced, followed by the arrow operator and the nested key *Anna*. The second arrow is not necessary, but may make the construct easier to follow. In fact, you don't need to use the arrow operator at all. This could have been written: *$$hashref{Math}{Anna}*.
6 Using the *$hashref* reference, you can also change or add new values to the *%science* hash. Lou's grade is changed.
7 The new grade is printed by dereferencing *$hashref*.

Anonymous Subroutines
An anonymous subroutine is created by using the keyword *sub* without a subroutine name. The expression is terminated with a semi-colon.

Example 10.11

(The Script)
```
    #!/bin/perl
1   $subref = sub { print @_ ; };
2   &$subref(a,b,c);
    print "\n";
```

Output

1 abc

Explanation

1 The scalar, *$subref*, is assigned an anonymous subroutine by reference. The only func-
   tion of the subroutine is to print its arguments stored in the @_ array.
2 The subroutine is called via its reference and passed three arguments.

Filehandle References
One of the only ways to pass a filehandle to a subroutine is by reference. You can use typeglob to create an alias for the filehandle and then use the backslash to create a reference to
the typeglob. Wow…

Example 10.12

(The Script)
```
    #!/bin/perl
1   open(README, "/etc/passwd") || die;

2   &readit(\*README); # reference to a typeglob

3   sub readit {
4        my ($passwd)=@__;
5        print "\$passwd is a $passwd.\n";
6        while(<$passwd>){
7             print;
         }
8        close($passwd);
     }

9   seek(README,0,0) || die "seek: $!\n";
```

O u t p u t

5 *$passwd is a GLOB(0xb0594).*
7 *root:x:0:1:Super-User:/:/usr/bin/csh*
   daemon:x:1:1::/:
   bin:x:2:2::/usr/bin:
   sys:x:3:3::/:
   adm:x:4:4:Admin:/var/adm:
   lp:x:71:8:Line Printer Admin:/usr/spool/lp:
   smtp:x:0:0:Mail Daemon User:/:
   uucp:x:5:5:uucp Admin:/usr/lib/uucp:
   nuucp:x:9:9:uucp Admin:/var/spool/uucppublic:/usr/lib/uucp/uucico
   listen:x:37:4:Network Admin:/usr/net/nls:
   nobody:x:60001:60001:Nobody:/:
   noaccess:x:60002:60002:No Access User:/:
   nobody4:x:65534:65534:SunOS 4.x Nobody:/:
   ellie:x:9496:40:Ellie Quigley:/home/ellie:/usr/bin/csh
9 **seek: Bad file number**

E x p l a n a t i o n

1 The "/etc/passwd" file is attached to the README filehandle and opened for reading.
2 The *readit* subroutine is called. The filehandle is passed by creating a reference to a glob. First the filehandle symbol is globbed with the asterisk. Then the reference to the glob is created by prefixing the glob with a backslash.
3 The *readit* subroutine is defined.
4 The @_ variable contains the reference.   It is assigned to a local scalar variable called *$passwd*. *$passwd* is a reference to the filehandle.
5 The reference, *$passwd*, when printed, shows that it contains the address of a typeglob (alias).
6 The expression in the *while* loop causes a line to be read from the "/etc/passwd" file and assigned to the $_ variable. The line is printed to the screen. The loop will continue until all the lines have been read and printed.
7 The filehandle is closed via the reference. This is probably not a good idea, if the program still wants access to the file without having to reopen it. This is done just to show that the reference is really dealing with the real filehandle.
8 When the subroutine exits, and the program continues execution, the filehandle, README, is no longer available. It was closed via the reference. Now, in order to read from the filehandle, it must be reopened. The *seek* function failed.

10.1.4   The ref Function

The *ref* function is used to test for a reference. It returns true if its argument is a reference and the null string if not. The value returned is the type of the thing being referenced. Types that can be returned are:

```
REF
SCALAR
ARRAY
HASH
CODE
GLOB
```

E x a m p l e   1 0 . 1 3

(The Script)
```
    #!/bin/perl
1  sub gifts;  # Forward declaration
2  $num = 5;
3  $junk = "xxx";
4  @toys = qw/ Budlightyear Woody Thomas/ ;
5  gifts( \$num, \@toys, $junk );
6  sub gifts {
7      my( $n, $t, $j) = @_;
8      print "\$n is a reference.\n" if ref($n);
       print "\$t is a reference.\n" if ref($t);
9      print "\$j is a not a reference.\n" if ref($j);
10     printf"\$t is a reference to an %s.\n", ref($t);
   }
```

O u t p u t

```
8   $n is a reference.
    $t is a reference.
9
10  $t is a reference to an ARRAY
```

Explanation

1   The subroutine, *gifts*, is a forward declaration, allowing Perl to know it is a subroutine defined somewhere in the program. You will not need an ampersand to call the subroutine if it is declared before it is defined.

2   The scalar, *$num*, is assigned 5.

3   The scalar *$junk* is assigned the string "xxx".

4   The array *@toys* is assigned a list with the *qw* construct.

5   The subroutine *gifts* is called. The first two variables are passed as references by preceding them with a backslash and the last variable, *$junk* is not passed as a reference.

6   The subroutine *gifts* is defined.

7   The values assigned to the *@_* array, in this case, two references (addresses) and one non-reference, will be assigned to *$n, $t*, and *$j*, respectively, and made local with the *my* function.

8   The *ref* function is called with a reference, *$n*, as its argument. The line will be printed only if the variable *$n* is a reference.

9   *$j* is not a reference. The return value for the *ref* function is null.

10   The *printf* function prints the value of what is returned from *ref*, the name of the type the reference points to.

11

Bless Those Things!
(Object-Oriented Perl5)

11.1 The OOP Paradigm

11.1.1 Packages and Modules Revisited

The big addition to Perl5 is the ability to do object-oriented programming, called OOP for short. OOP is centered around the way a program is organized. The program is designed to encapsulate (hide) the data and the functions that manipulate that data into classes. This is not really a new idea for Perl since data is already encapsulated in packages. If you recall, in our short discussion of packages, a package gives a sense of privacy to your program. Each package has its own symbol table, a hash that contains all the names in the "current" package. This makes it possible to create variables and subroutines that have their own namespace and thus protects the accidental clobbering of other variables of the same name in the program. The idea of hiding data in packages then is inherently part of Perl and is also one of the basic tenants of object-oriented programming. Every Perl program has at least one package called main where Perl statements are internally compiled.

The standard Perl library consists of a number of files, all of which contain packages. The notion of modules was introduced in Perl5. A module is really just a fancy package that is reusable. The reuse of code is done through inheritance; i.e., a package can inherit characteristics from a parent package and thus extend or restrict its own capabilities. The ability to extend the functionality of a class is called polymorphism. Along with hiding data (encapsulation), inheritance and polymorphism are considered the other basic tenants of the object-oriented philosophy.

To create a Perl module, you still use the *package* keyword and the scope is from the declaration of the package to the end of the block. Packages normally are the size of one file and can be stored in libraries. The files can be recognized as modules if their names end with a .pm extension and if the first letter of the module is capitalized. Pragmas are another special kind of module (the name is spelled in lowercase but still has the *.pm* extension) which directs the compiler to behave in a specified way. Whether the package is called a module or a pragma, it has some special features that differentiate it from an ordinary package. Those special features introduced in Perl5 give you the ability to model your programs with that kind of abstract thinking called object-oriented.

Tom Christianson, from his Web page called "Easy Perl5 Object Intro" says about Perl and objects, "Some people shy away from highly convenient Perl5 modules because they sometimes deal with objects...but some problems very much lend themselves to objects. This scares people. It shouldn't. There's a tremendous difference between merely knowing enough OO programming to merely use someone else's modules versus knowing enough to actually design and implement one yourself. People are afraid of having to be the latter just to get at the former. This is far from the case..." So, if you are not interested in writing programs that take advantage of the OOP features of Perl but still need to use Perl5 modules that do utilize objects, then you can skip to the end of this chapter and follow the examples provided there. (Section 11.6.)

11.1.2 Some Object-Oriented Lingo

Object-oriented programming is a huge subject. Thousands of books have been written on OOP programming, design, and methodology. Many programmers of the 90's have moved away from traditional top-down structured programming toward object-oriented programming languages for building complex software. This is not a book on object-oriented design or programming. However, there are some basic key words associated with OOP that should be mentioned before tackling Perl's OOP features. They are listed in Table 11.1.

TABLE 11.1   Key oop words

Word	Perl Meaning
Data encapsulation	hiding data and subroutines from the user, as in a package
Inheritance	the reuse of code, usually from a library where a package inherits from other packages
Polymorphism	literally "many forms" and specifically, the ability to extend the functionality of a class
Object	a referenced type that knows what class it belongs to
Method	a subroutine that manipulates objects.
Class	a package that contains objects and methods.
Constructor	a method that creates and initializes an object.
Destructor	a method that destroys an object.

11.2 Objects, Methods, and Classes

11.2.1 Classes and Privacy

A Perl class is just a package. The terms are interchangeable. But if you want to distinguish between the two terms, a class is a package containing special subroutines called methods that manipulate objects.

Since a class is really just a package, it has its own symbol table and yet the data or routines in one class can be accessed in another via the double colon (Perl5) or the single apostrophe (Perl4). Larry Wall says about privacy, "Perl does not patrol private/public borders within its modules--unlike other languages such as C++, Ada, and Modula-17, Perl isn't infatuated with enforced privacy...a Perl module would prefer that you stayed out of its living room because you weren't invited, not because it has a shotgun."[1] To keep variables private the *my* function is used. The *my* variables exist only within the innermost enclosing block, subroutine, eval or file. The *my* variables cannot be accessed from another package by using the double colon or single apostrophe because *my* variables are not related to any package; they are not stored on the symbol table of the package in which they are created.

Example 11.1

```
#!/bin/perl
1  package main;

2  $name = "Susan";
3  my $birthyear = 1942;

4  package nosy;
5  print "Hello $main::name.\n";
6  print "You were born in $main::birthyear?\n";
```

Output

```
5  Hello Susan.
6  You were born in ?
```

Explanation

1 The package is main.
2 The scalar, *$name,* is global in scope within this package.
3 The scalar, *$birthyear*, is local to this and any enclosing inner blocks.
4 The package *nosy* is declared. Its scope is from the declaration to the bottom of the file.
5 The global variable *$name* can be accessed by qualifying it with its package name and two colons.
6 The variable, *$birthyear,* is inaccessible to this package. It was declared with the *my* function in a different package, *main.*

11.3 Objects—Blessed References

To begin with, an object in Perl is created by using a hard reference. A reference, if you recall, is a scalar that holds the address of some variable. It's a pointer. A reference might also point to a variable or subroutine that has no name, called an anonymous variable. For example, here is a reference called "worker" to an anonymous hash:

$worker = { Name => "Tom", Salary => 25000 };

And to access a value in the anonymous hash, the reference *$worker* can be dereferenced by using the arrow operator as follows:

$worker->{Name}

To make a Perl object, first a reference is created. The reference normally is assigned the address of an anonymous hash (although it could be assigned the address of an array or scalar). The hash will contain the data members of the object. In addition to storing the address of the hash, the reference must know what package it belongs to. This is done by creating the reference and then "blessing" it into a package. The *bless* function blesses the "thing" being referenced into the package, not the reference itself. The following example (11.2) merely illustrates how to create an anonymous hash, bless it into a package, and then to use the *ref* function to see if it is truly in the package. The reason for doing this will become clearer as we move on.

The bless Function.

The *bless* function assigns the "thing" a reference points to into a package (also called a class). This is how an *object* is created. If the package is not listed as the second argument, the *bless* function makes the reference an object of the current package, i.e., the one in which it is created. It returns the reference. An object can be blessed into one class and then *reblessed* into another and then another, etc.

Format:
> bless REFERENCE, CLASSNAME
> bless REFERENCE

Example:
> $reference = { };
> bless($reference, $class);

E x a m p l e   1 1 . 2

```
#!/bin/perl
```
1 **package Employee;**

2 **$clerk**={ name=>"Tom",   # Anonymous hash
                salary=>25000,   # Holds the object's data
            };

3 **bless($clerk, Employee);**   # The hash referenced by $clerk is blessed into the
                                 # package

4 print "clerk is an ", **ref($clerk)**,".\n";   # ref returns the package name
5 print "The clerk's name is $clerk->{name}.\n";

O u t p u t

4 *clerk is an Employee*
5 *The clerk's name is Tom.*

E x p l a n a t i o n

1 The *Employee* package is declared.
2 A reference, *$clerk,* is assigned the address of an anonymous hash, consisting of two key/value pairs.
3 The *bless* function takes either one or two arguments. The first argument is the reference and the second argument is the name of the package. If the second argument is missing, the current package is assumed. In this example, the current package is called *Employee*. The second argument could have been left out. Now the reference "knows" that what it references (the object) is in the *Employee* package.
4 The *ref* function returns the name of the package if its argument has been "blessed".
5 The *$clerk* reference is dereferenced with the arrow operator.

11.4 Methods

11.4.1 Definition

A *method* is a subroutine that belongs to a class and expects its first argument to be a reference to an object or a package name. There are two types of methods: class (or static) methods and instance (or virtual) methods.[2] The class method expects a class name as its first argument and the instance method expects an object reference as its first argument.

---

2. What you call a method type depends on what book you read. Larry Wall categorizes methods as class methods, instance methods and dual-nature methods.

11.4.2   Invoking Methods

A method can be invoked in two ways:

Class Method Invocation:
(Assuming the method name is called "new" and the object's reference is called "$ref")

    1) $ref = new class (list of arguments);
    2) $ref = class->new(list of arguments);[3]

Instance Method Invocation:
(Assuming the method name is called "display" and the object reference is called "$ref")

    1) display $ref (list of arguments);
    2) $ref->display(list of arguments);

    The first example for each method is called the *indirect syntax* and the second example, using the arrow operator, is called the *object-oriented syntax.*

11.4.3   The Class Method--Constructor

A constructor is an OOP term for a class method that creates and initializes an object into a class. There is no special syntax for a constructor. It is just a method that is used to get a reference blessed into a package. The first method in a Perl class (i.e., the first subroutine in a package) is the one that creates the reference (to the object) and blesses it into the package. This method is often called "new" since it makes a new "thing", but could be called anything you want such as "create", "construct", "initiate", etc. The object that is blessed in the "new" subroutine is usually an anonymous hash. The anonymous hash holds the data for the class which may or may not be initialized by the constructor method.

E x a m p l e   1 1 . 3

```
     #!/bin/perl
1    package Employee;   # class

2    sub new {      # class method called a constructor
3        my $class = shift;
4        my $worker={ Name=>undef,   # Values will be assigned later
                     Salary=>undef,
                };

5        bless($worker, $class);  # $worker now references an object in this
                                  # class
6        return $worker;   #The reference to the object is returned
     }
```

---

3. Could also use $ref=class::new (), or $ref=class:new, or you are not interested in the OO way.

```
7    package main;    #switch namespaces to main package

8    my $empref = new Employee;    # call the new method
9    # $ref = Employee->new();    another way to call the new method
10   $empref->{Name}="Dan Savage"; # Use the object
     $empref->{Salary}=75000;
11   print "\$empref in main belongs to class ", ref($empref),".\n";
12   print "Name is $empref->{Name}.\n";
13   print "Salary is $empref->{Salary}.\n";
```

O u t p u t

10 i$empref in main belongs to class Employee.

E x p l a n a t i o n

1   The package *Employee* is declared. It can be called a class because it contains a meth-
     od that will manipulate an object (anonymous hash).
2   The subroutine *new* is sometimes called a "constructor" in OOP lingo. The primary
     job of a constructor is to create and initialize an object. In Perl, it doesn't really have
     any special syntax. This is called a class method since its first argument is the name
     of the class it belongs to. It is a subroutine that blesses a referenced "thing" into a class
     and returns the reference. Since the subroutine blesses something, it can now be called
     a *method* and the "thing" it blessed is an *object*. The package is called a *class*.
3   The first argument received by this type of subroutine is the name of the package or
     class, in this case *Employee*. This is another difference between a method and a sub-
     routine. The first argument of a method is either the name of a class or an object.
4   The reference *$worker* is assigned the address of an anonymous hash. The keys are
     assigned *undef,* meaning the values at this time are undefined.
5   The reference, *$worker*, is blessed into the class, *$class*.
6   When this function is called, it will return a reference to the anonymous hash.
7   We now switch namespaces to package *main*.
8   The *new* method is called with the class/package name *Employee* as its first argument.
     It returns a reference, *$empref* which points to the anonymous hash, called an object.
9   This line is commented out. It demonstrates another way in which to invoke a method
     called the object-oriented syntax. Use either one.
10   A string value *Dan Savage* is assigned to the key *Name* in the associative array pointed
     to by the reference *$empref*, i.e., the object's data is being assigned a value.
11   The *ref* function returns the name of the package if the reference has been blessed into
     that class.
12   The *Name* value is accessed through the reference.
13   The *Salary* value is accessed through the reference.

11.4.4   The Class and Instance Methods

The class method, also called a static method, takes a class (package) name as its first argument. The *new* function is an example of a class method. It functions for the entire class, not just for a specific object. In the following example, the *new* method "blesses" a reference to an anonymous hash and returns the reference.

Object-oriented programs often use access functions to control the way the data is modified and displayed. Then if the data needs to be represented in a different way in one of the methods, the other methods need not be affected as long as the interface provided to the user remains the same. The instance methods in the following examples are used as access functions as they set and display the data members of the class. Instance methods take an object reference as their first argument.

Example 11.4

```
     #!/bin/perl
1    package Employee;

2    sub new{    # Class/Static method
3        my $class = shift;
4        my $worker={};   # Anonymous and empty hash

5        bless($worker);
6        return $worker;
     }
7    sub set_name{  # Instance/Virtual method
8        my $self = shift;
9        print "\$self is a class ", ref($self)," reference.\n";
10       $self->{Name} = shift;
     }
11   sub display_name {  #
12       my $self = shift;   # The object reference is the first argument
13       print $self->{Name},"\n";
     }
14   package main;

15   my $emp = new Employee;    # Call class method

16   set_name $emp("Tom Savage");   # Call instance method

17   display_name $emp;   # Call instance method
```

O u t p u t

9 *$self is a class Employee reference.*
13 *Tom Savage*

E x p l a n a t i o n

1 The package *Employee* is declared. This can also be called the class *Employee*.
2 The class method *new* is a constructor. It creates a reference and blesses it into the class *Employee*.
3 The *$class* variable is assigned the name of the class, the first argument in the new constructor.
4 The reference, *$worker,* is assigned an anonymous and empty hash.
5 The "thing" referenced by *$worker* is blessed into the class *Employee*.
6 The reference will be returned from the new method.
7 The instance access method, *set_name*, is defined.
8 The name of the object reference is shifted from the *@_* array into *$self*.
9 The return from *ref* is the name of the class *Employee*.
10 The second argument is shifted from the @_ array. "Tom Savage" is assigned as a value to the key *Name*.
11 The instance method *display_name* is called to print the value in *Name* field of the anonymous hash.
12 The object reference is the first argument to the method. It is shifted from the @_ array into *$self*.
13 The value in the key *Name* field is displayed.
14 Package *main* is declared.
15 The new constructor method is called and the reference to the object is returned, a reference to an anonymous hash in the *Employee* class.
16 The instance method, *set_name* is called. Its argument is "Tom Savage".
17 The *display* method is called, which displays the value of the anonymous hash, Thomas Savage.

11.4.5 Passing Parameters to Constructor Methods.

Any arguments passed to the constructor method are called *instance variables*. Instance variables are used to initialize the object when it is created. In this way, each time the object is created, it can be customized. Either an anonymous hash or an anonymous array is commonly used to hold the instance variables.

E x a m p l e   1 1 . 5

```perl
    #!/bin/perl
1   package Employee;
2   sub new{  # Constructor  method
3       my $class = shift;
4       my ($name, $salary) = @_;   # Instance variables

5       my $worker={Name=>$name,
                    Salary=>$salary,
                    };

6       bless($worker);
7       return $worker;
    }


8   sub display {               # An instance method
9       my $self = shift;       # The name of the object is passed
10      while( ($key, $value)=each %$self){
            print "$key: $value \n";
        }
    }
11  package main;

12  $emp = new Employee("Tom Savage", 250000);
    # Invoking the methods--two ways
13  display $emp;     # The indirect object syntax
14  $emp->display;  # The object-oriented syntax
```

O u t p u t

```
13  Name: Tom Savage
    Salary: 250000
14  Name: Tom Savage
    Salary: 250000
```

Explanation

1. The package *Employee* is declared.
2. The class method, *new*, is defined as a constructor.
3. The first argument to the class method is the name of the class (package).
4. The instance variables are created from the remainder of the argument list.
5. The address of an anonymous array is assigned to to the reference, *$worker*. The keys are hard coded and the values are supplied from the instance variables.
6. The "thing" that the reference, *$worker*, points to is blessed into the class.
7. The reference *$worker* will be returned when the method is called.
8. The subroutine, *display*, is an instance method. It is defined in this class.
9. The first argument to the instance method is the reference to the object.
10. The *while* loop is used with the *each* function to get both keys and values from the anonymous array (object) referenced by *$self*.
11. The package main is declared.
12. The *new* method is called with two arguments. The only request here is that the name value is the first argument and the salary value is the second argument. There is no error checking. The example simply shows how to pass arguments to a constructor. The value returned to *$emp* is a reference to the anonymous array.
13. The instance method is called using the indirect object syntax.
14. The instance method is called using the object-oriented syntax.

11.4.6 Passing Parameters to Instance Methods

The first argument to an instance method is the name of the object reference. This value is typically shifted from the @_ array and stored in a *my* variable called *$self* or *$this*, although it doesn't matter what you call the variable. The remaining arguments are then processed as they are in any regular subroutine.

Example 11.6

```
#!/bin/perl
# Program to demonstrate passing arguments to an instance method.
# When the method is called the user can select what he wants returned.
1 package Employee;

2 sub new{    # Constructor
        my $class = shift;
        my ($name, $salary, $extension) = @_;
        my $worker={Name=>$name,
                    Salary=>$salary,
                    Extension=>$extension,
                };
        bless($worker);
        return $worker;
```

```
  }
3 sub display {   # Instance method
4        my $self = shift;   # Object reference is the first argument
5        foreach $choice ( @__){
6                print "$choice: $self->{$choice}\n";
         }
  }
```

```
7   package main;
```

```
8   $emp = new Employee("Tom Savage", 250000, 5433);
```

```
9   $emp->display (Name, Extension);   # Passing arguments to instance method
```

O u t p u t

Name: Tom Savage
Extension: 5433

E x p l a n a t i o n

1 The package *Employee* is declared. Since this package deals with blessed references and methods, call it a class.
2 The *new* method is a constructor. It will bless an object referenced by *$worker* into the *Employee* class when called. *$worker* points to an anonymous array.
3 The instance method *display* is defined.
4 The first argument to the *display* instance method is a reference to an *Employee* object. It is shifted and returned to *$self.*
5 The *foreach* loop iterates through the remaining arguments in the @_ array, one at a time assigning each argument in turn to the variable *$choice*. The variable *$choice* is a key of the anonymous array.
6 The selected values from the associative array are printed.
7 The package *main* is declared.
8 The constructor method is called to create a new *Employee* object.
9 The instance method is called with arguments. The first argument received will be the name of the object's reference, *$emp*, and the rest of the arguments are in parentheses.

11.4.7   Destructors and Garbage Collection

Perl keeps track of the number of references to an object and when the count reaches 0, the object is automatically destroyed. When your program exits, Perl handles the garbage collection by destroying every object associated with the program and deallocating any memory that was used. So you don't have to worry about cleaning up memory.[4] However, you can define a DESTROY method in your program to get control of the object just before it goes away.

Example 11.7

```
    #!/bin/perl
1  package Employee;
    sub new{
        my $class = shift;
        $worker={Name=>undef,
                Salary=>undef,
                };
        bless($worker, $class);
        return $worker;}
```

```
2  sub DESTROY{
        my $self = shift;
3       print "$self->{Name}\n";
4       delete $self->{Name}; # Remove the (object);
5       print "Hash Name entry has been destroyed. Bailing out...\n" If ( ! exists
        $self->{Name});
    }
    }
```

```
6  package main;
7  $empref = new Employee;  # Create the object
    $empref->{Name}="Dan Savage";
    $empref->{Salary}=10000;
8  print "Name is $empref->{Name}.\n";
9  print "Salary is $empref->{Salary}.\n";
```

Output

```
8  Name is Dan Savage.
9  Salary is 10000.
3  Dan Savage
5  Hash Name entry has been destroyed. Bailing out...
```

Explanation

1 The *Employee* class is declared and its constructor method defined.
2 The DESTROY method is defined. This method is automatically called when the program ends. Since Perl destroys the objects anyway, this function is unnecessary. You might use it for debugging purposes.
3 The value for the *Name* key in the *Employee* hash is printed.

---

4. If you use self-referencing data structures, then you will be responsible for destroying those references.

4 The *Name* key and its associated value are released with *delete*. Its memory is freed for reuse.

5 This message is printed just before the program exits if the hash entry does not exist. Since the entry was deleted, the message is printed. The *exists* tests if the object exists.

6 Package *main* is declared.

7 The object reference *$empref* is created by calling the constructor method.

8 The value of the hash key, *Name*, is printed.

9 The value of the hash key, *Salary*, is printed.

11.5 Inheritance

Inheritance means that a new class can inherit methods from an existing class. The new class can then add to or modify existing code in order to customize the class without having to reinvent what has already been done. The principle is that a class may be subdivided into a number of sub classes that all share common features, but each subclass may provide its own additional features, refining what it borrows to a more specific functionality. The idea of this kind of organization is not new. You may have seen it in a biology class when learning about the plant and animal kingdoms and the breakdown of each phylum, kingdom, class, species, etc., or in procedural programs with the use of functions to combine the common elements of a program into specific tasks.

In object-oriented programming, once a class has been written and debugged, it can be stored in a library and reused by other programmers. The programmer can then add features and capabilities to the existing class without rewriting the whole thing. This is done through inheritance, that is, by deriving a new class from an already existing class. The reuse of software and the increased use of library classes where all this software is stored and organized have contributed to the wide popularity of OOP languages. Let's see how Perl implements inheritance.

11.5.1 The @ISA Array and Calling Methods

The classes (packages) listed in the @ISA array are the parent or base classes of the current class. This is how Perl implements inheritance. The @ISA array contains a list of packages where Perl will search for a method if it can't find it in the current package. If the method still isn't found, then Perl searches for an AUTOLOAD function and calls that method instead. And if that isn't found, then Perl searches for the last time in a special predefined package called UNIVERSAL. The UNIVERSAL class is a global base class for all packages, the highest class in the hierarchy of classes.

The @ISA array is not searched in a call to a normal subroutine, but in a call to a subroutine if it is called with the method invocation syntax.

E x a m p l e   1 1 . 8

```
#!/bin/perl
# Example of attempting inheritance without updating the @ISA array.
1  { package Grandpa;
2  $name = "Gramps";
3  sub greetme {
        print "Hi $Child::name I'm your $name from package Grandpa.\n";
   }

4  { package Parent;
   # This package is empty.
   }

5  {package Child;
6  $name = "Baby";
7  print "Hi I'm $name in the Child Package here.\n";
8  Parent->greetme();  # Use method invocation syntax
   }
```

O u t p u t

7 Hi I'm Baby in the Child Package here.
8 Can't locate object method "greetme" via package "Parent" at inher2 line 23.

E x p l a n a t i o n

1 The package *Grandpa* is declared.
2 The scalar *$name* is assigned "Gramps" in package *Grandpa*.
3 The subroutine *greetme* is defined and when called, the *print* statement will be executed. *$Child::name* refers to the scalar *$name* in the Child package.
4 The package *Parent* is declared. It is empty.
5 The package *Child* is declared. This package will try to call a method from another package. Although objects and methods aren't being used here, the purpose of this example is to show you what happens if you try to inherit a method from a class that this package doesn't know about.
6 Perl can't find the method *greetme* in package Parent and prints the error message.

E x a m p l e   11 . 9

```
#!/bin/perl
# Example of attempting inheritance by updating the @ISA array.
```
1 { **package Grandpa;**
```
$name = "Gramps";
sub greetme {
```
2   **print "Hi $Child::name I'm your $name from package Grandpa.\n";**
```
}
```

3 { **package Parent;**
4 **@ISA=qw(Grandpa);** # Grandpa is a package in the @ISA array.
```
# This package is empty.
}
```

5 {**package Child**;
```
$name = "Baby";
```
6 print "Hi I'm $name in the Child Package here.\n";
7 **Parent->greetme();** # Parent::greetme() will fail.
```
}
```

O u t p u t

Hi I'm Baby in the Child Package here.
Hi Baby I'm your Gramps from package Grandpa.

E x p l a n a t i o n

1 The package *Grandpa* is declared.
2 The subroutine *greetme* is defined and when called, the *print* statement will be executed. *$Child::name* refers to the scalar *$name* in the Child package.
3 The *Parent* package is declared.
4 The @ISA array is assigned the name of the package *Grandpa*. Now if a method is called from this *Child* package and Perl can't find it, it will try the *Grandpa* package listed in the @ISA array. If you try to call a normal subroutine without method invocation, Perl won't consult the @ISA array because it uses the @ISA array only when methods are being called. Even though the subroutines used here are not technically methods, by calling *greetme* as a class method, Perl will search the @ISA array.
5 The *Child* package is declared.
6 This line will be printed from the Child package.
7 The class method *greetme* is called in the *Parent* package. The @ISA array tells Perl to look in the *Grandpa* package if the method isn't in the Parent package.

11.5.2 $AUTOLOAD, sub AUTOLOAD, and UNIVERSAL

If a subroutine (or method) cannot be found in the current package or in the @ISA array, the AUTOLOAD function will be called. The $AUTOLOAD variable is assigned the name of the missing subroutine if it is used with the AUTOLOAD function. Arguments passed to the undefined subroutine are stored in the AUTOLOAD subroutine's @_ array. If you assign a function name to the $AUTOLOAD variable, that subroutine will be called if the AUTOLOAD subroutine is provided in place of the missing subroutine. If the $AUTO-LOAD variable is used with the AUTOLOAD subroutine, either the method or regular sub-routine syntax can be used. If all fails and Perl still can't find the subroutine, a final package called UNIVERSAL is searched for the missing method.

Example 11.10

```
    #!/bin/perl
1   {package Grandpa;
    $name = "Gramps";
    sub greetme {
2       print "Hi $Child::name I'm your $name from package Grandpa.\n";
    }
    }

3   {package Parent;
4     sub AUTOLOAD{
5       print "$_[0]: $_[1] and $_[2]\n";
6             print "You know us after all!\n";
7             print "The unheard of subroutine is called $AUTOLOAD.\n"
    };

8   {package Child;
9   $AUTOLOAD=Grandpa->greetme();
    $name = "Baby";
10  print "Hi I'm $name in the Child Package here.\n";
11  Parent->unknown("Mom", "Dad");   # undefined subroutine
    }
```

Output

2   *Hi I'm your Gramps from package Grandpa.*
10 *Hi I'm Baby in the Child Package here.*
5   *Parent: Mom and Dad*
6   *You know us after all!*
7   *The unheard of subroutine is called Parent::unknown.*

Explanation

1   The package *Grandpa* is declared. It contains one subroutine.
2   This line is printed from the *Grandpa* package.
3   The package *Parent* is declared. It contains an AUTOLOAD subroutine. An undefined
     subroutine is called on line 11. It has two arguments, "Mom", and "Dad". If Perl can't
     find this subroutine in the *Child* package, it will look in the @ISA array and if it is not
     there, Perl will look for an AUTOLOAD function.
4   The subroutine, AUTOLOAD, is defined.
5   Since this function was called as a class method, the first argument stored in the
     @_ array is the name of the class. The remaining arguments are "Mom" and "Dad".
6   This line is printed to show that we got here.
7   The $AUTOLOAD variable contains the value of the class and the unnamed subrou-
     tine.
8   The package *Child* is declared.
9   If the scalar variable $AUTOLOAD is assigned the name of a subroutine, Perl will au-
     tomatically call that subroutine.
10   This line is printed to show in what order the lines are executed.
11   The *Child* package wants to access a method in the *Parent* package. The *Parent* pack-
     age does not contain a method or subroutine called unknown. It does, on the other
     hand, contain an AUTOLOAD subroutine which will be executed because this subrou-
     tine can't be found.

Example 11.11

```perl
     #!/bin/perl
1    package Grandpa;
     $name = "Gramps";
     sub greetme {
2         print "Hi $Child::name I'm your $name from package Grandpa.\n";
     }

3    {package Parent;
          # This package is empty.
     }

4    {package Child;
     $name = "Baby";
5    print "Hi I'm $name in the Child Package here.\n";
6    Parent->greetme();
     }
```

```
7  package UNIVERSAL;
8  sub AUTOLOAD {
9      print "The UNIVERSAL lookup package.\n";
10     Grandpa->greetme();
   }
```

Output

2 *Hi I'm Baby in the Child Package here.*
9 *The UNIVERSAL lookup package.*
5 *Hi Baby I'm your Gramps from package Grandpa.*

Explanation

1 The package *Grandpa* is declared.
2 The subroutine *greetme* is defined in this package.
3 The package *Parent* is declared. It is empty.
4 The package *Child* is declared..
5 This line is printed to show the flow of execution in the program.
6 The *greetme* subroutine is called as one of the *Parent* package methods.
7 Since the method could not be found in its own class on the @ISA array, and an AUTO-
   LOAD function is not supplied in the *Parent* package, then Perl looks for package UNI-
   VERSAL as a last resort. Here the subroutine AUTOLOAD calls *greetme*.

11.5.3   Derived Classes

Inheritance is when one class can inherit methods from an existing class. The existing class
is called the base or parent class and the new class which inherits is called the derived or
child class. The base class has capabilities that all its derived classes inherit and the derived
class can then go beyond those capabilities. If a derived class inherits from one base class,
it is called single inheritance. For example, single inheritance in real life might be that a
child inherits his ability to draw from his father. If a derived class inherits from more than
one base class, this is called multiple inheritance. To continue the analogy, the child inherits
his ability to draw from his father and his ability to sing from his mother. In Perl, the derived
class inherits methods from its base class (package) and can add and modify these methods
when necessary.

The classes are inherited by putting them in the @ISA array and the methods to be
exported to other modules can be specified in either the @EXPORTER or the
@EXPORTER_OK arrays. The data itself is inherited by referencing keys and values in
the anonymous hash where the data was initially assigned. These variables are called
instance variables and are defined in the constructor method.

In the previous chapter, we saw modules from the Perl standard library and modules
which you could create yourself. In order to include a module or pragma into your program, the *use* function was called with the module name (minus the *.pm* extension). The

module had the ability to export symbols to other packages that might need to use the module. A special module called *Exporter.pm* handled the details for exporting and importing symbols between modules. This module also needs to be included in the @ISA array. If a module functions as a class, then its methods can be called without explicitly listing them in the @EXPORT array. Note in the following examples, the class method (new) and the instance method (*display*) are not exported.

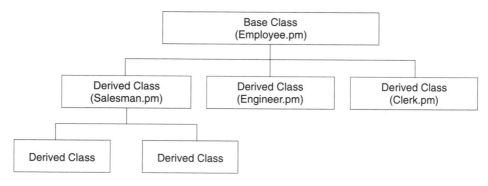

Inheritance Hierarchy

E x a m p l e   1 1 . 1 2

The Base Class:

```
1  $ cat Employee.pm
2  package Employee;  # Base class
3  @ISA = qw(Exporter);
4  require Exporter;

5  sub new {  # Constructor
6       my $class = shift;
7       my %params = @_;
8       my $self = {    Name=>$params{"Name"},
                        Address=>$params{"Address"},
                        Paycheck=>$params{"Paycheck"},
                };
9       bless ($self, $class);
   }
```

Explanation

1 At the shell prompt, the file Employee.pm is displayed. This file can be recognized as a Perl module because it ends with a .pm extension and the first letter of its name is uppercase.
2 The package is declared with the same name as the file, minus the extension. This is the base class. All employees have some common characteristics. In this example, they all have a name, an address, and a paycheck.
3 The @ISA array is updated to include the name of the Exporter module, a special Perl module that handles the semantics of importing and exporting of methods.
4 The Exporter module is loaded into the program.
5 The Employee constructor method is defined. It is called "new" by convention.
6 The name of the class will be shifted from the @_ array. This is a class method.
7 The rest of the parameters are stored in the hash *%params*.
8 The reference *$self* references an anonymous hash containing three keys and values which are provided from the argument list.
9 The object referenced by *$self* will be blessed into this class, Employee.

The Derived Class:

```
1   $ cat Salesman.pm
2   package Salesman;    # Derived class

3   require Exporter;
4   @ISA=qw(Exporter  Employee);
5   BEGIN{unshift(@INC, "./Baseclass");};

6   use Employee;

7   sub new {  # Constructor for the Salesman
        my $class = shift;
8       ($Name, $Address, $Basepay, $Commission ) = @_;
9       $Paycheck = &set_paycheck ( $Basepay, $Commission);
        # Not all employees get a commission
10      my $emp = new Employee ( Name=>$Name,
                                 Address=>$Address,
                                 Paycheck=>$Paycheck,
                               );
11      $emp->{Commission} = $Commission;  # Adding new properties
        $emp->{Basepay} = $Basepay;
12      bless ( $emp, $class );  # Rebless the object into this class
        }
```

```
13  sub set_paycheck {
        my ( $bp, $comm ) = @_;
        $pay = $bp + $comm;
14      return $pay;
    }

15  sub display{
        my $self = shift;
        print "\nSalesman's Statistics:\n";
16      foreach $key ( @_ ){
            print "$key: $self->{$key}\n";
            }
    }
```

Explanation

1   At the shell prompt, the contents of the file *Salesman.pm* are displayed.
2   The package (class) *Salesman* is declared.
3   The *Exporter* package is "required" for this package so that importing and exporting methods can be handled most efficiently. *Exporter.pm* is found in the standard Perl library.
4   The @ISA array contains the names of packages that will be used by this package. The Exporter and the Employee modules are two packages, base classes, that are needed by this Saleman module.
5   The BEGIN block is used to make sure the @INC array is updated at compile time so that it will be available in the search for the base classes. The *Employee.pm* module is located in a subdirectory called *Baseclass*.
6   The *use* function causes the *Employee* module to be loaded into the program.
7   The *Salesman* class defines a constructor method called *new*.
8   Arguments passed in are stored in the @_ and then assigned to the four scalars.
9   A call is made to the subroutine, *set_paycheck*.
10 The reference *$emp* in *Salesman* class is assigned the address of the anonymous hash by calling the *new* constructor from the base class, *Employee*. Values are obtained for the salesman and assigned to each of the keys. The *Employee* constructor creates the hash.
11 The derived class, *Salesman*, uses its reference $emp *to* add its own properties to the hash created by the *Employee* constructor.
12 The object that is referenced by *$emp* is now blessed into the *Salesman* class. Since it was first blessed into the base class, *Employee*, you can say it has been *reblessed* into the *Salesman* class.
13 The subroutine to calculate the paycheck is defined.

14   The pay has been calculated (this is not necessarily the way a salesman's commission is figured in, but it's just an example...) and is now returned from the function in the *$pay* variable.

15   The *display* method is defined. This is a instance method used to print out the keys and values in the hash for the *Salesman*.

16   The *foreach* loop iterates through the argument list, printing out each key and value referenced in the anonymous hash.

The Driver Program:

```
  #!/bin/perl
1 package main;

2 use Salesman;

3 print "Enter the salesman's name. ";
  chomp($name=<STDIN>);
4 print "Enter the salesman's address. ";
  chomp($address=<STDIN>);
5 print "Enter the salesman's basepay. ";
  chomp($basepay=<STDIN>);
6 print "Enter the salesman's commission. ";
  chomp($commission=<STDIN>);

7 $salesman = new Salesman ( $name, $address, $basepay, $commission );

8 $salesman->display( Name, Address, Paycheck );
```

O u t p u t

3   *Enter the salesman's name.* **Tommy Savage**
4   *Enter the salesman's address.* **1424 Hobart St.**
5   *Enter the salesman's basepay.* **55000**
6   *Enter the salesman's commission.* **3400**

8   *Salesman's Statistics:*

Name: Tommy Savage
Address: 1424 Hobart St.
Paycheck: 58400

E x p l a n a t i o n

1   This is package *main* of the driver program. The driver program will be using the *Salesman* module to create a new salesman employee. Even though the *Salesman* class was derived from the *Employee* class, this program doesn't have to know that. All this program needs to do is ask for the data and call the *Salesman* constructor with the correct arguments.

2   This line allows package *main* to use the *Salesman* module.

3   The user is asked for input in this and the next three lines

7   The constructor method for the *Salesman* module is called with the appropriate arguments. The arguments must be passed in the correct order when using this method. A reference to the new *Salesman* object is returned and assigned to *$salesman*.

8   The *Salesman* module's *display* method is called with selected arguments. The order and number of arguments can vary as long as the names passed are spelled correctly, since they represent the keys in the *Salesman* hash.

11.5.4   Multiple Inheritance

When a class inherits methods from more than one base or parent class, it is called multiple inheritance. In Perl, multiple inheritance is accomplished by adding more than one class to the @ISA array.

```
package  Child;
@ISA = qw ( Mother Father Teacher);
```

The search is depth-first so that Perl will search for classes in Mother and the hierarchy of classes it descends from, then Father and the hierarchy of classes it descends from, and finally Teacher and all its ancestors.

11.5.5   Overriding a Parent Method

There are times when two classes may have a method with the same name. If a derived class has a method with the same name as the base class, its method will take precedence over the base method. To override the method in the derived class so that you can access the method in the base class, the name of the method must be fully qualified with the class name and two colons.

Example 11.13

```perl
#!/bin/perl
1   package Employee;  # Base class
2   sub new {
        my $class = shift;
        my %params = @_;
        my $self = {  Name=>$params{"Name"},
                      Salary=>$params{"Salary"},
        };
        bless ($self, $class);
    }
3   sub display {  # Instance method
        my $self = shift;
4   #   print "The class using this display method is ", ref($self),"\n";
        foreach $key ( @  ){
5           print "$key: $self->{$key}\n";
        }
    }
```

```perl
5   package Salesman;  # Derived class
6   @ISA=qw (Exporter Employee);
7   sub new {   # Constructor in derived class
        my $class = shift;
        my (%parms) = @_;
8       my $self = new Employee(@_);  # Call constructor in base class
        $self->{Commission}=$parms{"Commission"},
        bless ( $self, $class );  # Rebless the object into the derived class
    }
    sub set_Salary {
        my $self = shift;
        $self->{Salary}=$self->{Salary} + $self->{Commission};
    }
9    sub display{  # Override method with subroutine
10      print "Stats for the Salesman\n";
        print "-" x 25, "\n";
11      Employee::display(@_);  # Access to the overridden method.
    }
    package main;
     $emp = new Salesman ( Name, "Tom Savage",
                           Salary, 50000,
                           Commission, 1500
                           );
     $emp->set_Salary;
12  $emp->display( Name, Salary);  # Call Salesman's display
```

O u t p u t

10 *Stats for the Salesman*

----

12 *Name: Tom Savage*
    Salary: 51500

E x p l a n a t i o n

1   The class *Employee* is declared. It contains a constructor method called *new* and an
     instance method called *display.*
2   The constructor method is defined.
3   The *display* method is defined.
4   The *Salesman* class is declared.
6   The @ISA array includes the names of the classes it needs: the *Exporter* class and the
     base class, *Employee*.
7   The constructor for the *Salesman* class is defined.
8   A reference is created in the *Salesman* class with the constructor from the base class,
     Employee.
9   This *display* subroutine takes precedence here in the derived class because it belongs
     to class *Salesman* and was called by using a reference to a *Salesman* object.
10   The printout is coming from the derived class (*Salesman*) subroutine, *display.*
11   By qualifying the name of the method to be of class *Employee*, this display method will
     override the current display method in package *Salesman.*
12   The *display* method is called. Since there is a *display* subroutine in this class, it is the
     one that will be called even though it is not an instance method, but merely a simple
     subroutine.

11.6 Using Objects from the Perl Library

In Chapter 9, we first looked into the standard Perl library that was provided with this distribution, Perl5.003. In that library there were a number of *.pl* and *.pm* files. The examples
covered dealt with packages that did not require knowledge about Perl's use of objects.
Those files utilized standard subroutines, not methods. Now that you know how objects and
methods are used in Perl, the following examples will demonstrate how to use those modules that require the OOP methodology.

11.6.1   Another Look at the Standard Perl Library

The @INC array contains the pathnames to the libraries Perl will search. After looking at
the library listings, we will *cd* into the standard Perl library and list the files found there.
You'll notice that some of the files end with the *.pm* extension and some end with the *.pl*
extension. The files that utilize objects (end in *.pm)* were introduced in Perl5 and are the
modules that support OOP programming. The files that do not have an extension are the

names of directories where Perl has stored modules that fit into that category. For example, the *File* and *Math* subdirectories contain modules that pertain to those respective subjects.

1 $ **perl -e 'print "@INC"'**
/opt/pkgs/perl/lib
/usr/dist/pkgs/perl,v5.003
/lib/sun4-solaris/5.003
/usr/dist/pkgs/perl,v5.003
/lib /usr/dist/pkgs/perl,v5.003
/lib/site_perl/sun4-solaris /usr/
dist/pkgs/perl,v5.003/lib/site_perl .

2 $ **cd /opt/pkgs/perl/lib**

3 $ **ls**

AnyDBM_File.pm	*POSIX.pm*	*chat2.inter*	*open2.pl*
AutoLoader.pm	*POSIX.pod*	*chat2.pl*	*open3.pl*
AutoSplit.pm	*Pod*	*complete.pl*	*overload.pm*
Benchmark.pm	*SDBM_File.pm*	*ctime.pl*	*perl5db.pl*
Carp.pm	*Safe.pm*	*diagnostics.pm*	*pod*
Cwd.pm	*Search*	*dotsh.pl*	*pwd.pl*
Devel	*SelectSaver.pm*	*dumpvar.pl*	*shellwords.pl*
DirHandle.pm	*SelfLoader.pm*	*exceptions.pl*	*sigtrap.pm*
DynaLoader.pm	*Shell.pm*	*fastcwd.pl*	*site_perl*
English.pm	*Socket.pm*	*find.pl*	*splain*
Env.pm	*Symbol.pm*	*finddepth.pl*	*stat.pl*
Exporter.pm	*Sys*	*flush.pl*	*strict.pm*
ExtUtils	*Term*	*ftp.pl*	*subs.pm*
Fcntl.pm	*Test*	*getcwd.pl*	*sun4-solaris*
File	*Text*		
getopt.pl	*sun4-sunos*		
FileCache.pm	*Tie*	*getopts.pl*	*syslog.pl*
FileHandle.pm	*Time*	*hostname.pl*	*tainted.pl*
Getopt	*abbrev.pl*	*i86pc-solaris*	*termcap.pl*
I18N	*assert.pl*	*importenv.pl*	*timelocal.pl*
IPC	*auto*	*integer.pm*	*validate.pl*
Math	*bigfloat.pl*	*less.pm*	*vars.pm*
NDBM_File.pm	*bigint.pl*	*lib.pm*	
Net	*bigrat.pl*	*look.pl*	
ODBM_File.pm	*cacheout.pl*	*newgetopt.pl*	

4 $ **cd Math**
   $ **ls**
   BigFloat.pm   *BigInt.pm*   *Complex.pm*

Explanation

1 The elements of the @INC array are printed to assure that the standard Perl library is
   included in Perl's library search path.
2 We go to the directory where the library modules are stored.
3 The library routines are listed.
4 Any file not ending in *.pl* or *.pm* is a subdirectory. We change to the *Math* subdirectory.
5 The contents of the directory are listed, showing three math modules.

11.6.2   An Object-Oriented Module from the Standard Perl Library

The following module, *BigFloat.pm*, allows the use of floating-point numbers of arbitrary
length. Number strings have the form /[+-]\d*\.?\d*E[+-]\d+/. When NaN is returned, it
means that a non-number was entered as input, that you tried to divide by zero, or that you
tried to take the square root of a negative number. BigFloat uses the *overload* module which
allows Perl's built-in operators to be assigned methods that will cause the operators to
behave in a new way. The operator is the key and the method assigned is the value. (See
overload.pm in the standard Perl library).

E x a m p l e   11 . 14

The File: **BigFloat.pm**

```
1 package Math::BigFloat;
2 use Math::BigInt;

  use Exporter;   # just for use to be happy
  @ISA = (Exporter);

3 use overload
4 '+'        =>      sub {new Math::BigFloat &fadd},
  '-'        =>      sub {new Math::BigFloat
                           $_[2]? fsub($_[1],${$_[0]}) : fsub(${$_[0]},$_[1])},
  '<=>'      =>      sub {new Math::BigFloat
                           $_[2]? fcmp($_[1],${$_[0]}) : fcmp(${$_[0]},$_[1])},
  'cmp'      =>      sub {new Math::BigFloat
                           $_[2]? ($_[1] cmp ${$_[0]}) : (${$_[0]} cmp $_[1])},
  '*'        =>      sub {new Math::BigFloat &fmul},
  '/'        =>      sub {new Math::BigFloat
                           $_[2]? scalar fdiv($_[1],${$_[0]}) :
                           scalar fdiv(${$_[0]},$_[1])},
  'neg'      =>      sub {new Math::BigFloat &fneg},
  'abs'      =>      sub {new Math::BigFloat &fabs},
```

```
    qw(
    ""      stringify
    0+      numify)          # Order of arguments unsignificant
    ;
```

5 **sub new** {
```
        my ($class) = shift;
        my ($foo) = fnorm(shift);
```
6
```
        panic("Not a number initialized to Math::BigFloat") if $foo eq "NaN";
```
7
```
        bless \$foo, $class;
    }
```

< Methods continue here. Module was too long to put here>
```
    # addition
```
8 **sub fadd** { #(fnum_str, fnum_str) return fnum_str
```
        local($x,$y) = (fnorm($_[$[]),fnorm($_[$[+1]));
        if ($x eq 'NaN' || $y eq 'NaN') {
            'NaN';
        } else {
            local($xm,$xe) = split('E',$x);
            local($ym,$ye) = split('E',$y);
            ($xm,$x e,$ym,$ye) = ($ym,$ye,$xm,$xe) if ($xe < $ye);
            &norm(Math::BigInt::badd($ym,$xm.('0' x ($xe-$ye))),$ye);
        }
    }
```

< Methods continue here>
```
    # divisionbb
    #   args are dividend, divisor, scale (optional)
    #   result has at most max(scale, length(dividend), length(divisor)) digits
```
9 **sub fdiv** #(fnum_str, fnum_str[,scale]) return fnum_str
```
    {
        local($x,$y,$scale) = (fnorm($_[$[]),fnorm($_[$[+1]),$_[$[+2]);
        if ($x eq 'NaN' || $y eq 'NaN' || $y eq '+0E+0') {
            'NaN';
        } else {
            local($xm,$xe) = split('E',$x);
            local($ym,$ye) = split('E',$y);
            $scale = $div_scale if (!$scale);
            $scale = length($xm)-1 if (length($xm)-1 > $scale);
            $scale = length($ym)-1 if (length($ym)-1 > $scale);
            $scale = $scale + length($ym) - length($xm);
            &norm(&round(Math::BigInt::bdiv($xm.('0' x $scale),$ym),$ym),
            $xe-$ye-$scale);
        }
    }
```

Explanation

1   The *BigFloat* class is declared. It resides in the *Math* subdirectory of the standard Perl library.

2   The *BigFloat* class also needs to use the *BigInt* module.

3   The *overload* function allows you to change the meaning of the built-in Perl operators. If, for example, you use the + operator, the + is a key and its value is an anonymous subroutine that creates an object and calls the *&fadd* subroutine.

4   The + operator is overloaded. See previous explanation.

5   This is *BigFloat*'s constructor method for creating an object.

6   If the value is not a number, this panic message is printed.

7   The object is blessed into the class.

8   This is the subroutine that performs addition on the object.

9   This is the subroutine that performs division on the object.

11.6.3   Using a Module with Objects from the Standard Perl Library

Example 11.15

```
1    $ export PERL5LIB="/opt/pkgs/perl/lib"
2    $ cat mymathprog

     #!/bin/perl
3    use Math::BigFloat;  # BigFloat.pm is in the Math directory

4    $number = "000.95671234e-21";
5    $mathref = new Math::BigFloat("$number");  # Create the object

6    print "\$mathref is in class ", ref($mathref), "\n"; # Where is the object

7    print $mathref->fnorm(), "\n";  # Use methods from the class

8    print "The sum of $mathref + 500 is: ", $mathref->fadd("500"),"\n";
9    print "Division using overloaded operator: ", $mathref / 200.5, "\n";
10   print "Division using fdiv method:", $mathref->fdiv("200.5"), "\n";

11   print "Enter a number ";
     chop($numstr = <STDIN>);

12   if ( $mathref->fadd($numstr) eq "NaN" ){ print "You didn't enter a num-
     ber.\n"};

     # Return value of Nan means the string is not a number ,or you divided by zero, or
     you took the square root of a negative number.
```

O u t p u t

6   *$mathref is in class Math::BigFloat*

7   *+95671234E-29*

8   *The sum of .0000000000000000000095671234 + 500 is:*
    +50000000000000000000000095671234E-29

9   *Division using overloaded operator:*
    .000000000000000000000004771632618453865336658354114713216957606

10 *Division using fdiv method:*
    +4771632618453865336658354114713216957606E-63

11 *Enter a number **hello***

12 *You didn't enter a number.*

E x p l a n a t i o n

1   At the shell prompt (Korn shell) the PERL5LIB environment variable is assigned the full path name of the standard Perl library. This updates the @INC array.

2   The contents of the program are displayed.

3   The *use* function loads the module *BigFloat.pm* into the program. Since this module is in a subdirectory of the library called *Math*, that subdirectory is included by prepending its name to the module with two colons.

4   A large number (e notation) is assigned to *$number.*

5   Now the methods from the module are utilized. The *BigFloat* constructor is called. A reference to the object is returned and assigned to *$mathref.*

6   The *ref* function returns the name of the class.

7   The *fnorm* method returns the "normal" value of *$number* in signed scientific notation. Leading zeros are stripped off.

8   The *fadd* method adds 500 to the number.

9   In this example an overloaded operator is used. The / operator is assigned a class method, *fdiv*, to perform the division. See code from *BigFloat.pm* shown above.

10 This time the *fdiv* method is called directly without using overloading to perform the division. The output is slightly different.

11 The user is asked to enter a number.

12 If NaN (not a number) is returned from the *fadd* method, the message is printed. This is a way you could check that user input is a valid numeric value.

12

Interfacing with the System

12.1 System Calls

Those migrating from Shell programming to Perl often expect that a Perl script is like a Shell script—just a sequence of UNIX commands. However, UNIX utilities are not accessed directly in Perl programs as they are in Shell scripts. Of course, to be effective there must be some way in which your Perl program can interface with the operating system. Perl has a set of functions, in fact, that specifically interfaces with the operating system and is directly related to the UNIX system calls so often found in C programs.

A *system call* requests some service from the operating system (kernel) such as getting the time of day, creating a new directory, removing a file, creating a new process, terminating a process, etc. A major group of system calls deals with the creation and termination of processes, how memory is allocated and released, and sending information (e.g., signals) to processes. Another function of system calls is related to the file system: file creation, reading and writing files, creating and removing directories, creating links, etc.[1]

The UNIX system calls are documented in Section 2 of the UNIX manual pages. Perl's system functions are almost identical in syntax and implementation. If a system call fails, it returns a -1 and sets the system's global variable, *errno,* to a value that contains the reason the error occurred. C programs use the *perror* function to obtain system errors stored in *errno*; Perl programs use the special $! variable. (See Section 12.5, "Error Handling.")

The following Perl functions allow you to perform a variety of calls to the system when you need to manipulate or obtain information about files or processes. If the system call you need is not provided by Perl, you can use Perl's *syscall* function, which takes a UNIX system call as an argument. (See Section 12.4.1, "The syscall Function.")

---

1. System calls are direct entries into the kernel, whereas library calls are functions that invoke system calls. Perl's system interface functions are named after their counterpart UNIX system calls in Section 2 of the UNIX manual pages.

12.2 Directories and Files

The most common type of file is a regular file. It contains data, an ordered sequence of bytes. The data can be text data or binary data. Information about the file is stored in a system data structure called an *inode*. The information in the inode consists of such attributes as the link count, the owner, the group, mode, size, last access time, last modification time, and type. The UNIX *ls* command lets you see the inode information for the files in your directory. This information is retrieved by the *stat* system call. Perl's *stat* function also gives you information about the file.

A directory is a specific file maintained by the UNIX kernel. It is composed of a list of filenames. Each filename has a corresponding number which points to the information about the file. The number, called an inode number, is a pointer to an inode. The inode contains information about the file as well as a pointer to the location of the file's data blocks on disk.

Directory Entry	
Inode #	Filename

The following functions allow you to manipulate directories, change permissions on files, create links, etc.

12.2.1 Making and Removing Directories

Creating a Directory

The mkdir Function

The *mkdir* function creates a new, empty directory with the specified permissions (mode). The permissions are set as an octal number. The entries for the . and .. directories are automatically created. The *mkdir* function returns 1 if successful and 0 if not. If *mkdir* fails, the system error is stored in Perl's $! variable.

Format:

```
mkdir(FILENAME, MODE);
```

Example 12.1

(The Command Line)
```
1  $ perl −e 'mkdir("joker", 0755)'
2  $ ls −ld joker
   drwxr−xr−x  2 ellie       512 Mar  7 13:43 joker
```

E x p l a n a t i o n

1   The first argument to the *mkdir* function is the name of the directory. The second argument specifies the *mode* or permissions of the file. The permissions, octal *0755*, specify that the file will have read, write, and execute permission for the owner, read and execute for the group, and read and execute for the others. (Remember that without execute permission, you cannot access a directory.)

2   The *ls -ld* command prints a long listing of the directory file with information about the file, the inode information. The leading 'd' is for directory, and the permissions are: *rwxr-xr-x*.

E x a m p l e   1 2 . 2

```
# This script is called "makeit"
1   die "$0 <directory name> " unless $#ARGV == 0;
2   mkdir ($ARGV[0], 0755 ) || die "mkdir: $ARGV[0]: $!\n";
```

(At The Command Line)
```
$ makeit
makeit <directory name> at makeit line 3.
$ makeit joker
makeit: joker: File exists
$ makeit cabinet
$ ls -d cabinet
cabinet
```

E x p l a n a t i o n

1   If the user doesn't provide a directory name as an argument to the script, the *die* function prints an error message and the script exits.

2   Unless the directory already exists, it will be created.

Removing a Directory

The rmdir Function
The *rmdir* function removes a directory, but only if it is empty.

Format:

```
rmdir(DIRECTORY);
rmdir DIRECTORY;
```

E x a m p l e   1 2 . 3

(At the Command LIne)
1 **$ perl –e 'rmdir("joke") II die "rmdir: $!\n"'**
   rmdir: Directory not empty
2 **$ perl –e 'rmdir("joker") II die "rmdir: $!\n"'**
   rmdir: No such file or directory

E x p l a n a t i o n

1 The directory, *joke*, contains files. It cannot be removed unless it is empty. The $! variable contains the system error, "Directory not empty".
2 The directory, *joker*, does not exist; therefore, it cannot be removed. The system error is stored in $!.

Changing Directories.   Each process has its own present working directory. When resolving relative path references, this is the starting place for the search path. If the calling process (e.g., your Perl script) changes the directory, it is changed only for that process, not the process that invoked it, normally the Shell. When the Perl program exits, the Shell returns with the same working directory it started with.

The chdir Function

The *chdir* function changes the current working directory. Without an argument, the directory is changed to the user's home directory. The function returns 1 if successful and 0 if not. The system error code is stored in Perl's $! variable.

Format:

```
chdir (EXPR);
chdir EXPR;
chdir;
```


E x a m p l e   1 2 . 4

1 **$ pwd**
   /home/jody/ellie
2 **$ perl –e 'chdir "/home/jody/ellie/perl"; print `pwd`"**
   /home/jody/ellie/perl
3 **$ pwd**
   /home/jody/ellie
4 **$ perl –e 'chdir " fooler" II die "Cannot cd to fooler: $!\n"'**
   Cannot cd to fooler: No such file or directory

E x p l a n a t i o n

1 This is the present working directory for the Shell.
2 The directory is changed to *home/jody/ellie/perl*. When the *pwd* command is enclosed in back quotes, command substitution is performed, and the present working directory for this process is printed.
3 Since the Perl program is a separate process invoked by the Shell, when Perl changes the present working directory, the directory is changed only while the Perl process is in execution. When Perl exits, the Shell returns and its directory is unchanged.
4 If the attempt to change the directory fails, the *die* function prints its message to the screen. The system error is stored in the $! variable and then printed.

Accessing a Directory via the Directory Filehandle.   The following Perl directory functions are modeled after the UNIX system calls sharing the same name. Although the traditional UNIX directory contained a two-byte inode number and a 14-byte filename (Figure 12.1), not all UNIX systems have the same format. The directory functions allow you to access the directory regardless of its internal structure.

FIGURE 12.1   A Directory

Inode	Filename
10	.
22	..
32	memo
45	mbox
23	notes
12	src

The opendir Function

The *opendir* function opens a named directory and attaches it to the directory filehandle. This filehandle has its own name space, separate from the other types of filehandles used for opening files and filters. The *opendir* function initializes the directory for processing by the related functions *readdir()*, *telldir()*, *seekdir()*, *rewinddir()*, and *closedir()*. The function returns 1 if successful.

Format:

```
opendir(DIRHANDLE, EXPR)
```

E x a m p l e   1 2 . 5

```
1 opendir(MYDIR, "joker");
```

E x p l a n a t i o n

1   The file *joker* is attached to the directory filehandle, MYDIR, and is opened for reading.
The directory, "joker", must exist and must be a directory. (See the example at the end
of this section.)

The readdir Function

A directory can be read by anyone who has read permission on the directory. You can't
write to the directory itself even if you have write permission. The write permission on a
directory means that you can create and remove files from within the directory, not alter the
directory data structure itself.

When we speak about reading a directory with the *readdir* function, we are talking about
looking at the contents of the directory structure maintained by the system. If the *opendir*
function opened the directory, in a scalar context, *readdir* returns the next directory entry.
The *readdir* function returns the <u>next</u> directory entry. In an array context, it returns the rest
of the entries in the directory.

Format:

```
readdir(DIRHANDLE);
readdir DIRHANDLE;
```

The rewinddir Function

The *rewinddir* function sets the position of DIRHANDLE back to the beginning of the
directory opened by *opendir*. It is not supported on all machines.

Format:

```
rewinddir(DIRHANDLE);
rewinddir DIRHANDLE;
```

The closedir Function

The *closedir* function closes the directory that was opened by the *opendir* function.

Format:

```
closedir (DIRHANDLE);
closedir DIRHANDLE;
```

E x a m p l e   1 2 . 6

(The Script)
```
1 opendir(DIR, "..") || die "Can't open: $!\n";   #open parent directory
2         @parentfiles=readdir(DIR);   #gets a list of the directory contents
3 closedir(DIR);   #closes the  filehandle
4 foreach $file ( @parentfiles )   # prints each element of the array
      { print "$file\n";}
```

O u t p u t

```
.

..

filea
fileb
filec
.sh_history
stories
```

E x p l a n a t i o n

1   The *opendiro* function opens the directory structure and assigns it to DIR, the directory filehandle. The .. (parent) directory is opened for reading.
2   The *readdir* function assigns all the rest of the entries in the directory to the array *@parentfiles*.
3   The *closedir* function closes the directory.
4   The files are printed in the order they are stored in the directory structure. This may not be the order that the *ls* command prints out the files.

The telldir Function

The *telldir* function returns the current position of the *readdir()* routines on the directory filehandle. The value returned by *telldir* may be given to *seekdir()* to access a particular location in a directory.

Format:

```
telldir(DIRHANDLE);
```

The seekdir Function

The *seekdir* sets the current position for *readdir()* on the directory filehandle. The position is set by the a value returned by *telldir()*.

Format:

```
seekdir(DIRHANDLE, POS);
```

E x a m p l e   1 2 . 7

(The Script)
```
1  opendir(DIR, ".");  # opens the current directory
2  while( $myfile=readdir(DIR) ){
3          $spot=telldir(DIR);
4          if ( "$myfile" eq ".login" ) {
                   print "$myfile\n";
                   last;
           }
   }
5  rewinddir(DIR);

6  seekdir(DIR, $spot);
7  $myfile=readdir(DIR);
   print "$myfile\n";
```

O u t p u t

```
.login
.cshrc
```

E x p l a n a t i o n

1 The *opendir* function opens the present working directory for reading.
2 The *while* statement is executed, and the *readdir* function returns the next directory entry from the directory filehandle and assigns the file to the scalar, *$myfile*.
3 After the *readdir* function reads a file name, the *telldir* function marks the location of that read and stores the location in the scalar, *$spot*.
4 When the *.login* file is read, the loop is exited.
5 The *rewinddir* function resets the position of the DIR filehandle to the beginning of the directory structure.
6 The *seekdir* function uses the results of the *telldir* function to set the current position for the *readdir* function on the DIR filehandle.
7 The next directory entry is read by the *readdir* function and assigned to the scalar, *$myfile*.

12.2.2 Permissions and Ownership

There is one owner for every UNIX file. The one benefit the owner has over everyone else is the ability to change the permissions on the file, thus controlling who can do what to the file. A group may have a number of members, and the owner of the file may change the group permissions on a file so that the group will enjoy special privileges.

Every UNIX file has a set of permissions associated with it to control who can read, write, or execute the file. There are a total of 9 bits that constitute the permissions on a file. The first 3 bits control the permissions of the owner of the file, the second set controls the permissions of the group, and the last set controls the rest of the world, e.g., everyone else. The permissions are stored in the *mode* field of the file's inode.

The chmod Function. The *chmod* function changes permissions on a list of files. The user must own the files to change permissions on them.[2] The files must be quoted strings. The first element of the list is the numeric octal value for the new mode. (Today the binary/ octal notation has been replaced for a more convenient mnemonic method for changing permissions. Perl does not use the new method.)

Table 12.1 illustrates the eight possible combinations of numbers used for changing permissions if you are not familiar with this method.

TABLE 12.1   Permission Modes

Octal	Binary	Permissions	Meaning
0	000	none	All turned off
1	001	--x	Execute
2	010	-w-	Write
3	011	-wx	Write, execute
4	100	r--	Read
5	101	r-x	Read, execute
6	110	rw-	Read, write
7	111	rwx	Read, write, execute

Make sure the first digit is a *0* to indicate an octal number. Do not use the mnemonic mode (e.g., +rx, because all the permissions will be turned off).

The *chmod* function returns the number of files that were changed.

Format:

```
chmod(LIST);
chmod LIST;
```

---

2. The caller's effective id must match the owner's userid of the file, or the owner must be superuser.

Example 12.8

1 $ perl –e '$count=**chmod 0755, "foo.p", "boo.p"** ;print "$count files changed.\n"'
2 *2 files changed.*
3 $ **ls –l foo.p boo.p**
   –rwxr–xr–x 1 ellie   0 Mar 7 12:52 boo.p*
   –rwxr–xr–x 1 ellie   0 Mar 7 12:52 foo.p*

Explanation

1 The first argument is the octal value *0755*. It turns on rwx for the user, r and x for the group and others. The next two arguments, "foo.p" and "boo.p", are the files affected by the change. The scalar, *$count*, contains the number of files that were changed.
2 The value of *$count* is *2* because both files were changed to *0755*.
3 The output of the UNIX, *ls -l*, command is printed, demonstrating that the permissions on files *foo.p* and *boo.p* have been changed to *0755*.

The chown Function.   The *chown* function changes the owner and group of a list of files. Only the owner or superuser can invoke it.[3] The first two elements of the list must be a numerical *uid* and *gid*. Each authorized UNIX user is assigned a *uid*, user identification number, and a *gid*, group identification number in the password file.[4] The function returns the number of files successfully changed.

Format:

```
chown(LIST);
chown LIST;
```

Example 12.9

(The Script)
1 $ uid=9496;
2 $ gid=40;
3 **$number=chown($uid, $gid, 'foo.p', 'boo.p');**
4 print "The number of files changed is $number\.n";

Output

4 *The number of files changed is 2.*

---

3. On BSD UNIX only the superuser can change ownership.
4. To get the uid or gid for a user, the *getpwnam* or *getpwuid* functions can be used.

Explanation

1   The user identification number, 9496, is assigned.
2   The group identification number, 40, is assigned.
3   The *chown* function changes the ownership on files "foo.p" and "boo.p" and returns the number of files changed.

The umask Function.   When a file is created it has a certain set of permissions by default. The permissions are determined by what is called the system mask. On most systems this mask is *022* set by the login program.[5] A directory has *777* by default (rwxrwxrwx) and a file has *666* by default (rw-rw-rw). The *umask* function is used to remove or subtract permissions from the existing mask.

To take *write* permission away from the "others", the umask value is subtracted from the maximum permissions allowed per directory or file:

777 (directory)	666 (file)
-002 (umask value)	-002 (umask value)
775	664

The *umask* function sets the umask for this process and returns the old one. Without an argument, the *umask* function returns the current setting.

Format:

```
umask(EXPR)
umask EXPR
umask
```

Example 12.10

1   **$ perl -e 'printf("The umask is %o.\n", umask);'**
    The umask is 22.
2   **$ perl -e 'umask 027; printf("The new mask is %o.\n", umask);'**
    The new mask is 27.

Explanation

1   The *umask* function without an argument prints the current *umask* value.
2   The *umask* function resets the mask to octal 027.

---

5.   The user can also set the umask in the .profile (sh or ksh) or .cshrc (csh) initialization files.

12.2.3 Hard and Soft Links

When you create a file it has one *hard* link, one entry in the directory. You can create additional links to the file, which are really just different names for the same file. The kernel keeps track of how many links a file has in the file's inode. As long as there is a link to the file, its data blocks will not be released to the system. The advantage to having a file with multiple names is that there is only one set of data or master file and that file can be accessed by a number of different names. A hard link cannot span file systems and must exist at link creation time.

A soft link is also called a *symbolic* link and sometimes a *symlink*. A symbolic link is really just a very small file (it has permissions, ownership, size, etc.). All it contains is the name of another file. When accessing a file that has a symbolic link, the kernel is pointed to the name of the file contained in the symbolic link. For example, a link from *thisfile* to */usr/bin/joking/otherfile* links the name *thisfile* to */usr/bin/joking/otherfile*. When *thisfile* is opened, *otherfile* is the file really accessed. Symbolic links can refer to files that do or don't exist and they can span file systems and even different computers. They can also point to other symbolic links.[6]

The link and unlink Functions.   The *link* function creates a hard link (i.e., two files that have the same name). The first argument to the link function is the name of an existing file; the second argument is the name of the new file (cannot previously exist) to be linked. Only the superuser can create a link that points to a directory. Use *rmdir* when removing a directory.

Format:

        link(OLDFILENAME, NEWFILENAME);

E x a m p l e   1 2 . 1 1

```
1  $ perl -e 'link("dodo", "newdodo");'
2  $ ls -li dodo newdodo
   142726 -rw-r-r- 2 ellie      0 Mar  7 13:46 dodo
   142726 -rw-r-r- 2 ellie      0 Mar  7 13:46 newdodo
```

E x p l a n a t i o n

1 The old file "*dodo*" is given an alternate name, "*newdodo*".
2 The *i* option to the *ls* command gives the inode number of the file. If the inode numbers are the same, the files are the same. The old file, *dodo*, started with one link. The link count is now two. Since *dodo* and *newdodo* are linked they are the same file, and changing one will then change the other. If one link is removed, the other still exists. To remove a file, all hard links to it must be removed.

---

6. Symbolic links originated in BSD and are supported under many ATT systems. They may not be supported on your system.

The *unlink* function deletes a list of files, like the UNIX *rm* command. If the file has more than one link, the link count is dropped by one. The function returns the number of files successfully deleted. To remove a directory, use the *rmdir* function, since only the superuser can unlink a directory with the *unlink* function.

Format:

```
unlink (LIST);
unlink  LIST;
```

E x a m p l e   1 2 . 1 2

(The Script)
```
1  unlink('a','b','c') || die "remove: $!\n";
2  $count=unlink <*.c>;
   print "The number of files removed was $count\n";
```

E x p l a n a t i o n

1   The files *a, b,* and *c* are removed.
2   Any files ending in *.c* (C source files) are removed. The number of files removed is stored in the scalar, *$count*.

The symlink and readlink Functions.   The *symlink* function creates a symbolic link. The symbolic link file is the name of the file that is accessed if the old filename is referenced.

Format:

```
symlink(OLDFILE, NEWFILE)
```

E x a m p l e   1 2 . 1 3

```
1  $ perl -e 'symlink("/home/jody/test/old", "new");'
2  $ ls -ld new
   lrwxrwxrwx  1 ellie   8 Feb 21 17:32 new  -> /home/jody/test/old
```

E x p l a n a t i o n

1   The *symlink* function creates a new filename, "new", linked to the old filename, */home/jody/test/old*.
2   The *ls-ld* command lists the symbolically linked file. The symbol *->* points to the new filename. The 'l' preceding the permissions also indicates a symbolic link file.

The *readlink* function returns the value of the symbolic link and is undefined if the file is not a symbolic link.

Format:

```
readlink(SYMBOLIC_LINK);
readlink SYMBOLIC_LINK;
```

E x a m p l e   1 2 . 1 4

1 **$ perl -e 'readlink("new")'**;
  /home/jody/test/old

E x p l a n a t i o n

1 The file *new* is a symbolic link. It points to */home/jody/test/old*, the value returned by the *readlink* function.

12.2.4   Renaming Files

The rename Function.   The *rename* function changes the name of the file, like the UNIX *mv* command. The effect is to create a new link to an existing file and then delete the existing file. The *rename* function returns 1 for success and returns 0 for failure. This function does not work across filesystem boundaries. If a file with the new name already exists, its contents will be destroyed.

Format:

```
rename(OLDFILENAME, NEWFILENAME);
```

E x a m p l e   1 2 . 1 5

1 **rename ("tmp", "datafile");**

E x p l a n a t i o n

1 The file, *tmp*, is renamed *datafile*. If *datafile* already exists, its contents are destroyed.

12.2.5   Changing Access and Modification Times

The utime Function

The *utime* function changes the access and modification times on each file in a list of files, like the UNIX *touch* command. The first two elements of the list must be the numerical access and modification times, in that order. The *time* function feeds the current time to the *utime* function. The function returns the number of files successfully changed. The inode modification time of each file in the list is set to the current time.

Format:

```
utime (LIST);
utime LIST;
```

Example 12.16

(The Script)
```
1   print "What file will you touch (either create or change time stamp)? ";
    chop($myfile=<STDIN>);
2   $now=time;  # This example makes the file if it doesn't exist.
3   utime( $now, $now, $myfile) || open(TMP,">>$myfile");7
```

(The Command Line)
```
$ ls -l brandnewfile
brandnewfile: No such file or directory

$ update.p
1   What file will you touch ( either create or update time stamp) ? brandnewfile

$ ls -l brandnewfile
2   -rw-r--r--  1  ellie      0 Mar   6  17:13 brandnewfile
```

Explanation

1   The user will enter the name of a file either to update the access and modification times or, if the file does not exist, to create it.
2   The variable, *$now*, is set to the return value of the *time* function, the number of non-leap seconds since January 1, 1970, UTC.
3   The first argument to *$now* is the access time, the second argument is the modification time, and the third argument is the file affected. If the *utime* function fails because the file does not exist, the *open* function will create the file, using TMP as the filehandle, emulating the UNIX *touch* command.

---

7. Larry Wall, *Programming Perl* (Sebastopol, CA: O'Reilly).

12.2.6 File Statistics

The information for a file is stored in a data structure called an inode, maintained by the kernel. For UNIX users, much of this information is retrieved with the *ls* command. In C and Perl programs, this information may be retrieved directly from the inode with the *stat* function.

The stat and lstat Functions.   The *stat* function returns a 13-element array containing statistics retrieved from the file's inode.The last two fields, dealing with blocks, are defined only on BSD UNIX systems.[8]

The *lstat* function is like the *stat* function, but if the file is a symbolic link, *lstat* returns information about the link itself rather than about the file that it references. If your system does not support symbolic links, a normal *stat* is done.

The 13-element array returned, contains the following elements. (The order is a little different from the UNIX system call, *stat.*)

The special *underscore* file handle is used to provide *stat* information from the file most previously *stat*'ed. This information is stored in the *stat* structure as follows:

device number
inode number
mode
link count
user id
group id
for a special file, the device number of the device it refers to
size in bytes, for regular files
time of last access
time of the last modification
time of last file status change
preferred I/O block size for file system
actual number of 512 byte blocks allocated

Format:

```
stat(FILEHANDLE);
stat FILEHANDLE;
stat(EXPR);
```

---

8. Ibid., p. 188.

E x a m p l e   1 2 . 1 7

(The Script)
```
1   open(MYFILE, "perl1") || die "Can't open: !$\n";
2   @statistics=stat(MYFILE);
3   print "@statistics\n";
    close MYFILE;

4   @stats=stat("perl1");
5   printf("The inode number is %d and the uid is %d.\n", $stats[1], $stats[4]);
6   print "The file has read and write permissions.\n", if -r _ && -w _;
```

O u t p u t

3   *1819 142441 33261 1 9496 40 -21335 75 761965998 727296409 8192 2*
5   *The inode number is 142441 and the uid is 9496.*
6   *The file has read and write permissions.*

E x p l a n a t i o n

1   The file, *perl1*, is opened via the filehandle, MYFILE.
2   The *stat* function retrieves information from the file's inode and returns that information to a 13-element array, *@statistics*.
3   The 13-element array is printed. The last two elements of the array are the blocksize and the number of blocks in 512 byte blocks. The size and number of blocks may differ because unallocated blocks are not counted in the number of blocks. The negative number is an NIS device number.
4   This time the *stat* function takes the file name as its argument, rather than the filehandle.
5   The second and fifth elements of the array are printed.
6   The special underscore filehandle is used to retrieve the current file statistics from the previous *stat* call. The file, *perl1*, was *stat*ed last. The file test operators, *-r* and *-w,* use the current *stat* information of *perl1* to check for read-and-write access on the file. (Chapter 8)

12.2.7   Low Level File I/0

The read Function (fread).   The *read* function reads a specified number of bytes from a filehandle and puts the bytes in a scalar variable. If you are familiar with C's standard I/O *fread* function, Perl's *read* function handles I/0 buffering in the same way. To improve efficiency, rather than reading a character at a time, a block of data is read and stored in a temporary storage area. C's *fread* function and Perl's *read* functions then transfer data, a byte at a time, from the temporary storage area to your program. (The *sysread* function is used to emulate C's low level I/0 *read* function.) The function returns the number of bytes read or an undefined value if an error occurred. If eof (end of file), 0 is returned.

In Perl, the *print* function (<u>not</u> the *write* function) is used to output the actual bytes returned by the *read* function. Perl's *print* function emulates C's *fwrite* function.

Format:

```
read(FILEHANDLE, SCALAR, LENGTH, OFFSET);
read(FILEHANDLE, SCALAR, LENGTH);
```

E x a m p l e   1 2 . 1 8

(The Script)
```
1  open(PASSWD, "/etc/passwd") || die "Can't open: $!\n";
2  $bytes=read (PASSWD, $buffer, 50);
3  print "The number of bytes read is $bytes.\n";
4  print "The buffer contains: \n$buffer";
```

O u t p u t

3 *The number of bytes is 50.*
4 *The buffer contains:*
   root:YhTLR4heBdxfw:0:1:Operator:/:/bin/csh
   nobody:

E x p l a n a t i o n

1   The */etc/passwd* file is opened for reading via the PASSWD filehandle.
2   The *read* function attempts to read 50 bytes from the filehandle and returns the number of bytes *read* to the scalar, *$bytes*.

The sysread and syswrite Functions.   The *sysread* function is like C's *read* function. It bypasses the standard I/0 buffering scheme and reads bytes directly from the filehandle to a scalar variable. Mixing *read* and *sysread* functions can cause problems, since the *read* function implements buffering and the *sysread* function reads bytes directly from the filehandle.

The *syswrite* function writes bytes of data from a variable to a specified filehandle. It emulates C's *write* function.

Format:

```
sysread(FILEHANDLE, SCALAR, LENGTH, OFFSET);
sysread(FILEHANDLE, SCALAR, LENGTH);

syswrite(FILEHANDLE, SCALAR, LENGTH, OFFSET);
syswrite(FILEHANDLE, SCALAR, LENGTH);
```

The seek Function.   Perl's *seek* function is the same as the *fseek* standard I/O function in C. It allows you to randomly access a file. It sets a position in a file, measured in bytes from the beginning of the file, where the first byte is byte 0. The function returns 1 if successful, 0 if not.

Format:

```
seek(FILEHANDLE, OFFSET, POSITION);
```

POSITION=The absolute position in the file where:
                0 = Beginning of file
                1 = Current position in file
                2 = End of file

OFFSET= Number of bytes from POSITION. A positive offset advances the position forward in the file. A negative offset moves the position backward in the file. A negative OFFSET sets the file position for POSITION 1 or 2.

Example 12.19

(The Script)
```
1   open(PASSWD, "/etc/passwd") || die "Can't open: $!\n";
2   while ( chop($line = <PASSWD>) ){
3          print "---$line---\n" if $line =~ /root/;
    }
4   seek(PASSWD, 0, 0) || die "$!\n";  # start back at the beginning of the file at first
                                       # byte
5   while(<PASSWD>){print if /ellie/;}
6   close(PASSWD);
```

Output

```
3   ---root:YhTLR4heBdxfw:0:1:Operator:/:/bin/csh---
5   ellie:aVD17JSsBMyGg:9496:40:Ellie Savage:/home/jodyellie:/bin/csh
```

Explanation

1   The */etc/passwd* file is opened via the PASSWD filehandle.
2   The *while* statement loops through the PASSWD filehandle, reading a line at a time until end of file is reached.
3   The line is printed if it contains the regular expression *root*.
4   The *seek* function sets the file position at position 0, the beginning of the file, byte offset 0. Since the filehandle was not closed, it remains opened until closed with the *close* function.

5 The *while* statement loops through the file.
6 The PASSWD filehandle is officially closed.

The tell Function.   The *tell* function returns the current byte position of a filehandle for
a regular file. The position can be used as an argument to the *seek* function to move the file
position to a particular location in the file.

Format:

```
tell (FILEHANDLE);
tell FILEHANDLE;
tell;
```

E x a m p l e   1 2 . 2 0

(The Script)
```
1  open(PASSWD, "/etc/passwd") || die "Can't open: $!\n";
   while ( chop($line = <PASSWD>) ){
        if ( $line =~ /sync/){
2              $current = tell;
           print "---$line---\n";
   }
3  printf "The position returned by tell is %d.\n", $current;
4  seek(PASSWD, $current, 0);
   while(<PASSWD>){
5       print;
   }
```

O u t p u t

2 *--sync::1:1::/:/bin/sync--*
3 *The position returned by tell is 296.*
5 *sysdiag:*:0:1:Old System Diagnostic:/usr/diag/sysdiag/sysdiag*
   sundiag::0:1:System Diagnostic:/usr/diag/sundiag/sundiag*
   ellie:aVD17JSsBMyGg:9496:40:Ellie Savage:/home/jodyellie:/bin/csh

E x p l a n a t i o n

1 The */etc/passwd* file is opened via the PASSWD filehandle.
2 When the line containing the regular expression, *sync*, is reached, the *tell* function will
   return the current byte position to the scalar *$current*. The current position is the next
   byte after the last character read.
3 The byte position returned by the *tell* function is printed.
4 The *seek* function locates the current position starting from the beginning of the file to
   the offset position returned by the *tell* function.

12.2.8 Packing and Unpacking Data

Not all files are text files. Some files, for example, may be packed into a binary format to save space, store images, or in a uuencoded format to ease in sending a file through the mail. These files are not readable as is the text on this page. The *pack* and *unpack* functions can be used to convert the lines in a file from one format to another.

The pack and unpack Functions. The *pack* and *unpack* functions have a number of uses. These functions are used to pack a list into a binary structure and then expand the packed values back into a list. When working with files, you can use these functions to create uuencode files, relational databases, and binary files.

The *pack* function converts a list into a scalar value that may be stored in machine memory. The TEMPLATE is used to specify the type of character and how many characters will be formatted. For example, the string "c4" or "cccc", packs a list into 4 unsigned characters and "a14" packs a list into a 14 byte ASCII string, null padded. The *unpack* function converts a binary formatted string into a list. The opposite of *pack* puts a string back into Perl format.

TABLE 12.2   The Template Pack and Unpack—Types and Values[9]

a	An ASCII string, will be null padded if packed and an ASCII string when unpacked.
A	An ASCII string, will be space padded if packed and an ASCII string without padding if unpacked.
b	A bit string, low-to-high order.
B	A bit string, high-to-low order.
h	A hexadecimal string, low nybble first.
H	A hexadecimal string, high nybble first.
c	A signed char value.
C	An unsigned char value.
s	A signed short value.
S	An unsigned short value.
i	A signed integer value.
I	An unsigned integer value.
l	A signed long value.
L	An unsigned long value.
n	A short in "network" order.
N	A long in "network" order.
f	A single precision float in the native format.
d	A double precision float in the native format.
p	A pointer to a string.
x	A null byte.
X	Back up a byte.
@	Null-fill to absolute position.
u	A uuencoded string for pack; a uudecoded string for unpack

---

9. Larry Wall and Randal L. Schwartz, *Programming Perl* (Sebastopol, CA: O'Reilly), pp. 166–67.

Format:

```
$string=pack(Template, @list );
@list = unpack(Template, $string );
```

Example 12.21

(The Script)
```
1       $bytes=pack("c5", 80,101,114, 108, 012);
2       print "$bytes\n";
```

Output

Perl

Explanation

1 The first element in the list, the Template (see Table 12.2), is composed of the type and the number of values to be packed, in this example, four signed characters. The rest of the list consists of the decimal values for characters 'P', 'e', 'r', and 'l' and the octal value for the newline. This list is packed into a binary structure. The string containing the packed structure is returned and stored in *$bytes*. (See your ASCII table.)
2 The four-byte character string is printed.

Example 12.22

(Script)
```
1       $string=pack("A15A3", "hey","you");  # ASCII string,  space padded
2       print "$string";
```

Output

2   *h e y   y o u*

Explanation

1 The two strings, "hey" and "you", are packed into a structure using the template A15A3. A15 will convert the string "hey" into a space-padded ASCII string consisting of 15 characters. A3 converts the string "you" into a 3-character space-padded string.
2 The strings are printed according to the pack formatting template. They are left justified.

E x a m p l e   1 2 . 2 3

(The Script)
```
  #!/bin/perl
  # Program to uuencode a file and then uudecode it.
1 open(PW, "/etc/passwd") || die "Can't open: $!\n";
2 open(CODEDPW, ">codedpw") || die "Can't open: $!\n";

3 while(<PW>){
4       $uuline=pack("u*", $_);
5       print CODEDPW $uuline;
  }
  close PW;
  close CODEDPW;

6 open(UUPW, "codedpw") || die "Can't open: $!\n";
  while(<UUPW>){
7       print;
  }
  close UUPW;
  print "\n\n";

8 open(DECODED, "codedpw") || die;
9 while(<DECODED>){
10      @decodeline = unpack("u*", $_);
11      print "@decodeline";
  }
```

O u t p u t

```
7 E<F]O=#!IX.C`Z,3I3=7!E<BU5<V5R.B\Z+W5S<B]B:6XO8W-H"@``
  19&%E;6]N.G@Z,3HQ.CHO.@H`
  58FEN.G@Z,CHR.CHO=7-R+V)I;CH*
  .<WES.G@Z,SHS.CHO.@H`
  :861M.G@Z-#HT.D%D;6EN.B]V87(O861M.@H`
  L;`Z>#HW,3HX.DQI;F4@4')I;G1E<B!!9&UI;CHO=7-R+W-P;V]L+VQP.@H`
  ?<VUT<#!IX.C`Z,#I-86EL($1A96UO;B!5<V5R.B\Z"@!R
  E=75C<#!IX.C4Z-3IU=6-P($%D;6EN.B]U<W(O;&EB+W5U8W`Z"@!L
  M;G5U8W`Z>#HY.CDZ=75C<<"!!9&UI;CHO=7-R+W-P;V]L+W5U8W!!P=6)L
  P;V]L+W5U8W!!P=6)L:6,Z
  5+W5S<B]L:6(O=75C<<"]U=6-I8V\*
  J;&ES=&5N.G@Z,S<Z-#I.971W;W)K(($%D;6EN.B]U<W(O;F5T+VYE=#HH*
  ?;F]B;V1Y.@H`;VUQ-#$-86EN+V1Z-"`:6XO8V%T:"`:"`$Z3F]B;V1Y.B\Z"@`O
  I;F]A8V-E<W,@,W>#HV.#HV-#IO;V%C8V5S<R\Z;F]L:6X@:F5T+6EN=7-H.@H`
```

J;F]B;V1Y-#IX.C8U-3,T.C8U-3,T.E-U;D]3(#0N>"!.;V)O9'DZ+SH*
M96QL:64Z>#HY-
#DV.C0P.D5L;&EE(%%U:6=L97DZ+VAO;64O96QL:64Z+W5S
*<B]B:6XO8W-H"@!C

11 root:x:0:1:Super-User:/:/usr/bin/csh
daemon:x:1:1::/:
bin:x:2:2::/usr/bin:
sys:x:3:3::/:
adm:x:4:4:Admin:/var/adm:
lp:x:71:8:Line Printer Admin:/usr/spool/lp:
smtp:x:0:0:Mail Daemon User:/:
uucp:x:5:5:uucp Admin:/usr/lib/uucp:
nuucp:x:9:9:uucp Admin:/var/spool/uucppublic:/usr/lib/uucp/uucico
listen:x:37:4:Network Admin:/usr/net/nls:
nobody:x:60001:60001:Nobody:/:
noaccess:x:60002:60002:No Access User:/:
nobody4:x:65534:65534:SunOS 4.x Nobody:/:
ellie:x:9496:40:Ellie Quigley:/home/ellie:/usr/bin/csh

Explanation

1   The local *passwd* file is opened for reading.
2   Another file called *codepw* is opened for writing.
3   Each line of the filehandle is read into the $_ until the end of file.
4   The *pack* function uuencodes the line ($_) and assigns the coded line to the scalar, $uuline. *uuencode* is often used to convert a binary file into an encoded representation that can be sent using mail.
5   The uuencoded string is sent to the filehandle.
6   The file containing the uuencoded text is opened for reading and attached to the UUPW filehandle.
7   Each line of uuencoded text is printed.
8   The uuencoded file is opened for reading.
9   Each line of the file is read from the filehandle and stored in $_.
10 The *unpack* function converts the uuencoded string back into its original form and assigns it to @*decodeline*.
11 The uudecoded line is printed.

E x a m p l e   1 2 . 2 4

(The Script)
```
    #!/bin/perl
1 $ints=pack("i3", 5,-10,15);
2 open(BINARY, "+>binary" ) || die;
3 print BINARY "$ints";
4 seek(BINARY, 0,0) || die;
    while(<BINARY>){
5         ($n1,$n2,$n3)=unpack("i3", $_);
6         print "$n1 $n2 $n3\n";
    }
```

O u t p u t

6 *5 -10 15*

E x p l a n a t i o n

1   The three integers, 5 , -10, and 15, are packed into 3 signed integers. The value returned is a binary structure assigned to *$ints*.
2   The BINARY filehandle is opened for reading and writing.
3   The packed integers are sent to the file. This file is compressed and totally unreadable. To read it, it must be converted back into an ASCII format. This is done with *upack*.
4   The *seek* function puts the file pointer back at the top of the file at byte position 0.
5   We're reading from the file one line at a time. Each line, stored in $_, is unpacked and returned to its original list values.
6   The original list values are printed.

12.3 Processes

Your Perl script is a program that resides on disk. When the program is placed in memory and starts execution, it is called a *process*. Each process has a number of attributes that are inherited from its parent, the calling process. Perl has a number of functions that will allow you to retrieve the information about the process. Before examining these functions, a short discussion about processes may help you to understand (or recall) the purpose of some of Perl's system calls.

Every process has a unique process ID, a positive integer, called the *pid*. Every process has a parent except process 0, the swapper. The first process init, PID 1, is the ancestor of all future processes, called descendants, or more commonly, child processes.

In the following diagram, the Perl process is a descendant of the Shell (sh).

FIGURE 12.2

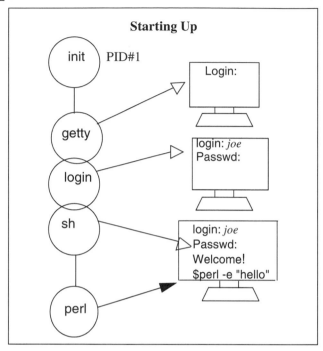

Each process also belongs to a *process group*, a collection of one or more processes, used for job control and signal handling. Each process group also has a unique PID and a process leader. When you log on, the process group leader may be your login shell. Any process created from your shell will be a member of this process group. The terminal opened by the process group leader is called the controlling terminal, and any processes it spawns inherits it. Any signals sent to the process will be sent to all processes in the group. That is why, when you press Ctrl-C, the process you are running and any of its children will terminate. Perl provides functions to obtain the process group id and to set the process group.

When a process is created, it is assigned four numbers, indicating who owns the process. They are the real and effective user id, and the real and effective group id. The user ID, called the *real uid*, is a positive integer that is associated with your login name. The real uid is the third field in the */etc/passwd* file. When you log on, the first process created is called the login shell, and it is assigned the user ID. Any processes spawned from the shell also inherit this *uid*. Any process running with the uid of zero is called a root or superuser process with special privileges.

There is also a group ID number, called the *real gid*, which associates a group with your login name. The default gid is the fourth field in the password file, and it is also inherited by any child process. The system administrator can allow users to become members of other groups by assigning entries in the */etc/group* file.

The following is an entry from the *passwd* file, illustrating how the *uid* and *gid* values are stored (fields are separated by colons).

E x a m p l e   1 2 . 2 5

(Entry from */etc/passwd*)
john:aYD17lsSjBMyGg:9495:41:John Doe:/home/dolphin/john:/bin/ksh

E x p l a n a t i o n

(The Fields)
1 login name
2 encrypted password
3 uid
4 gid
5 gcos
6 home directory
7 login shell

The *effective uid* (euid) and *effective guid* (guid) of a process are normally set to the same number as the real uid and real gid of the user who is running the process. UNIX determines what permissions are available to a process by the effective uid and gid. If the euid or guid of a file is changed to that of another owner, when you execute a program, you essentially become that owner and get his access permissions. Programs in which the effective uid or effective gid have been set are called *set user id* programs or *setuid* programs. When you change your password, the */bin/passwd* program has a setuid to root, giving you the privilege to change your password in the *passwd* file which is owned by root.

12.3.1   The Environment

When you log on, your Shell program inherits a set of environment variables initialized by either the login program or one of Shell's startup files (.profile or .login). These variables contain useful information about the process, such as the search path, the home directory, the user name, and the terminal type. The information in environment variables, once set and exported, is inherited by any child processes that are spawned from the process (parent) in which they were initialized. The Shell process will pass the environment information on to your Perl program.

The special associative array, *%ENV*, contains the environment settings. If you change the value of an environment setting in your Perl script, it is set for this process and any of its children. The environment variables in the parent process, normally the Shell, will remain untouched.

E x a m p l e   1 2 . 2 6

(The Script)
```
1 foreach $key (keys(%ENV)){
2                 print "$key\n";}
3 print "Your login name is $ENV{'LOGNAME'}\n";
4 $pwd=$ENV{'PWD'};
  print "/The present working directory is $pwd, "\n";
```

O u t p u t

```
2  OPENWINHOME
   MANPATH
   FONTPATH
   LOGNAME
   USER
   TERMCAP
   TERM
   SHELL
   PWD
   HOME
   PATH
   WINDOW_PARENT
   WMGR_ENV_PLACEHOLDER
3  Your login name is ellie
4  The present working directory is /home/jody/ellie
```

E x p l a n a t i o n

1 The *keys* function is used to get all the currently set environment variables from the *%ENV* array. These variables were inherited from the parent process, the Shell.
2 Each environment variable is printed.
3 The value of *LOGNAME*, the user name, is printed.
4 The value of *PWD*, the present working directory, is assigned to *$pwd* and printed.

Processes and Filehandles.   As discussed in Chapter 8, processes can be opened in Perl via either an input or output filehandle. For example, if you want to see all the currently running processes on your machine, you could create a filehandle for the UNIX *ps* command. (See Chapter 8 for details. See also Section 12.4.3, "The system Function," at the end of this chapter.)

E x a m p l e   1 2 . 2 7

(The Script)
1 **open(PROC, "ps -aux |")** || die "$!\n";   # *if running System V, use ps -ef*
2 print STDOUT <PROC>;

O u t p u t

```
2 ellie    3825 6.4 4.5 212  464 p5 R   12:18  0:00 ps –aux
  root         1 0.0 0.0  52    0 ?  IW  Feb 5 0:02 /sbin/init
  root        51 10.0 0.0 52    0 ?  IW  Feb 5 0:02 portmap
  root         2 10.0 0.0 52    0 ?  D Feb 5 0:02 pagedaemon
  root        90 10.0 0.0 52    0 ?  IW  Feb 5 0:02 rpc.statd
                < more processes here>
  ellie    1383 0.8 8.4 360  876 p4 S   Dec 26 11:34 /usr/local/OW3/bin/xview
  ellie    173 0.8 13.4 1932 1392 co S   Dec 20389:19 /usr/local/OW3/bin/xnews
  ellie    164 0.0 0.0 100    0 co IW  Dec 20 0:00 –c
                < some of the output was cut to save space >
  ellie    3822 0.0 0.0   0    0 p5 Z   Dec 20 0:00 <defunct>
  ellie    3823 0.0 1.1  28  112 p5 S   12:18  0:00 sh –c ps –aux | grep '^'
  ellie    3821 0.0 5.6 144  580 p5 S   12:18  0:00 /bin/perl checkon ellie
  ellie    3824 0.0 1.8  32  192 p5 S   12:18  0:00 grep ^ellie
```

E x p l a n a t i o n

1 The *PROC* filehandle is opened for reading. It is called an input filter. The output from
   the *ps* command is piped to Perl via the *PROC* filehandle.
2 The contents of the filter are printed to *STDOUT*.

Login Information.

The getlogin Function

The *getlogin* function returns the current login from */etc/utmp*. If null is returned from
getlogin, use *getpwuid*. The *getpwuid* function takes the uid of the user as an argument and
returns an entry from the *password* file associated with that uid.

The $< variable evaluates to the real uid of this process.

Format:

```
getlogin;
```

E x a m p l e   1 2 . 2 8

(The Script)
1 $loginname=**getlogin** || (getpwuid($<))[0]|| die "Not a user here!!";
2 print "Your loginname is $loginname.\n";

O u t p u t

2 *Your loginname is john.*

E x p l a n a t i o n

1 The *getlogin* function returns the login name from */etc/utmp* and, if that fails, retrieves
   it from the password file with the *getpwuid* function. The $< variable contains the real
   uid of this process.
2 The scalar, *$loginname*, contains the user's login name, the first entry of the password
   file.

Special Process Variables (pid, uid, euid, gid, euid).   Perl provides some special variables that store information about the Perl process executing your script. If you want to
make your program more readable, you can use the *English* module in the standard Perl
library to represent these variables in English.

$$	The process id of the Perl program running this script
$<	The real uid of this process
$>	The effective uid of this process
$(	The real gid of this process
$)	The effective gid of this process

The Parent Process ID.

The getppid Function and the $$ Variable
Each process on the system is identified by its process identification number (PID), a
positive integer. The special variable $$ holds the value of the PID for this process. This
variable is also used by the Shell to hold the process id number of the current process.
   The *getppid* function returns the process–ID of the *parent* process.

E x a m p l e   1 2 . 2 9

(The Script)
1 print "The pid of this process is $$\n";
2 print "The parent pid of this process is ", getppid,"\n";

O u t p u t

1 *The pid of this process is 3304*
2 *The parent pid of this process is 2340*

(At the Command Line)
3 $ **echo $$**
2340

E x p l a n a t i o n

1 The process identification number (*pid*) for this process, this Perl script, is printed.
2 The process that spawned this process is ordinarily the Shell, the parent process. The parent's pid is called the *ppid*.
3 After the Perl script exits, the $$ is used to print the *pid* of the Shell. The *ppid* for the Perl script was *2340*, the value of its parent's *pid*, that of the Shell.

The Process Group ID.

The pgrp Function

The *pgrp* function returns the current group process for a specified PID. Without an argument or with an argument of 0, the process group id of the current process is returned.

Format:

```
getpgrp(PID);
getpgrp PID;
getpgrp;
```

E x a m p l e   1 2 . 3 0

(The Script)
1 print "The PID of the Perl program running this script is ", $$;
2 printf "The PPID, parent's pid (Shell) , is %d\n", getppid;
3 **printf "The process group's pid is %d\n", getpgrp(0);**

O u t p u t

1 The PID of the Perl program running this script is 6671
2 The PPID, parent's pid (Shell), is 6344
3 The process group's pid is 6671

Process Priorities and Niceness.   The kernel maintains the scheduling priority selected for each process. Most interactive and short running jobs are favored with a higher priority. The UNIX *nice* command allows you to modify the scheduling priority of processes (BSD, pre-System V). On moderately or heavily loaded systems, it may be to your advantage to make CPU-intensive jobs run slower so that jobs needing higher priority get faster access to the CPU. Those jobs that don't hog the processor are called "nice."

The nice value is used in calculating the priority of a process. A process with a positive nice value runs at a low priority, meaning that it receives less than its share of the CPU time. A process with a negative number runs at a high priority, receiving more than its share of the processor. The nice values range from -20 to 19. Most processes run at priority zero, balancing their access to the CPU. (Only the superuser can set negative nice values.)

The following functions, *getpriority* and *setpriority*, are named for the corresponding system calls, found in Section 2 of your UNIX manual pages.

The getpriority Function

The *getpriority* function returns the current priority(nice value) for a process, process group, or a user. Not all systems support this function. If not implemented, *getpriority* produces a fatal error. WHICH is one of three values: 0 for the process priority, 1 for the process group priority, and 2 for the user priority. WHO is interpreted relative to the process identifier for the process priority, process group priority, or user priority. A value of zero represents the current process, process group, or user.

Format:

```
getpriority(WHICH, WHO);
```

Example 12.31

(The Script)
1 **$niceval = getpriority(0,0);**
2 **print "The priority, nice value, for this process is $niceval\n";**

Output

2 *The priority, nice value, for this process is 0.*

Explanation

1 The *getpriority* function will return the *nice* value for the current process.
2 The *nice* value for this process is zero. This gives the process no special favor when taking its share of time from the CPU.

The setpriority Function (nice)

The *setpriority* function sets the current priority (nice value) for a process, a process group, or a user. It modifies the scheduling priority for processes. If the *setpriority* system call is not implemented on your system, *setpriority* will return an error.

WHICH is one of three values: 0 for the process priority, 1 for the process group priority, and 2 for the user priority. WHO is interpreted relative to the process identifier for the process priority, process group priority, or user priority. A value of zero represents the current process, process group, or user. NICEVALUE is the *nice* value. A low nice value raises the priority of the process and a low high value decreases the priority of the process. (Confusing!)

Unless you have superuser privileges, you cannot use a negative *nice* value. Doing so will not change the current *nice* value.

Format:

```
setpriority(WHICH, WHO, NICEVALUE);
```

E x a m p l e   1 2 . 3 2

(The Script)
```
1  $niceval = getpriority(0,0);
2  print "The nice value for this process is $niceval.\n";
3  setpriority(0,0, ( $niceval + 5 ));
4  print "The nice value for this process is now", getpriority(0,0);
```

O u t p u t

```
2  The nice value for this process is 0.
4  The nice value for this process is now 5.
```

E x p l a n a t i o n

1   The *getpriority* function will return the nice value for the current process.
2   The nice value is printed.
3   The *setpriority* function adds *5* to the *nice* value of the current process. The process will have a lower priority. It is being "nice."
4   The new *nice* value returned by the *getpriority* function is 5.

12.3.2   Password Information

The following functions iterate through the */etc/passwd* file and retrieve information from that file into an array. These functions are named for the same functions found in the system library (Section 3 of the UNIX manual) and perform the same tasks. If you are interested in obtaining information about the */etc/group* file, the Perl functions *getgrent, getgrgid, getgrnam* all return a four-element array with information about group entries. A description of these functions can be found in the UNIX manual pages. Here is an example of an */etc/passwd* file:

```
root:YhTLR4heBdxfw:0:1:Operator:/:/bin/csh
nobody:*:65534:65534::/:
sys:*:2:2::/:/bin/csh
bin:*:3:3::/bin
uucp:*:4:8::/var/spool/uucppublic:
news:*:6:6::/var/spool/news:/bin/csh
sync::1:1::/:/bin/sync
ellie:aVD17TSsBMfYg:9496:40:Ellie Shellie:/home/jody/ellie:/bin/ksh
```

Getting a Password Entry.

The getpwent Function

The *getpwent* function retrieves information from the */etc/passwd* file. The return value from *getpwent* is a nine-element array consisting of:

> login name
> encrypted password
> user id
> group id
> quota
> comment
> gcos (user information)
> home directory
> login shell

Format:

```
($name, $passwd, $uid, $gid, $quota, $comment, $gcos,
    $dir, $shell )=getpwent;
```

Example 12.33

(The Script)
```
1  while( @info=getpwent) {
2      print "$info[0]\n" if $info[1]=~/\*+/;
       }
```

Output

```
2  nobody
   daemon
   sys
   bin
   uucp
```

Explanation

1   The *getpwent* function gets a line from the */etc/passwd* file and stores it in the array, *@in-fo*. The loop continues until *getpwent* cannot read another entry from */etc/passwd*.
2   If the second element of the array contains at least one star (*), the first element, the user name, is printed.

Getting a Password Entry by Username.

The getpwnam Function

The *getpwnam* function takes the user name as an argument and returns a nine-element array corresponding to that user's name field in the */etc/passwd* file.

Format:

```
getpwnam(loginname);
```

Example 12.34

```
(The Script)
    #!/bin/perl
1   foreach $name ( "root", "bin", "ellie" ){
2        if (($login, $passwd, $uid)=getpwnam($name)){
3          print "$login--$uid\n";
              }
        }
```

Output

```
3   root--0
    ellie--9496
    bin--3
```

Explanation

1   The *foreach* loop contains login names in its list, each to be processed in turn.
2   The *getpwnam* function retrieves information from */etc/passwd* and stores the first three fields of information in the array elements *$login, $passwd,* and *$uid*, respectively.
3   The *login name* and the *uid* are printed.

Getting a Password Entry by UID.

The getpwuid Function

The *getpwuid* function takes a numeric user id (uid) as an argument and returns a nine-element array corresponding to that user's uid entry in the */etc/passwd* file.

Format:

```
getpuid(UID)
```

Example 12.35

```
(The Script)
1   foreach $num ( 1 .. 10 ){
2       if (($login, $passwd, $uid)=getpwuid($num)){
3           print "$login--$uid\n";}
    }
```

Output

```
3   daemon--1
    sys--2
    bin--3
    uucp--4
    news--6
    ingres--7
    audit--9
```

Explanation

1   The *foreach* loop contains a range of *uid* numbers from 1 to 10 in its list, each to be processed in turn.
2   The *getpwuid* function retrieves information from */etc/passwd* and stores the first three fields of information in the array elements, *$login, $passwd,* and *$uid*, respectively.
3   The *login* name and its corresponding *uid* are printed.

12.3.3   Time and Processes

When working in a computer environment, programs often need to obtain and manipulate the current date and time. UNIX systems maintain two types of time values: calendar time and process time.

The calendar time counts the number of seconds since 00:00:00 January 1, 1970, UTC (Coordinated Universal Time).

The process time, also called CPU time, measures the resources a process utilizes in clock time, user CPU time, and system CPU time. The CPU time is measured in clock ticks per second.

Perl has a number of time functions that interface with the system to retrieve time information.

The times function. The *times* function returns a four-element array consisting of the CPU time for a process, measured in:

> User time—Time spent executing user's code
> System time—Time spent executing system calls
> Children's user time—Time spent executing all terminated child processes
> Children's system time—Time spent executing system calls for all terminated child processes

Format:

```
($user, $system, $cuser, $csystem) = times;
```

Example 12.36

(The Script)
```
    #!/bin/perl
1   printf "User time in this program %2.3f seconds\n", (times)[0];
2   printf "System time in this program %2.3f seconds\n", (times)[1];
```

Output

```
3   User time in this program 0.217 seconds
4   System time in this program 0.600 seconds
```

Explanation

1 The *time* function returns a four-element array and the first element is printed, the user time.
2 The *time* function returns a four-element array and the second element is printed, the system time.

The time function. The *time* function returns the number of non-leap seconds since January 1, 1970, UTC (Greenwich Mean Time). Its return value is used with the *gmtime* and *localtime* functions (see below) to put the time in a human readable format. The *stat* and *utime* functions also use the *time* functions when comparing file modification and access times.

The gmtime Function.   The *gmtime* function converts the return value of the *time* function to a nine-element array consisting of the numeric values for the Coordinated Universal Time (UTC), a new name for Greenwich Mean Time. If you are a C programmer, you will recognize that these values are taken directly from the *tm structure* found in the header file, */usr/include/time.h.* (See Table 12.3.)

Format:

```
gmtime(EXPR);
gmtime EXPR;
($sec, $min, $hour, $monthday, $month, $year, $weekday,
    $yearday, $isdaylight)=gmtime;
```

TABLE 12.3   Return Values for the gmtime Function

List Element	Meaning
$sec	Seconds after the minute - [0, 59]
$min	Minutes after the hour - [0, 59]
$hour	Hour since midnight - [0, 23]
$monthday	Day of the month - [1, 31]
$month	Months since January - [0, 11]
$year	Years since 1900
$weekday	Days since Sunday - [0, 6]
$yearday	Days since January 1 - [0, 365]
$isdaylight	Flag for daylight saving time

E x a m p l e   1 2 . 3 7

(The Script)
```
    #!/bin/perl
1  ($sec, $min, $hour, $monthday, $month, $year, $weekday, $yearday,
       $isdaylight) = gmtime;
2  print "The weekday is $weekday and the month is $month.\n";
3  print "The time in California since midnight is ", `date "+%H:%M"`;
4  print "The Greenwich Mean Time is $hour:$min since midnight\n";
5  print "Daylight saving is in effect.\n" if $isdaylight;
```

O u t p u t

```
2  The weekday is 2 and the month is 6.
3  The time in California since midnight is 20:35.
4  The Greenwich Mean Time is 3:35 since midnight.
5
```

Explanation

1 The *gmtime* function returns an array as defined in the table above.
2 The weekday and the month are printed for Greenwich Mean Time.
3 The time in California is printed by utilizing the UNIX "date" command.
4 The Greenwich Mean Time is printed.
5 If daylight saving is in effect, the value of *$isdaylight* is set to non-zero. Daylight time
   is not in effect. Nothing prints.

The localtime Function.   The *localtime* function converts the UTC time to a nine-element array with the local time zone.

Format:

```
localtime(EXPR);
localtime EXPR;
($sec, $min, $hour, $mday, $mon, $year, $wday, $yday,
    $isdst)=localtime(time);
```

Example 12.38

(The Script)
```
    #!/bin/perl
1  ($sec, $min, $hour, $mday, $mon, $year, $wday, $yday, $isdst)=
       localtime(time);
2      % weekday=(
       "0"=> "Sunday",
       "1"=>"Monday",
       "2"=>"Tuesday",
       "3"=>"Wednesday",
       "4"=> "Thursday",
       "5"=>"Friday",
       "6"=>"Saturday",
       );
       if ( $hour > 12 ){
3          print "The hour is ", $hour – 12 ," $min: o'clock.\n";
       else {
           print "The hour is $hour o'clock.\n";
4          print qq/The day is $weekday{"$wday"}.\n/;  # day starts at zero
5          print "The year is 19$year.\n";
6          print "The isdst is $isdst.\n";
       }
```

Output

3 *The hour is 9:52 o'clock.*
4 *The day is Wednesday.*
5 *The year is 1997.*
6 *The isdst is 0.*

Explanation

1 The *localtime* function converts the return of the time function to the local time.
2 An associative array, *%weekday*, associates a number of the weekday with the string weekday.
3 The hour and the minutes are printed.
4 The scalar, *$wday*, returned from the localtime function is a number. It is used as an index into the associative array, *%weekday*, to get the string "Wednesday".
5 The year is printed.
6 The *$isdt* element of the array prints 0 if daylight saving is not in effect.

12.3.4 Process Creation

What happens when your Perl program starts executing? Here is a brief sketch of what goes on. Normally, the Perl program is executed from the Shell command line. You type the name of your script (and its arguments) and then press carriage return. At that point, the Shell starts working. It first creates (forks) a new process called the child process   The child is essentially a copy of Shell that created it. There are now two processes running, the parent and child Shell. After the child process is created, the parent Shell normally sleeps (waits), while its child process gets everything ready for your Perl program, that is, handles redirection, if necessary, pipes, background processing, etc. When the child Shell has completed its tasks, it then executes (execs) your Perl program in place of itself. When the Perl process completes, it exits (exit) and its exit status is returned to the waiting parent process, the Shell. The Shell wakes up, and a prompt appears on the screen. If you type in a UNIX command, this whole process is repeated.

It's conceivable that your Perl program may want to start up a child process to handle a specific task, for example, a database application or a client/server program.

12.3.5 The fork Function

The *fork* function is used to create processes on UNIX systems. The *fork* function is called once and returns twice. It creates a duplicate of the parent (calling) process. The new process is called the child process. The child process inherits its environment, open files, real and user ids, masks, current working directory, and signals, etc. Both processes, parent and child, execute the same code, starting with the instruction right after the *fork* function call.

The *fork* function lets you differentiate between the parent and child because it returns a different value to each process. It returns 0 to the child process and the pid of the child to the parent process. It is not guaranteed which process will execute first after the call to the *fork* function.

Normally the *wait, exec*, and *exit* functions work in conjunction with the *fork* function so that you can control both what the parent and the child are doing. The parent, for example, waits for the child to finish performing some task, and after the child exits, the parent resumes where it left off.

Figure 12.3 illustrates how the UNIX Shell uses the *fork* system call to create a new process. After you type the name of your Perl program at the Shell prompt, the Shell forks, creating a copy of itself called the child process. The parent Shell sleeps (wait). The child Shell executes (execs) the Perl process in its place. The child never returns. Note that ENV variables, standard input, output, and standard error are inherited. When the Perl program completes, it exits and the parent Shell wakes up. The Shell prompt reappears on your screen. The Perl program could use the *fork* function to spawn off another application program.

Format:

```
fork;
```

E x a m p l e   1 2 . 3 9

(The Script)
```
1 $return_val=fork;
2 if ( $return_val == 0 ){
        print "This is the child process; return value  is $return_val.\n";
        }
3 elsif ( defined $return_val ){
        print "This is the parent process; return value is $return_val.\n";
   }
   else{
4       die "fork error: $!\n";
   }
```

O u t p u t

2   *This is the child process; return value is 0.*
3   *This is the parent process; return value is 3512.*

E x p l a n a t i o n

1   The *fork* function is called to create a copy of this process.
2   The return value is checked. If the return value is 0, the child's code is in execution.
3   If the return value is non-zero, the parent process is executing.
4   This statement is executed if the *fork* function fails. It might fail if the process table is full, that is, if the system has reached its maximum number of allowed processes.

FIGURE 12.3   Perl Process Creation from the Shell

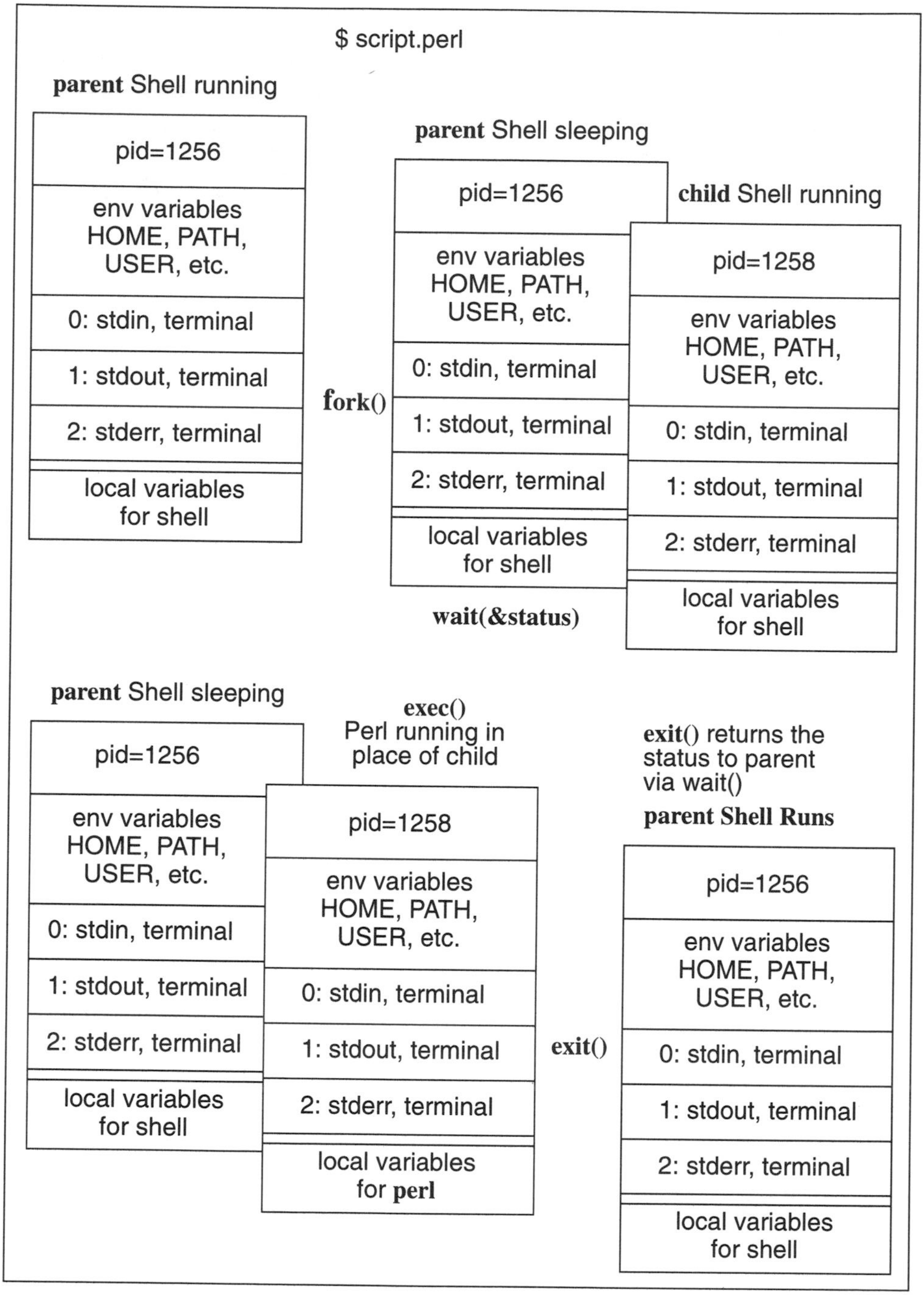

12.3.6 The exec Function

Whereas *fork* creates a brand new process, the *exec* function is used to initiate a new program in place of the currently running program. Normally, the *exec* function is called after *fork*. Perl inherits attributes from the Shell, and a process that is executed from within Perl also inherits Perl's attributes, such as PID, gid, uid, signals, directories, etc. If, then, the *exec* function is called directly (no fork) from within a Perl script, the new program executes in place of the currently running Perl program. When that program completes, you do not return to your Perl program. Since *exec* does not flush the output buffer, the $| variable needs to be set to ensure command buffering.

The filehandles, STDIN, STDOUT, and STDERR, remain open following a call to the *exec* function.

At the system level there are six different *exec* functions used to initiate new programs. Perl calls the C library function *execvp* if more than one argument is passed to the *exec* function. The arguments are the name of the program to execute and any other arguments that will be passed to that program. If a single scalar is passed to the *exec* function and it contains any Shell metacharacters, the Shell command, */bin/sh -c*, is passed the command for interpretation.

Format:

```
exec(UNIX COMMAND);
exec UNIX COMMAND;
```

E x a m p l e   1 2 . 4 0

(The Script)
1 **exec 'echo hi there you!'**;
2 print "hello";

O u t p u t

1 hi there you

(The Script)
1 **exec 'ls *.c'**;
2 print "hello.";

O u t p u t

a.c b.c c.c

Explanation

1 In both examples, the *exec* function will execute the UNIX command.
2 In both examples, the print statement will not be executed because *exec* never returns.
   The UNIX commands were executed in place of the Perl program.

12.3.7   The wait and waitpid Functions

The *wait* function waits for a child process to finish execution. After a *fork* call, both processes, parent and child, execute. The *wait* function forces the parent to wait until its child is finished and returns the pid of the child process to the parent. If there are no child processes, *wait* returns a -1.[10]

Format:

```
wait;
```

Example 12.41

(The Script)
```
1  $return_val=fork;
2  if ( $return_val == 0 ){  # In child
        print "This is the child process; return value  is $return_val.\n";
3       exec "/bin/date" || die "exec failed: $!\n";
        }
4  elsif ( defined $return_val ){   # In parent
        print "This is the parent process; return value is $pid.\n";
5       $pid = wait;
        print "Back in parent process.\n";
        print "The deceased child's pid is $pid.\n";
    }
   else{
6       die "fork error: $!\n";
        }
```

Output

```
4  This is the parent process; return value is 3530.
2  This is the child process; return value is 0.
3  Wed Mar 26 23:57:18 PST 1997.
5  Back in the parent process.
   The deceased child's pid is 3530.
```

---

10. The *waitpid* function also waits for a child process to finish execution, but it can specify which child it will wait for, and it has special flags that control blocking.

E x p l a n a t i o n

1 The *fork* function is called creating a copy of the current process. Now there are two processes running, the parent Perl process and the child Perl process. They are both executing the code directly following the fork call. The return value is assigned 0 in the child and the pid of the child in the parent.
2 If in the child process, the *if* statement block is executed.
3 The *exec* function executes the UNIX *date* command and does not return.
4 If in the parent process, the *elsif* statement block is executed. The value of *$return_val* is the pid of the child process.
5 The *wait* function is called by the parent who waits for the child to finish.   The pid of the deceased child is returned.
6 If the *fork* failed (no more processes?), the *die* function will print the error message and the program will exit.

12.3.8   The exit Function

The *exit* function causes the program to exit. It can be given an integer argument ranging from values between zero and 255. The exit value is returned to the parent process via the *wait* function call. By convention, UNIX programs exiting with a zero status are successful, and those exiting with non-zero failed in some way. (Of course, the criteria for success for one programmer may not be the same as those for another.)

Format:

```
exit (Integer);
exit Integer;
```

E x a m p l e   1 2 . 4 2

(The Script)
    #The name of the script is args.p
1 **exit 12** if $#ARGV == 0;

O u t p u t

1 **$ args.p**
2 **$ echo $?**
    12

E x p l a n a t i o n

1 The script is missing an argument.
2 The Shell's $? variable contains the exit status of the Perl program. If using C Shell, the exit status is stored in *$status*.

12.4 Other Ways to Interface with UNIX

If the system functions are still not enough, Perl offers a number of alternate ways to deal with the operating system. You can use the *syscall* function, command substitution, the *system* function, and the *here document* to get system information.

12.4.1   The syscall Function and the h2ph Script

The *syscall* function calls a specified system call with its arguments. If the C system call is not implemented, a fatal error is returned.   The first argument is the name of the system call preceded by *&SYS_*. The remaining arguments are the actual parameters that are required by the real system call. If the argument is numeric, it is passed as a C integer. If not, the pointer to the string value is passed. You may have to coerce a number to integer by adding 0 to it if it is not a literal and cannot be interpreted by context.

Before using the *syscall* function, you should run a script called *h2ph* that comes with the Perl distribution. At the bottom of the *h2ph* script (after __END__) are the manual pages for *h2ph*, including an explanation on how to run the script. This script converts the proper C header files to the corresponding Perl header files. These files must be added to the Perl library if you are using functions that require them. All the files created have the *.ph* extension. After running the *h2ph* script, make sure that the *@INC* array in your program includes the path to these library functions.[11]

Format:

```
syscall (&SYS_NAME, LIST);
```

Example 12.43

(At the Command Line)
1 $ cd /usr/include; /usr/local/bin/perl/h2ph * sys/*

(In Script)
```
    #!/bin/perl
    #The name of the script is args.p
2  push(@INC, "/usr/local/lib");
3  require "syscall.ph";
4  $bytes=syscall(&SYS_getpagesize);
5  printf "The pagesize for this Sparc Sun Workstation is %d bytes \n",$bytes;
```

Output

5 *The pagesize for this Sparc Sun Workstation is 4096 bytes.*

---

11. See also the *h2xs* script that comes with Perl5 distribution for building a Perl extension from any C header file.

E x p l a n a t i o n

1 The *h2ph* is executed so that the necessary C header files are converted to Perl header files. The files created are placed in */usr/local/lib* and end with a *.ph* extension.
2 The directory containing the *.ph* files is pushed onto the @INC array.
3 The file *syscall.ph* is required for using C system calls.
4 The Perl *syscall* function will call the *getpagesize* system call. The prefix, *&SYS_*, is necessary Perl syntax. It must be prepended to the real system call name.
5 The page size for this Sun4c is 4096 bytes.

12.4.2 Command Substitution—The Back Quotes

Although we have already discussed command substitution and back quotes in Chapter 4, a quick review might be in order here because command substitution is yet another way for Perl to interface with operating system commands.

Like the Shell, enclosing a command in back quotes causes it to be executed. Unlike the Shell, if double quotes surround the back-quoted string, command substitution will <u>not</u> occur. Unlike the C Shell, if the output resulting from executing the command is saved in a variable, it is stored as a scalar string, not an array.

E x a m p l e   1 2 . 4 4

(The Script)
```
   #!/bin/perl
1  print "The hour is ",`date`;

2  @d=`date`;
3  print $d[0]'

4  @d=split(/ /,`date`);
5  print "$d[0]\n"
6  $machine=`uname –n`;
7  print "$machine\n"'
```

O u t p u t

1 *The hour is Thu Mar 27 20:47:17 PST 1997*
3 *Thu Mar 27 20:59:11 PST 1997*
5 *Thu*
7 *dolphin*

Explanation

1 The UNIX *date* command is enclosed in back quotes. It is executed and appended to the string "The hour is ".

2 The array, *@d*, is set to the output of the *date* command. The output is stored as a single string, unlike the Shells, where the output is stored as a list.

3 Since the output of the command is stored as a single string, *$d[0]*, is the entire string.

4 The *split* command creates a list from the output returned from the *date* command.

5 Now the first element of the array is the first word in the list, *Thu*.

6 The scalar, *$machine*, is assigned the value of the UNIX command, *uname -n*, which contains the name of the host machine (*hostname* on BSD).

7 The name of the host machine is printed.

The Shell.pm Module (Perl5)

This module lets you use UNIX commands that you normally type at the Shell prompt in a Perl script. The commands are treated like Perl subroutines. Arguments and options are passed to the commands as a list of strings.

Example 12.45

(The Script)
```
    #!/bin/perl
1   use Shell qw(pwd ls date);   #Shell commands listed
2   print "Today is ", date();
3   print "The time is ", date("+%T");
4   print "The present working directory is ", pwd;
5   $list=ls( "-aF");
6   print $list;
```

Output

```
2   Today is Fri Mar 28 13:41:56 PST 1997
3   The time is 13:41:57
4   The present working is /home/ellie/sockets
6   ./
    ../
    sh.test*
    shellstuff
    timeclient*
    timeclient5*
    timeserver*
    timeserver5*
```

E x p l a n a t i o n

1   The *Shell.pm* module will be used in this program. The three UNIX shell commands, *pwd, ls,* and *date* will be treated as ordinary Perl subroutines.

2   The *date* command is executed as a subruoutine. This is an alternative to using back-quotes.

3   Arguments passed to the *date* command are strings enclosed in quotes.

4   The *pwd* command is executed.

5   The output of the *ls* command is assigned to scalar, *$list*. The argument is passed to the function as a single string.

6   The output of *ls -aF* is a list of files in the present working directory. The *-a* switch includes the dot files and the *-F* causes the executable scripts to be marked with an asterisk and the directories with a /.

12.4.3   The system Function

Like its C counterpart, the *system* function takes a UNIX command as its argument, sends the command to the UNIX shell for interpretation, and returns control back to the calling program, your script. This is just like the *exec* functions, except that a fork is done first, so that control is returned to the Perl script. Because it does not flush the output buffer, the special Perl variable $| is set to 1 to force a flush of the buffer after *print* or *write* statements. [12]

Format:

```
system("UNIX command");
system "UNIX command";
```

E x a m p l e   1 2 . 4 6

(The Command Line)
1   $ perl –e '**system("cal 1 1998")**;print "Happy New Year!\n";'
    January 1998
    S M   Tu W Th F S
    *   1   2 3*
    4   5   6   7 8   9 10
    11 12 13 14 15 16 17
    18 19 20 21 22 23 24
    25 26 27 28 29 30 31

    Happy New Year!

---

12. A fork is done, the script waits for the command to be executed, and control is then returned to the script.

Explanation

1 The *system* function executes the UNIX *cal* command to print out the calendar for the month of January, 1998.

Example 12.47

(The Script)
```
1  print "Hello there\n";
2  print "The name of this machine is ";
3  system ("uname –n"); # buffer is not  flushed
4  print "The time is ", `date`;
```

Output

```
1  Hello there
3  jody
2,4  The name of this machine is The time is Fri Mar 28 13:39:35 PST 1997
```

Explanation

1 The first *print* statement is executed as expected.
2 Since Perl depends on the default I/O buffering mechanism, the buffer may not be flushed immediately after the *print* statement; the results of the *system* function, executed by the Shell, are printed first.
3 The *system* function causes the Shell to execute the UNIX command, *uname -n*.
4 This *print* statement is printed directly after the print statement in line 2.

Example 12.48

(The Script)
```
   #!/bin/perl
1  $l=1;   #set special variable to flush the output buffer
2  print "Hello there\n";
3  print "The name of this machine is ";
   system ("uname –n");
4  print "The time is ", 'date';
```

Output

```
2  Hello there
3  The name of this machine is jody
4  The time is Tue Jan 26 13:43:54 PST 1998
```

Explanation

1 The $| special variable, when set to non-zero, forces the output buffer to be flushed after every *write* or *print*.

12.4.4 Here Documents

The Perl *here document* is derived from the Shell here document. Like the Shell, the Perl here document is a line-oriented form of quoting, requiring the << operator followed by an initial terminating string. There can be no spaces after the <<. If the terminating string is not quoted or double-quoted, variable expansion is performed. If the terminating string is single-quoted, variable expansion is not performed. Each line of text is inserted between the first and last terminating string. The final terminating string must be on a line by itself, with no surrounding whitespace.

Perl, unlike the Shell, does not perform command substitution (back quotes) in the text of a here document. Perl, on the other hand, does allow you to execute commands in the *here* document if the terminator is enclosed in back quotes.

Example 12.49

(The Script)

```
    #!/bin/perl
    $price=100;
1   print <<EOF;  # no quotes around terminator EOF are same as double quotes
2   The price of $price is right. # Variables are expanded
3   EOF

4   print <<'FINIS';
5   The price of $price is right. # The variable is not expanded  if terminator is
    enclosed in single quotes
6   FINIS

7   print << x 4;  # prints the line 4 times
8   Christmas is coming!
        # Blank line is necessary here as terminating string
9   print <<`END`;  # If terminator is in back quotes, will execute UNIX commands
10  echo hi there
11  echo -n "The time is "
12  date
13  END
```

Output

2   *The price of 100 is right.*
5   *The price of $price is right.*
8   *Christmas is coming!*
    Christmas is coming!
    Christmas is coming!
    Christmas is coming!
10 *hi there*
11 *The time is Mon Jan 25 11:58:35 PST 1993*

12.4.5   Globbing (Filename Expansion and Wild Cards)

If you are a Shell programmer or even a UNIX novice, you have been introduced to the Shell metacharacters used to expand filenames. The asterisk (*) is used to match all characters in a filename, the question mark (?) to match one character in a filename, and brackets ([ ]) to match one of a set of characters in a filename. The process of expanding these Shell metacharacters to a filename is called *globbing*.

Perl supports globbing if the filenames are placed within angle brackets, the read operators. There is also a function (Perl5) for globbing. (See Section 12.5.1)

Example 12.50

(The Script)
```
  #!/bin/perl
1 @myfiles=<*.[1-5]>;
2 print "@myfiles\n";
3 foreach $file ( <p??l[1-5]*>){
4       print "$file\n" if -T $file;
  }
```

Output

2 *exer.3 exer.4 exer.5 fileter.1 format.1 format.2 format.3 perl.4 perl.4.1*
4 *perl1*
   perl2
   perl3
   perl4
   perl4.1
   perl5

Explanation

1 In an array context, after the globbing is performed, a list of all the matched files is returned, and returned to the array, *@myfiles*. The list consists of any files that start with zero or more of any character, followed by a period, ending with a number between 1 and 5.

2 The list of matched files is printed.

3 The *foreach* loop is entered. Each time through the loop, the scalar, *$file*, is set to the next file that is successfully globbed, that is, any file starting with a 'p', followed by any two characters, followed by an 'l', followed by a number between 1 and 5, and ending in zero or more of any character.

4 If the file is a text file (-T), its name is printed.

The glob Function. The *glob* function does the same thing as the <*> operator. It expands the filename metacharacters just as the shell does and returns the expanded filenames.

Example 12.51

(Command Line)
```
1  $ perl –e 'while(glob("p???[1–5]")) {print "$_\n";}'
   perl1
   perl2
   perl3
   perl4
   perl5
```

(In Script)
```
2  while ( glob("p???[1–5]")){
3       print "$_\n";
   }
```

Output

```
3  perl1
   perl2
   perl3
   perl4
   perl5
```

E x p l a n a t i o n

1 At the command line, the *glob* function will "glob" onto any files in the current working directory whose name begins with a 'p', followed by any three characters (???), followed by any number between 1 and 5 ([1-5]). Each filename that matches the expression is assigned to $_ and then printed.
2 This time *glob* is being used in a script. The behavior is exactly the same as in the first example.
3 The expanded filenames are printed.

12.5 Error Handling

There are a number of occasions when a system call can fail, for example, when you try to open a file that doesn't exist, or remove a directory when it still contains files, or when you try to read from a file for which you do not have permission. Although we have used the *die* function in earlier examples, now we will go into more detail about error handling and functions you can use to handle errors. The functions are the *die* function, the *warn* function, and the *eval* function.

The *die* function is used to quit the Perl script if a command or filehandle fails.

The *warn* function is like the *die* function, but it does not exit the script.

The *eval* function has multiple uses, but it is primarily used for exception handling.

You may remember that the *short–circuit* operators, && and ||, evaluate the operands on the left and then evaluate the operands on the right. If the operand to the left of the && is true, the right-hand side is evaluated. If the operand to the left of the || is false, the right-hand side is evaluated.

12.5.1 The die Function

If a system call fails, the *die* function prints a string to STDERR and exits with the current value of $!. The $! variable yields the current value of *errno*, the UNIX global variable containing a number indicating a system error. The only time that *errno* is updated is when a system call <u>fails</u>. When a system call fails, a code number is assigned to *errno* to indicate the type of error. If the newline is omitted in the string, the message is printed with its line number. (See /usr/include/sys for a complete list.)

Example from */usr/include/sys/errno.h*:

```
#define EPERM   1      /* Not owner */
#define ENOENT  2      /* No such file or directory */
#define ESRCH   3      /* No such process */
#define EINTR   4      /* Interrupted system call */
#define EIO     5      /* I/O error */
    ...
```

Format:

```
die(LIST)
die LIST
die
```

Example 12.52

(In Script)
1 die "Can't cd to junk: $!\n" unless chdir "/usr/bin/junk";

Output

1 *Can't cd to junk: No such file or directory*

Explanation

1 The *chdir* failed. The $! contains the error message from *errno*. The newline causes the string after the *die* function to be printed with the value of the $! variable.

Example 12.53

(In Script)
1 die unless chdir '/poop' ;

Output

1 *Died at croak.perl line 4.*

Explanation

1 The *chdir* function failed. This time the $! was not included in the *die* string. The line where the error took place is printed.

Example 12.54

(In Script)
1 chdir '/poop' || die "Stopped";

Output

1 *Stopped at croak.perl line 4.*

12.5.2   The warn Function

The *warn* function (operator) is just like the *die* function except that the program continues to run. If in an eval block, the die function is called, the argument string given to the die will be assigned to the special variable $@. After a die this variable can be passed as an argument to warn. The output is sent to STDERR. (See eval, Section 12.5.3.)

The Carp.pm Module.   There are many ways to die. Perl5's Carp module extends the functionality of die. (See Example 9.22.)

12.5.3   The eval Function

The *eval* function is used for exception handling, catching errors. The block following *eval* is treated and parsed like a separate Perl program, except that all variable settings, and subroutine and format definitions remain after *eval* is finished.

The value returned from the *eval* function is that of the last expression evaluated. If there is a compile or runtime error, or the die statement is executed, an undefined value is returned and a special variable, $@, is set to the error message. If there is no error, $@ is a null string.

Evaluating Perl Expressions with eval

E x a m p l e   1 2 . 5 5

```
(The Script)
    #!/bin/perl
    # The eval function will evaluate each line you type and return the result
    # It's as though you are running a little independent Perl script.
    # Script name: plsh

1  print "> ";  # print the prompt
2  while(<STDIN>){
3        $result=eval ;   # eval evaluates the expression $_
4        warn $@ if $@; # If an error occurs, it will be assigned to $@
5        print "$result\n if $result";
6        print "> ";        # print the prompt
   }
```

O u t p u t

(The Command line)
   $ plsh
2 *> hello*
5 *hello*
2 *> bye*
5 *bye*
2 *> 5 + 4*
5 *9*
2 *> 8 / 3*
5 *2.66666666666667*
2 *> 5 / 0*
4 ***Illegal division by zero at (eval 5) line 3, <STDIN> line 5.***
   > "Oh I see
   Can't find string terminator '""' anywhere before EOF at (eval 6) line 1,
   <STDIN> line
   > exit

E x p l a n a t i o n

1 This line prints a prompt for the user. This program is like a little Perl shell. It can help you in evaluating an expression before putting it in a program, especially if you're not sure how Perl will handle it.
2 The *while* loop is entered. Each time the loop is entered it will read a line of input from the user and assign it to $_.
3 The *eval* function, without an argument, will evaluate the expression in $_ and assign the result of the evaluation to *$result*.
4 If the *eval* finds a syntax error or a system error results from the evaluation of the expression, the error message returned will be assigned to the $@ variable. If there is no error, the $@ variable is assigned a null string.
5 If the expression was successfully evaluated, the result will be printed.
6 The prompt is displayed and the loop re-entered.

Using Eval to Catch Errors in a Program

E x a m p l e   1 2 . 5 6

(In Script)
```
    #!/bin/perl
    print "Give me a number.";
    chop($a=<STDIN>);
    print "Give me a divisor.";
    chop($b=<STDIN>);
1   eval{ die unless $answer = $a/$b ; };
2   warn $@ if $@;
3   printf "Division of %.2f by %.2f is %.2f.\n",$a,$b,$answer if $answer ;
4   print "I'm here now. Good–day!\n";
```

O u t p u t

> *Give me a number.45*
> *Give me a divisor.6*
> 3 *Division of 45.00 by 6.00 is 7.50.*
> 4 *I'm here now. Good–day!*

O u t p u t

> *Give me a number.5*
> *Give me a divisor.0*
> 2 *Illegal division by zero at ./eval.p line 8, <STDIN> line 2.*
> 4 *I'm here now. Good–day!*

E x p l a n a t i o n

1 The *eval* function will evaluate the division (*$a/$b*) and store the result in *$answer*. Note that *$answer* is first used inside the *eval* function. It remains after *eval* is finished.
2 If all went well, and the division was completed, this line is ignored. If there was an error (e.g., division by zero), the $@ variable is set to the system error. The warn function then prints the message to STDERR, and the program resumes. If the *die* function is called in an *eval* block, the program does not exit but continues execution after the *eval* block exits.
3 The result of the division is printed, if successful.
4 This line is printed just to show you that the program continued execution even after a failure, since the *warn* function does not cause the script to exit.

The eval Function and the Here Document.

Example 12.57

(The Script)
```
    #!/bin/perl
1   eval<<"EOF";
2       chdir "joker" || die "Can't cd: $!\n";
3   EOF
4   print "The error message from die: $@";
5   print "Program $0 still in progress.\n";
```

Output

```
4   The error message from die: Can't cd: no such file or directory
5   Program ./eval4.p still in progress.
```

Explanation

1 The *here document* is like a special form of quoting. The eval function will get every-thing between the first EOF to the terminating EOF.
2 If the *chdir* function fails the *die* function is called and the program resumes after the last EOF of the *here document*.
3 EOF terminates the here document.
4 The error message from the *die* function is stored in the $@ variable.
5 The program continues.

12.6 Signals

A signal sends a message to a process and normally causes the process to terminate, usually due to some unexpected event, such as illegal division by zero, a segmentation violation, bus error, or a power failure. The kernel also uses signals as timers, for example, to send an alarm signal to a process. The user sends signals when he hits the BREAK, DELETE, QUIT, or STOP keys.

The kernel recognizes 31 different signals, listed in */usr/include/signal.h*. You can get a list of signals by simply typing "kill -l" at the UNIX prompt. (See Table 12.4.)

TABLE 12.4   Signals (BSD)*

Name	Number	Default	Description
SIGHUP	1	Terminate	Hangup
SIGINT	2	Interrupt	Interrupt
SIGQUIT	3	Terminate	Quit / Produces core file
SIGILL	4	Terminate	Terminate

*This is a partial listing of the signals.

Catching Signals. Signals are asynchronous events, that is, the process doesn't know when a signal will arrive. Programmatically you can ignore certain signals coming into your process or set up a signal handler to execute a subroutine when the signal arrives. In Perl scripts, any signals you specifically want to handle are set in the *%SIG* associative array. If a signal is ignored, it will be ignored after *fork* or *exec* function calls. (For a real application, see Appendix B.)

Format:

```
$SIG{'signal'};
```

E x a m p l e   1 2 . 5 8

(The Script)
```
    #!/bin/perl
1       sub handler{
2       local($sig) = @_;  # first argument is signal name
3       print "Caught SIG$sig—shutting down\n";
4       exit(1);
    }
5 $SIG{'INT'} = 'handler';  # Catch ^C
6 $SIG{'HUP'}='IGNORE';
7 print "Here I am!\n";
    sleep(10);
8 $SIG{'INT'}='DEFAULT';[13]
```

O u t p u t

7 *Here I am*
        < ^C is pressed while the process sleeps >
3 Caught SIGINT--shutting down

E x p l a n a t i o n

1 The subroutine called "handler" is defined.
2 The *local* function sets the first argument, the signal name, to the scalar, $*sig*.
3 If the signal arrives, the handler routine is executed and this statement is printed.
4 The program exits with a value of 1, indicating that something went wrong.
5 A value for the *$SIG* associative array is set. The key is the name of the signal without the 'SIG' prefix. The value is the name of the subroutine that will be called. If ^C, the interrupt key, is pressed during the run of the program, the handler routine is called.

---

13. Larry Wall, *Programming Perl* (Sebastopol, CA: O'Reilly).

6 IGNORE will ignore the hangup signal.

7 The *print* statement is executed and the process sleeps for 10 seconds. If the signal, Ctrl-C, arrives, the signal handler routine is called.

8 The SIGINT signal is reset to its default state, which is to terminate the process when ^C is pressed.

Sending Signals to Processes.

The kill Function

If you want to send a signal to a process or list of processes, the *kill* function is used. The first element of the list is the signal. The signal is a numeric value or a signal name if quoted. The function returns the number of processes that received the signal successfully. A process group is killed if the signal number is negative. You must own a process to kill it, that is, the effective uid and real uid must be the same for the process sending the kill signal and the process receiving the kill signal.

For complex signal handling, see the POSIX module in the Perl standard library

Format:

```
kill(LIST);
kill LIST;
```

E x a m p l e   1 2 . 5 9

```
1    $ sleep 100&
2    $ jobs -l
     [1] + 6505 Running              sleep 100&
3    $ perl -e 'kill 9, 6505'
     [1]    Killed                   sleep 100
```

E x p l a n a t i o n

1 At the UNIX shell prompt, the *sleep* command is executed in the background. The *sleep* command causes the shell to pause for 100 seconds.

2 The *jobs* command lists the processes running in the background. The *sleep* process is pid #6505.

3 Perl is executed at the command line. The *kill* function takes two arguments. The first one, signal 9, guarantees that the process will be terminated. The second argument is the pid of the *sleep* process.

The alarm Function

The *alarm* function tells the kernel to send a SIGALARM signal to the calling process after some number of seconds. Only one alarm can be in effect at a time. If you call *alarm* and an alarm is already in effect, the previous value is overwritten.

Format:

```
alarm (SECONDS);
alarm SECONDS;
```

E x a m p l e   1 2 . 6 0

(The Script)
1 **alarm(1)**;
2 print "In a Forever Loop!";
3 for (; ;){ printf "Counting...%d\n", $x++;}

O u t p u t

2 *In a Forever Loop!*
3 *Counting...0*
  Counting...1
  Counting...2
  Counting...3
  Counting...4
      ...
  Counting...294
  Counting...295
4 *Alarm Clock*

E x p l a n a t i o n

1 A SIGALARM signal will be sent to this process after one second.
2 This statement is printed.
3 The loop starts. We wait for one second. The resolution on the actual second may be off. The *syscall* function can be used to call other functions, for example, *setitimer (2)*and *getitimer (2)*, with better timing resolution.
4 When the alarm goes off, the message *'Alarm Clock'* is printed by the function.

The sleep Function

The *sleep* function causes the process to sleep for a number of seconds or forever if a number of seconds is not specified. It returns the number of seconds that the process slept. You can use the *alarm* function to interrupt the sleep.

Format:

```
sleep(SECONDS);
sleep SECONDS;
sleep;
```

Example 12.61

(The Script)
```
#!/bin/perl
1  $|=1  # flush output buffer
2  alarm(5);
   print "Taking a snooze...\n";
3  sleep 100;
4  print "\07 Wake up now.!\n";
```

Output

2 *Taking a snooze...   #Program pauses now for 5 seconds.*
4 *(Beep) Wake up now.*

Explanation

1 The $| variable forces the output buffer to be flushed after writes and prints.
2 The *alarm* function tells the kernel to send a SIGALARM signal to the process in 5 seconds.
3 The process goes to sleep for 100 seconds or until a signal is sent to it.
4 The \07 causes a beep to sound before the statement, "Wake up now!"

13

Report Writing with Pictures

PERL is the Practical Extraction and Report Language. After you have practically extracted and manipulated all the data in your file, you may want to write a formatted report to categorize and summarize this information. If you have written reports with the Awk programming language, you may find Perl's formatting a little "peculiar" at first.

13.1 The Template

In order to write a report, Perl requires that you define a template to describe visually how the report will be displayed, i.e., how the report is to be formatted. Do you want left-justified, centered, or right-justified columns? Do you have numeric data that needs formatting? Do you want a title on the top of each page or column titles? Do you have some summary data you want to print at the end of the report?

We'll start with a simple template for a simple report and build on that until we have a complete example.

A format template is structured as follows:

format FILEHANDLE=

Picture Line
Value Line (Text–to–be–formatted)

.

write;

13.1.1   Steps in Defining the Template

The steps for defining a template are:

1. Start the format with the keyword, *format*, followed by the name of the output filehandle and an equal sign. The default filehandle is STDOUT, the screen. The template definition can be anywhere in your script.

   format FILEHANDLE=

2. Although any text in the template will be printed as is, the template normally consists of a *picture line* to describe how the output will be displayed. The picture consists of symbols that describe the type of the fields (see Table 13.1). The fields are either left, center, or right justified (see Table 13.2). The picture line can also can be used to format numeric values (see Table 13.2).

TABLE 13.1   Field Designator Symbols

Field Designator	Purpose
@	Indicates the start of a field
@*	Used for multiline fields
^	Used for filling fields

TABLE 13.2   Field Display Symbols

Type of Field Symbol	Type of Field Definition
<	Left justified
>	Right justified
|	Centered
#	Numeric
.	Indicates placement of decimal point

3. After the field designator, the @ symbol, the *type* of field symbol is repeated as many times as there will be characters of that type. This determines the size of the field. If >>>>>> is placed directly after the @ symbol, it describes a six-character right-justified field. Strange, huh? Any real text is not placed directly after the @ symbol, or the field type is not interpreted.

4. After the picture line, which breaks the line into fields, comes the *value line*, text that will be formatted as described by the picture. Each text field is divided by a comma and corresponds, one to one, with the field symbol in the picture line. Any whitespace in the value line is ignored.

5. When you are finished creating the template, <u>a period (dot) on a line by itself terminates</u> the template definition.

6. After the template has been defined, the *write* function invokes the format and sends the formatted records to the specified output filehandle. For now, the default filehandle is STDOUT.

Example 13.1

(The Script)
```
   #!/bin/perl
1  $name="Tommy";
   $age=25;
   $salary=50000.00;
   $now="03/14/97";
   # Format Template
2  format STDOUT=
3  ———————————————REPORT————————————————

4  Name: @<<<<<< Age:@##Salary:@#####.## Date:@<<<<<<<<<<
5          $name,         $age,         $salary,         $now
6  .   # End Template

7  write;
8  print "Thanks for coming. Bye.\n";
```

Output

```
             ———————————————REPORT————————————————
   Name: Tommy   Age: 25 Salary: 50000.00 Date:03/14/97
   Thanks for coming. Bye.
```

Explanation

1 Variables are assigned.
2 The keyword, *format*, is followed by STDOUT, the default and currently selected file-handle, followed by an equal sign.
3 This line will be printed as is. Any text in the format that is not specifically formatted will print as is.
4 This line is called the *picture* line. It is a picture of how the output will be formatted. The @ defines the start of a field. There will be four fields. The first one is a left-justified six-character field, preceded by the string "*Name:* " and followed by the string "*Age:*" . The second field consists of two digits followed by "*Salary:*"; The third field consists of 7 digits with a decimal point inserted after the 5th digit, followed by the string, "*Date*".
5 These are the variables that are formatted according to the picture. Each variable is separated by a comma and corresponds to the picture field above it.
6 The dot ends the template definition.
7 The *write* function will invoke the template to display the formatted output to STDOUT.

13.2 Changing the Filehandle

If you want to write the report to a file, instead of to the screen, the file is assigned to a file-handle when it is opened. This same filehandle is used for the format filehandle when defining the template. To invoke the format, the *write* function is called with the name of the output filehandle as an argument.

E x a m p l e   1 3 . 2

```
    #!/bin/perl
1   $name="Tommy";
    $age=25;
    $salary=50000.00;
    $now="03/14/94";

2   open(REPORT, ">report" ) || die "report: $!\n";
    # REPORT filehandle is opened for writing
3   format REPORT=         # REPORT is also used for the format filehandle
    _____
      | EMPLOYEE INFORMATION |
    _____

4   Name: @<<<<<<
5          $name
    _____

    Age: @###
           $age
    _____

    Salary: @#####.##
            $salary
    _____

    Date: @>>>>>>>>>>
           $now
    _____

6   .
7   write REPORT;      # The write function sends output to the file associated
                       # with the REPORT filehandle
```

O u t p u t

I EMPLOYEE INFORMATION I

Name: Tommy

Age: 25

Salary: 50000.00

Date: 03/14/94

E x p l a n a t i o n

1. Variables are defined.
2. The file "report" is opened and attached to the REPORT filehandle.
3. The *format* keyword is followed by the output filehandle, REPORT.
4. The picture line describes the text string *"Name: "*, followed by a six-character left-justified field.
5. The scalar variable, *$name*, will be formatted as described in the picture line corresponding to it (see above).
6. The dot ends the format template definition.
7. The *write* function will invoke the format called REPORT and write formatted output to that filehandle. If the filehandle is not specified, the filehandle, REPORT, does not receive the formatted output because the *write* function has not been told where the output should go.

13.3 Top-of-the-Page Formatting

In the following example, the title, *"EMPLOYEE INFORMATION"*, is printed each time the format is invoked. It might be preferable to print only the title at the top of each page. Perl allows you to define a *top-of-the-page format* that will be invoked only when a new page is started. The default length for a page is 60 lines. After 60 lines are printed, Perl will print the top-of-the-page format at the top of the next page. (The default length can be changed by setting the special variable $= to another value.) In the following example, the *write* function sends all output to STDOUT each time the *while* loop is entered.

E x a m p l e   1 3 . 3   (**Before** Top-of-Page Formatting)

(The File)
$ cat datafile
Tommy Tucker:55:500000:5/19/66
Jack Sprat:44:45000:5/6/77
Peter Piper:32:35000:4/12/93

(The Script)
```
  #!/bin/perl
1 open(DB, "datafile" ) || die "datafile: $!\n";
2 format STDOUT=
  _____

  | EMPLOYEE INFORMATION |
  _____

        Name: @<<<<<<<<<<<<
              $name
  _____

        Age:@##
            $age
  _____

        Salary:@#####.##
               $salary
  _____

        Date:@>>>>>>>>>>
             $start
  .
3 while(<DB>){
4     ($name, $age, $salary, $start)=split(":");
5     write ;
  }
```

O u t p u t

_____

| EMPLOYEE INFORMATION |
_____

Name: Tommy Tucker
_____

Age:55
_____

Salary: 50000.00
_____

Date: 5/19/66

| EMPLOYEE INFORMATION |

Name: Jack Sprat

Age:44

Salary: 45000.00

Date: 5/6/77

| EMPLOYEE INFORMATION |

Name: Peter Piper

Age:32

Salary: 35000.00

Date: 4/12/54

Explanation

1 The file, "*datafile*", is opened for reading via the DB filehandle.
2 The format for STDOUT is created with picture lines and data.
3 The *while* loop reads one line at a time from the DB filehandle.
4 Each line is split by colons into an array of scalars.
5 The *write* function invokes the STDOUT format and sends the formatted line to STDOUT.

The next example illustrates the format for the *top of the page.*

Format:

```
format STDOUT_TOP=
     picture line
     value line (text to be formatted)
   .(End of template)
```

The keyword, *format*, is followed by the name of the filehandle appended with an underscore and the word *"TOP"*. If a picture line is included, the value line consists of the formatted text. Any text not formatted by a picture is printed literally. The period (dot) terminates the top-of-page format template.

The $% is a special Perl variable that holds the number of the current page.

E x a m p l e   1 3 . 4   **(After Top-of-Page Formatting)**

(The Script)

```
    #!/bin/perl
1   open(DB, "datafile" ) || die "datafile: $!\n";
2   format STDOUT_TOP=
3       – @||–
4         $%

            _____

5       | EMPLOYEE INFORMATION |
            _____

6   .
7   format STDOUT=

    Name: @<<<<<<<<<<<<
           $name
            _____

    Age: @##
           $age
            _____

    Salary:@#####.##
           $salary
            _____

    Date:@>>>>>>>
           $start
    .
8   while(<DB>){
9       ($name, $age, $salary, $start)=split(":");
10      write ;
    }
```

O u t p u t

```
                          – 1 –
        _____

        | EMPLOYEE INFORMATION |
        _____

        Name: Tommy Tucker
        _____

        Age: 55
        _____

        Salary: 50000.00
        _____
```

Date: 5/19/66

Name: Jack Sprat

_____

Age: 44

_____

Salary: 45000.00

_____

Date: 5/6/77

Name: Peter Piper

_____

Age: 32

_____

Salary: 35000.00

_____

Date: 4/12/93

Example 13.5

(The Script)

```
   #!/bin/perl
1  open(DB, "datafile" ) || die "datafile: $!\n";
2  open(OUT, ">outfile" )|| die "outfile: $!\n";
3  format OUT_TOP= # New Filehandle

4         – @||–
5              $%
        _____

       | EMPLOYEE INFORMATION |
        _____

       .
   format OUT=
   Name: @<<<<<<<<<<<<<
              $name
        _____

   Age: @##
              $age
        _____

   Salary: @#####.##
              $salary
        _____
```

```
    Date:@>>>>>>>
              $start
```

```
    .
    while(<DB>){
        ($name, $age, $salary, $start)=split(":");
6       write OUT;
    }
```

O u t p u t

$ cat outfile
               − 1 −

```
| EMPLOYEE INFORMATION |
```

```
Name: Tommy Tucker
```

```
Age: 55
```

```
Salary: 50000.00
```

```
Date: 5/19/66
```

```
Name: Jack Sprat
```

```
Age: 44
```

```
Salary: 45000.00
```

```
Date: 5/6/77
```

```
Name: Peter Pumpkin
```

```
Age: 32
```

```
Salary: 35000.00
```

```
Date: 4/12/93
```

13.4   **The select Function**

The *select* function is used to set the default filehandle for the *print* and *write* functions. When you have <u>selected</u> a particular filehandle with the *select* function, the *write* or *print* functions do not require an argument. The selected filehandle becomes the default when a format is invoked or when the print function is called.

The *select* function returns the scalar value of the *previously* selected filehandle.

If you have a number of formats with different names, the $~ variable is used to hold the name of the report format for the currently selected output filehandle. The *write* and *print* functions will send their output to the currently selected output filehandle.

The $^ variable holds the name of the top-of-page format for the currently selected output filehandle.

The $. variable holds the record number (similar to the NR variable in *awk*).

E x a m p l e   1 3 . 6

```
(The Script)
     #!/usr/bin/perl
     # write an awklike report
1    open(MYDB, "> mydb") || die "Can't open mydb: $!\n";
2    $oldfillehandle= select(MYDB);   # MYDB is selected as the filehandle
                                      # for write

3    format MYDB_TOP =
                    DATEBOOK INFO

     Name          Phone      Birthday     Salary
     _____.


4    format MYDB =
     @<<< @<<<<<<<<<<<<<<< @<<<<<<<<<<< @||||||| @######.##
       $.,     $name,              $phone,     $bd,    $sal
     .

5    format SUMMARY =
     _____

6    The average salary for all employees is $@######.##.
                                    $total/$count
     The number of lines left on the page is @###.
                                    $-
     The default page length is @###.
                       $=
```

```
7   .
    open(DB,"datebook") || die "Can't open datebook: $!\
    while(<DB>){
        ( $name, $phone, $address, $bd, $sal )=split(/:/);
8       write ;
        $count++;
        $total+=$sal;
    }
    close DB;

9   $~=SUMMARY;    # New report format for MYDB filehandle
10  write;

11  select ($oldfilehandle); #STDOUT is now selected for further writes or prints
12  print "Report Submitted On" , 'date';
```

Output

16 *Report Submitted On Sat Mar 26 11:52:04 PST 1994*

(The Report)
   $ cat mydb

                    DATEBOOK INFO

Name	Phone	Birthday	Salary
1 Betty Boop	245–836–8357	6/23/23	14500.00
2 Igor Chevsky	385–375–8395	6/18/68	23400.00
3 Norma Corder	397–857–2735	3/28/45	245700.00
. . .			
25 Paco Gutierrez	835–365–1284	2/28/53	123500.00
26 Ephram Hardy	293–259–5395	8/12/20	56700.00
27 James Ikeda	834–938–8376	12/1/38	45000.00

The average salary for all employees is $82572.50.
The number of lines left on the page is 32.
The default page length is 60.

Explanation

1   The filehandle, MYDB, is opened for writing.
2   The *select* function sets the default filehandle for the *write* and *print* functions to the filehandle, MYDB. The scalar, *$oldfilehandle*, is assigned the value of the <u>previously</u> assigned filehandle. The previously defined filehandle, in this example, is the default, STDOUT.
3   The top-of-the-page template is defined for filehandle, MYDB.

4   The format for the body of the report is set for filehandle, MYDB.

5   Another format template is defined with a new name, SUMMARY. This format can be invoked by assigning the format name, SUMMARY, to the special variable $~. (See line 19.)

6   The picture line is defined.

7   The format template is terminated.

8   The format is invoked and output is written to the currently selected filehandle, MYDB.

9   The $~ variable is assigned the new format name. This format will be used for the currently selected filehandle, MYDB.

10   The *write* function invokes the format, SUMMARY, for the currently selected filehandle, MYDB.

11   The *select* function sets the filehandle to the value of *$oldfilehandle*, STDOUT. Future *write* and *print* functions will send their output to STDOUT unless another output filehandle is selected.

12   This line is sent to the screen.

13.5 Multiline Fields

If the value line contains more than one newline, the @* variable is used to allow multiline fields. It is placed in a format template on a line by itself, followed by the multiline value.

E x a m p l e   1 3 . 7

(The Script)
```perl
    #!/bin/perl
1  $song="To market,\n
   to market, \nto buy a fat pig.\n";
2  format STDOUT=
3  @*
4  $song
5  @*
6  "\nHome again,\nHome again,\nJiggity, Jig!\n"
   .
   write;
```

O u t p u t

> *To market,*
> *to market,*
> *to buy a fat pig.*
> *Home again,*
> *Home again,*
> *Jiggity, Jig!*

Explanation

1 The scalar, *$song*, contains newlines.
2 The format template is set for STDOUT.
3 The @* fieldholder denotes that a multiline field will follow.
4 The value line contains the scalar, *$song*, which evaluates to a multiline string.
5 The @* fieldholder denotes that a multiline field will follow.
6 The value line contains a string embedded with newline characters.
7 End template definition.

13.6 Filling Fields

The caret (^) fieldholder allows you to create a filled paragraph containing text that will be placed according to the picture specification. If there is more text than will fit on a line, the text will wrap to the next line, etc., until all lines are printed in a paragraph block format. Each line of text is broken into words. Perl will place as many words as will fit on a specified line.   The value line variable can be repeated over multiple lines. Only the remaining text for each line is printed rather than reprinting the entire value over again.   If the number of value lines is more than the actual number of lines to be formatted, blank lines will appear.

Extra blank lines can be suppressed by using the special tilde (~) character, called the suppression indicator. If two consecutive tildes are placed on the value line, the field that is to be filled (preceded by a ^) will continue filling until all text has been blocked in the paragraph.

Example 13.8

```
(The Script)
    #!/bin/perl
    $name="Hamlet";
    print "What is your favorite line from Hamlet? ";
1   $quote = <STDIN>;
2   format STDOUT=
3   Play: @<<<<<<<<<Quotation: ^<<<<<<<<<<<<<<<<<
4           $name,              $quote
5           ^<<<<<<<<<<<<<<<<<
            $quote
            ^<<<<<<<<<<<<<<<<<
            $quote
6   ~       ^<<<<<<<<<<<<<<<<<
            $quote
    .
    write;
```

O u t p u t

What is your favorite line from Hamlet? *To be or not to be, that is the question:*
Whether 'tis nobler to in the mind to suffer the slings and arrows of outrageous
fortune...

Play:	*Hamlet*	*Quotation:*	*To be or not to be, that is the question: Whether 'tis nobler in the mind to suffer the slings and arrows of outrageous fortune...*

E x p l a n a t i o n

1   The user is asked for input and should type a line from Shakespeare's *Hamlet*. (The line wraps.)
2   The format template for STDOUT is defined.
3   The picture line contains two fields, one for the name of the play, *Hamlet*, and one for the line of user input, *$quote*. The ^ fieldholder is used to create a filled paragraph. The quote will be broken up into words that will fit over four lines. If there are more words than value lines, they will not be formatted. If there are less words than lines, blank lines will be suppressed due to the ~ character preceding the last picture line.
4   The value line contains the variables to be formatted according to the picture above them.
5   The second line contained in *$quote* is placed here if all of it did not fit on the first line.
6   If we run out of text after formatting three lines, the blank line will be suppressed.

E x a m p l e   1 3 . 9

(The Script)

```
    #!/bin/perl
    $name="Hamlet";
    print "What is your favorite line from Hamlet? ";
    $quote = <STDIN>;
    format STDOUT=
    Play: @<<<<<<<<<<Quotation:  ^<<<<<<<<<<<<<<<<<<<
1            $name,                 $quote
2   ~~                              ^<<<<<<<<<<<<<<<<<<<
                                    $quote
    .
3   write;
```

Output

What is your favorite line from Hamlet? *To be or not to be, that is the question: Whether 'tis nobler to in the mind to suffer the slings and arrows of outrageous fortune...*

Play: *Hamlet*	*Quotation:* *To be or not to be, that is the question: Whether 'tis nobler in the mind to suffer the slings and arrows of outrageous fortune...*

Explanation

1 The value line is set. It will contain the name of the play and the quotation.
2 Using two tildes (suppression indicators) tells Perl to continue filling the paragraph until all of the text in *$quote* is printed or a blank line is encountered.
3 The *write* function invokes the format.

13.7 Formatting Perl DBM Databases

The Perl distribution comes with a set of database management library files, called DBM, short for database management. DBM database files are stored as key/value pairs, an associative array which is mapped into a disk file. They can handle very large databases (a billion blocks or more). The nice thing about storing data with DBM functions is that the data is persistent, i.e., any program can access the file as long as the DBM functions are used. The disadvantage is that there is no filelocking or reliable buffer flushing, making concurrent reading and updating risky.[1] (Perl also provides special modules to interface with databases such as Sybase and Oracle. See Appendix for further information.)

Before a database can be accessed, it must be opened by using the *dbmopen* function. This binds the DBM file to an associative array (hash). The database is stored in two files. One file is a directory containing an index and has *.dir* as its suffix. The second file contains all data and has *.pag* as its suffix. Data is added to the hash, just as with any Perl hash, and an element is removed with Perl's *delete* function.

The DBM file can be closed with the *dbmclose* function.

Format:

```
dbmopen(hash, databasename, mode);
```

---

1. Although Perl's *tie* function wil probably replace the *dbmopen* function, for now we'll use this function because it's easier than *tie*.

Example:

dbmopen(%myhash, "mydbfile", 0666);

Perl's report writing mechanism is very useful for generating formatted data from one of the DBM databases. The following examples not only illustrate how to create, add, delete, and close a DBM database, but also how to create a Perl-style report.

Creating the Database

E x a m p l e   1 3 . 1 0

(The Script)
```perl
#!/usr/bin/perl
# Program name: makestates
# This program creates the database using the dbm functions
```

1 **use AnyDBM_File;**

2 **dbmopen(%states, "statedb", 0666) || die;**

3 TRY: {
4   print "Enter the abbreviation for your state. ";
         chomp($abbrev=<STDIN>);
         $abbrev = uc $abbrev; # Make sure abbreviation is uppercase
         print "Enter the name of the state. ";
         chomp($state=<STDIN>);
         lc $state;
5   **$states{$abbrev}="\u$state";** #Make first letter of state uppercase
         print "Another entry? ";
         $answer = <STDIN>;
6   redo TRY if $answer =~ /Y|y/;
     }

7 **dbmclose(%states);**

(The Command line)
8 $ **ls**
   makestates statedb.dir statedb.pag

O u t p u t

Enter the abbreviation for your state. CA
Enter the name of the state. california
Another entry? y
Enter the abbreviation for your state. me
Enter the name of the state. maine
Another entry? y
Enter the abbreviation for your state. NE
Enter the name of the state. nebraska
Another entry? y
Enter the abbreviation for your state. nm
Enter the name of the state. New Mexico
Another entry? n

E x p l a n a t i o n

1   Perl comes with a set of standard DBM packages. So that you don't have to figure out which package to use, the *AnyDBM_File.pm* module will get the appropriate package for your system from the standard set.

2   The *dbmopen* function will create or open an existing DBM file from the the disk. It needs a hash name, a database name, and a set of permissions. The user, group and others will be given read and write here.

3   This is a *labeled* block. The label is used with the *redo* statement on line number 6 so that the user can continue to add data to the database if he types *y* or *Y*.

4   The user is asked for input. He will input both the key and the value pairs for the hash.

5   The value is assigned to the hash. The *uc* function returns all uppercase.

6   If the user selects *y* or *Y*, the *redo* statement returns control to the labeled block.

7   The *dbmclose* function closes the database associated with the *%states* hash.

8   The data base is stored in two files. One file is a directory containing an index and has *state.dir* as its suffix. The second file contains all data and has *state.pag* as its suffix. The files are not in a readable format. The *dbm* functions are used to access the data.

Accessing the Database and Writing a Report

E x a m p l e   1 3 . 1 1

(The Script)

```
      #!/usr/bin/perl
      # Program name: getstates
      # This program fetches the data from the database and generates a report

1     use AnyDBM_File;

2     format STDOUT_TOP=
3     Abbreviation    State
      ==============================
4     .

5     format STDOUT=
6     @<<<<<<<<<<<<<<@<<<<<<<<<<<<<<<
7     $key,                $value
8     .

9     format SUMMARY=
      ==============================
          Number of states:@###
                           $total

      .

10    dbmopen(%states, "statedb", 0666);

11    @sortedkeys=sort keys %states;
12    foreach $key ( @sortedkeys ){
          $value=$states{$key};
          $total++;
13        write;
      }
14    dbmclose(%states);

15    $~=SUMMARY;
16    write;
```

O u t p u t

Abbreviation   State

==================================

    AZ   Arizona
    CA   California
    ME   Maine
    NE   Nebraska
    NM   New Mexico
    WA   Washington

==================================
        Number of states: 6

E x p l a n a t i o n

1   The *AnyDBM_File.pm* module will get the appropriate DBM package for your system
     from the standard set.
2   This is a top-of-the-page STDOUT format declaration for generating a report.
3   The picture line defines how the data will look when printed. Each of the keys and val-
     ues of the *%states* array will be formatted according to the picture line.
4   Period ends the format declaration.
5   This is the STDOUT format declaration for the body of each page.
6   This is the picture line that determines how the body of the program will look. Each
     key and value will be printed out as left justified strings.
7   These two values will be printed according to the picture line.
8   The period marks the end of the format declaration.
9   This is a new format declaration that will be assigned to a selected filehandle in order
     to invoke this format. It contains summary information for the report.
10   The *dbmopen* function will open the database on disk called *statedb* and assign its keys
     and values to the *%states* hash. The database is opened with read and write permis-
     sions for everyone (0666).
11   The keys in the *%states* hash are sorted and returned to *@sortedkeys*.
12   The *foreach* loop is used to loop through each of the sorted keys and values in the
     @sortedkeys array.
13   The *write* function invokes the format.
14   The *dbmclose* function closes the database.
15   The $~ variable is assigned the new format name. This format will be used for the cur-
     rently selected filehandle, STDOUT.
16   The new format is invoked. The summary information is printed.

Removing Data From the Database and Writing a Report

E x a m p l e   1 3 . 1 2

(The Script)
```
     #!/usr/bin/perl
1  use AnyDBM_File;

2  dbmopen(%states, "statedb", 0666) || die;

   TRY: {
       print "Enter the abbreviation for the state to remove. ";
       chomp($abbrev=<STDIN>);
       $abbrev = uc $abbrev;  # Make sure abbreviation is uppercase
3      delete $states{"$abbrev"};
       print "$abbrev removed.\n";
       print "Another entry? ";
       $answer = <STDIN>;
       redo TRY  if $answer =~ /Y|y/;
   }

4  dbmclose(%states);
```

O u t p u t

```
5  $ remstates
   Enter the abbreviation for the state to remove. NM
   NM removed.
   Another entry? n

6  $ getstates
   Abbreviation    State
   ===============================
   AZ          Arizona
   CA          California
   ME          Maine
   NE          Nebraska
   WA          Washington
   ===============================
                   Number of states:  5
7  $ ls
   getstates   makestates  yemstates    statedb.dir  statedb.pag
```

Explanation

1 The *AnyDBM_File.pm* module will get the appropriate DBM package for your system from the standard set.

2 The *dbmopen* function will create or open an existing DBM file from the the disk. It needs a hash name, a database name, and a set of permissions. The user, group and others will be given read and write.

3 An entry is deleted from the database with Perl's *delete* function.

4 The database is closed.

5 At the command line, the *rmstates* script is started. The user is asked to enter the entry he wants to delete. The key for *New Mexico*, *NM*, is entered.

6 The *getstates* script is then executed to retrieve the data from the database and print out a report. The report displays the data showing that New Mexico has been deleted.

7 The *ls* command lists the files associated with the database, *statedb.dir, statedb.pag*, and the three Perl scripts: *getstates, makestates*, and *yemstates*.

14

Send It over the Net and Socket to 'em!

14.1 Networking and Perl

Because sharing information and transferring files among computers are so inherently a part of everything we do, Perl offers a number of functions to obtain network information in your program. In order to write programs utilizing interprocess communication (sockets, message queues, etc.), it is essential to understand some of the basic terminology associated with the network. The following discussion is merely an introduction to some of the common networking vernacular, so that when you try to dissect or write Perl programs that require these functions, you will not have to search through all your C books or wade through the manual pages to figure out what is going on.

14.2 Client/Server Model

Most network applications use a client/server model. The server provides some service to one or more clients. The client may request a service from a server on the same machine or on a remote machine. Server programs provide such services as *e-mail, telnet,* and *ftp.* In order for the client and server to talk to each other, a connection is made between the two processes, often by utilizing sockets. Today, one of the most well-known client/server models is the client (browser)/server (HTTP) model used by the Web.

14.3   Network Protocols (TCP/IP)

When sending data over a network, there must be some reliable way to get the data from one machine to another. In order to facilitate this complicated process, networks are organized in a series of layers, each layer offering a specific networking service to the next layer. The layers are independent and have clearly defined interfaces defining their functions to the next layer. A high layer passes data and information to the layer below it, until the bottom layer is reached. At the bottom layer, two machines can physically communicate with each other. The rules and procedures used for one network layer on a machine to communicate with its counterpart network layer on another machine are called *protocols*. The most popular software networking UNIX protocols are TCP, UDP, IP, and Ethernet.

14.3.1   Ethernet Protocol (Hardware)

The Ethernet layer is the physical layer of the network. Any host connected to the Ethernet bus has physical access to data sent over the network. The Ethernet protocol prepares the data for transmission across a wire. It organizes the data in frames using 48-bit Ethernet source and destination addresses. The Ethernet layer, the lowest layer, represents the transfer of data on the physical network.

14.3.2   Internet Protocol (IP)

The IP (Internet Protocol) layer is above the Ethernet layer and prepares the data for routing on independent networks. IP uses a 4-byte Internet protocol address, and data is organized in pieces of information called *packets*. A packet contains an IP header with source and destination addresses, a protocol type, and a data portion. Although the IP protocol is more complicated than the Ethernet protocol, it is connectionless and unreliable in delivering packets. It doesn't guarantee how and that the data will be received, but if the data being sent is too large, IP will break it down into smaller units. The IP protocol hides the underlying differences among the different networks from the user.

14.3.3   Transmission Control Protocol (TCP)

Although the IP layer provides some flow control, it is not guaranteed to be reliable; that is, the data may not be received in the same order it was sent or it may never get to its destination at all. The TCP (Transmission Control Protocol) protocol provides a reliable end-to-end service and flow of control analogous to making a phone call. Once the connection is made, both sides can communicate with each other, and even if they talk at the same time, the messages are received in the same order they were sent. Programs that use TCP are *rlogin*, *rsh*, *rcp*, and *telnet*.

14.3.4   User Datagram Protocol (UDP)

UDP is an alternative to TCP. It is used in applications that do not require a continuous connection and are sending short messages periodically with no concern if some of the data is lost. A UDP datagram is similar to sending a letter in the mail. Each packet has an address; there is no guaranteed delivery time or sequencing; and duplicate packets may be sent.[1] This method prevents programs from hanging when a return is expected. Examples of programs that use this protocol are *rwho* and *ruptime*.

14.4 Network Addressing

Networks consist of a number of interconnected machines called *hosts*. The system administrator assigns the hostname when a new machine is added to the network. Each host on a TCP/IP/Ethernet network has a name and three types of addresses: an Ethernet address, an IP address, and a TCP service port number. When information is passed from one layer to another in a network, the packet contains header information, including the addresses needed to send the packet to its next destination.

The pack and unpack Functions.   Often the addresses returned by the networking functions are in a binary structure. In order to convert those addresses into an ASCII format, the Perl's *unpack* function can be used. Conversely, in order to pack an array or list into a binary format, the *pack* function is used. Before getting into all the details, let's review how the pack function works. (See Section 12.2.8.)

Format:

```
pack(Template, Array);
```

E x a m p l e   1 4 . 1

(The Script)
```
1       $bytes=pack("c4", 80,101,114,108);
2       print "$bytes\n";
```

O u t p u t

Perl

---

1. Bill Rieken and Lyle Weiman, *Adventure in UNIX, Network Applications Programming* (New York: Wiley), p. 7.

Explanation

1   The first element in the list, the Template (see Table 14.1), is composed of the type and the number of values to be packed, in this example, four signed characters. The rest of the list consists of the decimal values for characters 'P', 'e', 'r', and 'l'. This list is packed into a binary structure. The string containing the packed structure is returned and stored in *$bytes* (see your ASCII table).

2   The four-byte character string is printed.

TABLE 14.1   The Pack Template—Types and Values[2]

a	An ASCII string, will be null padded.
A	An ASCII string, will be space padded.
b	A bit string, low-to-high order.
B	A bit string, high-to-low order.
h	A hexadecimal string, low nybble first.
H	A hexadecimal string, high nybble first.
c	A signed char value.
C	An unsigned char value.
s	A signed short value.
S	An unsigned short value.
i	A signed integer value.
I	An unsigned integer value.
l	A signed long value.
L	An unsigned long value.
n	A short in "network" order.
N	A long in "network" order.
f	A single precision float in the native format.
d	A double precision float in the native format.
p	A pointer to a string.
x	A null byte.
X	Back up a byte.
@	Null-fill to absolute position.
u	A uuencoded string.

Ethernet Addresses.   Since the Ethernet address is usually burned into the PROM when the machine is manufactured, it is not a number that is assigned by a system administrator. It is simply used to identify that particular piece of hardware. The */etc/ethers* (UCB) file contains the Ethernet addresses and hostnames for a particular network.

IP Addresses.   The *IP address* is a 32-bit number assigned by the system administrator to a particular host on the network. If a host is connected to more than one network, it must have an IP address for each of the networks. It consists of a set of four decimal numbers (often called a four-octet address) separated by dots (e.g., 129.150.28.56). The first part of the address identifies the network to which the host is connected, and the rest of the address represents the host part. The addresses are divided into classes (A through C). The classes determine exactly what part of the address belongs to the network and what part belongs to

---

2.   Larry Wall and Randal L. Schwartz, *Programming Perl* (Sebastopol, CA: O'Reilly), pp. 166–67.

the host. The */etc/hosts* file contains the Internet address of your host machine, the host's name and any aliases associated with it. (See the *gethostent* and related functions.)

Port Numbers.   When serving a number of user processes, a server machine may have a number of clients requesting a particular service that use either the TCP or UDP protocol. When delivering information to a particular application layer, these protocols use a 16-bit integer *port number* to identify a particular process on a given host. UDP and TCP port numbers between 0 and 255, called well-known ports, are reserved for common services. (Some operating systems reserve additional ports for privileged programs.)[3] The most common services are Telnet and FTP with TCP port numbers 23 and 21, respectively. If you write a server application that will use either the UDP or TCP protocols, the application must be assigned a unique port number. This port number should be some number outside the range of the special reserved port numbers. The */etc/services* file contains a list of the well-known port numbers.

14.4.1   Perl Protocol Functions

The following Perl functions allow you to retrieve information from the */etc/protocols* file. The functions are named after the system calls and library functions found in Sections 2 and 3 of the UNIX manual pages.

The getprotoent Function.   The *getprotoent* function reads the next line from the network protocols database, */etc/protocol,* and returns a list. The entries are the official names of the protocols, a list of aliases or alternate names for the protocol, and the protocol number. The *setprotoent* function opens and rewinds the */etc/protocols* file. If STAYOPEN is non-zero, the database will not be closed after successive calls to the *getprotoent*. The *endprotoent* function closes the database.

Format:

```
getprotoent;
setprotoent (STAYOPEN);
endprotoent;
```

E x a m p l e   1 4 . 2

(The Script)
```
1    while (($name, $aliases, $proto ) = getprotoent){
2         printf "name=%-5s,aliases=%-6sproto=%-8s\n", $name, $aliases, $proto;
     }
```

---

3. W. Richard Stevens, *TCP/IP Illustrated: The Protocols* (Addison-Wesley), p. 13.

O u t p u t

2   *name=ip,aliases=IP proto=0*
     name=icmp,aliases=ICMPproto=1
     name=igmp,aliases=OGMPproto=2
     name=ggp,aliases=GGPproto=3
     name=tcp,aliases=TCPproto=6
     name=pup,aliases=PUPproto=12
     name=udp,aliases=IDPproto=17

E x p l a n a t i o n

1 The *getprotoent* function gets an entry from the */etc/protocols* file. The loop will read
   through the entire file. The name of the protocol, any aliases associated with it, and the
   protocol number are retrieved.
2 Each entry and its values are printed.

The getprotobyname Function.   The *getprotobyname* function is similar to the *getprotoent* above in that it gets an entry from the */etc/protocols* file. The *getprotobyname* takes
the protocol name as an argument and returns its name, any aliases, and its protocol number.

Format:

```
getprotobyname(NAME);
```

E x a m p l e   1 4 . 3

(The Script)
1   **($name, $aliases, $proto) = getprotobyname('tcp');**
     print "name=$name\taliases=$aliases\t$protocol number=$proto\n",

O u t p u t

     name=tcpaliases=TCP   protocol number=6

E x p l a n a t i o n

1 The name of the protocol, any alias name, and the protocol number are retrieved from
   the */etc/protocols* function. The name of the protocol, tcp, is passed as the NAME argument.

The getprotobynumber Function.   The *getprotobynumber* function is similar to the getprotoent function above in that it gets an entry from the */etc/protocols* file. The *getprotobynumber* takes the protocol number as an argument and returns the name of the protocol,
any aliases, and its protocol number.

Format:

```
getprotobynumber (NUMBER)
```

E x a m p l e   1 4 . 4

(The Script)
1   **($name, $aliases, $proto) = getprotobynumber(0);**
       print "name=$name\taliases=$aliases\t$protocol number=$proto\n",

O u t p u t

   name=ip   aliases=IP   protocol number=0

E x p l a n a t i o n

1   The *getprotobynumber* retrieves an entry from the */etc/protocols* file based on the proto-
    col number passed as an argument. It returns the name of the protocol, any aliases, and
    the protocol number.

14.4.2   Perl's Server Functions

These functions let you look up information in the network services file, */etc/services*.

The getservent Function.   The *getservent* function reads the next line from the */etc/ser-
vices* file. If STAYOPEN is non-zero, the */etc/services* file will not be closed after each call.

Format:

```
getservent;
setservent (STAYOPEN);
endservent;
```

E x a m p l e   1 4 . 5

(The Script)
1   setservent(1);
2   **($name, $aliases, $port, $proto) = getservent;**
3   print "Name=$name\nAliases=$aliases\nPort=$port\nProtocol=$protocol\n";

       < program continues here >

4   ($name, $aliases, $port, $proto) = getservent; *# retrieves the next entry in
       /etc/services*
5   print "Name=$name\nAliases=$aliases\nPort=$port\nProtocol=$protocol\n";
6   endservent;

O u t p u t

3   *Name=tcpmux*
     Aliases=
     Port=1
     Protocol=tcp

5   *Name=echo*
     Aliases=
     Port=7
     Protocol=tcp

E x p l a n a t i o n

1 The *setservent* function guarantees that the */etc/services* file remains open after each call
   if the STAYOPEN flag is non-zero.
2 The *getservent* function returns the name of the service, any aliases associated with the
   services, the port number, and the network protocol.
3 The retrieved values are printed.
4 The second call to *getservent* retrieves the next line from the */etc/services* file.
5 The retrieved values are printed.
6 The *endservent* function closes the network file.

The getservbyname Function.   The *getservbyname* function translates the service port
name to its corresponding port number.

Format:

```
getservbyname(NAME, PROTOCOL);
```

E x a m p l e   1 4 . 6

   ($name,$aliases,$port,$protocol)=getservbyname('telnet', 'tcp');

E x p l a n a t i o n

1 The name of the service is *telnet* and the protocol is *tcp*. The service name, aliases, the
   port number, and the protocol are returned.

The getservbyport Function.   The *getservbyport* function retrieves information from the
/etc/services file.

Format:

```
getservbyport(PORT, PROTOCOL);
```

E x a m p l e   1 4 . 7

(The Script)
```
    #!/bin/perl
    print "What is the port number? ";
    chop($PORT=<>);

    print "What is the protocol? ";
    chop($PROTOCOL=<>);
```

1   **($name, $aliases, $port, $proto) = getservbyport($PORT, $PROTOCOL);**
```
    print "The getservbyport function returns:
        name=$name
        aliases=$aliases
        port number=$port
        prototype=$protocol \n";
```

O u t p u t

```
    What is the port number?  517
    What is the protocol?  udp
    The getservbyport function returns:
        name=talk
        aliases=talk
        port number=517
        prototype=udp
```

E x p l a n a t i o n

1   The well-known port number, 517, and the protocol name, *udp*, are passed to the *get-servbyport* function. The name of the service, any aliases, the port number, and the protocol name are returned.

14.4.3   Perl's Host Information Functions

These functions allow you to retrieve information from the */etc/hosts* file. They are named after the system library routines found in Section 3 of the UNIX manual pages.

The gethostent Function.   The *gethostent* function returns a list consisting of the next
line from the */etc/hosts* file. The entries are the official name of the host machine, a list of
aliases or alternate names for the host, the type of address being returned, the length, in
bytes, of the address, and a list of network addresses, in byte order, for the named host.

Format:

```
gethostent;
sethostent(STAYOPEN);
endhostent;
```

E x a m p l e   1 4 . 8

(The Script)
```
    #!/bin/perl
1   while ( ($name,  $aliases, $addrtype, $length, @addrs) = gethostent ){
2       ($a, $b, $c, $d) = unpack ( 'C4', $addrs[0]);
3       print "The name of the host is $name.\n";
4       print "Local host address (unpacked) $a.$b.$c.$d\n";
    }
```

O u t p u t

3   *The name of the host is localhost.*
4   *Local host address (unpacked) 127.0.0.1*
    The name of the host is jody.
    Local host address (unpacked) 129.150.28.56

E x p l a n a t i o n

1 The *gethostent* function retrieves the next entry from the /etc/hosts file.
2 The raw address returned by the *gethostent* function is unpacked into four bytes (C4) so
   that it can be printed.
3 The name of the host, *jody,* is printed.
4 The local host's Internet address is printed.

The gethostbyaddr Function.   The *gethostbyaddr* function translates a network address
to its corresponding names. It retrieves the information from the */etc/hosts* file for a host by
passing a raw address as an argument. The entry consists of the official name of the host
machine, a list of aliases or alternate names for the host, the type of address being returned,
the length, in bytes, of the address, and a list of network addresses, in byte order, for the
named host.

Format:

```
gethostbyaddr(ADDRESS, DOMAIN_NUMBER);
```

E x a m p l e   1 4 . 9

(The Script)
```
    #!/bin/perl
1   $address=pack("C4", 127,0,0,1);
2   ($name, $aliases, $addrtype, $length, @addrs) = gethostbyaddr
      ($address,2);
3   ($a, $b, $c, $d) = unpack ( 'C4', $addrs[0]);
4   print "Hostname Is $name and the Internet address Is $a.$b.$c.$d.\n";
```

O u t p u t

Hostname is localhost and the Internet address is 127.0.0.1.

E x p l a n a t i o n

1   The Internet address is 127.0.0.1. It is packed into 4 bytes and this address is used by the *gethostbyaddr* function.
2   The raw address and the value of AF_INET (found in */usr/lnclude/sys/socket.h*) are passed to the *gethostbyaddr* function.
3   The raw address is unpacked into 4 bytes.
4   The name of the host and Internet address are printed.

The gethostbyname Function.   The *gethostbyname* function returns an entry from the */etc/hosts* file for the name of a specific host passed as an argument. The entry consists of the official name of the host machine, a list of aliases or alternate names for the host, the type of address being returned, the length, in bytes, of the address, and a list of network addresses, in byte order, for the named host.

Format:

```
gethostbyname(NAME);
```

E x a m p l e   1 4 . 1 0

```
    ($name, $aliases, $addtrtype, $length, @addrs)=gethostbyname("dolphin");
```

E x p l a n a t i o n

(See the *gethostent* function above for explanation.)

14.5 Sockets

Sockets were first developed at Berkeley in 1982 in order to support interprocess communication on networks. The client/server model is used for interprocess communication through sockets. Not all are versions of UNIX support sockets. If your system is one of these, the socket examples shown here will not work.

Sockets are a software abstraction representing the endpoints between two communicating processes, a server and a client; in other words, sockets allow processes talk to each other. The communicating processes can be on the same machine or on different machines. The server process creates the socket. The client process knows the socket by name. In order to ensure where the data is coming from or going to on a network, the socket uses IP and port addresses. A program using a socket opens the socket (similar to opening a file), and once the socket is opened, I/O operations can be performed for reading and writing information to the communicating processes. When a file is opened, a file descriptor is returned. When a socket is opened, a socket descriptor is returned to the server and one is returned to the client. The socket interface, however, is a lot more complex than working with files since communication is often done across networks.

Remote login and file transfer programs are common utilities that communicate across a network through the use of sockets.

14.5.1 Types of Sockets

Every socket has a type of communication path to identify how the data will be transferred through the socket.   The two most common types of sockets, SOCK_STREAM and SOCK_DGRAM, utilize the TCP and UDP protocols, respectively.

There are other less common types of sockets, such as SOCK_SEQPACKET and SOCK_RAW, but we will not discuss those here.

Stream Sockets.   The stream socket, SOCK_STREAM type of socket, provides a reliable, connection-oriented, sequenced, two-way service. It provides for error detection and flow control, and it removes duplicate segments of data. The underlying protocol is TCP. (See Section 14.3.3, "TCP protocol.")

Datagram Sockets.   The datagram sockets, SOCK_DGRAM type of socket, provides a connectionless service. Packets sent may be received in any order or may not be received on the other end at all. There is no guarantee of delivery and packets may be duplicated. The underlying protocol is UDP. (See Section 14.3.4, "UDP protocol.")

14.5.2 Socket Domains

When a socket is opened, a number of system calls are issued describing how the socket is to be used. The process must specify a communication domain, also called an address family, to identify the way the socket is named and what protocols and addresses are needed in order to send or receive data. The domain of a socket identifies where the server and client reside—on the same machine, on the Internet, or on a XEROX network.

The two standard domains are the *UNIX domain* and the *Internet domain*. When using sockets for interprocess communication, the *UNIX domain* is used for processes communicating on the same machine, whereas the *Internet domain* is used for processes communicating on remote machines using the TCP/IP protocols. (The *AF_NS domain* is used for processes on a XEROX network.)

The UNIX Domain and the AF_UNIX Family.   If the communication is between two processes on a local machine, the address family (AF) is called AF_UNIX. The UNIX domain supports the SOCK_STREAM type and the SOCK_DGRAM socket type. The SOCK_STREAM type in the UNIX domain provides a bidirectional communication between processes, similar to the pipe facility. This is a reliable byte-stream transfer between processes. The datagram sockets are unreliable, not often used, and cause the socket to behave like message queues or telegrams.

Sockets in the UNIX domain have pathnames in the UNIX file system. The *ls -l* command lists the file as a socket if the first character is an 's' (see Example 14.11). In the system file */usr/include/sys/socket.h*, the AF_UNIX family is assigned the constant value, 1.

E x a m p l e   1 4 . 1 1

$ls -IF greetings
srwxrwxrwx   *1 ellie   0 Apr 26 09:31 greetings=*

The Internet Domain and the AF_INET Family.   The Internet domain sockets, identified as AF_INET, are used for interprocess communication between processes on different computers. The Internet domain also supports the socket types, SOCK_STREAM and SOCK_DGRAM.

The Internet socket is defined by its IP address to identify the Internet host and its port number to identify the port on the host machine.

The underlying protocol for SOCK_STREAM is TCP. The underlying protocol for SOCK_DGRAM is UDP. In the system file */usr/include/sys/socket.h*, the AF_INET family is defined as the constant 2.

Socket Addresses.   A socket, once created, needs an address so that data can be sent to it. In the AF_UNIX domain, the address is a filename, but in the AF_INET domain it is an IP address and a port number.

14.5.3   Creating a Socket

The *socket* function creates the socket and returns a filehandle for the socket. In the server this socket is called the rendezvous socket.

Format:

```
socket(SOCKET_FILEHANDLE, DOMAIN, TYPE, PROTOCOL);
```

Example 14.12

```
$AF_UNIX=1;
$SOCK_STREAM=1;
$PROTOCOL=0;
```

```
1    socket(COMM_SOCKET, $AF_UNIX, $SOCK_STREAM, $PROTOCOL);
```

Explanation

1 In this example, the *socket* function creates a filehandle called COMM_SOCKET. The domain or family is UNIX, the socket type is STREAM socket, and the protocol is assigned 0, which allows the system to choose the correct protocol for this socket type.

14.5.4   Binding an Address to a Socket Name

The bind Function.   The *bind* function attaches an address or a name to a SOCKET filehandle. (See sample programs at the end of this chapter.)

Format:

```
bind(SOCKET_FILEHANDLE, NAME);
```

Example 14.13

```
1        bind(COMM_SOCKET, "/home/jody/ellie/perl/tserv");
2        bind(COMM_SOCKET, $socket_address);
```

Explanation

1 When using the UNIX domain, the socket filehandle, COMM_SOCKET, is bound to a UNIX pathname.
2 When using the Internet domain, the socket filehandle, COMM_SOCKET, is bound to the packed address for the socket type.

14.5.5   Creating a Socket Queue

The listen Function.   The *listen* function waits for *accepts* on the socket and specifies the number of connection requests to be queued, before rejecting further requests. Imagine having call waiting on your phone with up to 5 callers queued.[4] If the number of client requests exceeds the queue size, an error is returned.   The function returns true if successful, false otherwise. Error code is stored as $!.

Format:

```
listen(SOCKET_FILEHANDLE, QUEUE_SIZE);
```

Example 14.14

```
1      listen(SERVERSOCKET, 5);
```

Explanation

1   The number of waiting connections in the queue is set to 5. The *listen* function queues the incoming client requests for the *accept* function (see below).

14.5.6   Waiting for a Client Request

The accept Function.   The *accept* function in the server process waits for a request from the client to arrive. If there is a queue of requests, the first request is removed from the queue when a connection is made. The *accept* function then opens a new socket filehandle with the same attributes as the original or generic socket, also called the rendezvous socket, and attaches it to the client's socket. The new socket is ready to communicate with the client socket. The generic socket is now available to accept additional connections. The *accept* function returns true if successful, false otherwise. Error code is stored as $!.

Format:

```
accept(NEWSOCKET, GENERICSOCKET);
```

Example 14.15

```
1    accept (NEWSOCK, RENDEZ_SOCK );
```

Explanation

1   The server process uses the *accept* function to accept requests from clients. It takes the first pending request from the queue and creates a new socket filehandle, NEWSOCK, with the same properties as RENDEZ_SOCK filehandle, also called the generic or rendezvous socket.

---

4. Larry Wall and Randal L. Schwartz, *Programming Perl* (Sebastopol, CA: O'Reilly), p. 158.

14.5.7   Establishing a Socket Connection

The connect Function.   The *connect* function uses the socket filehandle and the address of the server socket to which it will connect. It makes a rendezvous with the *accept* function in the server. After the connection is made, data can be transferred. If the UNIX domain is used, the pathname of the UNIX file is provided. If the Internet domain is used, the address is a packed network address of the proper type for the server. It returns true if successful, false otherwise. Error code is stored as $!.

Format:

```
connect(SOCKET, ADDRESS);
```

E x a m p l e   1 4 . 1 6

```
1    connect(CLIENTSOCKET, "/home/joe/sock" );
2    connect(CLIENTSOCKET, $packed_address);
```

E x p l a n a t i o n

1   In the UNIX domain, a UNIX pathname is attached to the filehandle, CLIENTSOCKET.
2   In the Internet domain, a packed network address is attached to the filehandle, CLIENT-SOCKET. The address is obtained from the *gethostbyname* function and is packed with the Perl *pack* function. For example:

```
$hostname="houston";
$port=9876;
$AF_INET=2;
$SOCK_STREAM=1;
($name, $aliases, $type, $len, $address)=gethostbyname($hostname);
$packed_address=pack(S n a4 x8, $AF_INET, $port, $address);
```

14.5.8   Socket Shutdown

The shutdown Function.   The *shutdown* function shuts down a socket connection as specified. If the HOW argument is 0, further receives on the socket will be refused. If the HOW argument is 1, further sends on the socket will be refused, and if the argument is 2, all sends and receives are stopped.

Format:

```
shutdown(SOCKET, HOW);
```

E x a m p l e   1 4 . 1 7

1   shutdown(COMM_SOCK, 2);

E x p l a n a t i o n

1   The socket filehandle, COMM_SOCK, will disallow further sends or receives. It is
shutdown.

FIGURE 14.1   **Sockets for a Server and Client Connection-Oriented Communication**

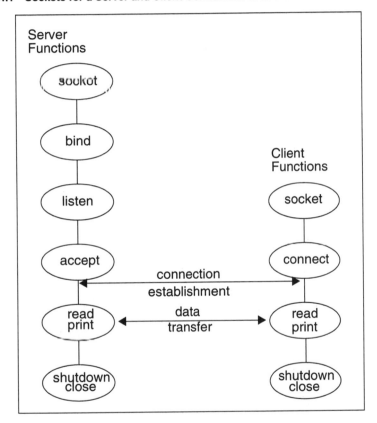

14.6 Client/Server Programs

The sample programs shown here were tested on Sun workstations running SunOS 4.1.3
and SunOS 5.3. These programs are examples of stream sockets for the UNIX and Internet
domains. Although datagrams (UDP protocol) are supported, they are unreliable and delivery of packets is not guaranteed. They are used in the Internet domain by programs such as
rwho and *ruptime*, but are rarely used in the UNIX domain.

14.6.1 Connection-Oriented Sockets on the Same Machine

The following scripts are very simple examples of the client/server model utilizing stream sockets for communication endpoints. Both client and server reside on the same machine, and the client simply reads a greetings message from the server and prints the message on the screen. There is little error checking or signal handling. The programs are simple demonstrations of how the above-named socket functions are used. (For socket functions not included in this chapter, see Appendix A.)

The Server Program.

E x a m p l e   1 4 . 1 8

(The Script)

```perl
#!/usr/bin/perl

# The server and the client are on the same machine.
print "Server Started.\n";
1    $AF_UNIX=1;   # The domain is AF_UNIX
2    $SOCK_STREAM=1; # The type is SOCK_STREAM
3    $PROTOCOL=0;   # Protocol 0 is accepted as the "correct protocol" by most
        systems.

4    socket(SERVERSOCKET, $AF_UNIX, $SOCK_STREAM, $PROTOCOL) ||
        die " Socket $!\n";
     print "socket OK\n";
5    $name="./greetings";   # The name of the socket is associated within the file
                            # system
     unlink "./greetings" || warn "$name: $!\n";

6    bind(SERVERSOCKET, $name) || die "Bind $!\n";
     print "bind OK\n";

7    listen(SERVERSOCKET, 5)|| die "Listen $!\n";
     print "listen OK\n";

     while(1){
8        accept(NEWSOCKET, SERVERSOCKET )|| die "Accept $!\n";
         # accept client connection
```

```
9       $pid=fork || die "Fork: $!\n";
10      if ($pid == 0 ){
11          print NEWSOCKET "Greetings from your server!!\n";

12          close(NEWSOCKET);
            exit(0);
        }
        else{
13          close (NEWSOCKET);
        }
    }
```

Explanation

1   The domain is set to UNIX. The client and server are on the same machine.
2   The socket type is SOCK_STREAM, a connection-oriented, byte-stream type of communication.
3   The *protocol* is set to 0. This value is handled by the system if set to 0.
4   The *socket* function is called. The filehandle, SERVERSOCKET, is created in the server.
5   The pathname of the file "greetings" is the name in the file system the socket FILE-HANDLE will be associated with. It will be the real name to which the socket filehandle is attached. If the file already exists, it will be removed with the *unlink* function.
6   The socket filehandle is bound to the UNIX file "greetings".
7   The *listen* function allows the process to specify how many pending connections it will accept from the client. The requests are queued and the maximum number that can be queued is five.
8   The *accept* function waits for a client request and creates a new socket filehandle, NEWSOCKET, with the same attributes as the original filehandle, SERVERSOCKET (also called the rendezvous socket). NEWSOCKET is the socket that actually communicates with the client. The rendezvous socket remains available to accept future connections.
9   A child process is created with the *fork* function. Now both parent and child are in execution.
10 If the *pid* returned is zero, the child is in execution. If the pid is non-zero, the parent is in execution.
11 If the child process is in execution (pid is zero), the greetings message is written to the socket, NEWSOCKET. The server is communicating with its client.
12 The NEWSOCKET filehandle is closed by the child and the child exits.
13 The NEWSOCKET filehandle is closed by the parent so that it can receive more client requests.

The Client Program.

Example 14.19

(The Script)
```perl
    #!/usr/bin/perl
    print "Hi I'm the client\n";

1   $AF_UNIX=1;
2   $SOCK_STREAM=1;
3   $PROTOCOL=0;

4   socket(CLIENTSOCKET, $AF_UNIX, $SOCK_STREAM, $PROTOCOL);
5   $name="./greetings";

    do{
        # client connects  with server
6       $result = connect(CLIENTSOCKET, "$name" );
        if ($result != 1 ){
            sleep(1);
        }
7   }while($result !=  1 );  # Loop until a connection is made
8   read(CLIENTSOCKET, $buf, 500);
9   print STDOUT "$buf\n";
10  close (CLIENTSOCKET);
    exit(0);
```

Explanation

1   The domain is AF_UNIX. The client and server reside on the same machine. The value assigned to the scalar is the value that is assigned to the AF_UNIX macro in the system file */usr/include/sys/socket.h*.   The *socket* function requires these values as arguments in order to create a socket.

2   The type of socket is SOCK_STREAM, a sequenced, reliable, bidirectional method of communication between the client and server. The value assigned to the scalar is the value that is assigned to the SOCK_STREAM macro in the system file */usr/include/sys/socket.h*. The *socket* function requires these values as arguments in order to create a socket.

3   The protocol value is handled by the system calls involved in creating the socket. It determines how the socket is implemented at a low level. By assigning 0 as the protocol value, the *socket* function considers this the "correct protocol"; that is, you don't have to worry about the details.

4   The *socket* function creates a socket filehandle called CLIENTSOCKET.

5   The socket filehandle, CLIENTSOCKET, will be associated with the UNIX file "greetings".

6   The *connect* function connects the CLIENTSOCKET filehandle to the UNIX file "greetings" so that the client can communicate with the server. The return from the function is true if it succeeded, and false otherwise.

7   Until the connection is made, the program loops.

8   Now that the connection has been made, the client reads as many as 500 bytes from the server socket and stores the bytes in the scalar, *$buf*.

9   The contents of *$buf* are printed to STDOUT.

10   The CLIENTSOCKET filehandle is closed. For more control, the *shutdown* function should be used.

FIGURE 14.2   The Output

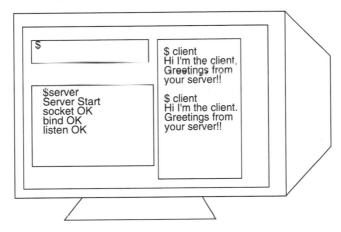

14.6.2   Connection-Oriented Sockets on Remote Machines (Internet Clients and Servers)

The following program was executed on two Sun workstations. The server's hostname is *scarecrow*, running SunOS 5.3, and the client's hostname is *houston*, running SunOS 4.1.3. In this program, the client on one machine asks the server on another machine for the time. The server sends the time to the client socket, and the client prints the time in readable format to the screen. These examples do not take advantage of Perl5's *Socket.pm* module in the standard library. All values are hardcoded and therefore are not necessarily portable from one machine to another.   (See Section 14.7.)

```
#!/usr/local/bin/perl
# timeserver — a Time Server program,
# opens a Rendezvous Socket on port 9876
# and waits for a client to connect.
# When each client connects, this server determines the machine
# time on its host and writes the value on the communication
# socket to the client.
```

```
       #
       #                Usage: timeserver [port number]
       #
1      ($port)=@ARGV;
2      $port=9876 unless $port;
3      $AF_INET=2;
4      $SOCK_STREAM = 1;
5      $sockaddr = 'S n a4 x8';
6      ($name,$aliases,$proto)=getprotobyname('tcp');
7      if($port !~ /^\d+$/){
8          ($name, $aliases, $port)=getservbyport($port,'tcp');
       }
       print "Port = $port\n";
9      $this = pack($sockaddr, $AF_INET, $port, "\0\0\0\0");
10     select(COMM_SOCK); $l = 1; select (stdout);
       # Create R_SOCKET, the rendezvous socket descriptor
11     socket(R_SOCKET, $AF_INET, $SOCK_STREAM, $proto ) || die "socket:
       $!\n";
       # Bind R_SOCKET to my address, $this
12     bind(R_SOCKET, $this) || die "bind: $!\n";
13     listen(R_SOCKET, 5) || die "connect: $!\n";
       # Infinite loop – wait until client connects, then serve the client
       while(1){
14         accept(COMM_SOCK, R_SOCKET) || die "$!\n";
15         $now = time;
16         print COMM_SOCK $now;
       }
```

Explanation

1   A hostname may be passed as a command line argument (see line 7).

2   If the *ARGV* array is empty, the scalar, *$port*, is assigned the value 9876. This port number is assigned by the programmer to a number outside the reserved port numbers. On a Sun, port numbers through 1024 are reserved. The port number 9876 is also called an ephemeral port, short lived.

3   The scalar $AF_INET is assigned the value 2, the constant value assigned to the macro AF_INET in */usr/include/sys/socket.h*. This number represents the Internet domain, AF_INET.

4   The type of socket is SOCK_STREAM, assigned the value of 1 in */usr/include/sys/socket.h*.

5   The *pack* function will use this format for the socket address.

6   The *getprotobyname* function returns the official protocol name, any aliases, and the protocol number using the *tcp* protocol as the name.

7   If the scalar, *$port*, is not an assigned number, but the name of the server machine was passed in at the command line, the *getservbyport* function will return the correct port number for the server using the *tcp* protocol.

8 The *port number* is printed.

9 The address for this Internet domain and port number is packed into a binary structure consisting of an unsigned short, a short in "network" order, four ASCII characters, and 8 null bytes. In comparable C programs, you will note that the method for getting addresses is by using a *sockddr* (see line 5) structure (see */usr/include/sys/socket.h*). Perl handles most of this for you.

10 The *socket* filehandle is selected as the current default handle for output. The $I special variable is set to 1, forcing buffers to be flushed on every *write* or *print*. The *stdout* filehandle is normally line buffered when sending output to a terminal and block buffered otherwise. When output is going to a pipe or socket, the buffers will be flushed.

11 The *socket* function creates the rendezvous socket filehandle, R_SOCKET.

12 The *bind* function binds the socket filehandle to the correct address for the server.

13 The *listen* function sets the queue limit to 5, the maximum for pending requests from the client.

14 The *accept* function waits for a client request, and when it gets one, accepts it by creating a new socket filehandle called COMM_SOCK with all the same attributes as R_SOCKET. COMM_SOCK is the server socket that will communicate with the client.

15 The *time* function returns the number of non-leap year seconds since Jan. 1, 1970, UTC.

16 The *time* is sent to the socket filehandle, COMM_SOCK.

```perl
#!/usr/local/bin/perl
# timeclient—a client for the Time Server program,
# creates a socket and connects it to the server on port 9876.
# The client then expects the server to write the server's
# host  time onto the socket. The client simply does
# a read on its socket, SOCK, to get the server's time.
#
#          Usage: timeclient [server_host_name]
#
      print "Hi, I'm in Perl program \'client\' \n";
1     ($them) = @ARGV;
2     $them = 'localhost' unless $them;
3     $port = 9876 ;  # timeserver is at this port number
4     $AF_INET = 2;
5     $SOCK_STREAM = 1;
6     $sockaddr = 'S n a4 x8';
7     ($name, $aliases, $proto) = getprotobyname('tcp');
8     ($name,$aliases, $port, $proto)=getservbyname($port, 'tcp') unless $port
        =~ /^\d+$/;

9     ($name,$aliases, $type, $len, $thataddr)=gethostbyname($them);
10    $that = pack($sockaddr, $AF_INET, $port, $thataddr);
      # Make the socket filehandle.
```

```
11    if ( socket(SOCK, $AF_INET, $SOCK_STREAM, $proto ) ){
      print "socket ok\n";
      }
      else { die $!; }
      # Call up the server.
12    if(connect(SOCK, $that)){
      print "connect ok.\n";
      }
      else { die $!;}
      # Set socket to be command buffered.
13    select(SOCK); $l = 1; select (STDOUT);
      # Now we're connected to the server, let's read her host time
14    $hertime = <SOCK>;
      close(SOCK);
      print "Server machine time is: $hertime\n";
15    @now = localtime($hertime);
      print "\t$now[2]:$now[1] ", $now[4]+1,"/$now[3]/$now[5]\n";
```

Explanation

1   The server's hostname may be passed as a command line argument.
2   If the *ARGV* array is empty, the hostname is set to 'localhost'.
3   To identify the server process, the client needs to know the server's port number.
4   The domain is Internet.
5   The type of socket is SOCK_STREAM, assigned the value of 1 in */usr/include/sys/ socket.h*.
6   The pack function will use this format for the socket address.
7   The *getprotobyname* function returns the official protocol name, any aliases, and the protocol number, using the *tcp* protocol as the name.
8   The *getservbyname* function returns the name of the official name of the server, any aliases, the port number, and the protocol name, unless *$port* contains already assigned digits.
9   The raw network address information is obtained from the host by *gethostname*.
10   The address for the server's Internet domain and port number is packed into a binary structure, consisting of an unsigned short, a short in "network" order, four ASCII characters, and 8 null bytes. In comparable C programs, you will note that the method for getting addresses is by using a *sockddr* structure (see */usr/include/sys/socket.h*).
11   The *socket* function creates an Internet domain, connection-oriented socket filehandle, SOCK.
12   The *connect* function connects the client's socket to the server's address.
13   The SOCK filehandle is selected. Buffers will be flushed after prints and writes.
14   Perl reads from the SOCK filehandle. The server's time is retrieved.
15   The time is converted to local time and printed.

FIGURE 14.3   Connection-Oriented Sockets on Remote Machines

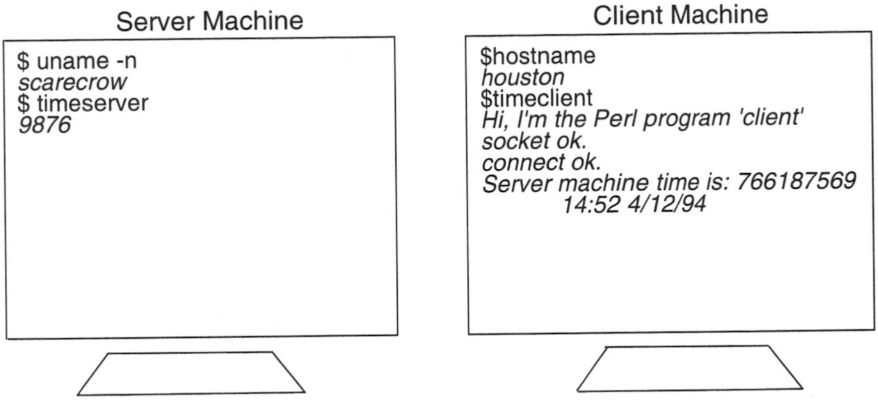

Server Machine

```
$ uname -n
scarecrow
$ timeserver
9876
```

Client Machine

```
$hostname
houston
$timeclient
Hi, I'm the Perl program 'client'
socket ok.
connect ok.
Server machine time is: 766187569
          14:52 4/12/94
```

14.7 The Socket.pm Module

Although sockets were originally an idea started at Berkeley for UNIX systems, they are now supported on many other operating systems. Perl5 introduced a special module to deal with sockets called *Socket.pm*. This makes it much easier to port programs from one machine to another because the necessary functions and constants needed for your machine are handled in the module, thus allowing you to get away from hard coding values into the program as seen in the examples above. However, a caveat...you must understand the way the Socket module works before using it. The names of constants are not intuitive and the later versions of Perl5 have introduced more functionality to the module. The following examples demonstrate how to write the previous TCP/IP server and client programs by taking advantage of *Socket.pm* and some of the other pragmas offered in Perl5 to better secure the programs when used on a network.

The Server.

E x a m p l e 1 4 . 2 0

(The Server Script)
```
1    #!/bin/perl -Tw
2    require 5.000;
3    use strict;
4    use Socket;
5    use FileHandle;
     # timeserver -- a Time Server program, opens a Rendezvous Socket on port
     # 9688 and waits for a client to connect.
```

```
       # When each client connects, this server determines the machine
       #        time on its host and writes the value on the communication
       #        socket to the client.
       #
       #               Usage: timeserver
       #
6      my($this, $now);
7      my $port = shift || 9688;

8      $this = pack('Sna4x8', AF_INET, $port, "\0\0\0\0");
       print "Port = $port\n";
9      my $prototype = getprotobyname('tcp');
10     socket(SOCKET, PF_INET, SOCK_STREAM, $prototype) || die "socket:
       $!\n";
       print "Socket o.k.\n";

11     bind(SOCKET, $this) || die "bind: $!\n";
       print "Bind o.k.\n";

12     listen(SOCKET, SOMAXCONN) || die "connect: $!\n";
       print "Listen o.k.\n";

13     COMM_SOCKET->autoflush;
       SOCKET->autoflush;

       # Infinite loop - wait until client connects, then serve the client
14     while(1){
          print "In loop.\n";
15        accept(COMM_SOCKET, SOCKET) || die "$!\n";
          print "Accept o.k.\n";
16        $now = time;
17        print COMM_SOCKET $now;
       }


       }
```

Explanation

1   The -w switch sends diagnostics to stderr if an identifier is mentioned only once, a sca-
    lar is used before being set, a non-number is used as a number, etc. The -T switch turns
    on taint checking to prevent data coming into your program from affecting something
    inside your program. If using a directory path, the taint mode checks to see if the di-
    rectory is writeable by others, and it checks arguments coming into the program. Once
    tainted, the data (or any variable that references the tainted data) cannot be used in

any command that invokes a subshell. It is suggested that taint checking is turned on for server programs and CGI scripts, i.e., programs that are run for someone else.

2   The *require* uses the version number as an argument. This ensures that programs prior to 5.000 will abort.

3   The *strict* pragma ensures that your program does not use unsafe constructs. It disallows symbolic references, that variables must be declared with the *my* function, that barewords are not allowed.

4   The *Socket* module will be used in this program. The module is designed to make the use of sockets more portable.

5   The *FileHandle* module is used here to take advantage of its method *autoflush* which will force the proper flushing of buffers when writing to the socket.

6   These variables will be used later in the program. They must be declared with *my* because the *strict* pragma enforces this as a safety feature.

7   A hostname may be passed as a command line argument and shifted into the $*port* variable. If the *ARGV* array is empty, the scalar, $*port*, is assigned the value 9688; a number well outside the range of reserved port numbers.

8   AF_INET is a constant defined in the Socket module to represents the Internet domain. The pack function packs the IP address and port number for the server socket into $*this*.

9   The *getprotobyname* function returns the official protocol name, any aliases, and the protocol number, using the *tcp* protocol as the name.

10   The *socket* function creates the rendezvous socket filehandle, SOCKET.

11   The *bind* function binds the socket filehandle to the correct address for the server.

12   The *listen* function sets the queue limit to SOMAXCONN, the maximum for pending requests from the client (usually 5).

13   The *autoflush* method from the FileHandle class forces buffers to be flushed as soon as something is written to the socket.

14   An infinite loop is started. The server is now waiting for a client request.

15   The *accept* function waits for a client request, and when it gets one, accepts it by creating a new socket filehandle, called COMM_SOCK, with all the same attributes as SOCKET.

16   Server calls the *time* function to get the current time and assigns that value to $*now*.

17   Server sends the time to COMM_SOCK. Client will get it at its end.

The Client

```
    #!/usr/local/bin/perl -w
    require 5.003;
1   use Socket;
    use FileHandle;
2   use strict;
3   my($remote, $port, @thataddr, $that,$them, $proto,@now, $hertime);
```

```perl
# timeclient --  a client for the Time Server program,
#          creates a socket and connects it to the server on
#          port 9688.
#          The client then expects the server to write server's
#          host time onto the socket, so the client simply does
#          a read on its socket, SOCK, to get the server's time
#
#
#                 Usage:  timeclient [server_host_name]
#
     print "Hi, I'm in perl program \'client\' \n";
4    $remote = shift || 'localhost' ;
5    $port =  9688 ;  # timeserver is at this port number
6    @thataddr=gethostbyname($port, $remote);

7    $that = pack('SnC4x8', AF_INET, $port, $thataddr[4]);

8    $proto = getprotobyname('tcp');

     # Make the socket filehandle.

9 if ( socket(SOCK, PF_INET, SOCK_STREAM, $proto ) ){
             print "socket ok\n";
     }
     else { die $!; }

     # Call up the server.
10   if (connect(SOCK, $that)) {
          print "connect ok.\n";
     }
          else { die $!;}

     # Set socket to be command buffered.
11   SOCK->autoflush;

# Now we're connected to the server, let's read her host time
12   $hertime = <SOCK>;
13 close(SOCK);

14   print "Server machine time is: $hertime\n";
15   @now = localtime($hertime);
16   print "\tTime-$now[2]:$now[1] ", "Date-",$now[4]+1,"/$now[3]/$now[5]\n";
```

Explanation

1   The Socket module will be used in this program.

2   The *strict* pragma is used to ensure that variables used in this program are "safe".

3   These variables will be used later in the program. They must be declared with *my* because the *strict* pragma enforces this as a safety feature.

4   A server's hostname may be passed as a command line argument and shifted into the *$port* variable. If the *ARGV* array is empty, the scalar, *$port*, is assigned 'localhost'.

5   The client gets the server's port number if it was assigned a value.

6   Now the client gets the server's official address. The raw network address information is obtained by *gethostbyname*.

7   The address for the server's Internet domain and port number is packed into a binary structure, consisting of an unsigned short, a short in "network" order, four ASCII characters, and 8 null bytes.

8   The *tcp* protocol information is returned.

9   The *socket* function creates an Internet domain, connection-oriented socket filehandle, SOCK.

10   The *connect* function connects the client's socket to the server's address.

11   The *autoflush* method forces the socket's buffers to be flushed after prints and writes.

12   Perl reads from the SOCK filehandle. The server's time is retrieved via the socket.

13   The socket is closed.

14   The time value (number of non-leap-year seconds since 1/1/1970, UTC) retrieved from the server is printed.

15   The time is converted to local time and assigned to array @now.

16   The converted time is printed.

Output

```
$ perl timeserver
Port = 9688
Socket o.k.
Bind o.k.
Listen o.k.
In loop.

$ perl timeclient
Hi, I'm in perl program 'client'
socket ok
connect ok.
Server machine time is: 859584967
    Time-13:36 Date-3/28/97
```

FIGURE 14.4   Server-Client and Socket.pm

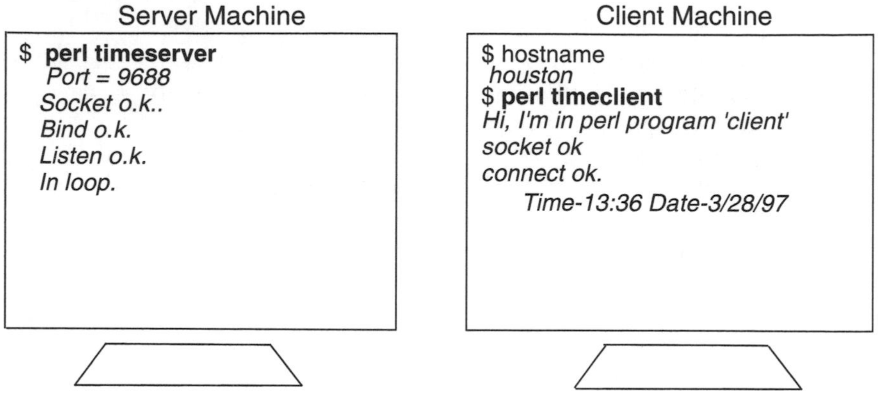

Server Machine

```
$  perl timeserver
   Port = 9688
   Socket o.k..
   Bind o.k.
   Listen o.k.
   In loop.
```

Client Machine

```
$ hostname
 houston
$ perl timeclient
Hi, I'm in perl program 'client'
socket ok
connect ok.
     Time-13:36 Date-3/28/97
```

15

Message Queues, Semaphores, and Shared Memory

15.1 The IPC Objects

The three types of communication objects found in System V IPC are message queues, semaphores, and shared memory. These forms of communication are restricted to the same host machines but can serve unrelated processes. They may be used for transaction processing and database applications to communicate requests and control the way the resources are allocated. Message queues are used to send data to other processes; shared memory allows processes to simultaneously share a common memory segment; semaphores allow processes to synchronize their activities and control the way processes access and release shared resources.[1]

15.1.1 Common Features

Creating Objects and Keys. Each IPC object has a *get* function for creating the object, and each *get* function expects a key as its first argument. The key, a long integer, is the name of the object and is assigned by the programmer who is creating the object. Any process that wants to use the object must know its key; just as if you want to use a file, you must know its name. Each type of object has its own name space, so that keys for a semaphore, a message queue, or a shared memory segment do not share the same namespace. If you create a message queue, for example, it is given a unique key in order to identify it, and other message queues cannot have this key. However, a shared memory segment or a sema-

---

1. If you need to use any System IPC objects, your kernel must be configured to support them. A number of UNIX systems, other than System V systems, support IPC. These examples were used on a UNIX system running SunOS, a Berkeley version.

phore could have the same key as the message queue because they have their own namespace.

The *key* is converted by the kernel to an *id* number. The id number is used by any of the other object functions to identify the object. The key itself is only used by different processes that need access to an object with any of the *get* functions. If the object already exists, the process can get access to it if it has the right key; otherwise, the key will be used to create a new object.

To create a unique key, you can use the &IPC_PRIVATE flag. The kernel will create a new IPC object and return a new identification number.

Identifying Objects and ID Number.   The identification number or IPC ID number is the value (nonnegative integer) returned from successful calls to any of the *get* functions, similar to file descriptors.   It is stored in a table in the kernel and is used to identify the object when using object functions other than the *get* functions (e.g., *msgsnd*, *shmread*, or *semop*). To send or retrieve messages from a message queue, for example, the functions need just the id number of the object to identify it.

Controlling Objects and Permissions.   Objects are global. Once created, an object resides in the kernel and is available to other processes. Even if the process that created the object dies or is no longer using the object, the object remains in the system. The IPC control functions can be used to remove objects and change permissions on objects.

The permissions on an object are similar to the permissions on files; they determine who can do what to the object. But unlike files, there is not only an owner uid and group uid, but also a creator uid and group id. To change the values of the uid, gid, or permission modes, the process must be the creator of the IPC object or superuser. Ownership can be assigned to another process, but only the creator of the object retains the right to destroy it.

The permission modes correspond to file modes, but execute permission has no significance. Shared memory and message queues use read and write permissions, whereas semaphores use read and alter permissions.

Each type of object also has control (ctrl) functions that allow the object to change the uid and gid values of an object as well as the permissions, similar to *chown* and *chmod* when using files.

Flags.   The PIC functions are modified by flag arguments. They are shown in Tables 15.1 and 15.2.

TABLE 15.1   The get (create) Functions

Flag	Function
&IPC_CREAT	Create an IPC object (with a key) if it does not already exist.
&IPC_EXCL	Create an IPC object (with a key) if it does not exist and return an error if it does exist.
0600	Set the permissions for the new object. In this case, the object has read and write permissions for the owner.
0	The object is there already. You just want access.

TABLE 15.2   The ctl (control) Functions

Flag	Functions
&IPC_STAT	Gets the values of each member of the data structure of a given IPC object.
&IPC_SET	Sets the values of members of the data structure of a given IPC object. Used to set the uid, gid, and permission modes.
&IPC_RMID	Removes an IPC object from the system.

15.1.2   IPC User Commands

The UNIX *ipcs* command lists the System V IPC objects currently active on your system. (See Table 15.3.)

TABLE 15.3   The ipcs Command[2]

-q	Prints information about message queues
-m	Prints information about memory segments
-s	Prints information about semaphores
-b	Prints current allowed size information
-c	Prints creator's login name and group name
-o	Prints outstanding usage information
-p	Prints process id information
-t	Prints time information
-a	Prints all above information

The *ipcrm* command removes an IPC object by identification number. (See Table 15.4.)

TABLE 15.4   The ipcrm Command to Remove an ID or Key

-q msqid	Removes message queue identifier and queue
-m shmid	Removes shared memory segment identifier and segment
-s semid	Removes semaphore identifier and semaphore set information
-Q msgkey	Removes message queue associated with key
-M shmkey	Removes shared memory segment associated with key
-S semkey	Removes semaphore set associated with key

Example 15.1

```
$ ipcs
IPC status from jody as of Sat May 21 07:27:17 1994
T  ID    KEY       MODE       OWNER    GROUP
Message Queues:
Shared Memory:
m  2400 0x0000000a —rw———— ellie    40
Semaphores:
s  230 0x0000000a —ra–ra–ra– ellie    40
```

2. See UNIX manual pages for more detailed information.

```
$ ipcrm —m 2400
$ ipcrm —s 230
$ ipcs
IPC status from jody as of Sat May 21 07:27:54 1994
T   ID   KEY    MODE    OWNER    GROUP
Message Queues:
Shared Memory:
Semaphores:
```

15.1.3 Size Limits

The IPC objects have built-in configuration limits. On BSD, see */usr/include/sys/msg.h,* */usr/include/sys/sem.h,* or */usr/include/sys/shm.h.* On SVR4, see */etc/conf/cf.d/mtune.*

15.1.4 Required Header Files—The h2ph Script

When using the IPC functions, it is necessary to include the Perl library header file "ipc.ph". In addition, message queues require the header file "msg.ph"; semaphores require the "sem.ph" header file; shared memory requires "shm.ph". These files are obtained by running the script, *h2ph,* that comes with the Perl distribution. The script converts C header files to the corresponding Perl header files. If you read the script, there are instructions on how to run it and what files must be included. Larry Wall, Perl author, suggests that to run the script you type:

```
cd /usr/include ; h2ph * sys/*
```

This script will create a long list of ".ph" files and put them in a directory called */usr/local/ lib/perl.* These files are required when using the Perl *ipc* functions.

You may also check that the @INC array contains the correct path for these files. To include the Perl library functions, use the *require* function:

```
require "ipc.ph";
require "msg.ph";
require "sem.ph";
require "shm.ph";
```

You may find that the *.ph* files created by running *h2ph* on all the files in */usr/include* and */sys* are not enough. When executing your *ipc* program, you may receive the Perl message, "*Have you run h2ph?*" There are a number of subdirectories under */usr/include* that may be required. For example, to use shared memory, I needed the header files in */usr/include/ machine.* To get those files, type:

```
cd /usr/include; h2ph machine/*
```

15.2 **Message Queues**

Message queues provide a way to send data called messages from one process to another. They consist of a list of messages stored within the kernel and identified by an identification number. Messages are identified by type, length, and the actual message. The message can consist of any kind of data, but it must begin with a long integer. When a message is created, it is added to a new or existing queue. When a message is sent, it is added to the end of the message queue. Messages can be retrieved in a first-in, first-out order, or in any order you want, if the type of the message is named. The message queue is analogous to a mailbox stored in the kernel. If it has permission, any process can reach into the mailbox and retrieve a message.

When a process quits, the message queue is not automatically removed because the IPC objects are not part of the process memory. The *msgctl* function is used to remove a message. The Perl functions associated with message queues are based on the system calls described in Section 2 of the UNIX manual pages.

The msgget Function.   The *msgget* function calls the System V IPC *msgget()* system call and returns a message queue id number. Creating a message queue is similar to opening a file and getting back a file descriptor, except that the message queue is accessible to any process that knows the id. A key is passed as an argument, and the message queue id is returned. A message queue for a specified key is created if the &IPC_CREAT flag is on. If the &IPC_EXCL flag is set, and the message queue already exists with the specified key, an error is returned.

Format:

```
id=msgget(key, flags);
```

Example 15.2

1 require "ipc.ph";
   require "msg.ph";

2 $PERMISSIONS=0600;
3 $ipckey=&IPC_PRIVATE;
4 **$msgid=msgget($ipckey, &IPC_CREAT | &IPC_EXCL | $PERMISSIONS);**

Explanation

1 The Perl library functions are required in order to use the IPC functions.
2 The permissions are set to read and write for the owner/creator of the message queue.
3 The key is set with the &IPC_PRIVATE flag to make it unique. The kernel will create a unique identifier if it does not already exist.
4 The *msgget* function is called. The first argument is the key, followed by the flags and permissions. A message id is returned if successful, and an undefined value if not.

The msgctl Function.   The *msgctl* function calls the *msgctl* system call(). It is used to retrieve information about the message queue, set permissions, or by setting a flag, remove the queue. The first argument is the message id; the second argument, CMD, specifies the command to be performed; the last argument is used if the CMD is specified with the flag, &IPC_STAT. The command arguments are issued with flags &IPC_STAT, &IPC_SET, and &IPC_RMID.

The &IPC_STAT flag creates a uid structure which is stored in ARG as a scalar. ARG contains the members of the message queue structure.

The &IPC_SET function sets the uid, gid, mode, and number of bytes in the queue.

The &IPC_RMID flag removes the message queue and all its data from the kernel. If any other process attempts to send or receive messages from the queue, it will receive an error.

These last two flags can only be set if the effective user ID of the process equals the message queue's owner or creator effective uid or guid, or the process has superuser privileges.

The return values for the *msgtl* function are the same as for the *ioctl* and *fcntl* functions. (See Appendix A.) (See Table 15.5.)

TABLE 15.5   Return Values for the msgctl Function

System Call Returns	Meaning	Perl Function Returns
-1	Failure	Undefined value
0	Success	String "0 but true"
Otherwise	A number	

Format:

```
msgctl(MSGID, CMD, ARG);
```

Example 15.3

1 require "ipc.ph";
   require "msg.ph";

2 ($ret_val=msgctl($msgid, &IPC_RMID, 0)) || ($ret = -1);
   print "System returned $ret_val.\n";

Explanation

1 The Perl library functions must be included in order to use the IPC functions.
2 The *msctl* function will remove (&IPC_RMID) the message queue associated with the message queue id, *$msgid*. The third argument is NULL if the command is not &IPC_STAT. The returned value is either an undefined value if the function fails, *0 but true* if a structure is not returned. The value returned from the operating system can be stored in a variable.

The msgsnd Function.   The *msgsnd* function calls the *msgsnd()* system call. It adds a message to the message queue associated with the message id. The MESSAGE argument consists of the type (long integer) followed by the *text* of the message. Perl's *pack* function allows you to specify the *type* (as a long integer) and the message as null padded ASCII text. The FLAGS are defined in the IPC header files. If the flag is set to 0, the function blocks if the queue is full. If the flag &IPC_NOWAIT (non-blocking) is specified and the queue is full, the *msgsnd* function returns immediately with an error.

The *message type* is a positive integer that can be used by the retrieving process for selecting a particular type of message (see Table 15.6).

Format:

```
msgsnd(MSGID, MESSAGE, FLAGS);
```

E x a m p l e   1 5 . 4

(The Script)
```
1  require "ipc.ph";
   require "msg.ph;
2  $msg_type=1;
3  $msg=pack("L a*", $msg_type, "Hello out there!");

4  msgsnd($msgid, "$msg", 80, &IPC_NOWAIT);
```

E x p l a n a t i o n

1 The *ipc.ph* and *msg.ph* header files must be included.
2 The message type is *1*.
3 The *pack* function creates a string by combining a long integer (type) and the actual message as an ASCII string *-a**.
4 The *msgsnd* function adds the message to the queue. The arguments are the message queue id, the actual message, the size in bytes of the message, and the flags. The &IPC_NOWAIT flag is turned on so that if the queue is full, the function will return immediately with an error.

The msgrcv Function.   The *msgrcv* function calls the *msgrcv()* system call. It retrieves a message from the message queue into a variable by the type and size of the message. The function returns true if successful and false if there is an error, storing the error code is $!.

TABLE 15.6   Type Values

Type	Definition
0	The first message on the queue is returned
> 0	The first message on the queue of that type is returned
< 0	The first message on the queue, where type is less than or equal to the absolute value of type, is returned.

Format:

```
msgrcv(MSGID, VARIABLE, SIZE, TYPE, FLAGS);
```

E x a m p l e   1 5 . 5

(The Script)
```
1  require "ipc.ph";
   require "msg.ph";
```

2 msgrcv($msgid, $var, 100, 3, 0) II die "msgrcv: $!\n";

E x p l a n a t i o n

1 The Perl library IPC functions must be included.
2 The *msgrcv* function has five arguments: *$msgid*, the message id; *$var*, the variable that will hold the retrieved message; the size (100 bytes) of the message; the type of the message; the flags. The *type* of the message is 3. Type 3 messages will be retrieved from the message queue (see Table 15.6).

Message Queue Example.   The following program is used to illustrate the Perl message queue functions. The parent process creates the message queue with the *msgget* function, and gets a message id. The parent calls the *fork* function to start a child process. The child process creates a list of seven messages in an associative array.   The child uses the *msgsnd* function to add these messages to the queue. The parent then retrieves the messages from the queue with the *msgrcv* function and prints them out. Lastly, the *msgctl* function is used to remove the queue. Since both parent and child are executing in a forever loop, the program is exited by pressing the interrupt key, ^C, at which time the signal handling routine, "cleanup", is called.

E x a m p l e   1 5 . 6

```
   #!/usr/bin/perl
1  $l=1;
2  unshift(@INC, "/home/local/lib/perl/sys");
   print "@INC\n";
3  require "syscall.ph";
   require "ipc.ph";
   require "msg.ph";
   $NULL=0;
4  $ipckey=$$;  # Create the key with the process id of this Perl program
5  $msgid=msgget($ipckey, &IPC_CREAT| 0600);  # Create the queue and get
      # the message id
```

```
6    $SIG{'INT'}='cleanup';
7    $pid=fork;
8    if ( $pid == −1 ){ die  "fork failed: $!\n";}
9    elsif ( $pid == 0 ) {
     $SIG{'INT'}='DEFAULT';
10       %message_send = (        # The type and the message are assigned to an
                                  # associative array
                 '1', "Monday's child is fair of face.",
                 '2', "Tuesday's child is full of grace.",
                 '3', "Wednesday's child is full of woe.",
                 '4', "Thursday's child has far to go.",
                 '5', "Friday's child is loving and giving. ",
                 '6', "Saturday's child has to work for a living. ",
                 '7', "But the child who's born on the Sabbath day..."
             );

        while(1){
           $type=&gettype;
11         $msg=pack("L a*", $type, $message_send{"$type"});
12         msgsnd($msgid, "$msg", 80, &IPC_NOWAIT);  # send a message
            sleep(1);
           }
     }
     else{
     while(1){
13      msgrcv($msgid, $var, 80, −7, 0 );  # receive  a message
14      $msgtype=unpack("L a*", $var);
             printf("Type %d: %s\n",$msgtype, $var);
           }
     }

     sub cleanup {
         local($signal)=@_;
         print "Removing message queue.\n";
15       ($ret=msgctl($msgid, &IPC_RMID, $NULL)) || ($ret = −1);
         print "System returned $ret.\n";
         exit(0);
     }
     sub gettype{
         local( $type ) = int(rand(7)) + 1 ;
         $type;  # return the type, a random number between 1 and 7
     }
```

O u t p u t

/home/local/lib/perl/sys /usr/local/lib/perl .
Type 4: Thursday's child has far to go.
Type 2: Tuesday's child is full of grace.
Type 3: Wednesday's child is full of woe.
Type 4: Thursday's child has far to go.
Type 7: But the child who's born on the Sabbath day...
Type 2: Tuesday's child is full of grace.
Type 5: Friday's child is loving and giving.
Type 2: Tuesday's child is full of grace.
Type 4: Thursday's child has far to go.
Type 1: Monday's child is fair of face.
Type 1: Monday's child is fair of face.
Type 3: Wednesday's child is full of woe.
Type 2: Tuesday's child is full of grace.
^CRemoving message queue.
System returned 0 but true.

E x p l a n a t i o n

1   $| is set to 1 to make sure buffers are flushed after every print statement; this is a good idea when forking another process to keep standard I/0 buffers flushed.

2   The @*INC* array is prepended with "/home/locla/lib/perl/sys" to include all the *.ph* files in the path.

3   The required header files are included in the script. (See Section 12.4.1, "h2ph".)

4   The key is set to the pid of the Perl process running this script.

5   The *msgget* function will create the message queue with read and write permissions for the creator/owner and return the message queue id number, if successful.

6   A signal handler is created for the Interrupt, C^, signal.

7   The *fork* function is called. The scalar, $pid, will receive 0 from the child process, and the pid of the parent from the parent process. (See Section 12.3.5, "System Interface.")

8   If the return from the fork function is -1, the script will die with a reason for the failure.

9   If the value of $pid == 0, we are running in the child process.

10   An associative array, %*mesage_send*, is created. The key will be the message type, and the value will be the actual message.

11   The Perl *pack* function creates a string beginning with a long integer, followed by the actual message. The type is randomly chosen by the *gettype* subroutine.

12   The message is sent to the message queue. If & IPC_NO_WAIT flag is set, the function returns immediately with an error if the queue is full.

13   The parent will retrieve a message (the *msgrcv* function) from the queue and store it in the scalar, *$var*. The size of the message is 80 bytes; the type of the message is -7. A -7 message type means that if there are message types less than or equal to type 7, the lowest type will be retrieved from the queue first.

14   The *unpack* function is being used here to unpack a single value, the message type, and
     to store that value in the scalar, *$msgtype*.

15   The *msgctl* function will remove the message queue from the kernel's memory. If the
     function is successful, "0 but true", is returned.

15.3 Semaphores

A semaphore is really just a counter, created in the kernel and used for efficiently managing
and synchronizing shared resources. If, for example, two processes are using shared memory and both try to write to the memory at the same time, the semaphore is used to lock the
memory segment while one process is using it and to release the lock when that process has
finished. Semaphores only have meaning if all the processes sharing the resource volunteer
to use them. Processes that don't use semaphores will not be locked out of a shared region
as long as they have access to it.

A semaphore is a data structure containing the semaphore value, the process id of the
last process that performed a semaphore operation, the number of processes waiting for the
value of the semaphore value to be greater than 0, and the number of processes waiting for
the value of the semaphore to be equal to zero. (See below, "The semop Function.")

A *binary* semaphore is a commonly used type of semaphore. It controls a single resource
and has one of two values, 0 or 1. If the process controlling the resource, process A, has
performed an operation that waits for the semaphore value to become zero, and if the value
of the semaphore is zero, then process A will not release the resource until the value of the
semaphore is greater than zero. The value of the semaphore cannot be less than zero. When
the value is greater than zero, another process, process B, may acquire the resource. Process
A will sleep until the semaphore value is zero again. The processes use semaphore operations to adjust the value of the semaphore.

The semget Function.   The *semget* function calls the System V IPC *semget()* system call
and returns a semaphore id number. A key is passed as an argument and the semaphore id
is returned. A semaphore data structure for a specified key is created if the &IPC_CREAT
flag is on. If the &IPC_CREAT flag is off, the semaphore must already exist.

The NSEMS argument is the number of semaphores in the set. The set is treated as an
array, starting with element 0.

Format:

```
semget ( KEY, NSEMS,  FLAGS );
```

Example 15.7

```
1  require "ipc.ph";
   require "sem.ph";

2  $PERMISSIONS=0666;
3  $ipckey=&IPC_PRIVATE;
4  $semid=semget($ipckey, 1, &IPC_CREAT | &IPC_EXCL | $PERMISSIONS);
```

Explanation

1 The Perl library functions must be included in order to use the IPC functions.
2 The permissions are set to *read* and *alter* (instead of write) for any process using the semaphore.
3 The key is set with the &IPC_PRIVATE flag (in Perl, it must be preceded with an ampersand) to make it unique. The kernel will create a unique identifier.
4 The *semget* function is called. The first argument is the key, followed by the number of semaphores in the set (an array of semaphore structures). If the flag &IPC_CREATE is specified, the semaphore is created with the permissions given. With &IPC_EXCL set, an error is returned if the semaphore already exists. A semaphore id is returned if successful and an undefined value if not.

The semop Function.   The *semop* function calls the *semop()* system call to manipulate semaphores. It is this function that determines whether a shared resource should be acquired or released by a process. The function returns true if successful, false otherwise. On error, the $! variable is set to the error code.

When setting the semaphore option string in Perl, there are three values to consider: the *number of semaphores* in the set, the *semaphore operation*, and the *flag* values. The *pack* function is used to pack all of these values into one string.

The *semaphore operation* is the most important setting since it determines whether to acquire or release the resource. It is this operation that adjusts the current value of the semaphore. The *adjustment value* of the operation can be negative, 0, or positive.

If a binary semaphore is being used,[3] the semaphore value is either 0 or 1. The process calling the *semop* function with an adjustment value of zero will wait for the value of the semaphore to become 0. (The initial value of the semaphore is zero.) If the value of the semaphore is zero, that process controls the resource. Another process waits for the semaphore value to become greater than zero; in the case of a binary semaphore, it waits for the value to become 1. By selecting a positive adjustment value (the *semop* function), the controlling process will add that amount to the value of the semaphore, causing the value to be greater than zero. The resource is released and the controlling process now waits for the semaphore value to become zero again. A negative adjustment can decrement the value of the semaphore, but it can never cause the value of a semaphore to be negative. Such an oper-

---

3.   In these examples, binary semaphores are used. System V IPC allows lists of semaphore operations.

ation would cause the process to block until the operation results in either a zero or positive value (Table 15.7).

TABLE 15.7   Semaphore Operations-Controlling Process

Value of Semaphore	Adjustment Value(semop)	Result
0	0	Acquire the resource; keep it until value of semaphore > 0.
0	1	Increment semaphore value by 1; release the resource; wait (block) until the semaphore value is 0.
0	-1	Decrement value of semaphore by one; can't have a negative semaphore value; process blocks.

The flags &IPC_NOWAIT and &IPC_UNDO may be used to affect the semaphore operations. If &IPC_NOWAIT is used, the process is not forced to wait, the kernel undoes the operations performed on the semaphore, and returns an error. The &IPC_UNDO flag forces the process to release a resource if it terminates and undoes any operations that process performed on the semaphore before it exited.

Format:

```
semop ( SEMID, SEMOPSTRING);
```

E x a m p l e   1 5 . 8

```
1  require "ipc.ph";
   require "sem.ph";

   < Perl script Here>

2  $semnum=0;  # Number of the semaphore (first element of an array is 0 )
3  $semflags=0; # Blocking flag
4  $semop=0;  # The adjustment value for the semaphore
5  $semopstring=pack("s*", $semnum, $semop,$semflags);
6  semop($semid, $semopstring ) || die "semop: $!\n";
```

E x p l a n a t i o n

1 The library header files are loaded into the script.
2 The scalar, *$semnum*, is set to the number of the semaphore in the set to which the operation applies. There is only one semaphore in the array; the value of *semnum* is the first element in the array (starting at 0).
3 The value of the flags can be IPC_NOWAIT or SEM_UNDO. A value of zero blocks until the operation can be performed.

4 The semaphore operation is set to zero. The value of the semaphore is tested. If the semaphore value is not zero, the process blocks until it becomes zero.
5 The Perl pack function is used to create a packed array of *semop* values (in C, this is
   called the *sembuf* structure).
6 The first argument to the *semop* function is the semaphore id which identifies the semaphore to the kernel. The second argument consists of a string created by the *pack* function with the semaphore values and flags.

E x a m p l e   1 5 . 9

```perl
      #!/usr/bin/perl
      # Using Binary Semaphores
1     $l=1;
2     unshift(@INC, "/home/local/lib/perl/sys");
      print "@INC\n";
3     require "syscall.ph";
      require "ipc.ph";
      require "sem.ph";

4     $ppid=$$;
5     $ipckey=&IPC_PRIVATE; # Create a key
6     $semid=semget($ipckey, 1, &IPC_EXCL | &IPC_CREAT | 0666);
      # get a semphore id
7     $semnum=0;
8     $semflags=0;
9         print "\nParent: So you're the one who  took the car last night!\n\n";
10    $pid=fork;
      if (undefined ($pid)){die  "fork failed: $!\n";}
      elsif ( $pid == 0 ) { # In child

11        for($i=1;$i<=10;$i++){
12            $semop=0;
13            $semopstr=pack("s*", $semnum, $semop, $semflags);
14            die "Semaphore 1: $!\n" unless semop($semid, $semopstr);
15            print "Child: \"I did not.\"\n";
16            $semop=2;
              $semopstr=pack("s*", $semnum, $semop, $semflags);
17            die "Semaphore:2 $!\n" unless semop($semid, $semopstr);
      }
      }
      else{
          for($i=1; $i<= 10; $i++){
              $semop=-1;
```

```
                $semopstr=pack("s*", $semnum, $semop, $semflags);
18              die "$i Semaphore 3: $!\n" unless semop($semid, $semopstr);
                print "Parent: \"Yes you did.\"\n";
                $semop=-1;
                $semopstr=pack("s*", $semnum, $semop, $semflags);
19              die "Semaphore 4: $!\n" unless semop($semid, $semopstr);
        }


        }
     if ( $ppid==$$){
         print "\nParent gets the last word.\n";
20       semctl($semid, 0, &IPC_RMID, 0);
     }
```

O u t p u t

/home/local/lib/perl/sys /usr/local/lib/perl .
Parent: So you're the one who took the car last night!
Child: "I did not."
Parent: "Yes you did."
Child: "I did not."
Parent: "Yes you did."
Child: "I did not."
Parent: "Yes you did."
Child: "I did not."
Parent: "Yes you did."
Child: "I did not."
Parent: "Yes you did."
Child: "I did not."
Parent: "Yes you did."
Child: "I did not."
Parent: "Yes you did."
Child: "I did not."
Parent: "Yes you did."
Child: "I did not."
Parent: "Yes you did."
Child: "I did not."
Parent: "Yes you did."
Child: "I did not."
Parent: "Yes you did."
Parent gets the last word.

E x p l a n a t i o n

1   $| is set to 1 to make sure buffers are flushed after every *print* statement; this is a good idea when forking another process to keep standard i/o buffers flushed.

2   The *@INC* array is prepended with "*/home/local/lib/perl/sys*" to include all the *.ph* files in the path.

3   The required header files are included in the script (see Section 15.1.4, "h2ph").

4   The scalar, *$ppid*, is set to the process id of the Perl process, the parent.

5   A unique key is created.

6   The *semget* function is called. A binary semaphore will be created and its id number returned.

7   The scalar, *$semnum*, is set to the number of the semaphore in the set to which the operation applies. There is only one semaphore in the array; the value of *semnum* is the first element in the array (starting at 0).

8   The value of the flags can be &IPC_NOWAIT or &SEM_UNDO. A value of zero blocks until the operation can be performed.

9   The parent process prints the string.

10 The parent forks a new process.

11 If we are in the child process, a *for* loop is started.

12 The scalar, *$semop*, is set to 0.

13 The *pack* function creates a semaphore structure by combining the semaphore scalar values, *$semnum*, *$semop*, and *$semflags*, into a string called *$semopstr*.

14 The semaphore operation is set to zero. The value of the semaphore is tested. If the semaphore value is not zero, the process blocks until it becomes zero. The semaphore value is initially set to zero by the system.

15 Since the value of the semaphore is 0, the child process prints, "I did not."

16 The value of the scalar, *$semop*, is set to 2.

17 The semaphore operation is now 2. Two is added to the value of the semaphore. When the loop is entered, a *semaphore operation* of 2 causes the child to block, because the value of the semaphore is now 2. The child won't gain control until the semaphore value is zero. (Remember, a semaphore value is adjusted by the semaphore operation.)

18 The parent gets control and will call the *semop* function with a negative value (-1). The value of the semaphore is decremented by 1. The value is now one. The parent controls.

19 The semaphore operation is -1. The value of the semaphore is decremented again. The value of the semaphore is 0. When the parent enters the loop, the semaphore operation of -1 will cause the parent to block, since the value of the semaphore is now 0. (Another -1 operation would cause the value of the semaphore to be less than zero. A semaphore value can never be less than zero.) The parent blocks. The child gets control. This procedure continues until both parent and child have looped ten times.

20 When both parent and child have exited their respective for loops, the script will check to see if parent process is in execution and will remove the semaphore set with the *semctl* function.

15.4 Shared Memory

Shared memory allows a common segment of memory to be shared by a number of processes. The shared memory is used for communication between two simultaneously running processes (see Figure 15.1). The memory is created by the kernel and resides in kernel memory. It can be of any size within the size limitations of your system. Processes can attach and detach themselves from the memory at any time, and the shared memory will remain in the system even if the process that created it dies or if there are no processes attached to it. In Perl programs the *shmread* and *shmwrite* functions allow a process to attach itself to a segment of memory, read from or write to the segment, and then detach from the segment.

There is no guaranteed method for controlling access to shared memory segments in System V IPC. One process might write to the memory segment before another process could read what was already there. To coordinate the way in which processes access shared memory, semaphores are often used.

FIGURE 15.1   A Shared Memory Segment

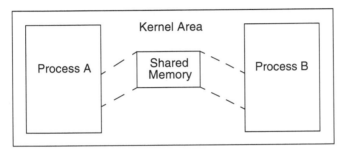

The shmget Function.   The *shmget* function calls the System V IPC *shmget( )* system call and returns an id number.   A key is passed as an argument and the shared memory id is returned. A shared memory segment is created for a specified key if the &IPC_CREAT flag is on. If the segment exists, the &IPC_EXCL flag returns an error code, stored in the $! variable, if the memory segment corresponding to the specified key already exists. If the &IPC_EXCL flag is off and the segment already exists, the *shmid* for the existing segment is returned. Then the shared memory segment must already exist or an error is returned and stored in the $!. The size argument specifies that the segment will be of at least SIZE number of bytes. *Read* permission on a shared memory segment allows data to be retrieved from the segment, whereas *write* permission allows data to be stored and retrieved from the segment.

Format:

```
id=shmgett(KEY, SIZE, FLAGS);
```

Example 15.10

```
1 require "ipc.ph";
  require "shm.ph";

2 $PERMISSIONS=0600;
3 $ipckey=10;
4 $size=100;
5 $shmid=shmget($ipckey, $size, $PERMISSIONS | &IPC_CREAT |
    &IPC_EXCL );
```

Explanation

1 The Perl library functions must be included in order to use the IPC functions.
2 The permissions are set to *read* and *write* for the owner/creator of the shared memory; that is, data can be fetched from and stored into the new memory segment.
3 The *key* is set to 10. In order to access the shared memory segment, any process must use this key.
4 The size of the memory segment is 100 bytes.
5 The *shmget* function returns the identification for the shared memory stored in the kernel.

The shmctl Function.   The *shmctl* function calls the *shmctl* system call. The first argument is the shared memory id number; the second argument, CMD, specifies the command to be performed; and the last argument is used if the CMD is specified with the flag, &IPC_STAT. The command arguments are issued with flags & IPC_STAT, &IPC_SET, and &IPC_RMID.

IPC_STAT creates a shared memory data structure which is stored in ARG as a scalar.

The IPC_SET function sets the uid, gid, and permission mode.

The IPC_RMID flag removes the shared memory segment and all its data from the kernel if there are no processes attached to it. If any other processes attempt to send or receive messages from the queue, they will receive an error.

These last two flags can only be set if the effective user ID of the process equals the shared memory's owner or creator effective uid or gtud or if the process has superuser privileges.

The return values for the *msgtl* function are the same as for the *ioctl* and *fcntl* functions (see Table 15.8).

TABLE 15.8   Return Values for the shmctl Function

System Call Returns	Meaning	Perl Function Returns
-1	Failure	Undefined value
0	Success	String "0 but true"
Otherwise	A number	

Format:

```
shmctl(SHMID, CMD, ARG);
```

Example 15.11

```
1  require "ipc.ph";
   require "shm.ph";
```

```
2  ( $ret_val=shmctl($shmid, &IPC_RMID, 0)) II ( $ret = -1 );
   print "System returned $ret_val.\n";
```

Explanation

1   The Perl library functions must be included in order to use the IPC functions.
2   The *shmctl* function will remove (&IPC_RMID), the message queue associated with the message queue id, *$msgid*. The third argument is NULL if the command is not IPC_STAT. The returned value is either -1 if the function fails or 0 but true if a structure is not returned. In this example, the return is "0 but true".

The shmread Function.   The *shmread* function reads SIZE bytes from the shared memory segment starting at a specified address. Using a POS, position of 0, lets the kernel select an address where the memory will be attached. The memory is attached, the bytes read, and the memory then detached. (This Perl function replaces the *shmat* system call that returns a pointer to the address you selected.) The function returns true if successful, and false if there is an error, storing the error code is $!.

Format:

```
shmread(SHMID, STRING, POS, SIZE);
```

Example 15.12

(The Script)
```
1      require "ipc.ph";
       require "shm.ph";
```

```
           < Perl Script Here>
```

```
2  shmread($shmid, $string, 0,80)II die "shmread: $!\n";
```

Explanation

1 The Perl library IPC functions must be included.
2 The *shmread* function will read 80 bytes from position 0 of the shared memory and store the results in the scalar, *$string*.

The shmwrite Function.   The *shmwrite* function writes the shared memory segment ID starting at position, POS, for a memory segment size of SIZE bytes. It attaches, writes data into the segment, and detaches the process from the memory segment. (This replaces the *shmat* system call.) The function returns true if successful, and false if there is an error, storing the error code is $!. If the string is too short, it is filled with null bytes to fill what is left.

Format:

```
shmwrite(ID, STRING, SIZE, POS, SIZE);
```

Example 15.13

(In The Script)
1   require "ipc.ph";
         require "shm.ph";

             < Perl Script Here>

2   **shmwrite($shmid, "Hello out there from process $$",0,80)|| die
         "shmwrite: $!\n";**

Explanation

1 The Perl library IPC functions must be included.
2 The *shmwrite* function sends the string to the shared memory segment, starting at position 0, for a size of 80 bytes.

Shared Memory Example.   The example consists of two programs. The first program, Process A, will create a shared memory segment. Processes A and B will communicate with each other via this memory segment. To control access to the memory, a semaphore is used. Since Process A's first semaphore operation is 0 and the value of the semaphore is initially set to zero by the system, Process A goes first. Process A sends a string to the shared memory segment, goes to sleep, and waits for Process B to read what was written there. After Process B fetches the data from the shared memory segment, it sends the data to a UNIX file. Process B then writes its own message to the segment and sleeps. Process A wakes up and reads what is in the shared memory segment and sends the data to another UNIX file. Process A then sends another string to the shared memory segment and sleeps. This goes on 20 times until the looping stops.

E x a m p l e   1 5 . 1 4   (Process A)

(The Script)

```
    #!/usr/bin/perl
    $|=1;
1   unshift (@INC, "/home/local/lib/perl/sys");
    print "@INC\n";
2   require "syscall.ph";
    require "ipc.ph";
    require "sem.ph";
    require "shm.ph";
    # Process A
    $SIG{'INT'}='cleanup';
    sleep 2;
3   $ipckey=10;
4   $shmid = shmget($Ipckey, 80, 0600I&IPC_CREAT I &IPC_EXCL );
        # get a memory segment
5   $semid = semget($ipckey, 1, &IPC_EXCL I &IPC_CREAT I 0666);
        #get a semaphore
6   open(FROM_B, "> data_f_B") II die "Can't open: $!\n";  # open a file
7   print FROM_B "Hi,  I'm Process A. I got this data from process B\n";
        # print to a file

    for($cnt = 1; $cnt <= 20; $cnt++)
    {
    $semop=0;
    $semopstr=pack("s*", 0, $semop, 0);
8   die "Semaphore 1: $!\n" unless semop($semid,$semopstr);
        # semaphore operation is 0; semaphore value is 0; process A is in control
9   shmwrite($shmid, "data $cnt from process A", 0,80)II die "shmwrite:
    $!\n";
        # write this string to the shared memory segment
    $semop=2;
    $semopstr=pack("s*", 0, $semop, 0);
10  die "Semaphore 2: $!\n" unless semop($semid, $semopstr);
        # semaphore operation increases the semaphore value to 2.
    $semop=0;
    $semopstr=pack("s*", 0, $semop, 0);
11  die "Semaphore 3: $!\n" unless semop($semid,$semopstr);
        #semaphore operation is 0; semaphore value is 2; process A blocks.
12  shmread($shmid, $string, 0, 80) II die "shmread: $!\n";
        # read from the shared memory segment what Process B put there
13  print FROM_B "$string\n";
        # print what was read from shared memory to the file
```

```
    }
    sub cleanup {
        local($signal)=@_;
        $|=1;
20      shmctl($shmid, &IPC_RMID, 0);
        semctl($semid, 2, &IPC_RMID, 0);
        exit(0);
    }
```

Explanation

1   The *@INC* array is prepended with "/home/local/lib/perl/sys" to include all the .ph files in the path.

2   The required header files are included in the script. (See Section 15.1.4, "h2ph".)

3   The key is created. It is assigned a value of 10.

4   The *shmget* function is called. A memory segment of 80 bytes will be created and its id number returned.

5   The *semget* function will create 1 semaphore. This binary semaphore will be used to control the shared memory. The semaphore uses the same key, but the kernel maintains a separate name space for each IPC object.

6   A filehandle is opened for file "data_f_B".

7   This line is printed into the file "data_f_B" via the filehandle, FROM_B.

8   This process requests a semaphore operation of 0. The value of the semaphore is initially zero.This process gets control.

9   The *shmwrite* function attaches the memory segment, writes the string to the segment, and then detaches the process from the shared memory segment.

10   A semaphore operation with an adjustment value of 2 will increment the value of the semaphore by 2.

11   Then a semaphore operation of 0 will cause the process to block, because a semaphore operation of 0 must wait until the value of the semaphore is 0. Process A will go to sleep; Process B now gets control and will read what Process A just stored in the shared memory segment. (See Process B program on the following page.)

12   When Process A gets control again, it will read from the shared memory and store what it fetched in the variable, *$string*. The shared memory segment contains what Process B stored there while this process was sleeping. Process A will then send the contents of *$string* to the file.

13   The value of the flags can be IPC_NOWAIT or SEM_UNDO. A flag value of zero blocks until the operation can be performed.

Example 15.15

(The Script)

```perl
#!/usr/bin/perl
$I=1;
unshift (@INC, "/home/local/lib/perl/sys");
print "@INC\n";
require "syscall.ph";
require "ipc.ph";
require "sem.ph";
require "shm.ph";
# Process B
$SIG{'INT'}='cleanup';
```

1   `$ipckey=10;  # This process must know the key value`
2   **`$shmid = shmget($ipckey, 80, 0 );   # get the segment`**
3   `$semid = semget($ipckey, 1, 0);`
4   `open(FROM_A, "> data_f_A") || die "Can't open: $!\n";`
5   `print FROM_A "Hi, I'm Process B. I got this data from process A\n",`
```perl
     for($cnt = 1; $cnt <= 20; $cnt++)
     {
         $semop = -1;
           $semopstr=pack("s*", 0, $semop, 0);
```
6   `    die "Semaphore 1: $!\n" unless semop($semid,$semopstr);`
```perl
     # read from shared memory segment
```
7   **`shmread($shmid, $string, 0,80)`**`|| die "shmread: $!\n";`
8   **`shmwrite($shmid, "data $cnt from process B",0,80)`**`|| die "shmwrite: $!\n";`
```perl
     print FROM_A "$string\n";
     $semop=-1;
     $semopstr=pack("s*", 0, $semop, 0);
```
9   `die "Semaphore 2: $!\n" unless semop($semid, $semopstr);`
```perl
     }
```
10   `close(FROM_A);`
```perl
     sub cleanup {
     local($signal)=@_;
```
     `shmctl($shmid, &IPC_RMID, 0);`
```perl
      semctl($semid, 2, &IPC_RMID, 0);
      exit(0);
      }
```

Explanation

1   The *key* is set to 10, as it was in Process A.
2   The *shmget* function gets the id for the shared memory segment.
3   The *semid* function gets the id for semaphore with the key.
4   The UNIX file, "data_f_A" is opened via the filehandle, FROM_A.
5   The string, "Hi, I'm Process B. I got this data from process A." is printed to the UNIX file.
6   The semaphore operation decrements the value of the semaphore by one. If this operation would cause the semaphore value to become negative, the process blocks.
7   If the process is not blocked, the *shmread* function will fetch what is in the shared memory segment and store it in *$string*.
8   After reading from the shared message segment, the *shmwrite* function will send the string to the shared memory segment.
9   The semaphore operation adjusts the semaphore value by decrementing it by one. If the value of the semaphore is adjusted so that it becomes negative, the process blocks.
10 The UNIX file is closed.

Output

```
$ more data_f_A
Hi I'm Process B. I got this data from process A
data 1 from process A
data 2 from process A
data 3 from process A
data 4 from process A
data 5 from process A
data 6 from process A
data 7 from process A
data 8 from process A
data 9 from process A
data 10 from process A
data 11 from process A
data 12 from process A
data 13 from process A
data 14 from process A
data 15 from process A
data 16 from process A
data 17 from process A
data 18 from process A
data 19 from process A
data 20 from process A
```

```
$ more data_f_B
```
Hi, I'm Process A. I got this data from process B
data 1 from process B
data 2 from process B
data 3 from process B
data 4 from process B
data 5 from process B
data 6 from process B
data 7 from process B
data 8 from process B
data 9 from process B
data 10 from process B
data 11 from process B
data 12 from process B
data 13 from process B
data 14 from process B
data 15 from process B
data 16 from process B
data 17 from process B
data 18 from process B
data 19 from process B
data 20 from process B

16

The Hyper Dynamic Duo
<u>(CGI and Perl)</u>

16.1   What is CGI

Now that the informational spider web called Internet has become a commercial shopping center, it seems like everyone has a home page hanging out there. And if you don't have one now, you probably will by the time this book gets out on the market. There are zillions of books and software programs on how to navigate, surf, master web sites, design Web pages, unleash HTML, Java, CGI, Perl, and any other topic related to the Internet. What do you need to get started with all this? Well, as you know, you need a computer hooked up to a phone line, a browser program such as Netscape, Mosaic, or Internet Explorer, and access to a server program such as Apache, Cern, or Netscape etc., etc. After connecting to the Net, you learn rather quickly how to navigate your way around and unless you have a job or some other life, you could surf around forever and never see it all.

So what makes up a Web page? A Web page is a file that contains HTML tags and text, formatting instructions, and underlined phrases called links that connect you to other documents either on the same machine or to some other machine on the network. The document (called a hypertext document) tells the browser on your system how to display the document, e.g., whether or not it has a blue background with big white letters or a white background with pink borders and a photograph of your face, an order form for buying a new computer, a registration form for a local college, or an image of you dancing around in your living room to old Beatles songs. The page, as you know, may contain what is called hypermedia, which includes images, sound, movies, and hot links to other documents. A Web page is created in a text editor and the resulting HTML file is called the source file. So that the browser recognizes the file, its name ends in either *.html* or *.htm*. The HTML tags tell the browser how to display the document on your screen. Learning the basics of HTML is not difficult, but developing an artistic and interesting design is another story, and now there are companies devoted to creating these masterpieces for other companies doing competitive business over the net.

There are two types of pages: static pages and dynamic pages. The static pages do not require interaction with the user. The most they can do is send already existing documents to users. They are more like a page in a book and usually describe the services some individual or company offers. They can be very artistic and interesting, but they can't handle information on demand. Dynamic pages on the other hand are "alive". They can accept and retrieve information from the user, produce specialized and customized content, search through text, query databases, and generate documents on the fly. They can manage information that is constantly changing, based on the requests of different users. These dynamic pages require more than an HTML text file. They are driven by programs or scripts that interact with the Web server, which then transfers information to your browser. To send the information back and forth between the program and the server, a gateway program is used. The server itself relays user requests to a program which in turn manages the information, e.g., it retrieves data from a file or database as a result of a user request and then sends it back to the server. The CGI (Common Gateway Interface) protocol defines how the server communicates with these programs. Its function is to allow the WWW server to go beyond its normal boundaries for retrieving and accessing information from external databases and files. It is, then, a specification that defines how data can be transferred from the script to the server and from the server to the script. Gateway programs, called CGI scripts, can be written in any programming language, but Perl has become the *de facto* standard language, mainly because it is flexible and easy to use. By now, if you have read the previous chapters, you know that the Perl interpreter is easy to get. You know that it is portable. And you know about Perl's ability to handle regular expressions, files, sockets, and I/O. Once you know Perl, writing CGI scripts is relatively easy. The critical part is making sure the server and Perl have been properly installed and that your scripts are placed in the directory where the server will look for them. So that the server knows where you are storing the scripts and how to reach the necessary libraries, the pathnames must also be set correctly. All efforts are to no avail if any of the necessary steps from installation to implementation are incorrect in any way. It is very frustrating to see the browser whining about not finding a requested file or server or scolding that you are forbidden to run a program.

This chapter is not written to make you a master Web designer; it is to give you some understanding of how Perl fits into the CGI scheme and how the dynamic pages for the Web are created. Sometimes, seeing the overall picture is the key to understanding the purpose and plan of the more detailed design. There is a plethora of Web information available on the Internet and in trade books to fill in the details.

Browser / Server / CGI

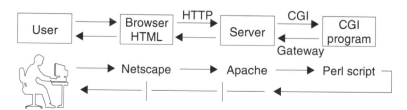

16.2 The HTTP Server

We discussed the client/server model and the TCP/IP protocols for regulating network operations in Chapter 14. On the Internet, communication is also handled by a TCP/IP connection. The Web is based on this model. The server side responds to client (browser) requests
and provides some feedback, either by sending back a document or by executing a CGI program, or issuing an error message. The network protocol that is used by the Web so that the
server and client know how to talk to each other is the Hypertext Transport Protocol or
HTTP. This does not preclude the TCP/IP protocol's being implemented. HTTP objects
are mapped onto the transport data units, a process that is beyond the scope of this discussion; it is a simple, straightforward process that is unnoticed by the typical Web user. (See
http://www.cis.ohio-state.edu/htbin/rfc2068.html for a technical description of HTTP.) The
HTTP protocol was built for the Web to handle hypermedia information; it is object oriented and stateless. In object-oriented terminology, the documents and files are called
objects and the operations that are associated with the HTTP protocol are called *methods*.
When a protocol is stateless, neither the client nor the server stores information about each
other, but manages its own state information.

   Once a TCP/IP connection is established between the Web server and client, the client
will request some service from the server. Web servers are normally located at well-known
TCP port 80. The client tells the server what type of data it can handle by sending *Accept*
statements with its requests. For example, one client may accept only HTML text, whereas
another client might accept sounds and images as well as text. The server will try to handle
the request (requests and responses are in ASCII text) and send back whatever information
it can to the client (browser). The response confirms what HTTP version was used, the status code describing the results of the server's attempt (did it succeed or fail?), a header and
data. The header part of the message indicates whether the request is OK and what type of
data is being returned, e.g., the content type may be *html/text*. The user then sees a formatted page on the screen that may contain highlighted hyperlinks to some other page.
Whether the user clicks on a hyperlink or not, once the document is displayed, that transaction is completed and the TCP/IP connection will be closed. Once closed, a new connection will be started if there is another request. What happened in the last transaction is of
no interest to either client or server, i.e., the protocol is stateless.

   HTTP is also used to communicate between browsers, proxies, and gateways to other
Internet systems supported by FTP, Gopher, WAIS and NNTP protocols.

16.2.1 The URL (Uniform Resource Locator)

A URL is the way you get around on the Web. You click on a hotlink and you are trans-
ported to some new page, or you type in a URL in browser's Location box and a file opens
up or a script runs. It is a virtual address that specifies the location of pages, objects, scripts,
etc. It refers to an existing protocol such as HTTP, Gopher, FTP, Telnet, mailto, or news
(Table 16.2). A typical URL for the popular Web HTTP protocol looks like this:

```
http://www.comp.com/dir/text.html
```

The two basic pieces of information provided in the URL are the protocol, *http*, and the data needed by the protocol, *www.comp.com/dir/files/text.html*. The parts of the URL are further defined in the following chart (Table 16.1).

TABLE 16.1   Parts of a URL

Part	Description
protocol	service such as http, gopher, ftp, telnet, news, etc,. protocol
host/IP number	DNS host name or its IP number
port	TCP port number used by server, normally port 80
path	path and filename reference for the object on a server
parameters	specific parameters used by the object on a server
query	the query string for a CGI script
fragment	reference to subset of the object

The default HTTP network port is 80; if a HTTP server resides on a different network port, e.g., 12345 on www.comp.com, then the URL becomes:

```
http://www.comp.com.12345/dir/text.html
```

TABLE 16.2   Web Protocols

Protocol	Function	Example
http:	Hyper Text Transfer Protocol; open Web page or start CGI script	http://www.nnic.noaa.gov/cgi-bin/netcast.cgi
ftp:	File Transfer Protocol	ftp://jague.gsfc.nasa.gov/pub
mailto:	Mail Protocol by email address	mailto:debbiej@aol.com
file:	Open a local file	file://opt/apache/htdocs/file.html
telnet:	Open telnet session	telnet://nickym@netcom.com
news:	Opens a news session by news server Name or Address	news:alt..fan.john-lennon

Not all parts of a URL are necessary. If you are searching for a document in the Locator box in the Netscape browser, the URL may not need the port number, parameters, query, or fragment parts. If the URL is part of a hotlink in the HTML document, it may contain a relative path to the next document, that is, relative to the root directory of the server. If the user has filled in a form, the URL line may contain information appended to a question mark in the URL line. It really depends on what protocol you are using and what operation you are trying to accomplish that affects the appearance of the URL.

Example 16.1

1 http://www.cis.ohio-state.edu/htbin/rfc2068.html
2 http://127.0.0.1/Sample.html
3 ftp://oak.oakland.edu/pub/
4 file:/opt/apache_1.2b8/htdocs/index.html
5 http//susan/cgi-bin/form.cgi?string=hello+there

E x p l a n a t i o n

1   The protocol is HTTP.
   The hostname *www.cis.ohio-state.edu* consists of[1]:
       The hostname translated to an IP address by the Domain Name Service, DNS.
       The domain name: *ohio-state.edu.*
       The top-level domain name: *edu.*
   The directory where the HTML file is stored is *htbin.*
   The file to be retrieved is *rfc20868.html,* an HTML document.
2   The protocol is HTTP.
   The IP address is used instead of the hostname; this is the IP address for a local host.
   The file is in a subdirectory of the server name. The file consists of HTML text.
3   The protocol is *ftp.*
   The host *oak.oakland.*
   The top-level domain is *edu.*
   The directory is *pub.*
4   The protocol is file. A local file will be opened.
   The hostname is missing. It then refers to the local host.
   The full path to the file *index.html* is listed.
5   The information after the question mark is the query part of the URL, which resulted
   from submitting input into a form. The query string is URL encoded. In this example,
   a plus sign has replaced the space between "hello" and "there". The server stores this
   query in an environment variable called QUERY_STRING. It will be passed on to a CGI
   program called from the HTML document. (See GET method.)

File URLs and the Server's Root Directory

If the protocol used in the URL is *file*, the server assumes that file is on the local machine.
A full pathname followed by a file name is included in the URL. When the protocol is followed by a server name, all pathnames are relative to the document root of the server. The
document root is the directory defined as the main directory for your Web server. The leading slash that precedes the path is not really part of the path as in the UNIX absolute path
that starts at the root directory. Rather the leading slash is used to separate the path from
the hostname. An example of a URL leading to documents in the server's root directory:

        http://www.myserver/index.html

The full UNIX pathname for this might be:

        /usr/bin/www.myserver/htdocs/index.html

A shorthand method for linking to a document on the same server is called a partial or
relative URL. For example, if a document called *http://www.myserver/stories/webjoke.html*

---

1. Most WEB severs run on hostnames starting with *www,* but this is only a convention.

contains a link to *images/webjoke.gif*, this is a relative URL. The browser will expand the relative URL to its absolute URL, *http://www.myserver/stories/images/webjoke.gif*, and make a request for that document if asked.

16.3 Short Introduction to HTML

In order to write Web pages, you must learn at least some of what makes up the HTML language. There are volumes written on this subject. Here we will cover just enough to introduce you to HTML and give you the basics so that you can write some simple dynamic pages with forms and CGI scripts.

Web pages are written as ASCII text files in a language called the HyperText Markup Language, HTML. HTML consists of a set of instructions called tags that tell your Web browser how to display the text in the page.[2] When you type in the URL or click on a hyperlink on a page, the browser (client) communicates to the server that it needs a file and the file is sent back to the browser. The file contains text written in HTML that may contain text, images, audio, video, and hyperlinks. It's the browser's job to interpret the HTML tags and display the formatted page on your screen. (To look at the source file for a Web page, you can use the "View Document" menu under "View" in the Netscape browser and see the HTML tags used to produce the page.)

The HTML source file can be created in any text editor. Its name ends in *.html* or *.htm* to indicate that it is an HTML file. The HTML tags that describe the way the document looks are enclosed in angle brackets < >. The tags are easy to read. If you want to create a title, for example, the tag instruction is enclosed in brackets, the actual text for the title is sandwiched between the marker that starts the instruction, <TITLE>, and the tag that ends the instruction, </TITLE>. The following line is called a TITLE element, consisting of the <TITLE> start tag, the enclosed text, and the </TITLE> end tag. The tag may also have attributes to describe its function further. For example, a text input area may allow a specified number of rows and columns, or an image may be aligned and centered at the top of the page. The elements and attributes are case-insensitive.

```
<TITLE>War and Peace</TITLE>
```

When the browser sees this instruction, the title will be printed in the bar at the top of the browser's window as a title for the page. To put comments in the HTML document, the commented text is inserted between <!-- and -->.

Because HTML is a structured language, there are rules about how to place the tags in a document.

---

2. If you have ever used the UNIX programs nroff and troff for formatting text, you'll immediately recognize the tags used for formatting with HTML.

Creating Links.

Links or hyperlinks are images or text enclosed within anchor tags to produce point-to-point references to other documents. The links can be created to connect one section of a Web page to another resource on the Internet. The text is usually underlined and colored blue.

A hyperlink to another resource on the Web requires two tags starting and ending with the "A" element. The inital <A tag is followed by the HREF attribute. The HREF attribute is assigned the URL of the designated link file. The URL is enclosed in double quotes. Next is the hotlink. It consists of a word or words, after the right angle bracket > and the closing </A> tag. The hotlink will be underlined when the HTML document is displayed. The pathnames are case-sensitive but the tag elements are not.

Example 16.2

```
1   <A HREF="http://www.apache.org/">Apache</A>
2   <a href="http://www.fas.harvard.edu/~john/httpd/docs/index.html">
    Click here to see the Web Development Links page</a>
```

Explanation

1   'A' is an anchor element. HREF is assigned the URL, the address of the file that will be linked if the user clicks on the word *Apache*. The text, *Apache*, is enclosed between an opening angle bracket and the end tag for element 'A'. It is placed right after the URL. Any text enclosed in these angle brackets will be underlined and colored blue by the Netscape browser. (See Example 16.5.)
2   The elements are case-insensitive, but the URL is not. This is another hotlink to an HTML file, *index.html*, at the Internet address *www.fas.harvard.edu* in john's home directory under *httpd/docs*.

Image Formats

There are two types of images that can be embedded in an HTML document: inline images and external images. In fact, other media such as sound and video cannot be loaded directly by the browser; they come from somewhere else.

Inline images are loaded when you load the Web page and are often files called *gif* files. They are just part of the Web page itself.

External images are downloaded at the user's request by clicking on some hotlink. There are a number of image formats that a browser may be configured to handle. Assuming you have already created an image in the *gif* format, the HTML IMG element is used. The IMG element allows the inclusion of any graphical images from other files anywhere on the Internet.

E x a m p l e   1 6 . 3

```
1   <IMG SRC="/icons/redball.gif">
2   <img src="apache_pb.gif">
```

E x p l a n a t i o n

1   The IMG element is used to load in an image file. SRC is assigned the pathname and
    file, *redball.gif*, a GIF image file in the directory *icons* under the root directory of the
    server.
2   The tags are not case sensitive. This image is located in a file on this server under the
    server's root directory.

E x a m p l e   1 6 . 4

Netscape: Source of: file:/opt/apache_1.2b8/htdocs/index.html

```
<HTML><HEAD>
<TITLE>Test Page for Apache</TITLE>
</HEAD><BODY>

<H1>It Worked!</H1>

If you can see this, then your
<A HREF="http://www.apache.org/">Apache</A> installation was
successful.  You may now add content to this directory and
replace this page.

<P>
The Apache <A HREF="manual/index.html">documentation has been
included with this distribution.</A>

<P>
You are free to use the image below on an Apache-powered web
server.  Thanks for using Apache!

<P>
<img src="apache_pb.gif">

</BODY></HTML>
```

Example   16.5

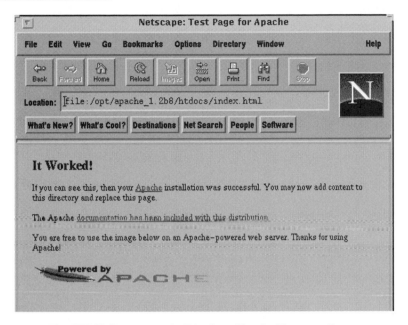

The HTML Document As Displayed by the Netscape Browser.

TABLE 16.3   Simple HTML Tags and What They Do

Tag Element	Function
<!-- text -->	Commented text; nothing is displayed.
<BASE HREF="http://www.bus.com/my.html">	Where this document is stored.
<HTML>document</HTML>	Found at the beginning and end of the document, indicating to a browser that this is an HTML document.
<HEAD>headinginfo</HEAD>	First element inside the document. Normally contains the title and is displayed outside of the main window of the browser.
<TITLE>title of the document</TITLE	Title of the document; displayed outside the document text in a window frame or top of the screen. Can be placed in the bookmark list.
<BODY>document contents</BODY>	Contains all the text and other objects to be displayed.
<H1>heading type</H1>	Heading elements, for levels 1 through 6, create bold face headings. The levels elements are: H1, H2, H3, H4, H5, and H6. The largest, outermost heading is H1.
<P>text</P>	Paragraph tag. Marks the beginning of a paragraph. Inserts break after a block of text. Can go anywhere on the line. Ending paragraph tags are optional. Paragraphs end when a new <P>or another tag marking a new block of text is encountered.
<B>text</B>	**Bold** text.
<I>test</I>	*Italic* text.
<TT>text</TT>	`Typewriter text.`
<U>text</U>	<u>Underlined text.</u>

TABLE 16.3   Simple HTML Tags and What They Do (continued)

Tag Element	Function
\<BR\>	Line break.
\<HR\>	Horizontal shadow line.
\<UL\>	Start of an unordered (bulleted) list.
\<LI\>	An item in a list.
\<LI\>	Another item in a list.
\</UL\>	The end of the list.
\<OL\>	Start of an ordered list.
\<DL\>	Descriptive list.
\<DT\>	An item in a descriptive list.
\<DT\>	Another item in a descriptive list.
\</DL\>	End of the descriptive list.
\<STRONG\>	**Bold text.**
\<EM\>	*Italics text.*
\<BLOCKQUOTE\>text\</BLOCKQUOTE\>	Italicized blocked text with spaces before and after quote.
\<A HREF SRC="URL"\>	Creates hotlink to a resource at address in URL on the Web.
\<IMG SRC="URL"\>	Loads an image into a Web page. URL is the image file.

16.3.1   HTTP Status Codes and the Logfiles

When the server responds to the client, it sends information which includes the way it handled the request. Most Web browsers handle these codes silently if they fall in the range between 100, 200, and 300. The codes within the 100 range are informational, indicating that the server's request is being processed. The most common status code is 200, indicating success, i.e., the information requested was accepted and fulfilled.

TABLE 16.4   HTTP Status Codes

Status	CodeMessage
100	Continue
200	Success, OK
204	No Content
301	Document Moved
400	Bad Request
401	Unauthorized
403	Forbidden
404	Not Found
500	Internal Server Error
501	Not Implemented
503	Service Unavailable

Check your server's access log to see what status codes were sent by your server after a transaction was completed.[3] The following example consists of excerpts taken from the Apache server's access log. This log reports information about a request handled by the

---

3. For more detailed information on status codes, see:
http://www.w3.org/hypertext/WWW/Protocols/HTTP/HTRESP.html

server and the status code generated as a result of the request. The error log contains any standard error messages that the program would ordinarily send to the screen, such as syntax or compiler errors.

E x a m p l e   1 6 . 6

(From Apache's Access log)
1   susan - - [06/Jul/1997:14:32:23 -0700] "GET /cgi-bin/tryit.cgi HTTP/1.0" **500** 633
2   susan - - [16/Jun/1997:11:27:32 -0700] "GET /cgi-bin/hello.cgi HTTP/1.0" **200** 1325
3   susan - - [07/Jul/1997:09:03:20 -0700] "GET /htdocs/index.html HTTP/1.0" **404** 170

E x p l a n a t i o n

1   The server hostname is *susan*, followed by two dashes indicating unknown values, such as user id and password. The time the request was logged, the type of request is GET (See Section 16.8), and the file accessed was *hello.cgi*. The protocol is HTTP/1.0. The status code sent by the server was 500, *Internal Server Error,* meaning that there was some internal error, such as syntax error in the program, *hello.cgi.* The browser's request was not fulfilled. The number of bytes sent was 633.
2   Status code 200 indicates success! The request was fullfilled.
3   Status code 404, *Forbidden,* means that the server found nothing matching the URL requested.

16.4 A Simple HTML Document

The following HTML file is created in your favorite text editor and consists of a simple set of tagged elements.

E x a m p l e   1 6 . 7

(The Html Text File)
1   **<HTML>**
2   <HEAD>
3   <TITLE>Hyper Test</Title>
4   </HEAD>
5   <BODY>
6   <H1>Hello To You and Yours!</H1>
7   <H2 ALIGN="center">Welcome
8   </H2>
9   <P>Life is good. Today is <I>Friday.</I></P>
10 </BODY>
11 **</HTML>**

Explanation

1   All of the text for the HTML document is between the <HTML> tag and the </HTML> tag. Although HTML is the standard language for Web creating pages, there are other markup languages that look like HTML. The HTML tag distinguishes between the other types of markup languages. You can omit these tags, and your browser will not complain. It's just more official to use them.

2   The HEAD tag contains information about the document, such as the title. This information is not displayed with the rest of the document text. This tag always comes right after the HTML start tag.

3   The TITLE tag produces a title at the top of the window.

4   The closing tag for the HEAD element is </HEAD>. Note the forward slash.

5   This is the BODY start tag. This part of the document appears in the main browser window.

6   A Level 1 heading is enclosed between the H1 start and end tags.

7   This is a Level 2 heading. The ALIGN attribute tells the browser to center the heading on the page.

8   This is the end tag for a level 2 heading.

9   The <P> tag starts a paragraph. The string, *Friday*, will be printed in italics text. </P> marks the end of the paragraph.

10 This tag marks the end of the body of the HTML document.

11 This tag marks the end of the HTML document.

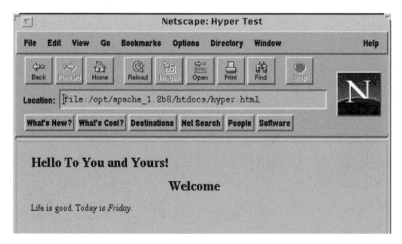

The HTML Document Displayed by the Netscape Browser

16.5 How HTML and CGI Work Together

HTML is the markup language used to determine the way a Web page will be displayed. CGI is a protocol that allows the server to extend its functionality. A CGI program is executed on behalf of the server mainly to process forms such as a registration form or a shopping list. When a browser (client) makes a request of the server, the server examines the URL. If the server sees *cgi-bin* as a directory in the path, it will go to that directory, open a pipe, and execute the CGI program. The CGI program gets its <u>input from the pipe</u> and sends its <u>standard output back though the pipe to the server</u>. <u>Standard error</u> is sent to the server's <u>error log</u>. If the CGI program is to talk to the server, it must speak the Web language, since this is the language that is ultimately used by the browser to display a page. The CGI program then will format its data in HTML and send it back to the HTTP server. The server will then return this document to the browser to be displayed to the user.

FIGURE 16.1   The Client/Server/CGI Program Relationship

16.5.1   A Simple CGI Script

The following Perl script consists of a series of print statements, most of which send HTML output back to stdout (piped to the server). This program is executed directly from the CGI directory, *cgi-bin*. Some servers require that CGI script names end in *.cgi* so that they can be recognized as CGI scripts. After creating the script, the execute permission for the file must be turned on. For UNIX systems, type at the prompt:

chmod 755 scriptname

or

chmod +x scriptname

The URL entered in the browser *Location* window includes the protocol, the name of the host machine, the directory where the CGI scripts are stored, and the name of the CGI script. Some servers expect that the CGI script ends in either a *.pl* or *.cgi* extension such as:

http:servername/cgi-bin/perl_script.cgi

The HTTP headers.

The first line of output for most CGI programs is an HTTP header that tells the browser what type of output the program is sending to it. Right after the header line, there must be a blank line and two newlines. The two most common types of headers, also called MIME types, are "Content-type: text/html\n\n" and "Content-type: text/plain\n\n". Another type of header is called the *Location* header, which is used to redirect the browser to a different Web page. And finally, *Cookie* headers are used to set cookies for maintaining state; i.e., keeping track of information that would normally be lost once the transaction between the server and browser is closed.

TABLE 16.5   HTTP Headers

Header	Type	Value
Content Type:	text/plain	Plain text
Content Type:	text/html	HTML tags and text
Content Type:	image/gif	Gif graphics
Location:	http://www....	Redirection to another Web page
Set-cookie: NAME=VALUE...	Cookie	Set a cookie on a client browser

Example 16.8

```
1  #!/opt/perl5/bin/perl
2  print "Content-type: text/html\n\n";
3  print "<HTML><HEAD><TITLE> CGI/Perl First Try</TITLE></HEAD>\n";
4  print "<BODY BGCOLOR=Black TEXT=White>\n";
5  print "<H1><CENTER> Howdy, World! </CENTER></H1>\n";
6  print "<H2><CENTER> It's ";
7  print "<!--comments -->";   # This is how HTML comments are included
8  print `date`;   # Execute the UNIX date command
9  print "and all's well.\n";
10 print "</H2></BODY></HTML>\n";
```

Explanation

1   This first line is critical. Many Web servers will not run a CGI script if this line is missing. This tells the server where Perl is installed.

2   This line is called the MIME header. No matter what programming language you are using, the first output of your CGI program must be a MIME header followed by two newlines. This line indicates what type of data your application will be sending. In this case, the CGI script will be sending HTML text back to the server. The \n\n cause a blank line to be printed. The blank line is also crucial to success of your CGI program.

3   The next lines sent from Perl back to the server are straight HTML tags and text. This line creates the header information, in this case, a title for the document.

4   This defines the background color as white and the textual material as navy blue.

5   <H1> is a Level 1 heading. It is the largest of the headings and prints in bold text. "Howdy, World!" will be formatted as a Level 1 heading and centered on the page.

6   All text from here until line 10 will be formatted as a Level 2, centered heading.

7   This is how comments are inserted into an HTML document. They are not displayed by the browser.

8   The UNIX *date* command is executed and its output is included as part of the centered, second level heading. (If this command is not implemented on your system, e.g., Windows 95 or Mac, you will have to find a workaround or skip this line.)

9   This line is printed as part of heading level 2.

10   These tags end the second level heading, the body of the document and the HTML document itself.

E x a m p l e   1 6 . 9

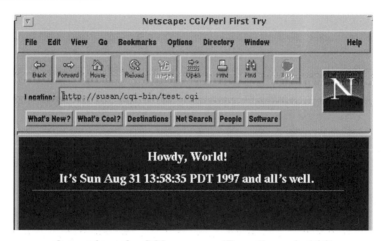

Output from the CGI program. (From Example 16.8)

16.6 Where to Find CGI Applications

There are a number of Web sites providing online resources to help you get started in writing your own CGI scripts. Browsing through some of following sites can give you a good idea of how Web pages are designed.

TABLE 16.6   Websites For CGI Beginners and Developers

The Website	What it Is
http://www.virtualville.com/library/cgi.html	An introduction to CGI
http://www.virtualville.com/library/scripts.html	Scripts to Go. A collection of CGI scripts
http://www.worldwidemart.com/scripts/	Matt Wright's Script Archive
http://www.eff.org/~erect/Scripts	Selena Sol's Public Domain CGI Script Archive
http://www.per.com/CPAN/	The Comprehensive Perl Archive Network
http://www.engr.iupui.edu/~dbewley/cgi/	Dale Bewley's CGI Scripts
http://www.bio.cam.ac.uk/cgi-lib/	The cgi-lib.pl Home Page
http://www.selah.net/cgi.html	The CGI Collection
http://www.yahoo.com/Computers_and_Internet/INternet/ World_Wide_Web/CGI_Common_Gateway_Interface/	Yahoo CGI Resources

16.7 Getting Information Into and Out the CGI Script

The server and the CGI script communicate in four major ways. Once the browser has sent a request to the server, the server can then send it on to the CGI script. The CGI script gets its input from the server as:

1. Environment Variables
2. Query Strings
3. Standard input
4 Extra path information

After the CGI program gets the input from the server, it parses it and processes it, and then formats so that the server can relay the information back to the browser. The CGI script sends output through the gateway by:

1. Generating new documents on the fly.
2. Sending existing static files to the standard output.
3 Using URL's that redirect the browser to go somewhere else for a document.

16.7.1 CGI Environment Variables

The CGI program is passed a number of environment variables from the server. The environment variables are set when the server executes the gateway program and are set for all requests. The environment variables contain information about the Server, the CGI program, the ports and protocols, path information, etc. User input is normally assigned to the QUERY_STRING environment variable. In the following example, this variable has no value because the user never was asked for input; i.e., the HTML document has no INPUT tags.

The environment variables are set for all requests and are sent by the server to the CGI program. In a Perl program, the environment variables are assigned to the %ENV associative array as key/value pairs. They are shown in Table 16.7.

TABLE 16.7   CGI Environment Variables

Name	Value	Example
DOCUMENT ROOT	The directory from which the server serves Web documents	/opt/apache//htdocs/index.html
GATEWAY_INTERFACE	The revision of the CGI used by the server	CGI/1.1
HTTP_ACCEPT	The MIME types accepted by the client	image/gif, image/jpeg, etc
HTTP_CONNECTION	The preferred HTTP connection type	Keep-Alive
HTTP_HOST	The name of the host machine	susan
HTTP_USER_AGENT	The browser (client) sending the request	Mozilla/3.01(X11;I; Sun05.5.1 sun4m)
REMOTE_HOST	The remote hostname of the user making a request	eqrc.ai.mit.edu
REMOTE_ADDR	The IP address of the host making a request	192.100.1.11
REMOTE_PORT	The port number of the host making a request	33015

TABLE 16.7 CGI Environment Variables (continued)

Name	Value	Example
REQUEST_METHOD	The method used to get information to the CGI program	GET, POST, etc
SCRIPT_FILENAME	The absolute pathname of the CGI program	/opt/apache/cgi-bin/hello.cgi
SCRIPT_NAME	The relative pathname of the CGI program; a partial URL	/cgi-bin/hello.cgi
SERVER_ADMIN	E-mail address of the system administrator	root@susan
SERVER_NAME	The server's host name, DNS alias, or IP address	susan, 127.0.0.0
SERVER_PORT	Server's port number where client request was sent	80
SERVER_PROTOCOL	The name and version of the protocol	HTTP/1.0
SERVER_SOFTWARE	Name and Version of the server software	Apache/1.2b8
QUERY_STRING	The string obtained from a GET request from the URL	http://susan/cgi-bin/ form1.cgi?Name=Christian+Dobbins
PATH_INFO	Extra path information passed to a CGI program.	
PATH_TRANSLATED	The PATH_INFO translated to its absolute path	
CONTENT_TYPE	The MIME type of the query data	text/html
CONTENT_LENGTH	The number of bytes passed from the server to CGI program	Content-Length=55

An HTML File with a Link to a CGI Script.

The following example is an HTML file that will allow the user to print out all the environment variables. When the browser displays this document, the user can click on the hotlink "here" and the CGI script, *env.cgi*, will then be executed by the server. In the HTML document the string "here" and the URL ("*http://susan/cgi-bin/env.cgi*") are enclosed in the "A" anchor tags. If the hotlink is ignored by the user, the browser displays the rest of the document. The following example is the HTML source file that will be interpreted by the browser. The browser's output is shown in the Netscape window below the example.

E x a m p l e   16.10

(The HTML file with a hotlink to a CGI script)
```
1   <HTML>
2   <HEAD>
3   <TITLE>TESTING ENV VARIABLES</TITLE>
    </HEAD>
    <BODY>
    <P>
    <H1> Major Test </H1>
4   <P> If you would like to see the environment variables<BR>
    being passed on by the server, click .

5   <A HREF="http://susan/cgi-bin/env.cgi">here</A>
    <P>Text continues here...
    </BODY>
    </HTML>
```

Explanation

1   The <HTML> tag says this document is using the HTML protocol.
2   The <HEAD> tag contains the title and any information that will be displayed outside the actual document.
3   The <TITLE> tag is displayed in the top bar of the Netscape window.
4   The <P> tag is the start of a paragraph. The <BR> tag causes the line to break.
5   The <A> tag is assigned the path to the CGI script, *env.cgi*, on server, *susan*. The word "here" will be displayed by the browser in blue underlined letters. If the user clicks on this word, the CGI script will be executed by the server. The script will print out all of the environment variables passed to the script from the server. This is one of the ways information is given to a CGI script by a Web server. The actual CGI script is shown below in Example 16.11.

Example 16.11

The Output of the HTML File with a Hotlink to the CGI Script

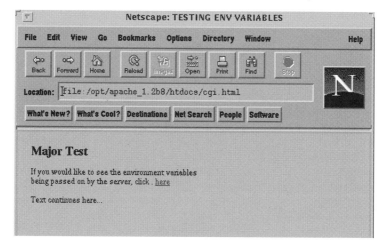

E x a m p l e   1 6 . 1 2

(The CGI Script)
```
1   #!/opt/perl5/bin/perl
2   print "Content type: text/plain\n\n";
3   print "CGI/1.1 test script report:\n\n";
4   print "argc is ", $#ARGV + 1, ". argv is @ARGV.\n";

5   # Print out all the environment variables

6   while(($key, $value)=each(%ENV)){
7          print "$key = $value\n";
    }
```

E x p l a n a t i o n

1 The #! line is important to your server if your server is running on a UNIX platform. It
   is the path to Perl. The line must be the correct pathname to your version of perl or you
   will receive the error message from your server: **Internal Server Error ...**

2 The first line generated by the CGI script is a valid HTTP header, ending with a blank
   line. The header contains a content type (also called a MIME type) followed by *text/
   plain*, meaning that the document will consist of plain text. If the script were to include
   HTML tags, the content type would be *text/html*.

3 The version of the Common Gateway Interface used by this server is printed.

4 If any arguments are passed to this script, the number of arguments (*$#ARGV + 1*), and
   the array of arguments (*@ARGV*) will be printed.

5 This is a Perl comment line.

6 The *%ENV* hash contains environment variables (keys and values) passed into the Perl
   script from the server. The each function will return both the key and the value and store
   them in scalars, *$key* and *$value*, respectively.

7 The *$key/$value* pairs are printed back to STDOUT, which has been connected to the
   server by a pipe mechanism.

E x a m p l e 1 6 . 1 3

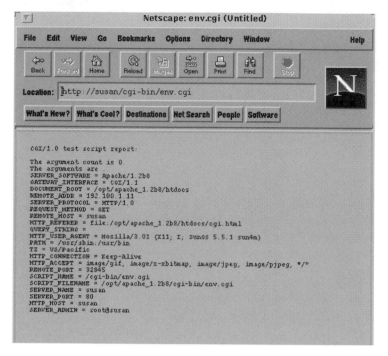

The Environment Variables. Output from the CGI Script.

16.8 Forms

Processing user input is one of the most common reasons for using a CGI script. This is normally done with forms. The form offers you a number of ways in which to accept input, called virtual input devices, such as radio buttons, checkboxes, pop-up menus, and text boxes. All forms are in HTML documents and begin with a <FORM> tag and end with a </FORM> tag. A method attribute may be assigned. The method attribute indicates how the form will be processed. The GET method is the default and the POST method is the most commonly used alternative. The GET method is preferable for operations that will not effect the state of the server, that is, simple document retrieval and database lookups, etc., whereas the POST method is preferred for handing operations that may change the state of the server, such as adding or deleting records from a database. These methods will be described in the next section. The ACTION attribute is assigned the URL of the CGI script that will be executed when the data is submitted by pressing the "Submit" button.

The browser gets input from the user by displaying fields that can be edited. The fields are created by the HTML <INPUT TYPE=key/value> tag.These fields might take the form of checkboxes, text boxes, radio buttons, etc. The data that is entered into the form is sent to the server in an encoded string format in a name/value pair scheme. The value represents the actual input data. The CGI programmer must understand how this input is encoded in order to parse it and use it effectively. First let's see how input gets into the browser by looking at a simple document and the HTML code to produce it. The user will be able to click on a button or enter data in the text box. The input in this example won't be processed thus causing an error to be sent to the server's error log when the submit button is selected. Nothing will be displayed by the browser. The default for obtaining input is the GET method.

A summary of the steps in producing a form is:

1. START: Start the form with the HTML FORM tag.
2. ACTION: The ACTION attribute of the FORM tag is the URL of the CGI script that will process the data input from the form.
3. METHOD: Provide a method on how to process the data input. The default is the GET method.
4. CREATE: Create the form with buttons and boxes and whatever looks nice using HTML tags and fields.
5. SUBMIT: Create a Submit box so that the form can be processed. This will launch the CGI script listed in the ACTION attribute.
6 END: End the form and the HTML document.

A Simple Form with Radio Buttons, Check Boxes, and Text Fields

E x a m p l e   1 6 . 1 4

```
1    <HTML>
     <HEAD>
2    <TITLE>Input Types for Forms</TITLE>
     </HEAD>
     <BODY>
3    <FORM ACTION="http://susan/cgi-bin/form.cgi"
4    <P><B>
     Type in a string here:
5    <INPUT TYPE="text" NAME="string" SIZE=50>
     <P>
6    Choose a menu item:
     </B>
     <P>
7    <MENU>
8    <LI><INPUT TYPE="radio" NAME="choice" VALUE="burger" > Hamburger
     <LI><INPUT TYPE="radio" NAME="choice" VALUE="fish" > Fish
     <LI><INPUT TYPE="radio" NAME="choice" VALUE="steak" > Steak
     <LI><INPUT TYPE="radio" NAME="choice" VALUE="yogurt"> Yogurt
9    </MENU>
     <P>
```

```
       <B>
       Choose a place:
       </B>
10     <MENU>
11     <INPUT TYPE="checkbox" NAME="place" VALUE="LA" > Los Angeles
       <BR>
       <INPUT TYPE="checkbox" NAME="place" VALUE="SJ" > San Jose
       <BR>
       <INPUT TYPE="checkbox" NAME="place" VALUE="SF" CHECKED> San
       Francisco
       <BR>
       </MENU>
       <P>
12     <INPUT TYPE=SUBMIT VALUE="Submit">
13     <INPUT TYPE=RESET VALUE="Clear">
       </FORM>
       </BODY>
14     </HTML>
```

Explanation

1   This tag says that this is the start of an HTML document.

2   The title tag. The title appears outside of the browser's main window.

3   The beginning of a FORM tag which specifies where the browser will send the input data and the method that will be used to process it. The default method is the GET method. When the data is submitted, the CGI script will be executed by the server, *susan*. The CGI script is located under the server's root directory in the *cgi-bin* directory, the directory where CGI scripts are normally stored.

4   The <P> tag starts a new paragraph. The <B> tag says the text will be in bold type.

5   The input type is a text box that will hold up to 50 characters.

6   The user is asked to pick from a series of menu items.

7   This tag starts a series of menu items in the form of a bulleted list of radio buttons and the corresponding values.

8   The first type item in the list is a set of radio buttons. The key/value pairs are used to build a query string to pass on to the CGI program after the submit button is pressed. The value of the NAME attribute "choice", for example, will be assigned "burger" if the user clicks on the Hamburger option. *choice=burger* is passed onto the CGI program.

9   This tag marks the end of the menu items.

10 This <MENU> tag starts a new menu.

11 The input type this time is in the form of checkboxes. When the user clicks on one of the checkboxes, the value of the NAME attribute will be assigned one of the values from the VALUE attribute; e.g., place may be assigned "LA" if "Los Angeles" is checked.

12 If the user clicks the "Submit" button, the CGI script listed in the forms ACTION attribute will be launched. In this example, the script wasn't programmed to do anything. An error message is sent to the server's error log.

13   If the "Clear" button is pressed, all of input boxes are cleared.

14   End the HTML document.

E x a m p l e   1 6 . 1 5

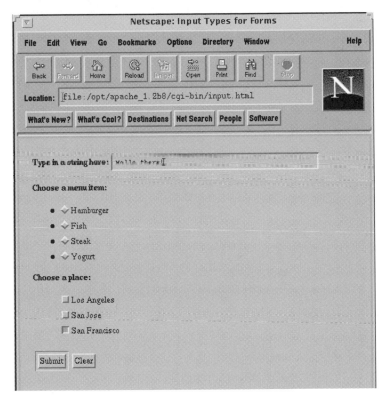

The HTML Page with Input Types

TABLE 16.8   Form Control types

Control type	Attributes	Description
TEXT	NAME	Creates a textbox for user input
	SIZE, MAXLENGTH	Specifies the size of the textbox
PASSWORD		Like textbox, but input is hidden
CHECKBOX	NAME, VALUE	Displays a square box that can be checked
		Creates name/value pairs from user input
RADIO	NAME, VALUE	Like checkboxes, except only one box can be checked.
HIDDEN	NAME, VALUE	Provides name/value pair without displaying an object on the screen
IMAGE	SRC	Displays the image pointed to by the src attribute
SUBMIT	NAME, VALUE	When pressed, executes the form; launches CGI script
RESET	NAME, VALUE	Resets the form to its original position; clears all input fields

16.8.1 The GET Method

The simplest and most widely supported type of form is created with what is called the GET method. If a method is not supplied, the GET method is the default. It is the only method used for retrieving static HTML files and images. Since HTML is an object-oriented language, you may recall that a method was a name for a subroutine.

The GET method passes data to the CGI program by appending the input to the program's URL, either as extra path information or as URL encoded string. The QUERY_STRING environment variable is assigned the encoded string.

The following example illustrates the HTML file used to produce a form. After filling out the form, if the user presses the Send (submit) box, the CGI script, *form1.cgi,* (assigned to the ACTION attribute) is executed.

E x a m p l e   1 6 . 1 6

(HTML file with a form tag and action attribute)
1   <HTML>
2   <HEAD>
3   <TITLE>First CGI Form</TITLE>
4   </HEAD>
5   <HR>
6   **<FORM ACTION="http://susan/cgi-bin/form1.cgi" METHOD=GET>**
    <! When user presses submit, cgi script is called to process input >
7   **Please enter your name:
**
8   **<INPUT TYPE="text" SIZE=50 NAME="Name">**
    <P>
    Please enter your phone:
9   **<INPUT TYPE="text" SIZE=50 NAME="Phone">**
    <P>

10 **<INPUT TYPE=SUBMIT VALUE="Send">**
    <INPUT TYPE=RESET VALUE="Clear">

    </FORM>
    </BODY>
    </HTML>

E x p l a n a t i o n

1   The start tag for an HTML document.
2   The start of the header information.
3   The title of the document.
4   The end of the header information.
5   The tag for a shadowed rule line.
6   The FORM tag specifies the URL and method that will be used to process a form.
     When a user submits the form, the browser will send to the Web server all the data it
     has obtained from the browser. The ACTION attribute tells the server to call a CGI

script at the location designated in the URL and send the data onto that program to be processed. The CGI program can do whatever it wants to with the data and, when finished, will send it back to the server. The server will then relay the information back to the browser for display.

7   The user is asked for input.

8   The input type is a text box that will hold up to 50 characters. The NAME attribute is assigned the string "Name". This will be the key part of the key/value pair. The user will type something in the text box. The value he types will be assigned to the "NAME" key. This *NAME=VALUE* pair will be sent to the CGI script in that format, e.g., *NAME=Christian*.

9   The NAME attribute for the input type is "Phone". Whatever the user types in the text box will be sent to the CGI program as *Phone=VALUE*, e.g., *Phone=510-456-1234*

10   The attribute SUBMIT for the input type causes the submit button to appear with the string "Send" written into the button. If this box is clicked on, the CGI program will be executed. The input is not sent to the CGI program. The RESET attribute allows the user to clear all the input devices by clicking on the "Clear" button.

Example 16.17

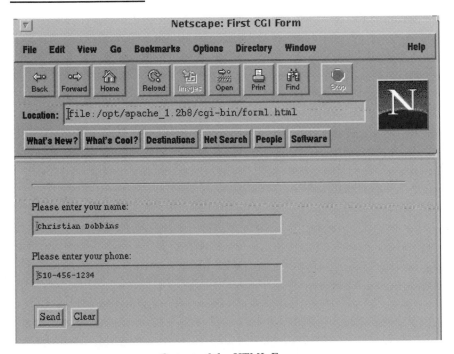

Output of the HTML Form

Example 16.18

```
1  #!/opt/perl5/bin/perl
   # The CGI script that will process the form information sent from server
2  print "Content type: text/plain\n\n";

   print "CGI/1.1 First CGI form :\n\n";
   # Print out all the environment variables

3  while(($key, $value)=each(%ENV)){
4      print "$key = $value\n" if $key eq "QUERY_STRING";
   }
```

Explanation

1 The #! line tells the server where to find the Perl interpreter.
2 The content type is plain text since there is no HTML to output in this simple script.
3 The while loop is used to loop through all of the ENV variables in the %ENV hash. These variables were passed into the Perl script from the Web server.
4 This line will be printed only when the value of the QUERY_STRING environment variable is found. It wasn't really necessary to loop through the entire list. It would have been sufficient just to type: *print "$ENV{QUERY_STRING}\n"*;

Example 16.19

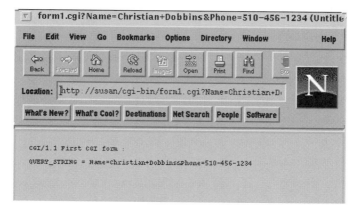

Output from CGI Script

16.8.2 The Encoded Query String

When using the GET method, information is sent to the CGI program in the environment variable, QUERY_STRING.[4] The string is URL encoded. Each key-value pair is separated by an ampersand (&) and spaces are replaced with plus signs (+). Any non-alphanumeric values are replaced with their hexadecimal equivalent preceded by a percent sign (%).

After you press the submit button on the previous example, you will see the input strings in your browser in the Location bar (Netscape); the URL line preceded by a question mark. The highlighted part in the following example is the part that will be assigned to the environment variable, QUERY_STRING. See Table 16.9.

http://susan/cgi-bin/form1.cgi?Name=Christian+Dobbin&Phone=510-456-1234

The QUERY_STRING environment variable will be passed to your Perl script in the %*ENV* hash. To access the key/value pair in your Perl script, type:

    print $ENV{QUERY_STRING};

TABLE 16.9   Encoding Symbols in a Query String

Symbol	Function
&	Separates key/value pairs
+	Replaces spaces
%xy	Represents any ASCII character with a value of less than 21 hexadecimal (33 decimal) or greater than 7f (127) and special characters ?, &, %, +, and = . These characters must be escaped with a %, followed by the hexadecimal equivalence (xy) of that character, e.g., %2F represents a forward slash and %2c represents a comma.

With Perl's many string manipulation functions, you can take this information and break it down into a set of key/value pairs. The Perl CGI script can use the information and then send it back to the server in a suitable format.

16.8.3   Decoding the Query String with Perl

Decoding the query string is not a difficult task because Perl has such a large number of string manipulation functions such as *tr, s, split, substr, pack,* etc. Once into your Perl program, you can split up the query string and do whatever you want with it.

For removing &, +, and = signs from the query string, the substitution command, *s,* the *split* function, and the translate function, *tr,* are useful. To deal with the hexadecimal to character conversion of those characters preceded by a % sign, the *pack* function is normally used.

E x a m p l e   1 6 . 2 0

(URL encoded strings)

1   **Name=Christian+Dobbins&Phone=510-456-1234&SIGN=Virgo**
    Christian Dobbins 510-456-1234 Virgo

2   **string=Joe+Smith%3A%2450%2c000%3A02%2F03%2F77**
    Joe Smith:$50,000:02/03/77

---

4. When using the POST method, the input is assigned to a variable from stdin and encoded the same way.

Explanation

1 The key/pair values show that the URL has three pieces of information separated by the ampersand (&): *NAME=Christian+Dobbins*; *PHONE=510-456-1234;* and *SIGN=Virgo*. The first thing to do would be to split up the line and create an array. (See *a.*)
   After splitting up the string by ampersands, remove the + with the *tr* or *s* functions and split the remaining string into key/value pairs with the split function, using the = as the split delimiter. (See *b.*)

   a.   @key_value = **split(/&/, $ENV{QUERY_STRING})**;
             print "@key_value\n";

             Output:
             Name=Christian+Dobbins Phone=510-456-1234 Sign=Virgo

   b.   foreach $pair (@key_value){
                   $pair =~ tr/+/ /;
                   ($key, $value) = **split(/=/, $pair)**;
                   print "\t$key: $value\n";
             }

             Ouput:
             Name: Christian Dobbins
             Phone: 510-456-1234
             Sign: Virgo

2 This string contains ASCII characters that are less than 33 decimal and greater than 127, the colon, the dollar sign, the comma, and the forward slash. The *pack* function is used to convert the hexadecimal coded characters back into character format. First the search side of the substitution, */%(..)/*, is a regular expression that contains a literal percent sign followed by any two characters (each dot represents one character) enclosed in parentheses. The parentheses are used so that Perl can store the two characters it finds in the special scalar, $1. On the replacement side, the *pack* function will first use the *hex* function to convert the two hexadecimal characters stored in $1 to their corresponding decimal values and then pack the resulting decimal values into unsigned characters. The result of this execution is assigned to the scalar, *$input*.

$input="string=Joe+Smith%3A%2450%2c000%3A02%2F03%2F77";

```
$input=~s/%(..)/pack("c", hex($1))/ge;
print $input,"\n";
```

             Output:
                 string=Joe+Smith:$50,000:02/03/77

E x a m p l e   1 6 . 2 1

(The HTML document)
1   <HTML>
2   <HEAD>
3   <TITLE>First Form</TITLE>
    </HEAD>
    <HR>
4   **<FORM ACTION="http://susan/cgi-bin/form2.cgi" METHOD=GET>**

5   Enter your name:
6   **<INPUT TYPE="text" SIZE=50 NAME="Name">**
    <P>
    Please enter your phone:
7   **<INPUT TYPE="text" SIZE=50 NAME="Phone">**
    <P>

    Please enter your birth sign:
    <INPUT TYPE="text" SIZE=50 NAME="SIGN">
    <P>
8   **<INPUT TYPE=SUBMIT VALUE="Send">**
9   **<INPUT TYPE=RESET VALUE="Clear">**

10 </FORM>
    </BODY>
    </HTML>

E x p l a n a t i o n

1   This is the start tag for an HTML document.
2   This is the head tag containing header information.
3   The title tag is part of the header, not displayed on the page but in the title bar.
4   This is the start of a Form tag. The action is to execute the CGI script called *form2.cg*i.
    The method used is the GET method. Input will be stored in the QUERY_STRING en-
    vironment variable. If a method is not supplied, the GET method is used by default.
5   The user is asked for input, followed by a line break.
6   The input type is a text box that will hold 50 characters of input. The NAME attribute
    is required. It holds the key portion of the key/value pair, e.g., *Name=Tom.*
7   The input type is a text box that will hold 50 characters. The NAME attribute again is
    required and holds the key portion in the key/value pair, e.g., *Phone=123-333-3333.*
8   The input type is a submit button within the form. The value on the button is "Send".
    When this button is pressed, the form is submitted and the CGI script is executed.
9   The input type is a reset button within the form. The value on the button is "Clear".
10 The end of form tag.

Example 16.22

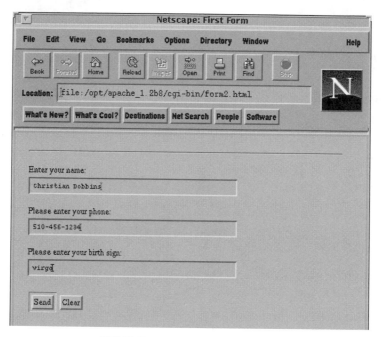

HTML Form Using Get Method

Example 16.23

```
1    #!/opt/perl5/bin/perl

2    print "Content type: text/plain\n\n";
     print "CGI/1.1 test script with query strings:\n\n";
     # Print out all the environment variables

3    while(($key, $value)=each(%ENV)){
4        print "$key = $value\n" if $key eq "QUERY_STRING";
     }

5    $QUERYSTRING=$ENV{'QUERY_STRING'};

6    @key_value=split(/&/, $QUERYSTRING);

7    print "@key_value\n";

     print "\n\nNow let's manipulate the query string to get what we want.\n\n";
8    foreach $pair ( @key_value){
9        $pair =~ tr/+/ /;
10       ($key, $value) = split(/=/, $pair);
11       print "\t$key: $value\n";
     }
```

E x p l a n a t i o n

1   This is the pathname for the Perl interpreter.

2   This header line describes the format of the data returned from this program to be plain text. The two newlines end the header information.

3   The *%ENV* hash contains the key/value pairs sent to this Perl program by the Web server. The *each* function returns both a key and a value from the *%ENV* hash. The *while* loop will iterate through all the key/value pairs.

4   The key/value pair will be printed if *$key* evaluates to QUERY_STRING.

5   The scalar, *$QUERYSTRING*, is assigned the value of the QUERY_STRING environment variable.

6   The scalar, *$QUERYSTRING*, is split by ampersands. The output returned is stored in the three element array, *@key_value*, as : *NAME=Christian+Dobbins PHONE=510-456-1234 SIGN=Virgo*.

7   The new array is printed.

8   The *foreach* loop is used to iterate through the array. Each element is separated by a space and assigned in turn to the scalar *$pair*.

9   The *tr* function replaces any plus signs with a space, e.g., *Christian+Dobbins* will become *Christian Dobbins*.

10 The scalar, *$pair*, is split by equal signs. Two values are returned. The first is assigned to *$key* and the second to *$value*, e.g., *$key* is assigned "NAME" and *$value* is assigned "Christian Dobbins".

11 The new key/value pair is printed and sent back to the Web server. The browser displays the output.

E x a m p l e   1 6 . 2 4

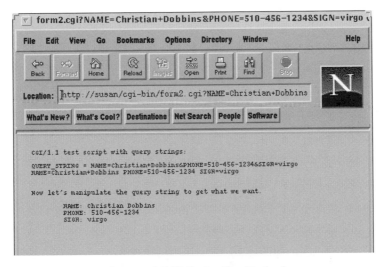

Output of CGI Script-Get Method

16.8.4   The POST Method

The only real difference between the GET and POST methods is the way that input is passed from the server to the CGI program. When the GET method is used, the server sends input to the CGI program in the QUERY_STRING environment variable. When the POST method is used, the CGI program gets input from standard input, *stdin*. One reason for using the POST method is that some browsers restrict the amount of data that can be stored in the QUERY_STRING environment variable. And the POST method doesn't store its data in the query string. Also, the GET method displays the input data in the URL line in the location box of the browser, whereas the POST method hides the data. Since the POST method does not append input to the URL, it is often used in processing forms where there is a lot of data being filled into the forms.

In the HTML document the FORM tag starts the form. The ACTION attribute tells the browser where to send the data that is collected from the user, and the METHOD attribute tells the browser how to send it. If POST is the method, the output from the browser is sent to the server and then to the CGI program's standard input.

The amount of data, i.e., the number of bytes taken as input from the user, is stored in the CONTENT_LENGTH environment variable. Rather than assigning the input to the QUERY_STRING environment variable, the browser sends the input to the server in a message body, similar to the way e-mail messages are sent. The server then encapsulates all the data and sends it on to the CGI program. The CGI program then reads the input data from the *stdin* stream via a pipe. The Perl *read* function reads the CONTENT_LENGTH amount of bytes, saves the input data in a scalar and then processes it the same way it processes input coming from the query string. It's not that the format for the input has changed; it's just how it got into the program. Note that after the POST method has been used, the browser's *Location* box does not contain the input in the URL, as it did with the GET method.

E x a m p l e   1 6 . 2 5

(The HTML file for POST method)
```
1   <HTML>
    <HEAD>
2   <TITLE>First POST METHOD Form</TITLE>
    </HEAD>
    <HR>
3   <FORM ACTION="http://susan/cgi-bin/form3.cgi" METHOD=POST>
4   Enter your name: <BR>
5   <INPUT TYPE="text" SIZE=50 NAME="NAME">
    <P>
    Please enter your phone: <BR>
6   <INPUT TYPE="text" SIZE=50 NAME="PHONE">
    <P>
    Please enter your birth sign: <BR>
```

```
7  <INPUT TYPE="text" SIZE=50 NAME="SIGN">
   <P>
8  <INPUT TYPE=SUBMIT VALUE="Send">
9  <INPUT TYPE=RESET VALUE="Clear">
   </FORM>
   </BODY>
10 </HTML>
```

Explanation

1   This is the start of the HTML document.

2   This is the title of the HTML document that appears at the top of the browser frame bar.

3   This is the beginning of an HTML form. The method attribute is POST, which means data will be sent to the input stream, *stdin*, of CGI script, *form3.cgi*, located at URL *http://susan/cgi-bin*

4   User is asked for input.

5   The INPUT TYPE is assigned a text attribute with a SIZE=50. The text window will display up to 50 characters. Whatever the user types as input will go into the "NAME" field of the NAME attribute.

6   The INPUT TYPE is assigned a text attribute with a SIZE=50. Whatever the user types as input will go into the "PHONE" field of the NAME attribute.

7   The INPUT TYPE is assigned a text attribute with a SIZE=50. The text window will display up to 50 characters. Whatever the user types as input will go into the "SIGN" field of the NAME attribute.

8   The INPUT TYPE is assigned a TYPE attribute of SUBMIT. The value, "Send", assigned to the VALUE attribute, will be written right in the SUBMIT button. If the submit button is clicked on by the user, the browser will gather all the input and put it in *name=value* pairs. The SUBMIT doesn't put the values for either submit or reset types in the query string.

9   If the Reset button is clicked by the user, the browser clears all the input fields so that the user can re-enter the data. The string "Clear" will be written right in the reset button.

10 This marks the end of the HTML document.

E x a m p l e   1 6 . 2 6

```
(The CGI script to process the Form)
1  #!/opt/perl5/bin/perl
2  print "Content type: plain/text\n\n";

   print "CGI/1.1 test script with query strings:\n\n";
   # Print out all the environment variables
3  while(($key, $value)=each(%ENV)){
           print "$key = $value\n" ;
   }
4  if ( $ENV{REQUEST_METHOD} eq 'GET' ){
           $buffer=$ENV{'QUERY_STRING'};
   }
   else{
5          read( STDIN, $buffer, $ENV{'CONTENT_LENGTH'});
   }
   print "\n\nNow let's manipulate the buffer to get what we want.\n\n";
6  foreach $pair ( split(/&/, $buffer)){
7          $pair =~ tr/+/ /;
8          ($name, $value) = split(/=/, $pair);
9          print "\t$key: $value\n";
   }
```

E x p l a n a t i o n

1 Don't forget the #! line to let the server know where to find the Perl interpreter in order to run this program.

2 The content type is plain text since there are not any HTML tags in this script.

3 All of the CGI environment variables, both keys and values, are printed.

4 If the value of the REQUEST_METHOD is equal to GET, the value of the QUERY_STRING is assigned to the scalar *$buffer*.

5 If the REQUEST_METHOD wasn't GET, then we'll assume it was POST and get the input data with the *read* function. The *read* function reads from *stdin* a specified number of bytes, CONTENT_LENGTH, into a scalar, *$buffer*. The *stdin* is piped into the CGI script from the server in the same encoded format as shown in the QUERY_STRING environment variable when the GET method was used.

6 The *split* function will split the input using the & as the field delimiter. This will create an array of name/value pairs separated by spaces, e.g., NAME=Christian+Dobbins&PHONE=510-456-1234&SIGN=Virgo will become:

   NAME=Christian+Dobbins PHONE=510-456-1234 SIGN=Virgo

   The *foreach* loop processes each element of the array by first assigning "*NAME=Christian+Dobbins*" to the scalar *$pair*. Each element of the array returned by the *split* function is separated by white space. The next iteration of the *foreach* loop will assign the string "*PHONE=510-456-1234*" to the scalar *$pair*, etc.

7 The *tr* function replaces each plus sign (+) with a single space. Remember that all spaces
   in the input data have been encoded with a plus sign. The value of *$pair* becomes
   "NAME=Christian Dobbins".

8 The *split* function will create an array by splitting the string *"NAME=Christian Dobbins"*, with the equal sign (=) as the field delimiter. The string *NAME* is assigned to
   $name and the string *"Christian Dobbins"* is assigned to *$value*.

Example 16.27

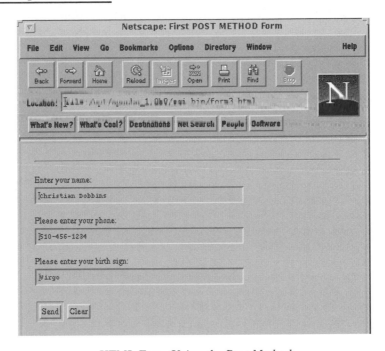

HTML Form Using the Post Method

Example 16.28

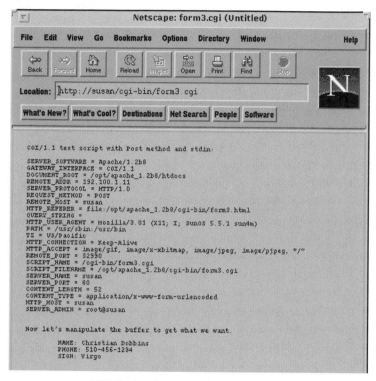

CGI Script Output—The Post Method

16.8.5 Extra Path Information

Information can also be provided to the CGI script by appending some extra path information to the URL of the HTML document. The path information starts with a forward slash so that the server can identify where the actual CGI script ends and the new information begins. The information can then be processed in the CGI script by parsing the value of the PATH_INFO environment variable where this extra information is stored.

If the information appended is a path to another file, the PATH_TRANSLATED environment variable is also set, mapping the PATH_INFO value to the document root directory. The document root directory is found in the DOCUMENT_ROOT environment variable. The path name is treated as relative to the root directory of the server.

Example 16.29

(The HTML Document)

```
1  <HTML>
2  <HEAD>
   <Title>testing Env Variables</title>
   </HEAD>
   <BODY>
   <P>
   <H1> Major Test </h1>
   <P> If You Would Like To See The Environment Variables<Br>
   Being Passed On By The Server, Click .
```

3 <A Href="Http://susan/cgi-bin/pathinfo.cgi/color=red/size=small">here</a>
```
   <P>
   Text Continues Here...
   </BODY>
   </HTML>
```

Example 16.30

(The CGI Script)

```
   #!/opt/perl5/bin/perl

1  print "Content type: text/html\n\n";

   print "CGI/1.0 test script report:\n\n";

   print "The argument count is ", $#ARGV + 1, ".\n";
   print "The arguments are @ARGV.\n";
   # Print out all the environment variables

2  while(($key, $value)=each(%ENV)){
3       print "$key = $value\n";
   }

   print "=" x 30, "\n";
4  print "$ENV{PATH_INFO}\n";
5  $line=$ENV{PATH_INFO};
6  $line=~tr/\// /;
7  @info = split(" ", $line);
8  print "$info[0]\n";
9  eval "\$$info[0]\n";
10 print $color;
```

Explanation

1   The content type is text/html.
2   The loop iterates through each of the ENV variables, assigning the key to *$key* and the corresponding value to *$value*.
3   Each key and value is printed.
4   The value for the $ENV{PATH_INFO} environment variable is printed.
5   The value of $ENV{PATH_INFO} variable is assigned to the scalar *$line*.
6   All forward slashes are replaced with spaces. */color=red/size=small* will become *color=red size=small* and assigned to $line.
7   The *split* function splits the scalar *$line* into an array, using spaces as the separator.
8   The first element of the array, *color=red*, is printed.
9   The eval function evaluates the expression and assigns *red* to *$color*.
10 When the scalar, *$color*, is printed, the value is *red.*

Example 16.31

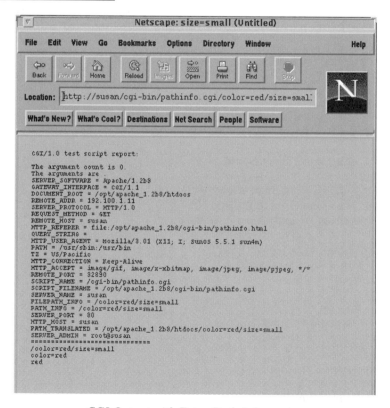

CGI Output with Extra Path Information

16.8.6   Server Side Includes

It is not always necessary to produce a full-blown CGI script just to get a small amount of data on the fly from a static HTML document. If you just wanted to know the name of a remote server, the current file, or the date and time, etc., it would seem silly to have to write a CGI script. Now most servers support a short-cut feature that allows the HTML document to output these small amounts of information without requiring an HTTP header. The feature is called SSI, short for Server Side Includes, really just HTML directives that are inserted into the HTML document, a file normally ending with a *.shtml* extension.

Format:
                `<!--command option=value -->`

Example:
                `<!--#exec cgi="/cgi-bin/joker/motto"-->`

Explanation:
Executes the CGI program enclosed in quotes as though called from an anchor link.

TABLE 16.10   Some Common SSI Commands.

Command	Example	Meaning
include	`<!--#include file="myfile.html"- ->`	Inserts a file in current directory or subdirectory.
config	`<!- - #config sizefmt="bytes" - ->`	Sets the format for display size of the file in bytes.
echo	`<!- -#echo var="DATE_GMT"- ->`	Prints the date in Greenwich Mean Time; other values are shown in example 10.21.
exec	`<!- -#exec cmd="finger"-->`	Executes shell command *finger*.
fsize	`<!- -#fsize file="test.html"- ->`	Prints the size of the file.
flastmod	`<!- -$flastmod file="test.html"- ->`	Prints the last modification time of the file.

The following example is the HTML source test file from a Web server *OmniHTTd*.

Example 16.32

```
<HTML>
<HEAD>
<Meta Http-equiv="Pragma" Content="No-cache">
<Title>cgi And Ssi Test</title>
</head>
<Body Bgcolor="#ffffff">
<H1>cgi And Ssi Test</h1>

<Hr>
<H2>standard Cgi Test</h2>
You Are Visitor # <Img Src="/cgi-bin/visitor.exe"><P>
<Hr>
```

1   `<H2>`**Server Side Includes**`</h2>`
     If Server Side Includes Are Enabled, You Will See Data Values Below:
     `<P>`
2   The Date Is: **`<!--#echo Var="Date_local"-->`**`<Br>`
3   The Current Version Of The Server Is: **`<!--#echo Var="Server_software"-->`**`<Br>`
4   The Cgi Gateway Version Is: **`<!--#echo Var="Gateway_interface"-->`**`<Br>`
5   The Server Name Is: **`<!--#echo Var="Server_name"-->`**`<Br>`
6   This File Is Called: **`<!--#echo  Var="Document_name"-->`**`<Br>`
7   This File's Uri Is: **`<!--#echo Var= "Document_uri"-->`**`<Br>`
8   The Query String Is: **`<!--# Echo Var= "Query_string_unescaped"-->`**`<Br>`
9   This File Was Last Modified: **`<!--#echo Var="Last_modified" -->`**`<Br>`
10   The Size Of The Unprocessed File Is **`<!--#fsize Virtual="/test.shtml"-->`**`<Br>`
11   You Are Using **`<!--#echo Var="Http_user_agent"-->`**`<Br>`
12   You Came From **`<!--#echo Var="Http_referer"-->`**`<P>`
     `<Br>`
     `<Input Type="Submit" Value="Go!">`
     `</FORM>`
     `<HR>`
     `</BODY>`
     `</HTML>`

O u t p u t

1   *Server Side Includes is enclosed in heading tags to print:*
     If server side includes are enabled, you will see data values below:

2   The date is: *Jul 22 1997*
3   The current version of the server is: *OmniHTTPd/2.0a2(Win32;i386)*
4   The CGI gateway version is: *CGI/1.1*
5   The server name is: *ellie.Learn1.com*
6   This file is called: *C:\HTTPD\HTDOCS\test.shtml*
7   This file's URI is: */test/shtml*
8   The query string is:
9   This file was last modified: *Jun24 1997*
10   The size of the unprocessed file is *1989*
11   You are using Mozilla/2.01KIT *(Win95; U)*
12   You came from *http://127.0.0.1/default.htm*

16.9 Using the CGI-lib.pl Library

The *CGI-lib.pl* library was written by Stephen Brenner and is the standard library for CGI programming routines for both Perl4 and Perl5. The main purpose of this library is to read all the form information and parse it so that it can be manipulated as an associative array without yo worrying about how to remove plus signs, equal signs, convert hexadecimal values, etc. There are routines that will also take care of header information, error messages, upload files, and print out all the environment variables.

TABLE 16.11   Library Subroutines from CGI-lib.pl

Subroutine Name	What it Does
&ReadParse	Read both Form and Get input variables into an associative array called %in. This is the primary subroutine in the library.
&PrintHeader	Returns the standard "Content-type: text/html\n\n header needed by all CGI programs.
&HtmlTop("Title of the Page")	Prints top page title in the head tags.
&HtmlBot	Prints the HTML footer at the bottom of the document.
&MethGet, &MethPost	Tests which method is being used; returns true or null.
&MyBaseUrl, MyUrl	Returns the URL of the current script.
&CGIError, &CGIDie	Converts an error message to HTML for the browser.
&PrintVariables(%ENV)	Prints contents of the associative array; in this example, the contents of the %ENV array are printed.

Example 16.33

```
   #!/opt/perl5/bin/perl
1  require "cgi-lib.pl";
2  print &PrintHeader;
3  print &HtmlTop("Hello to you all out there!!");
4   print &MyBaseUrl;
5  print "<p>Hi there.  I'm with ya!</p>\n";
   print "<p>How are you?</p>\n";
6  print &HtmlBot;
```

Explanation

1 To use the *cgi-lib* library, it must be included in your program with the "require" function. Make sure that the library is located in a directory that is listed in the *@INC* array.
2 This is the *PrintHeader* subroutine. It prints out the Content type and two newlines.
3 For the top of the page, this subroutine prints "Hello to you all out there!!" as a title for the document and as a level 1 heading in the body of the document.
4 The *MyBaseUrl* prints the URL for this CGI script.
5 These lines print HTML paragraph tags and text.
6 This line prints the footer at the bottom of the HTML document.

E x a m p l e   1 6 . 3 4

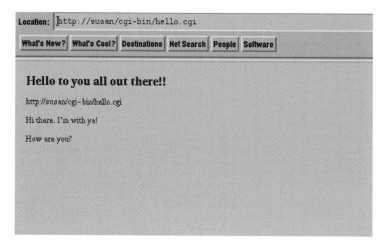

The HTML Produced by cgi.pl

E x a m p l e   1 6 . 3 5

The Output

16.10 The CGI-lib.pm Module

The most popular Perl5 library for CGI programs is the *CGI.pm* module written by Lincoln Stein which is compatible with most of the syntax in the *CGI-lib.pl* library function. *CGI.pm* takes advantage of the object oriented features that were introduced in Perl5. It provides methods to interpret query strings, handle forms, and hides the details of HTML syntax for handling forms with the GET and POST methods. For those migrating from the *cgi-lib.pl* library, *CGI.pm* has added a *ReadParse* subroutine, the primary function in the *cgi-lib.pl* library for reading and parsing input.

For a complete tutorial written by the author of the *CGI.pm* library module, L. Stein, see Website:

http://www-genome.wi.mit.edu/ftp/pub/software/WWW/cgi_docs.html

TABLE 16.12   CGI Methods

Method	Example	What it Does
new	$query = new CGI;	Parses input and puts it in object, *$query* for both GET and POST methods.
	$query = new CGI(INPUTFILE)	Reads contents of form from previously opened filehandle.
keywords	@keywords = $query->keywords	Obtains parsed keywords from the Isindex input string and returns an array.
param	@params = $query->param(-name=>'name', -value=>value);	Returns an array of parameter names passed into the script.
	$value = $query->('arg')	Returns a value (or list of values) for @values = $query->('arg')the parameter passed.
append	$query->append(-name=>'value');	Appends values to parameter.
delete	$query->delete('param');	Deletes a parameter.
delete_all	$query->delete	Deletes all parameters; clears the *$query*, the object.
import_names	$query->import_names('namespace')	Imports variables into namespace.
save	$query->save(FILEHANDLE)	Saves the state of a form to a file.
startform	$query->startform(-method=> -action=>, -encoding);	Returns a <FORM> tag with optional method, action, and encoding.
endform	$query->endform;	Ends the <FORM> tag.
textfield	$query->textfield(-name=>'field', -default=>'start', -size=>50, -maxlength=>90);	Creates a text field box.
textarea		Same as text field but includes multiline text entry box.
password_field	$query->password_field(-name=>'secret' -value=>'start', -size=>60, -maxlength=>80);	Creates a password field.
popup_menu	$query->popup_menu(-name=>'menu' -values=>'@items' -defaults=>'name', -labels=>\%hash);	Creates a pop-up menu.

TABLE 16.12   CGI Methods (continued)

Method	Example	What it Does
scrolling_list	$query->scrolling_list(-name=>'listname', -values=>[list], -default=> [sublist], -multiple=>'true', -labels=>\%hash);	Creates a scrolling list.
checkbox_group	$query->checkbox_group(-name=>'group_name', -values=>[list], -default=>[sublist], -linebreak=>'true', -labels=>\%hash)	Creates a group of checkboxes.
checkbox	$query->checkbox(-name=>'checkbox_name', -checked=>'checked',, -value=>'on',, -label=>'clickme')	Creates a standalone checkbox.
radio_group	$query->radio_group(-name=>'group_name', -values=>[list], -default=>'name', -linebreak=>'true', -labels=>\%hash);	Creates a group of radioboxes.
submit	$query->submit(-name=>'button', -value=>'value');	Creates the submit button for forms.
reset	$query->reset	Creates the reset button to clear the form boxes to former values.
defaults	$query->defaults	Creates a button that completely resets the form to its defaults.
hidden	$query->hidden(-name=>'hidden', -default=>[list]);	Creates a hidden from view text field.
image_button	$query->image_button(-name=>'button', -src=>'/source/URL', -align=>'MIDDLE');	Creates a clickable image button.
cookie	$query->cookie(-name=>'sessionID', -value=>'whatever', -expires=>'+3h', -path=>'/', -domain=>'ucsc.edu', -secure=>1);	Creates a Netscape cookie.
header	$query->header(-cookie=>'cookiename');	Puts cookie in the HTTP header.

E x a m p l e   1 6 . 3 6

```
     #!/opt/perl5/bin/perl
1    BEGIN { unshift(@INC, '/opt/perl5/lib');}
2    use CGI qw(:standard);

3    print header;
4    print start_html(-title =>'Trying the CGI.pm Module',
                      -BGCOLOR=>'blue');
     ),
5    h1('Talk About You!'),
6    start_form,
7         "What's your name? ",textfield('name'),
8    p,
          "What's is your occupation? ", textfield('job'),
     p,
9    "     Select a vacation spot. ", popup_menu(-name=>'place',
                            -values=>['Hawaii','Europe','Canada','Mexico']),
     p,
10   submit,
11   end_form,
     hr;

12   if (param()) {
          print
13                "Your name is ",em(param('name')),
                  p,
                  "Your occupation is ", em(param('job')) ,
                  p,
                  "Your vacation place is ",em(param('place')),
                  hr;
     }
```

E x p l a n a t i o n

1   The @INC array is updated at compile time by putting in the BEGIN subroutine block. This assures that modules can be loaded from the proper library. Remember, modules are loaded at compile time, not run time.

2   The *use* directive says that the *CGI.pm* module is being loaded and will import the *:standard* set of function calls which use a syntax new in library versions 1.21 and higher. This syntax allows you to call methods without explicitly creating an object with the *new* constructor method, i.e., the object is created for you.

3   The header method *header* returns the Content-type: header. You can provide your own MIME type if you choose, otherwise, it defaults to *text/html*.

4   This will return a canned HTML header and the opening <BODY> tag. Parameters are optional and are in the form -title, -author, and -base. Any additional parameters, such as the Netscape unofficial BGCOLOR attribute, are added to the <BODY> tag, e.g., *-BGCOLOR=>red*.

5   This will produce a level 1 heading tag. It's a shortcut and will produce the <H1> Html tag.

6   This method starts a form.

7   The *textfield* method creates a text field box. The first parameter is the NAME for the field; the second parameter representing the VALUE is optional. NAME is assigned "name" and VALLUE is assigned "".

8   The *p* is a shortcut for a paragraph <P>.

9   The *popup_menu* method creates a menu. The required first argument is the menu's name (-*name*). The second argument, -*values,* is an array of the menu items. It can be either anonymous or named.

10 The *submit* method creates the submit box.

11 This line ends the form.

12 If the *param* method returns non-null, each of the values associated with the parameters will be printed.

13 The *param* method returns the value associated with "name", i.e., what the user typed as input for that parameter.

E x a m p l e   1 6 . 3 7

The HTML Source Produced by the CGI.pm Module (Exercise 10.28)

Example 16.38

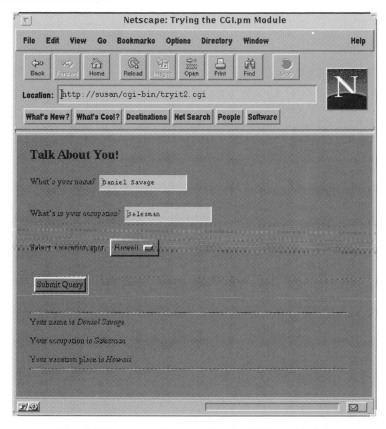

The CGI Program Produced by the CGI.pm Module

16.11 Cookies

16.11.1 What's a Cookie?

There's a place here in Chico, California, called Ray's Video where you can sign out movies for a day, three days, etc. In order to make the transaction, the first thing the clerk does is ask for your driver's license number. That number is used to identify you in the database, to find out if you have overdue movies, or owe money. In this way a record is kept of past transactions by using a unique identifier, your driver's license. A Web server or CGI script can save state information by using its own unique identifier, called a cookie.

The HTTP protocol, by design, is stateless in order to keep the connections brief. After a transaction is completed, the connection is lost and the browser and server have no recollection of what transpired from one session to the next. But now that the Internet is used as a huge shopping center it is often necessary to keep track of users and what they have purchased and their preferences, registration information, etc. Netscape Navigator introduced the idea of cookies in order to achieve persistent state, i.e., keep information around that would normally be lost at the end of a transaction. The cookie allows the server to keep client information on the client's (browser) machine in a cookie file (often called *cookie.txt* or just *cookie*) stored on the hard drive so that the information can be retrieved at some later time. A cookie is a *name=value* pair similar to the query string used by the GET method and its values are assigned to the HTTP_COOKIE environment variable. The cookie can be created by the server or a CGI script and sent back to the browser in an HTTP header. The browser maintains a list of cookies on disk that belong to a particular Web server and returns them to the server via the HTTP header during subsequent interactions. A cookie then is passed back and forth between a browser and a server.

There are two types of cookies: short-term and persistent cookies. A short-term cookie is good for the same transaction. A short-term cookie might be used if a user is browsing from one page to another, adding items to a shopping cart. But if you need to keep track of every time the user visits your site over a number of different sessions, then you need a persistent cookie. Since there may be a lot of information being stored, that information can be stored in a database on the server while the cookie itself can be used to record a session key or unique user id. Many browsers have begun to adopt the cookie idea and it is likely to become part of the HTTP standard. See:

>
> http://www.netscape.com/newref/std/cookie_spec.html
> *Persistent Client State HTTP Cookies A Preliminary Specification*

16.11.2   Making Cookies

To make a cookie, the HTTP *Set Cookie* response header is assigned a number of fields. If your server supports cookies, this header information will be sent from your CGI script to the server and assigned to the HTTP_COOKIE environment variable. Now what you do with this information is up to you.

TABLE 16.13   Set Cookie Fields (Netscape)

Field	Purpose
Name=Value	Required field. Name of the cookie and its value.
Expires=Date	Commands the browser to forget the cookie after this date. By default, the cookie expires when the current browser session terminates.
Domain=Domain	Domain name of the server from which the URL was fetched; defaults to the path of the URL sending the Set Cookie request header.
Path=Path	Limits the URL of the cookie to where the browser can let the server see it. Any program in this path will have access to the cookie.
Secure	Sends the server a cookie only if a secure HTTP connection has been established.

Cookies are limited. So when setting the *name=value* field, there is a limit of 4 kilobytes. There can be no more than 20 cookies from a domain or server, and there can be only 300 cookies per client. If a lot of information needs to be stored, the cookie is usually set to some unique identifier and used as a means to locate the data in an external database saved on the server side of the connection.

The following example merely illustrates how to use the *Set-Cookie* header and to see what values are stored in the HTTP_COOKIE environment variable. The easiest way to create and retrieve cookies is to use the *CGI.pm* library module, which contains methods to hide the details of the implementation.

E x a m p l e   1 6 . 3 9

```
    #!/opt/perl5/bin/perl
1   my $name = "Ellie";
    my $expiration_date = "Friday, 10-Aug-98 00:00:00: GMT";
    my $path = "/cgi-bin";

2   print "Set-Cookie: shopper=$name, expires=$expiration_date,
            path=@path";
    print "\n";

3   print "Set-Cookie: user=Joe";
    print "\n";

4   print "Content-type: text/html\n\n";

5   print "<html>";
    print "<head><title>Cookie Test</Title></head>";
    print "<body>";
    print "<h1>Cookie</h1>";
    print "<h3>Got Milk?</h3>";
    print "<hr>";
    print "<p>";
    print "Look at the HTTP_COOKIE environment variable.";
    print "<p><br>";

6   print $ENV{HTTP_COOKIE},"\n";

    print "<p>";
    print "<hr>";
    print "</Body></Html>";
```

Explanation

1 The local variables are set. These variables will be assigned to fields in the Set-Cookie response header. The expiration time specifies an expiration date and time for the cookie in the format Day, DD-Mon-YY HH:MM:SS GMT. This field is optional. In this example ,the cookie will expire on August 28, 1998, GMT (Greenwich Mean Time).

2 The *Set-Cookie* response header is set with the cookie name, shopper, and its corresponding value, *Ellie*. The expiration date of this cookie is set, and the path is set to the location where the cookie is valid. The root path "/" is most general and means that the cookie is valid in all directories below the Document root. In this example, the browser will send the cookie to every program in the *cgi-bin* directory.

3 This is another cookie. This header relies on defaults for the rest of its fields.

4 Now the standard HTML header is set.

5 This is the start of the HTML document.

6 The browser will display the values of the HTTP_COOKIE environment variable. Each of the cookies is separated by a semi-colon. This could be parsed with Perl functions such as *tr* and *s* to get whatever information is needed.

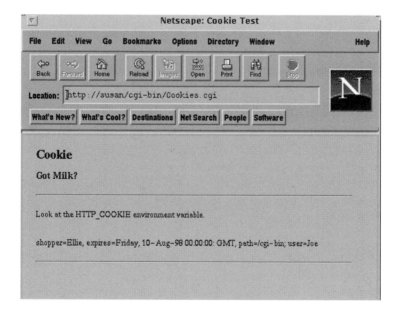

To summarize, CGI programs benefit both the user and the Web developer in that they allow static documents to become dynamic and interactive. But CGI is not a programming language. It is rather a set of conventions specifying how external programs can interface with a Web server. Although the external programs can be written in any language that adheres to these specifications, such as C, C++, Visual Basic, Shell, etc., Perl has become the chosen language by Web developers for writing CGI programs because it is relatively easy to learn, handles both high- and low-level operations, manages all kinds of text and databases, and is now reusable and extensible. And with security being a major concern with any program launched on the Internet, Perl has included a library module called *pgperl,* also known as Penguin, to protect sensitive data. And of course, last but not least, it's portable and free.

Appendix A

A.1 Perl Functions

The following is a complete list of Perl functions and a short description of what they do.

abs

abs VALUE
Returns the absolute value of its argument ($_ is the default). Ignores signs.

accept

accept(NEWSOCKET,GENERICSOCKET)
Accepts a socket connection from clients waiting for a connection. The GENERICSOCKET, a filehandle, has been previously opened by the *socket* function, is bound to an address, and is listening for a connection. NEWSOCKET is a filehandle with the same properties as GENERICSOCKET. The *accept* function attaches GENERICSOCKET to the newly made connection.
See accept(2)[1].

alarm

alarm(SECONDS)
alarm SECONDS
Sends a SIGALARM signal to the process after a number of SECONDS.
See alarm(3).[2]

---

1. The encircled text is a reference to the like-named UNIX system call found in Section 2 of the UNIX manual pages.
2. The like-named UNIX library function is found in Section 3 of the UNIX manual pages.

atan2

>
> **atan(X,Y)**
> Returns the arctangent of X/Y in the range <pi>.

bind

>
> **bind (SOCKET, NAME)**
> Binds an address, NAME, to an already opened unnamed socket, SOCKET. See
> bind(2).

binmode

>
> **binmode(FILEHANDLE)**
> **binmode FILEHANDLE**
> For operating systems that distinguish between text and "binary" mode (not UNIX).
> Prepares FILEHANDLE for reading in binary mode.

bless

>
> **bless (REFERENCE, CLASS);**
> **bless REFERENCE;**
> Tells the object referenced by REFERENCE that it is an object in a package
> (CLASS) in the current package if no CLASS is specified. Returns the reference.

caller

>
> **caller(EXPR)**
> **caller EXPR**
> **caller**
> Returns an array with information about the subroutine call stack, including the
> package, filename and line number. With EXPR, a number, goes back EXPR stack
> frames before current one.

chdir

>
> **chdir(EXPR)**
> **chdir EXPR**
> **chdir**
> Changes the present working directory to EXPR. If EXPR is omitted, changes
> directory to home directory. See chdir(2).

chmod

>
> **chmod (MODE, LIST)**
> **chmod MODE, LIST**
> Changes permissions of a list of files; first argument is the permission MODE
> number (octal); the remaining arguments are a list of file names. Returns the
> number of files changed.
> See chmod(2).

chomp

> **chomp(LIST)**
> **chomp(VARIABLE)**
> **chomp VARIABLE**
> **chomp**
> Chops off the last character of a string, VARIABLE, or the last character of each
> item in a LIST if that character corresponds to the current value of $/, by default set
> to the newline. Unlike chop (see below), it returns the number of characters
> deleted.

chop

> **chop(LIST)**
> **chop(VARIABLE)**
> **chop VARIABLE**
> **chop**
> Chops off the last character of a string, VARIABLE, or the last character of each
> item in a LIST and returns the chopped value. Without an argument, chops the last
> character off $_.

chown

> **chown(LIST)**
> **chown LIST**
> Changes owner and group of a list of files. First two elements in the list are the
> numerical uid and gid, respectively. The rest of the list are the names of files.
> Returns the number of files changed. See chown(2).

chr

> **chr NUMBER**
> Returns the ASCII value for NUMBER, e.g., chr(66) returns "B".

chroot

> **chroot (FILENAME)**
> **chroot FILENAME**
> Changes root directory for the current process to FILENAME, which is the starting
> point for pathnames starting with /. Must be superuser to do this. See chroot(2).

close

> **close(FILEHANDLE)**
> **close FILEHANDLE**
> Closes the file, socket, or pipe associated with FILEHANDLE.

closedir

closedir(DIRHANDLE)
closedir DIRHANDLE
Closes a directory structure opened by *opendir.* See directory(3).

connect

connect(SOCKET, NAME)
Connects a process with one that is waiting for an *accept* call. NAME is a packed network address. See connect(2).

cos

cos(EXPR)
cos EXPR
Returns the cosine of EXPR (in radians).

crypt

crypt(PLAINTEXT, SALT)
The password encryption function where PLAINTEXT is the user's password and SALT is a two character string consisting of characters in the set [a–zA–Z./]. See crypt(3).

dbmclose

dbmclose(%ASSOC_ARRAY)
dbmclose %ASSOC_ARRAY
Breaks the binding between a DBM file and an associative array. Only useful with NDBM, a newer version of NDBM, if supported. (See untie). Also see dbm(3).

dbmopen

dbmopen(%ASSOC_ARRAY, DBNAME, MODE)
Binds a DBM or NDMB file to an associative array. Before a database can be accessed, it must be opened by *dbmopen.* The files *file.dir* and *file.pag* must exist. DBNAME is the name of the file without the *.dir* and *.pag* extension. If the database does not exist and permission MODE is specified, the database is created. See dbminit(3). See tie.

defined

defined(EXPR)
defined EXPR
Returns a Boolean value, 1, if EXPR has a real value. Returns a Boolean value, 0, if EXPR does not have a real value. EXPR may be a scalar, array, hash, or subroutine. For a hash, checks only whether the value (not key) is defined.

delete

delete $ASSOC{KEY}

Deletes a value from an associative array. If successful, returns the deleted value; otherwise, an undefined value. If a value in %ENV is deleted, the environment will be modified. The *undef* function can also be used and is faster.

die

die(LIST)
die LIST
die

Prints the LIST to STDERR and exits with the value of $!, the system error message (errno). When in an *eval* function, sets the $@ value to the error message, and aborts *eval*. If the value of LIST does not end in a newline, the name of the current script, the line number, and a new line are appended to the message.

do

do BLOCK
do SUBROUTINE(LIST)
do EXPR

do BlOCK returns the value of the last command in the BLOCK.
do SUBROUTINE(LIST) calls a SUBROUTINE that has been defined.
do EXPR uses EXPR as a filename and executes the contents of the file as a Perl script. Used primarily to include subroutines from the Perl subroutine library.

dump

dump LABEL

Causes an immediate binary image core dump. Used for undumping a core file; *undump* is not part of this Perl distribution.

each

each (%ASSOC_ARRAY)
each %ASSOC_ARRAY

Returns a two element array, the key and value for the next value of an associative array, in random order.

eof

eof (FILEHANDLE)
eof()
eof

Returns 1 if next read on FILEHANDLE indicates the end of file. If FILEHANDLE is omitted, returns the end of file for the last file read.

eval

eval(EXPR)
eval EXPR

Evaluates expression as a Perl program in the context of the current Perl script. Often used for trapping errors. Eval is used to trap fatal errors. Syntax errors or runtime errors or those coming from the die function are returned to $@ variable. The $@ variable is set to null if there are no errors. The value returned is the value of the last expression evaluated.

exec

exec(LIST)
exec LIST

Executes a system command in LIST in context of the current program. Never returns. If LIST is scalar, checks for shell metacharacters and passes to /bin/sh. Otherwise, arguments are passed to the C function call, execvp. Does not flush output buffer.

exists

exists EXPR

Returns true if a specified key from an associative array exists, even if its corresponding value is undefined.

exit

exit(INTEGER)
exit INTEGER

Exits with script with status value of INTEGER. If INTEGER is omitted, exits with 0, meaning program exits with successful status. Non–zero status implies that something went wrong in the program.

exp

exp(EXPR)
exp EXPR

Returns e to the power of EXPR.

fcntl

fcntl(FILEHANDLE, FUNCTION, SCALAR)

Changes properties on an open file. Requires "*sys/fcntl.ph*". The FUNCTION can duplicate an existing file descriptor, get or set file descriptor flags, get or set file status flags, get or set asynchronous I/O ownership, and get or set record locks. SCALAR is an integer for flags. See fcntl(2).

fileno

fileno(FILEHANDLE)
fileno FILEHANDLE
Returns the integer file descriptor for FILEHANDLE. Descriptors start with STDIN, STDOUT, STDERR, 0, 1, and 2, respectively. May not be reliable in Perl scripts if a file is closed and reopened. See ferror(3).

flock

flock(FILEHANDLE, OPERATION)
Applies or removes advisory locks on files. OPERATION specifies an operation on a lock for a file, shared locks, exclusive locks, or nonblocking locks. The OPERATION to remove a file is unlock. See flock(2).

fork

fork
Creates a new (child) process. The child is a copy of the parent process. Both child and parent continue execution with the instruction immediately following the *fork*. Returns 0 to the child process and the pid of the child to the parent.

format

format NAME =
picture line
value list

   ...

.

Declares a set of picture lines to describe the layout of corresponding values. The *write* function uses the specified format to send output to a named filehandle represented by NAME. If NAME is omitted, the default is STDOUT.

formline

formline PICTURE, LIST
An internal function used by formats to format a list of values according to the picture line. Can also be called directly in a program.

getc

getc(FILEHANDLE)
getc FILEHANDLE
getc
Returns the next character from the input file associated with FILEHANDLE. Returns a null string at EOF. If FILEHANDLE is omitted, reads from STDIN.

getgrent

> **getgrent**
> **setgrent**
> **endgrent**
> Iterates through */etc/group* and returns an entry from */etc/group* as a list, including group name, password, group id, and members.See getgrent(3).

getgrgid

> **getgrgid(GID)**
> Returns a group entry file by group number. See getgrgid(3).

getgrnam

> **getgrnam(NAME)**
> Returns a group file entry by group name. See getgrent(3).

gethostbyaddr

> **gethostbyaddr(ADDRESS, AF_INET)**
> Translates a network address to its corresponding names and alternate addresses. Returns the hostname, aliases, addresstype, length, and unpacked raw addresses. See gethostbyaddr(3). AF_INET is always 2.

gethostbyname

> **gethostbyname(HOSTNAME)**
> Translates a hostname to an entry from the */etc/hosts* file as a list, including the hostname, aliases, addresses. See gethostbyname(3). In scalar context, returns only the host address.

gethostent

> **gethostent**
> **sethostent(STAYOPEN)**
> **endhostent**
> Iterates through */etc/hosts* file and returns the entry as a list,including name, aliases, addresss type, length, and alternate addresses. Returns a list from the network host database,*/etc/hosts*. See gethostent(3).

getlogin

> **getlogin**
> Returns the current login from */etc/utmp*, if there is such a file. See *getlogin(3)*. If getlogin does not work, try:$loginname = getlogin || (getpwuid($<))[0] || die "Not a user here.";

getnetbyaddr

getnetbyaddr(ADDR, ADDRESSTYPE)

Translates a network address to its corresponding network name or names. Returns a list from the network database, */etc/networks*. See getnetent(3). In scalar context, returns only the network name. In scalar context, returns only the network name.

getnetbyname

gatnetbyname(NAME)

Translates a network name to its corresponding network address. Returns a list from the network database, */etc/networks*. See *getnetent(3)*. In scalar context, returns only the network address.

getnetent

getnetent
setnetent(STAYOPEN)
endnetent

Iterates through the */etc/networks* file and returns the entry as a list. Returns a list from the network database, */etc/networks*. See getnetent(3). In scalar context, returns only the network name.

getpeername

getpeername(SOCKET)

Returns the packed *sockaddr* address of other end of the SOCKET connection. See getpeername(2).

getpgrp

getpgrp(PID)
getpgrp PID

Returns the current process group for the specified PID (PID 0 is the current process). Without EXPR, returns the process group of the current process. See *getpgrp(2)*.

getppid

getppid

Returns the PID of the parent process. If 1 is returned, that is the PID for init. Init adopts a process whose parent has died. See getpid(2).

getpriority

getpriority(WHICH, WHO)

Returns the current priority, nice value, for WHICH—a process, a process group, or a user. WHO is relative to which group. A WHO value of zero, denotes the current process, process group, or user. See *getpriority(2)*.

getprotobyname

>   **getprotobyname(NAME)**
>
>   Translates a protocol NAME to its corresponding number and returns a list
>   including the protocol name, aliases, and the protocol number. Returns a line from
>   the network protocol database, */etc/protocols*. See *getprotoent(3)*.

getprotobynumber

>   **getprotobynumber(NUMBER)**
>
>   Translates a protocol number to its corresponding name and returns a list including
>   the protocol name, aliases, and the protocol number. Returns a line from the
>   network protocol database, */etc/protocols*. See getprotoent(3).

getprotoent

>   **getprotoent**
>   **setprotent(STAYOPEN)**
>   **endprotoent**
>
>   Returns a list from the */etc/protocols* database, including the protocol name,
>   aliases, and the protocol number. If STAYOPEN flag is non-zero, the database will
>   not be closed during subsequent calls. The endprotoent function closes the file.
>   See *getprotoent(3)*. In scalar context, returns the protocol name.

getpwent

>   **getpwent**
>   **setpwent**
>   **endpwent**
>
>   Iterates through the */etc/passwd* file and returns the entry as a list, username,
>   password, uid, gid, quotas, comment, gcos field, home directory, and startup shell.
>   The endpwent function closes the file. See *getpwent(3)*. In scalar context, returns
>   the username.

getpwnam

>   **getpwnam(NAME)**
>
>   Translates a username to the corresponding entry in */etc/passwd* file. Returns a
>   list, including the username, password, uid, gid, quotas, comment, gcos field, home
>   directory, and startup shell. See *getpwent(3)*. In scalar context, returns the
>   numeric user ID.

getpwuid

>   **getpwuid(UID)**
>
>   Translates the numeric user id to the corresponding entry from the */etc/passwd* file.
>   Returns a list, including the username, password, uid, gid, quotas, comment, gcos
>   field, home directory, and startup shell. See *getpwent(3)*. In scalar context, returns
>   the username.

getservbyname

getservbyname(NAME,PROTOCOL)

From */etc/services* database, translates a port name to its corresponding port number as a scalar and, returns as an array, the service name, aliases, port where service resides, and protocol needed, from the */etc/services* database. See getservent(3). In scalar context, returns only the service port number.

getservbyport

getservbyport(PORT_NUMBER,PROTOCOL)

From */etc/services* database, translates a port number to its corresponding port name as a scalar and, returns as an array, the service name, aliases, port where service resides, and protocol needed, from the */etc/services* database. See getservent(3). In scalar context, returns only the service port number.

getservent

getservent
setservent(STAYOPEN)
endservent

Iterates through the */etc/services* database, returning the service name, aliases, port where service resides, and protocol needed. If STAYOPEN flag is non–zero, the database will not be closed during subsequent calls and endservent closes the file. See getservent(3). In scalar context, returns only the service port name.

getsockname

getsockname(SOCKET)

Returns the packed sockaddr address of the local end of the SOCKET connection. See getsockname(2).

getsockopt

getsockopt(SOCKET, LEVEL, OPTNAME)

Returns the requested options, OPTNAME, associated with SOCKET, at the specified protocol level. See getsockopt(2).

glob

glob EXPR

Performs filename expansion on EXPR as the shell does. Without EXPR, $_ is used. Uses the internal <*> operator.

gmtime

gmtime (EXPR)
gmtime EXPR

Converts the results of the *time* function to a 9 element array with the Greenwich Mean time zone including the second, minute, hour, month day, month, year, weekday, yearday, and 1 if daylight standard time is in effect. See ctime(3) and timegm() in the Perl library module *Time::Local*.

goto

> **goto LABEL**
> **goto EXPR**
> **goto &NAME**
> Program branches to the LABEL and resumes execution. Cannot goto any construct that requires intialization, such as a subroutine or foreach loop. Goto never returns a value. The form goto &NAME substitutes the currently running subroutine with a call to NAME (used by the AUTOLOAD subroutine).

grep

> **grep(EXPR, LIST)**
> **grep BLOCK LIST**
> Returns to a new array, any element in LIST where EXPR matches that element. Returns to a scalar, the number of matches.

hex

> **hex(EXPR)**
> **hex EXPR**
> Returns the decimal value of EXPR interpreted as a hexadecimal string. Without EXPR, uses $_.

import

> **import CLASSNAME LIST**
> **import CLASSNAME**
> Not a built-in function, but a class method defined by modules that will export names to other modules through the use function.

index

> **index(STR, SUBSTR, POSITION)**
> **index(STR,SUBSTR)**
> Returns the position of the first occurrence of SUBSTR in STR. POSITION specifies a starting position for the substring in the string starting with base 0.

int

> **int(EXPR)**
> **int EXPR**
> Returns the integer portion of EXPR. Without EXPR, $_ is used.

ioctl

> **ioctl(FILEHANDLE,FUNCTION,SCALAR)**
> Used to control I/0 operations, mainly terminal I/0. Requires "*sys/ioctl.ph*". FUNCTION is an I/O request. SCALAR will be read or written depending on the request. See ioctl(2).

join

join(EXPR, LIST)
Returns a single string by joining the separate strings of LIST into a single string where the field separator is specified by EXPR, a delimiter.

keys

keys(%ASSOC_ARRAY)
keys %ASSOC_ARRAY
Returns a normal array consisting of all the keys in the associative array.

kill

kill(SIGNAL, PROCESS_LIST)
kill PROCESS_LIST
Sends a signal to a list of processes. The signal can either be a number or a signal name (signal name must be quoted). (Negative signal number kills process group.) See kill(2).

last

last LABEL
last
The last command is comparable to C's break command. It exits the innermost loop, or, if the loop is labeled last LABEL, exits that loop.

lc

lc EXPR
Returns EXPR in lowercase. Same as \L \E escape sequence.

lcfirst

lcfirst EXPR
Returns EXPR with the first character in lowercase. Same as \l \E sequence.

length

length(EXPR)
length EXPR
Returns the length in characters of scalar EXPR, or if EXPR is omitted, returns length of $_. Not used to find the size of an array or associative array.

link

link (OLDFILE, NEWFILE)
Creates a hard link. NEWFILE is another name for OLDFILE. See link(2).

listen

listen(SOCKET, QUEUESIZE)
Listens for connections on a SOCKET with a queue size specifying the number of processes waiting for connections. See listen(2).

local

local(LIST)
Makes variables in LIST local for this block, subroutine or *eval*.

localtime

localtime(EXPR)
localtime EXPR
Converts the time returned by the *time* function to a 9–element array for the local timezone. See ctime(3).

log

log(EXPR)
log EXPR
Returns the logarithm (base e) of EXPR. If EXPR is omitted, returns log($_).

lstat

lstat(FILEHANDLE)
lstat FILEHANDLE
lstat(EXPR)
Returns a 14–element array consisting of file statistics on a symbolic link, rather than the file the symbolic link points to. The array consists of:
>   device
>   file inode number
>   file mode
>   number of hard links to the file
>   user ID of owner
>   group ID of owner
>   raw device
>   size of file
>   file last access time
>   file last modify time
>   file last status change time
>   preferred blocksize for file system I/O
>   actual number of blocks allocated

See stat(2)

map

map (BLOCK LIST)
map (EXPR, LIST)
Evaluates BLOCK or EXPR for each element of LIST and returns the list value containing the results of the evaluation. The following example translates a list of numbers to characters. @chars = map chr, @numbers;

mkdir

mkdir(NAME, MODE)
Creates a directory, NAME, with MODE permissions (octal). See mkdir(2).

msgctl

msgctl(MSGID, CMD, FLAGS)
Calls the *msgctl* system call, allowing control operations on a message queue. Has weird return codes. (See System V IPC.) Requires library file "*ipc.ph*" and "*msg.ph*". See also msgctl(2).

msgget

msgget(KEY, FLAGS)
Calls *msgget* system call. Returns the message queue id number, or if undefined, an error. (See System V IPC.) See also msgget(2).

msgrcv

msgrcv(MSGID, VAR, MSG_SIZE, TYPE, FLAGS)
Calls the *msgrv* system call. Receives a message from the message queue, stores the message in VAR. MSG_SIZE is the maximum message size and TYPE is the message type. (See System V IPC.) See also msgrcv(2).

msgsnd

msgsnd(ID, MSG, FLAGS)
Calls the *msgsnd* system call. Sends the message, MSG, to the message queue. MSG must begin with the message type. The *pack* function is used to create the message. (See System V IPC.) See also msgsnd(2).

my

my EXPR
my (EXPR1, EXPR2, ...)
Variables declared with the *my* function are made private, i.e., they exist only within the innermost enclosing block, subroutine, eval, or file. Only simple scalars, complete arrays, and hashes can be declared with *my*.

new

> **new CLASSNAME LIST**
> **new CLASSNAME**
> Not a built-in function, but a constructor method defined by the CLASSNAME
> module for creating CLASSNAME type objects. Convention taken from C++.

next

> **next LABEL**
> **next**
> Starts the next iteration of the innermost or loop labeled with LABEL. Like the C
> continue function.

no

> **no Module LIST**
> If a pragma or module has been imported with *use,* the *no* function says you don't
> want to use it anymore.

oct

> **oct(EXPR)**
> **oct EXPR**
> **oct**
> Returns the decimal value of EXPR, an octal string. If EXPR contains a leading 0x,
> EXPR is interpreted as hex. With no EXPR, $_ is converted.

open

> **open(FILEHANDLE, EXPR)**
> **open (FILEHANDLE)**
> **open FILEHANDLE**
> Opens a real file, EXPR, and attaches it to FILEHANDLE. Without EXPR, a scalar
> with the same name as FILEHANDLE must have been assigned that filename.
>
> | | |
> |---|---|
> | read | "FILEHANDLE" |
> | write | ">FILEHANDLE" |
> | read/write | "+>FILEHANDLE" |
> | append | ">>FILEHANDLE" |
> | pipe out | "\| UNIX Command" |
> | pipe in | "UNIX Command \|" |

opendir

> **opendir(DIRHANDLE, EXPR)**
> Opens a directory structure, named EXPR, and attaches it to DIRHANDLE for
> functions that examine the structure. See directory(3).

ord

> **ord(EXPR)**
> **ord**
> Returns the unsigned numeric ASCII values of the first character of EXPR. If EXPR is omitted, $_ is used.

pack

> **$packed=pack("TEMPLATE", LIST)**
> Packs a list of values into a binary structure and returns the structure. TEMPLATE is a quoted string containing the number and type of value.
>
> TEMPLATE is:
>
> | | |
> |---|---|
> | a | An ASCII string, null padded. |
> | A | An ASCII string, space padded. |
> | b | A bit string, low–to–high order. |
> | B | A bit string, high–to–low order. |
> | h | A hexadecimal string, low nybble first. |
> | H | A hexadecimal string, high nybble first. |
> | c | A signed char value. |
> | C | An unsigned char value. |
> | s | A signed short value. |
> | S | An unsigned short value. |
> | i | A signed integer value. |
> | I | An unsigned integer value. |
> | l | A signed long value. |
> | L | An unsigned long value. |
> | n | A short in "network" order. |
> | N | A long in "network" order. |
> | f | A single–precision float in native format. |
> | d | A double–precision float in native format. |
> | p | A pointer to a string. |
> | x | A null byte. |
> | X | Back up a byte. |
> | @ | Null–fill to absolute precision. |
> | u | A uuencoded string. |

package

> **package NAMESPACE**
> A package declaration creates a separate namespace (symbol table) for NAMESPACE, the Perl way of creating a class. The NAMESPACE belongs to the rest of the innermost enclosing block, subroutine, eval or file. If the package declaration is at the same level, the new one overrides the old one.

pipe

> **pipe(READHANDLE, WRITEHANDLE)**
> Opens a pipe for reading and writing, normally after a fork. See pipe(2).

pop

> **pop(ARRAY)**
> **pop ARRAY**
> Pops and returns the last element of the array. The array will have one less element.

pos

> **pos (SCALAR)**
> **pos SCALAR**
> Returns the offset of the character after the last matched search in SCALAR left off, i.e., the position where the next search will start. Offsets start at 0. If the $scalar is as signed "hello" and the search is $scalar =~ m/l/g, the pos function would return the position of the character after the first 'l', position 3.

print

> **print(FILEHANDLE LIST)**
> **print(LIST)**
> **print FILEHANDLE LIST**
> **print LIST**
> **print**
> Prints a string or a comma separated list of strings to FILEHANDLE, or to the currently selected FILEHANDLE, or to STDOUT, the default. Retuns 1 if successful, 0 if not.

printf

> **printf(FILEHANDLE FORMAT, LIST)**
> **printf(FORMAT, LIST)**
> Prints a formatted string to FILEHANDLE or, if FILEHANDLE is omitted, to the currently selected output filehandle. STDOUT is the default. See printf(3). Similar to C's printf, except * is not supported.

push

> **push(ARRAY, LIST)**
> Pushes the values in LIST onto the end of the ARRAY. The array will be increased. Returns the new length of ARRAY.

q, qq, qw, qx
    q/STRING/
    qq/STRING/
    qw/LIST/
    qx/COMMAND/
    An alternative form of quoting. The *q* construct treats STRING as if enclosed in
    single quotes. The *qq* construct treats STRING as if enclosed in double quotes.
    The *qw* construct treats each element of LIST as if enclosed in single quotes, and
    the *qx* treats COMMAND as if in back quotes.

quotemeta
    quotemeta EXPR
    Returns the scalar value of EXPR with all regular expression metacharacters
    backslashed.

rand
    rand(EXPR)
    rand EXPR
    rand
    Returns a random fractional number (scalar) between 0 and EXPR, where EXPR
    is a positive number. Without *srand* generates the same sequence of numbers.
    If EXPR is omitted, returns a value between 0 and 1. See rand(3).

read
    read(FILEHANDLE,SCALAR, LENGTH, OFFSET)
    read(FILEHANDLE, SCALAR, LENGTH)
    Reads LENGTH number of bytes from FILEHANDLE, starting at position OFFSET,
    into SCALAR and returns the number of bytes read, or 0 if *eof*. (Similar to fread
    system call.) See fread(3).

readdir
    readdir(DIRHANDLE)
    readdir DIRHANDLE
    Reads the next entry of the directory structure, DIRHANDLE, opened by *opendir*.
    See directory(3).

readlink
    readlink(EXPR)
    readlink EXPR
    Returns the value of a symbolic link. EXPR is the pathname of the symbolic link,
    and if omitted, $_ is used. See readlink(2).

recv

recv(SOCKET, SCALAR, LEN, FLAGS)
Receives a message of LEN bytes on a socket into SCALAR variable. Returns the
address of the sender. See recv(2).

redo

redo LABEL
redo
Restarts a loop block without reevaluting the condition. If there is a continue block,
it is not executed. Without LABEL, restarts at the innermost enclosing loop.

ref

ref EXPR
Returns a scalar true value, the data type of EXPR, if EXPR is a reference, else
the null string. The returned value depends on what is being referenced, a REF,
SCALAR, ARRAY, HASH, CODE, or GLOB. If EXPR is an object that has been
blessed into a package, return value is the package (class) name.

rename

rename(OLDNAME, NEWNAME)
Renames a file OLDNAME to NEWNAME. Does not work across filesystem
boundaries. If NEWNAME already exists, it is destroyed. See rename(2).

require

require(EXPR)
require EXPR
require
Includes file, EXPR, from the Perl library by searching the @INC array for the
specified file. Also checks that the library has not already been included. $_ is used
if EXPR is omitted.

reset

reset(EXPR)
reset EXPR
reset
Clears variables and arrays or, if EXPR is omitted, resets ?? searches.

return

return LIST
Returns a value from a subroutine. Cannot be used outside of a subroutine.

reverse

reverse(LIST)
Reverses the order of LIST and returns an array.

rewinddir

rewinddir(DIRHANDLE)
rewinddir DIRHANDLE
Rewinds the position in DIRHANDLE to the beginning of the directory structure.
See directory(3).

rindex

rindex(STRING, SUBSTR, OFFSET)
rindex(STRING, SUSSTR)
Returns the last position of SUBSTR in STRING starting at OFFSET, if OFFSET is
specified.

rmdir

rmdir(FILENAME)
rmdir FILENAME
Removes a directory, FILENAME, if empty.

s

s/SEARCH_PATTERN/REPLACEMENT/[g][i][e][o]
Searches for pattern and, if found, replaces the pattern with some text. Returns
the number of substitutions made. The g option is global across a line. The i option
turns off case sensitivity. The e option evaluates the replacement string as an
expression, e.g., *s/\d+/$&+5/e*;

scalar

scalar(EXPR)
Forces EXPR to be evaluated in a scalar context.

seek

seek(FILEHANDLE, POSITION, WHENCE)
Positions a file pointer in a file, FILEHANDLE, from some position, relative to its
position in the file, WHENCE. If WHENCE is 0, starts at the beginning of the file;
if WHENCE is 1, starts at the current position of the file, and if WHENCE is 2, starts
at the end of the file. POSITION cannot be negative if WHENCE is 0.

seekdir

seekdir(DIRHANDLE, POSITION)
Sets the position for the *readdir* function on the directory structure associated with
DIRHANDLE. See directory(3).

select

> **select(FILEHANDLE)**
> **select**
> Returns the currently selected filehandle if FILEHANDLE is omitted. With FILEHANDLE, sets the current default filehandle for *write* and *print*. (See Formatting.)

select

> **select(RBITS,WBITS,EBITS,TIMEOUT)**
> Examines the I/0 file descriptors to see if descriptors are ready for reading, writing, or have exceptional conditions pending. Bitmasks are specified and TIMEOUT is in seconds. See select(2).

semctl

> **semctl(ID,SEMNUM, CMD, ARG)**
> Calls the *semctl* system call, allowing control operations on semaphores. Has weird return codes. (See System V IPC.) Requires library file *"ipc.ph"* and *"sem.ph"*. See also semctl(2).

semget

> **semget(KEY, NSEMS, SIZE, FLAGS)**
> Returns the semaphore id associated with KEY, or undefined if an error. (See System V IPC.) Requires library files *"ipc.ph"* and *"sem.ph"*. See also semget(2).

semop

> **semop(KEY, OPSTRING)**
> Calls the *semop* system call, to perform operations on a semaphore identified by KEY. OPSTRING must be a packed array of *semop* structures. (See System V IPC.) Requires library files "ipc.ph" and "sem.ph". See also semop(2).

send

> **send(SOCKET, MSG, FLAGS,TO)**
> **send(SOCKET, MSG, FLAGS)**
> Sends a message on a SOCKET. See send(2).

setpgrp

> **setpgrp(PID, PGRP)**
> Sets the current process group for the specified process, process group, or user. See getpgrp(2).

setpriority

> **setpriority(WHICH,WHO, PRIORITY)**
> Sets the current priority, *nice* value, for a process, process group, or user. See getpriority(2).

setsockopt

setsockopt(SOCKET,LEVEL,OPTNAME,OPTVAL)

Sets the requested socket option on SOCKET. See getsockopt(2).

shift

shift(ARRAY)
shift ARRAY
shift

Shifts off the first value of the ARRAY and returns it, shortening the array. If ARRAY is omitted, the @ARGV array is shifted, and if in subroutines, the @_ array is shifted.

shmctl

shmctl(ID,CMD,ARG)

Calls the *shmctl* system call, allowing control operations on shared memory. Has weird return odes. (See System VIPC.) Requires library file "ipc.ph" and "shm.ph". See also shmctl(2).

shmget

shmget(KEY, SIZE, FLAGS)

Returns the shared memory segment id associated withthe KEY, or undefined if an error. The shared memory segment created is of at least SIZE bytes. Requires "*ipc.ph*" and "*shm.ph*". (See System V IPC.) See also shmget(2).

shmread

shmread(ID, VAR, POS, SIZE)

Reads from the shared memory ID starting at position, POS for SIZE. VAR is a variable used to store what is read.The segment is attached, data is read from, and the segment is detached. Requires "*ipc.ph*" and "*shm.ph*". (See System V IPC.) See also shmat(2).

shmwrite

shmwrite(ID, VAR, POS, SIZE)

Writes to the shared memory ID starting at position, POS for SIZE. VAR is a variable used to store what is written. The segment is attached, data is written to, and the segment is detached. Requires "*ipc.ph*" and "*shm.ph*". (See System V IPC.) See also shmat(2).

shutdown

shutdown(SOCKET, HOW)

Shuts down a SOCKET connection. If HOW is 0 further receives will be disallowed. If HOW is 1,further sends will be disallowed. If HOW is 2, then further sends and receives will be disallowed. See shutdown(2).

sin

sin(EXPR)
sin
Returns the sine of EXPR (expressed in radians). If EXPR is omitted, returns sine of $_.

sleep

sleep(EXPR)
sleep EXPR
sleep
Causes program to sleep for EXPR seconds. If EXPR is omitted, program sleeps forever. See sleep(3).

socket

socket(SOCKET, DOMAIN, TYPE, PROTOCOL)
Opens a socket of a specified type and attaches it to filehandle, SOCKET. See socket(2).

socketpair

socketpair(SOCKET, SOCKET2,DOMAIN,TYPE, PROTOCOL)
Creates an unamed pair of connect sockets in the specified domain, of the specified type. See socketpair(2).

sort

sort(SUBROUTINE LIST)
sort(LIST)
sort SUBROUTINE LIST
sort LIST
Sorts the LIST and returns a sorted array. If SUBROUTINE is omitted, sorts in string comparison order.If SUBROUTINE is specified, gives the name of a subroutine that returns an integer less than, equal to, or greater than 0, depending on how the elements of the array are to be ordered. The two elements compared are passed (by reference) to the subroutine as $a and $b, rather than @_. See Array Functions. SUBROUTINE cannot be recursive.

splice

splice(ARRAY,OFFSET,LENGTH,LIST)
splice(ARRAY,OFFSET,LENGTH)
splice(ARRAY,OFFSET)
Removes elements designated starting with OFFSET and ending in LENGTH from an array, and if LIST is specified, replaces those elements removed with LIST. Returns the elements removed from the list. If LENGTH is not specified, everything from OFFSET to the end of ARRAY is removed.

split

> **split(/PATTERN/,EXPR, LIMIT)**
> **split(/PATTERN/,EXPR)**
> **split(/PATTERN/)**
> **split**
> Splits EXPR into an array of strings and returns them to an array. The PATTERN
> is the delimiter by which EXPR is separated. If PATTERN is omitted, whitespace is
> used as the delimiter. LIMIT specifies the number of fields to be split.

sprintf

> **$string=sprintf(FORMAT, LIST)**
> Returns a string rather than sending output to STDOUT with same formatting
> conventions as the *printf* function. See printf(3).

sqrt

> **sqrt(EXPR)**
> **sqrt EXPR**
> Returns the square root of EXPR. If EXPR is omitted, the square root of $_ is
> returned.

srand

> **srand(EXPR)**
> **srand EXPR**
> **srand**
> Sets the random seed for the *rand* function. If EXPR is omitted, the seed is the time
> function. See rand(3).

stat

> **stat(FILEHANDLE)**
> **stat FILEHANDLE**
> **stat(EXPR)**
> Returns a 13–element array consisting of file statistics for FILEHANDLE or file
> named as EXPR. The array consists of:
>> the device
>> the file inode number
>> file mode
>> number of hard links to the file
>> user ID of owner
>> group ID of owner
>> raw device
>> size of file
>> file last access time
>> file last modify time
>> file last status change time

preferred blocksize for file system I/O
actual number of blocks allocated
See stat(2)

study

study(SCALAR)
study SCALAR
study
Uses a linked list mechanism to increase efficiency in searching for pattern matches that are to be repeated many times. Can only study one SCALAR at a time. If SCALAR is omitted, $_ is used. Most beneficial in loops where many short constant strings are being scanned.

sub

sub NAME BLOCK
sub NAME
sub BLOCK
sub NAME PROTO BLOCK
sub NAME PROTO
sub PROTO BLOCK
The first two declare the existence of named subroutines and return no value. Without a block, **sub NAME** is a forward declaration. The **sub BLOCK** is used to create an anonymous subroutine. The last three are like the first three, except they allow prototypes to describe how the subroutine will be called. A prototype will notify the compiler that a subroutine definition will appear at some later time and can tell the compiler what type and how many arguments the subroutine expects. For example, *sub foo ($$@)*, declares that the subroutine *foo* will take three arguments, two scalars and an array. An error will occur if, for example, fewer than three arguments are passed.

substr

substr(EXPR, OFFSET, LENGTH)
substr(EXPR, OFFSET)
Returns a substring after extracting the substring from EXPR starting at position OFFSET and if LENGTH is specifie that many characters from OFFSET. If OFFSET is negative, starts from the far end of the string.

symlink

symlink(OLDFILE, NEWFILE)
Creates a symbolic link. NEWFILE is symbolically linked to OLDFILE. The files can reside on different partitions. See symlink(2).

syscall

syscall(LIST)
syscall LIST
Calls the system call specified as the first element in LIST, where the system call is preceded with &SYS_ as in &SYS_system call. The remaining items in LIST are passed as arguments to the system call. Requires *"syscall.ph"*.

sysread

sysread(FILEHANDLE, SCALAR, LENGTH, OFFSET)
sysread(FILEHANDLE, SCALAR, LENGTH)
Reads LENGTH bytes into variable SCALAR from FILEHANDLE. Uses the read system call. See read(2).

sysopen

sysopen(FILEHANDLE, FILENAME, MODE)
sysopen(FILEHANDLE, FILENAME, MODE, PERMS)
Opens FILENAME using the underlying operating system's version of the open call, and assigns it to FILEHANDLE. The file modes are system dependent and can be found in the Fcntl library module. 0 means read-only, 1 means write-only, and 2 means read/write. If PERMS is omitted, the default is 0666. See open(2).

system

system(LIST)
system LIST
Executes a shell command from a Perl script and returns. Like the *exec* function, except forks first and the script waits until the command has been executed. Control then returns to script. The return value is the exit status of the program and can be obtained by dividing by 256 or right-shifting the lower 8 bits. See system(3).

syswrite

syswrite(FILEHANDLE, SCALAR, LENGTH, OFFSET)
syswrite(FILEHANDLE, SCALAR, LENGTH)
Returns the number of bytes written to FILEHANDLE. Writes LENGTH bytes from variable SCALAR, to FILEHANDLE, starting at position OFFSET, if OFFSET is specified. Uses the write system call. See write(2).

tell

tell(FILEHANDLE)
tell FILEHANDLE
tell
Returns the current file position, in bytes (starting at byte 0), for FILEHANDLE. Normally the returned value is given to the seek function in order to return to some position within the file. See lseek(2).

telldir

telldir(DIRHANDLE)
telldir DIRHANDLE
Returns the current position of the *readdir* function for the directory structure, DIRHANDLE. See directory(3).

tie

tie (VARIABLE, CLASSNAME, LIST)
Binds a VARIABLE to a package (CLASSNAME) that will use methods to provide the implemenation for the variable. LIST consists of any additional arguments to be passed to the new method when constructing the object. Most commonly used with associative arrays to bind them to databases. The methods have predefined names to be placed within a package. The predefined methods will be called automatically when the tied variables are fetched, stored, or destroyed, etc.

The package implementing an associative array provides the following methods:
        TIEHASH $classname, LIST
        DESTROY $self
        FETCH $self, $key
        STORE $self, $key
        DELETE $self, $key
        EXISTS $self, $key
        FIRSTKEY $self
        NEXTKEY $self, $lastkey

Methods provided for an array are:
        TIEARRAY $classname, LIST
        DESTROY $self
        FETCH $self, $subscript
        STORE $self, $subscript, $value

Methods provided for a scalar are:
        TIESCALAR $classname, LIST
        DESTROY $self
        FETCH $self
        STORE $self, $value

Example:
        $object = tie %hash, Myhashclass;
                while($key, $value)=each (%hash){
                print "$key, $value\n"; # invokes the FETCH method
        $object = tie @array, Myarrayclass;
                $array[0]=5; # invokes the STORE method
        $object = tie $scalar, Myscalarclass;
                untie $scalar; # invokes the DESTROY method

tied

> ### tied VARIABLE
> Returns a reference to the object that was previously bound with the *tie* function or undefined if VARIABLE is not tied to a package.

time

> ### time
> Returns a four–element array of non–leap seconds since January 1, 1970, UTC. Used with *gmtime* and *localtime* functions. See ctime(3).

times

> ### times
> Returns a four–element array giving the user and system CPU times, in seconds, for the process and its children. See times(3).

tr

> ### tr/SEARCHPATTERN/REPLACEMENT/[c][d][e]
> ### y/SEARCHPATTERN/REPLACEMENT/[c][d][e]
> Translates characters in SEARCHPATTERN to corresponding character in REPLACEMENT. Similar to UNIX *tr* command.

truncate

> ### truncate(FILEHANDLE, LENGTH)
> ### truncate(EXPR, LENGTH)
> Truncate FILEHANDLE or EXPR to a specified LENGTH. See truncate(2).

uc

> ### uc EXPR
> Returns EXPR (or $_ if no EXPR) in uppercase letters. Same as \U \E escape sequences.

ucfirst

> ### ucfirst EXPR
> Returns the first character of EXPR(or $_ if no EXPR) in uppercase. Same as \u escape sequence.

umask

> ### umask(EXPR)
> ### umask EXPR
> ### umask
> Sets the umask (file creation mask) for the process and returns the old umask. With EXPR omitted, returns the current umask value. See umask(2).

undef

> **undef(EXPR)**
> **undef EXPR**
> **undef**
> Undefines EXPR, an lvalue. Used on scalars, arrays, hashes, or subroutine names
> (&subroutine) to recover any storage associated with it. Always returns the
> undefined value. Can be used by itself when returning from a subroutine to
> determine if an error was made.

unlink

> **unlink(LIST)**
> **unlink LIST**
> **unlink**
> Removes a LIST of files. Returns the number of files deleted. Without an
> argument, unlinks the value stored in $_. See unlink(2).

unpack

> **unpack(TEMPLATE, EXPR)**
> Unpacks a string representing a structure and expands it to an array value,
> returning the array value, using TEMPLATE to get the order and type of values.
> Reverse of pack. See pack.

unshift

> **unshift(LIST)**
> **unshift**
> Prepends LIST to the beginning of an array. Returns the number of elements in the
> new array.

untie

> **untie VARIABLE**
> Breaks the binding (unties) between a variable and the package it is tied to.
> Opposite of tie.

use

> **use Module LIST**
> **use Module**
> **use pragma**
> A compiler directive that imports subroutines and variables from Module into the
> current package. LIST consists of specific names of the variables and subroutines
> the current package will import. The -m and -M flags can be used at the command
> line instead of *use*. Pragmas are a special kind of module that can affect the
> behavior for a block of statements at compile time. Three common pragmas are:
> *integer, subs*, and *strict*.

utime

> **utime(LIST)**
> **utime LIST**
> Changes the access and modification times on a list of files.The first two elements
> of LIST are the numerical access and modification times.

values

> **values(%ASSOC_ARRAY)**
> **values ASSOC_ARRAY**
> Returns an array consisting of all the values in an associative array,
> ASSOC_ARRAY in random order.

vec

> **vec(EXPR, OFFSET, BITS)**
> Treats a string, EXPR, as a vector of unsigned integers. Returns the value of the
> element specified   OFFSET is the number of elements to skip over in order to find
> the one wanted, and BITS is the number of bits per element In the vector. BITS
> must be one of of a power of two from 1 to 32, e.g., 1,2,4,8,16, or 32.

wait

> **wait**
> Waits for the child process to terminate. Returns the pid of the deceased process
> and −1 if no child processes. The status value is returned in the $? variable. See
> wait(2).

waitpid

> **waitpid(PID, FLAGS)**
> Waits for a child process to terminate and returns true when the process dies, or −
> 1 if there are no child processes, or if FLAGS specify non-blocking and the process
> hasn't died. $? gets the status of the dead process. Requires "sys/wait.ph". See
> wait(2).

wantarray

> **wantarray**
> Returns true if the context of the currently running subroutine wants an array value,
> i.e., the returned value from the subroutine will be assigned to an array. Returns
> false if looking for a scalar. Example: *return wantarray ? () : undef;*

warn

> **warn(LIST)**
> **warn LIST**
> Sends a message to STDERR, like the *die* function, but doesn't exit the program.

write

> **write(FILEHANDLE)**
> **write FILEHANDLE**
> **write**
> Writes a formatted record to FILEHANDLE or currently selected FILEHANDLE
> (See select), i.e., when called, invokes the format (picture line) for the
> FILEHANDLE; with no arguments, either goes to stdout or to the filehandle
> currently selected by the *select* call. Has nothing to do with the write(2) system call.
> See syswrite.

y

> **y/SEARCHPATTERN/REPLACEMENT/[c][d][e]**
> Translates characters in SEARCHPATTERN to corresponding character in
> REPLACEMENT. Also known as tr and similar to UNIX *tr* command or *sed* y
> command.

A.2   Special Variables

A.2.1   Filehandles

$| If non–zero, forces buffer flush after every write and print on the currently
     selected filehandle.
$%   Current page number of currently selected filehandle.
$=   Current page length of currently selected filehandle.
$–   Number of lines left on the page for currently selected filehandle.
$~   Name of current report format for currently selected filehandle.
$^   Name of current top–of–page format for currently selected filehandle.

A.2.2   Local to Block

$1.. $9 Contains remembered subpatterns that reference a corresponding set of
        parentheses. Same as \1..\9.
$&   The string matched by the last pattern match. (Like sed editor)
$`   The string preceding what was matched in the last pattern match.
$'   The string that follows whatever was matched by the last pattern match.
$+   The last pattern matched by the last search pattern.

Example:
$str="old and restless";

print "$&\n" if $str =~ /and/;
print "$`\n" if $str =~ /and/;
print "$'\n" if $str =~ /and/;

```
print "\nold string is: $str\n";
$str=~s/(old) and (restless)/$2 and $1/;
print "new string is: $str\n";
print "\nlast pattern matched: $+\n";
```

O u t p u t

and
old
restless

E x p l a n a t i o n

old string is: old and restless
new string is: restless and old
last pattern matched is. restless

A.2.3   Global

$_	Default input and pattern–searching space.
$.	Current input line number of last filehandle that was read. Must close the filehandle to reset line numbers for next filehandle.
$/	Input record separator, newline by default. (Like RS in awk.)
$\	Output record separator for the print function. Does not print a newline unless set: $\="\n".
$,	Output field separator for the print function. Normally delimiter is not printed between comma separated strings unless set: S,=" ".
$"	Same as $, but applies to printing arrays when in double quotes. Default is space.
$#	Output format for numbers printed with the print function. (Like OMFT in awk.)
$$	The process id number of the Perl program running this script.
$?	Status returned by last pipe closed, command in back quotes, or system function.
$*	Default is 0. Set to 1, does a multi–line match within a string; 0 for a match within a single line.
$0	Name of this Perl script.
$[	Index of first element of an array, and first character in a substring. Default is 0.
$]	The first part of the string is printed out when using perl –v for version information.
$;	The subscript separator for multi–dimensional array emulation. Default is \034. (Like SUBSEP in awk.)
$!	Yields the current value of errno (system error number). If numeric; and the corresponding system error string.

$@   Error message from the last eval, do, or require function.
$<   The real uid of this process.
$>   The effective uid of this process.
$(The real gid of this process.
$)   The effective gid of this process.
$:   The set of characters after which a string may be broken to fill
         continuation lines (starting with ^) in a format. Default is " \n–" to break
         on whitespace, newline, or colon.
$^D   Perl's debug flags when –D switch is used.
$^F   Maximum file descriptor passed to subprocess, usually two.
$^I   Current value of inplace–edit extension when –i switch is used. Use
         undef to disable inplace editing.
$^P   Internal Perl debugging flag.
$^T   Time of day when script started execution. Used by –A, –C, and –M test
         operators and be set to any number value returned by time to perform
         file tests relative to the current time.
$^W   The current value of the warning switch.
$^X   The full pathname by which this Perl was invoked.
_   An underscore. The special designator for file testing when stating files.
ARGV   The special filehandle array for looping over line arguments.
$ARGV   The variable containing the name of the current file when reading from
         <ARGV>.
@ARGV   The array containing command line arguments.
DATA   Special filehandle referring to anything following __END__.
@F   The array into which input lines are autosplit when the –a switch is used.
@INC   Array containing pathnames where require and do functions look for
         files that are to be included in this script.
%INC   Associative array containing entries for files that have been included by
         calling do or require. The key is the filename and the value is its
         location.
%ENV   Associative array containing the current environment.
%SIG   Associative array used to set signal handlers.
STDERR   Special filehandle for standard error (main'stderr).
STDIN   Special filehandle for standard input (main'stdin).
STDOUT   Special filehandle for standard output (main'stdout).

A.3 Perl Pragmas

A pragma is a special "pseudo" module that hints how the compiler should behave. The *use declaration* allows the importation of compiler directives called pragmas into your Perl program. Pragmas determine how a block of statements will be compiled. They are lexically scoped; the scope is limited to the current enclosing block and it can be "turned off" with the *no* directive. Pragma names are conventionally lowercase.

Pragma	What it Does
use integer	OK to use integer operations (float is the norm). All mathmatical operations will be handled in integer math and the decimal point on a number truncated.
use diagnostics	Forces verbose warning messages beyond the normal diagnostics issued by the Perl compiler and interpreter. Since it affects only the innermost block, the pragma is normally placed at the beginning of the program. Cannot use "no diagnostics".
use strict	'vars' With 'vars' as an argument, must use lexical (my) variables or fully qualified variable names with the package name and the scope operator or import ed variables. If not adhered to, will cause a compilation error.
use strict	'refs' Generates a runtime error if symbolic references are used, such as typeglobs.
use strict	'subs' Generates a compile-time error if a bare word is used and it is not a predeclared subroutine or filehandle.
use strict	Generates compile-time errors if symbolic references are used, if non-lexical variables are declared, if bare words that are not subroutines or filehandles are used.
use lib 'library path'	Loads in the library at compile time, not run time.
use sigtrap'signal names'	Initializes a set of signal handlers for the listed signals. Without an argument for a set of default signals. Prints a stack dump of the program and is sues an ABRT signal.
use subsqw(subroutine list)	Predeclares a list of subroutines allowing the subroutines listed to be called without parentheses and overrides built-in functions.
no integer	To turn off or unimport the pragma, the pragma name is preceded with "no"..

A.4 Perl Modules

TABLE A.1 General Programming

Module	Description
Benchmark	Checks and compares the speed of running code in CPU time.
Config	Accesses Perl configuration options from the *%Config* hash.
Env	Converts the *%ENV* hash to scalars containing environment variables, e.g., *$ENV{HOME}* becomes *$HOME*.
English	Provides scalars in English or awk names for special variables, e.g., $0 can be represented as *$PROGRAM_NAME*.
Getopt	Provides for processing of command line options and switches with arguments.
Shell	Used to run Shell commands within Perl scripts by treating the commands as subroutines, e.g., *$today=date();*
Symbol	Generates anonymous globs with gensym() and qualifies variable names with qualify().

TABLE A.2 Error Handling

Carp	Generates die-like error messages to report line numbers of the calling routine where the error occurred. The subroutines that can be called from this module are *carp()*, *croak()*, and *confess()*.
Sys::Syslog	Provides a Perl interface to the UNIX *syslog(3)* library calls.

TABLE A.3 File Handling

Cwd	Gets the pathname of the current working directory. Produces an error message if used with the -w switch.
DirHandle	Provides an object-oriented interface for directory handles.
File::Basename	Splits a filename into components or extracts a file name or a directory from full directory path.
File::CheckTree	Runs file tests on a collection of files in a directory tree.
File::Copy	Used to copy files or filehandles.
File::Find	Used to traverse a UNIX file tree.
File::Finddepth	Searches depth-first through a file system.
File::Path	Creates and removes a list of directories.
FileCache	Allows more files to be opened than permitted by the system.
FileHandle	Provides an object-oriented interface to filehandle access methods.
SelectServer	Saves and restores a selected filehandle.
flush.pl	Writes any data remaining in the filehandle's buffer or prints an expression and then flushes the buffer.
pwd.pl	Sets the PWD environment variable to the present working directory after using chdir.
stat.pl	Puts the values returned by the stat function into scalars—*$st_dev, $st_ino, $st_mode, $st_nlink, $st_uid, $st_rdev, $st_atime, $st_mtime, $st_ctime, $st_blksize, $st_blocks.*

TABLE A.4 Text Processing

Pod::Text	Converts POD documentation to ASCII formatted text.
Search::Dict	Searches for a string in a dictionary (alphabetically ordered) file and sets the file pointer to the next line.
Term::Complete	Provides a filename completion like interface for prompting a user for partial input that can be completed by pressing a tab key or a complete list of choices by pressing Ctrl-d.
Text::Abbrev	Creates an abbreviation table, a hash consisting of key/value pairs from a list. The key is the abbreviation and the value is the string that was abbbreviated, e.g., *ma/mail, mo/more.*
Text::ParseWords	Parses a line of text into a list of words like the shell does, stripping leading whitespace.

TABLE A.4   Text Processing (continued)

Module	Description
Text::Soundex	Maps words to four character length codes that roughly correspond to how the word is pronounced or sounds.
Text::Tabs	Expands tabs into spaces and unexpands tabs to spaces.
Text::Warp	Wraps text into a paragraph.

TABLE A.5   Database Interfaces

AnyDBM_File	A Unix based module providing framework for multiple DBMs.
DB_File	Provides access to Berkeley DB manager. See: *ftp//ftp.cs.berkeley.edu/ucb/4bsd*.
DBI	Returns a list of DBs and drivers on the system, and functions to interact with the database.
GDBM_File	Provides access to the GNU database manager. See: *ftp://prep.ai.mit.edu/pub/gnu*.
NDBM_File	A UNIX based module providing an interface to NDBM files.
ODBM_File	A UNIX based module providing an interface to ODBM files.
SDBM_File	A UNIX based module providing an interface to SDBM files

TABLE A.6   Math

Math::BigFloat	Supports arbitary-sized floating-point arithmetic.
Math::BigIn	Supports arbitrary-sized integer arithmetic.
Math::Complex	Supports complex numbers to demonstrate overloading
bigrat.pl	Enables infinite precision arithmetic on fractions.

TABLE A.7   Networking

chat2.pl	Allows Perl to manipulate interactive network services such as FTP.
comm.pl	Newer than *chat2.pl*. Allows Perl to manipulate interactive services.
IPC::Open2	Opens a process for reading and writing to allow data to be piped to and from an external program.
IPC::Open3	Opens a process for reading,writing, and error handling so that data can be piped to and from an external program.
Net::Ping	Checks whether a remote machine is up.
Socket	Creates sockets and imports socket methods for interprocess communication and loads socket.h header file.
Sys::Hostname	Gets the hostname for the system.

TABLE A.8   Time and Locale

Time::Local	Computes the UNIX time (the number of non-leap year seconds since January 1, 1970) from local and GMT time.
I18N::Collate	Compares 8-bit scalar data according to the current locale.

TABLE A.9   Terminals

Term::Cap	Provides low-level functions to manipulate terminal configurations as a terminal interface to the termcap database.

TABLE A.10   Object-Oriented Module Functions

Exporter	Used by other modules to make methods and variables available through importation.
Autoloader	For large modules, loads in only needed sections of a module. overload.
AutoSplit	Splits module into bite-sized chunks for autoloading.
Devel::SelfStubber	Generates stubs for SelfLoading modules to insure that if a method is called, it will get loaded.
DynaLoader	Used to automatically and dynamically load modules.
overload	Used to overload mathmatical operations.
Tie::Hash	Provides methods for tying a hash to a package.
Tie::Scalar	Provides methods for tying a scalar to a package.
Tie::SubstrHash	Provides a hash table-like interface to an array with constant key and record size.

TABLE A.11   Language Extension

ExtUtils::Install	For installing and deinstalling platform-dependent Perl extensions.
ExtUtils::Liblist	Determines what libraries to use and how to use them.
ExtUtils::MakeMaker	Creates a Makefile for a Perl extension in the extension's library.
ExtUtils::Manifest	Automates the maintenance of MANIFEST files, consisting of a list of filenames.
ExtUtils::Miniperl	Writes C code for *perlmain.c* that contains the bootstrap code for making archive libraries needed by modules available from within Perl.
ExtUtils::Mkbootstrap	Is called from the extension's Makefile to create a bootstrap file needed to do dynamic loading on some systems.
ExtUtils::Mksysmlists	Writes linker option files used by some linkers during the creation of shared libraries for dynamic extensions.
ExtUtils::MM_OS2	Overrides the implementation of methods causing UNIX behavior.
ExtUtils::MM_Unix	To be used with MakeMaker to provide methods for both UNIX and non-UNIX systems.
ExtUtils::MM_VMS	Overrides the implementation of methods causing UNIX behavior.
Fcntl	Translates the C fcntl header file.
POSIX	Provides the Perl interface to IEEE std 1003.1 identifiers.
Safe	Provides private compartments where unsafe Perl code can be evaluated.
Test::Harness	Used by MakeMaker to run test scripts for Perl extensions and produce diagnostics.

A.5   Command Line Switches

–a	Turns on autosplit mode when used with –n or –p, performing implicit split on whitespace. Fields are put in @F array.

date | perl –ane 'print "$F[0]\n";

–c	Checks Perl syntax without executing script.
–d	Turns on Perl debugger.
–D	Sets Perl debugging flags. (Check your Perl installation to make sure debugging was installed.) To watch how Perl executes a script, use –D14.
–e command	Used to execute Perl commands at the command line rather than in a script.
-F*pattern*	Specifies a pattern to use when splitting the input line. The pattern is just a regular expression enclosed in slashes, single or double quotes. For example, -F/:+/ splits the input line on one or more colons. Turned on if -a is also in effect.
-h	Prints a summary of Perl's command-line options.
–i*extension*	Enables in–place editing when using <> to loop through a file. If extension is not specified, modifies the file inplace. Otherwise renames the input file with the extension (used as a backup), and creates an output file with the original file name which is edited in place. This is the selected filehandle for all print statements.

–Idirectory	Used with –P to tell the C Preprocessor where to look for included files, by default */usr/include* and */usr/lib/perl* and the current directory.
–Idigits	Enables automatic line–ending processing. Chops the line terminator if –n or –p are used. Assigns $\ the value of digits (octal) to add the line terminator back on to print statements. Without digits specified, sets $\ to the current value of $/.(See special variables.)

-m[-]module

-M[-]module

-M[-]'module'

-[mM]module=arg[,arg]...

-m*module*	Executes the *use* module before executing the Perl script.
-Mmodule	Executes the *use* module before executing the Perl script. Quotes are used if extra text is added. The dash shown in square brackets means that the use directive will be replaced with *no*.
–n	Causes Perl to implicitly loop over a named file printing only lines specified.
–p	Causes Perl to implicitly loop over a named file printing all lines in addition to those specified
.–P	Causes script to be run through the C preprocessor before being compiled by Perl.
–s	Enables switch parsing after the script name but before filename arguments removing any switches found there from the @ARGV array. Sets the switch names to a scalar variable of the same name and assigns 1 to the scalar, e.g., –abc becomes $abc in the script.
–S	Makes Perl use the PATH environment variable to search for the script if the *#!/usr/bin/perl* line is not supported.
-T	Forces "taint" checks to be turned on for testing a script, which is ordinarily done only on setuid or setgid programs. Recommended for testing CGI scripts.
–u	Causes a core dump of script after compilation. (UNIX based).
–U	Allows Perl to do unsafe operations, e.g., unlinking directories if superuser.
–v	Prints Perl version information. (UNIX based.)

-V   Prints a summary of most important Perl configuration values and
                       the current value of the @INC array.

−w   Prints warnings about possible misuse of reserved words,
                       filehandles, and subroutines, etc.

−xdirectory   Any text preceding the #!/usr/bin/perl line will be ignored. If a
                       directory name is provided as an argument to the -x switch, Perl
                       will change to that directory before execution of the script starts.

A.6   Debugger

To invoke the Perl debugger, use the –d switch. It allows you to examine your program in
an interactive type environment after it has successfully compiled. After each line, the script
will stop and ask for a command. The line you will be looking at is the next line that will
be executed, not the previous one. The prompt contains the current package, function, file
and line number, and the current line. Following is a list of the debug commands.

    Once you start the debugger, all the debugging commands are listed by typing "h" at the
debug prompt.

    Here is a sample run. The debugger commands, obtained by typing 'h', are highlighted.

$ perl −d exer.1
Loading DB routines from $RCSfile: perldb.pl,v $$Revision: 4.0.1.2 $$Date: 91/11/
05 17:55:58 $
Emacs support available.
Enter h for help.
main'(exer.1:3):   print "Today is ", `date`;
  DB<1> h

T	Stack trace.
s	Single step.
n	Next, steps over subroutine calls.
r	Return from current subroutine.
c [line]	Continue; optionally inserts a one–time–only breakpoint at the specified line.
<CR>	Repeat last n or s.
l min+incr	List incr+1 lines starting at min.
l min−max	List lines.
l line	List line.
l	List next window.
−	List previous window.
w line	List window around line.
l subname	List subroutine.
f filename	Switch to filename.
/pattern/	Search forwards for pattern; final / is optional.

?pattern?	Search backwards for pattern.
L	List breakpoints and actions.
S	List subroutine names.
t	Toggle trace mode.
b [line] [condition]	Set breakpoint; line defaults to the current execution line; condition breaks if it evaluates to true, defaults to '1'.
b subname [condition]	Set breakpoint at first line of subroutine.
d [line]	Delete breakpoint.
D	Delete all breakpoints.
a [line] command	Set an action to be done before the line is executed. Sequence is: check for breakpoint, print line if necessary,do action, prompt user if breakpoint or step, evaluate line.
A	Delete all actions.
V [pkg [vars]]	List some (default all) variables in package (default current).
X [vars]	Same as "V currentpackage [vars]".
< command	Define command before prompt.
> command	Define command after prompt.
! number	Redo command (default previous command).
! –number	Redo number'th to last command.
H –number	Display last number commands (default all).
q or ^D	Quit.
p expr	Same as "print DB'OUT expr" in current package.
= [alias value]	Define a command alias, or list current aliases.
command	Execute as a Perl statement in current package.

```
  DB<1> l
3:      print "Today is ", `date`;
4:      print "The name of this \uperl script\e is $0.\n";
5:      print "Hello, The number we will examine is 125.5.\n";
6:      printf "The \unumber\e  is %d.\n", 125.5;
7:      printf "The \unumber\e  is %d.\n", 125.5;
8:      printf "The following number is taking up 20 spaces and is right justified.\n";
9:      printf "|%–20s|\n", 125;
10:     printf "\t\tThe number in hex is %x\n", 125.5;
11:     printf "\t\tThe number in octalis %o\n", 125.5;
12:     printf "The number in scientific notation is %e\n", 125.5;
  DB<1> q
```

A.7 Perl Translators

A.7.1 Awk to Perl Example

(The text file to be processed):

```
Betty Boop:245–836–8357:635 Cutesy Lane, Hollywood, CA 91464:6/23/23:14500
Igor Chevsky:385–375–8395:3567 Populus Place, Caldwell, NJ 23875:6/18/68:23400
Norma Corder:397–857–2735:74 Pine Street, Dearborn, MI 23874:3/28/45:245700
Jennifer Cowan:548–834–2348:583 Laurel Ave., Kingsville, TX 83745:10/1/35:58900
John DeLoach:345–124–5678:12 Dodo Lande, Pleasonton, CA 96547:5/12/55:600000
Fred Fardbarkle:674–843–1385:20 Park Lane, Deluth, MN 23850:4/12/23:78900
Lori Gortz:327–832–5728:3465 Mirlo Street, Peabody, MA 34756:10/2/65:35200
Paco Gutierrez:835–365–1284:454 Easy Street, Decatur, IL 75732:2/28/53:123500
Ephram Hardy:293–259–5395:235 Carlton Lane, Joliet, IL 73858:8/12/20:56700
James Ikeda:834–938–8376:23445 Aster Ave., Allentown, NJ 83745:12/1/38:45000
Fred Fardbarkle:674–843–1385:20 Park Lane, Deluth, MN 23850:4/12/23:78900
Lesley Kerstin:408–456–1234:4 Harvard Square, Boston, MA 02133:4/22/62:52600
Barbara Kerz:385–573–8326:832 Ponce Drive, Gary, IN 83756:12/1/46:268500
Wilhelm Kopf:846–836–2837:6937 Ware Road, Milton, PA 93756:9/21/46:43500
Sir Lancelot:837–835–8259:474 Camelot Boulevard, Bath, WY 28356:5/13/69:24500
```

(The awk Script):

```awk
# Awkscript to retrieve information

BEGIN{
    FS=":"
    OFS="\t";
    print "NAME     PHONE     ADDRESS        BIRTHDATE   SALARY"
    print "———————————————————————————————————————————————————"
}
    {printf "%–16s%–14s%–39s%–11s%10.2f\n", $1,$2, $3, $4, $5 }
    /CA/{count++}  # Count all people living in California
    {totalsal+=$5 }  # Total salaries

END{
    print "———————————————————————————————————————————————————"
    print "The number living in California is " count "."
    printf "The average salary is $%8.2f\n", totalsal/NR;
}
```

(The AWK Output):
$ nawk –f nawk.sc datebook

NAME	PHONE	ADDRESS	BIRTHDATE	SALARY
Betty Boop	245–836–8357	635 Cutesy Lane, Hollywood, CA 91464	6/23/23	14500.00
Igor Chevsky	385–375–8395	3567 Populus Place, Caldwell, NJ 23875	6/18/68	23400.00
Norma Corder	397–857–2735	74 Pine Street, Dearborn, MI 23874	3/28/45	245700.00
Jennifer Cowan	548–834–2348	583 Laurel Ave., Kingsville, TX 83745	10/1/35	58900.00
John DeLoach	345–124–5678	12 Dodo Lande, Pleasonton, CA 96547	5/12/55	600000.00
Fred Fardbarkle	674–843–1385	20 Park Lane, Deluth, MN 23850	4/12/23	78900.00
Lori Gortz	327–832–5728	3465 Mirlo Street, Peabody, MA 34756	10/2/65	35200.00
Paco Gutierrez	835–365–1284	454 Easy Street, Decatur, IL 75732	2/28/53	123500.00
Ephram Hardy	293–259–5395	235 Carlton Lane, Joliet, IL 73858	8/12/20	56700.00
James Ikeda	834–938–8376	23445 Aster Ave., Allentown, NJ 83745	12/1/38	45000.00
Fred Fardbarkle	674–843–1385	20 Park Lane, Deluth, MN 23850	4/12/23	78900.00
Lesley Kerstin	408–456–1234	4 Harvard Square, Boston, MA 02133	4/22/62	52600.00
Barbara Kerz	385–573–8326	832 Ponce Drive, Gary, IN 83756	12/1/46	268500.00
Wilhelm Kopf	846–836–2837	6937 Ware Road, Milton, PA 93756	9/21/46	43500.00
Sir Lancelot	837–835–8259	474 Camelot Boulevard, Bath, WY 28356	5/13/69	24500.00

The number living in California is 2.
The average salary is $116653.33

(The awk to Perl translation):

```
$ a2p nawk.sc > perl.sc
$ cat perl.sc
#!/usr/local/bin/perl
eval "exec /usr/local/bin/perl –S $0 $*"
    if $running_under_some_shell;
                # this emulates #! processing on NIH machines.
                # (remove #! line above if indigestible)

eval '$'.$1.'$2;' while $ARGV[0] =~ /^([A–Za–z_]+=)(.*)/ && shift;
                # process any FOO=bar switches

# Awkscript to retrieve information

$, = ' ';           # set output field separator
$\ = "\n";          # set output record separator

$FS = ':';
$, = "\t";
```

```
print 'NAME            PHONE        ADDRESS                        BIRTHDATE  SALARY';
print
     ,_____
                                                                                 ';

while (<>) {
($Fld1,$Fld2,$Fld3,$Fld4,$Fld5) = split(/[:\n]/, $_, 9999);
    printf "%–16s%–14s%–39s%–11s%10.2f\n", $Fld1, $Fld2, $Fld3, $Fld4, $Fld5;
    if (/CA/) {
       $count++;
    }
    # Count all people living in California
    $totalsal += $Fld5;
    # Total salaries
}

print

     ,_____
                                                                                 ';
print 'The number living in California is ' . $count . '.';
printf "The average salary is \$%8.2f\n", $totalsal / $.;
```

(Output of Perl translation Script):

```
$ perl.sc datebook
$ chmod +x perl.sc
$ perl.sc datebook
```

NAME	PHONE	ADDRESS	BIRTHDATE	SALARY
Betty Boop	245–836–8357	635 Cutesy Lane, Hollywood, CA 91464	6/23/23	14500.00
Igor Chevsky	385–375–8395	3567 Populus Place, Caldwell, NJ 23875	6/18/68	23400.00
Norma Corder	397–857–2735	74 Pine Street, Dearborn, MI 23874	3/28/45	245700.00
Jennifer Cowan	548–834–2348	583 Laurel Ave., Kingsville, TX 83745	10/1/35	58900.00
John DeLoach	345–124–5678	12 Dodo Lande, Pleasonton, CA 96547	5/12/55	600000.00
Fred Fardbarkle	674–843–1385	20 Park Lane, Deluth, MN 23850	4/12/23	78900.00
Lori Gortz	327–832–5728	3465 Mirlo Street, Peabody, MA 34756	10/2/65	35200.00
Paco Gutierrez	835–365–1284	454 Easy Street, Decatur, IL 75732	2/28/53	123500.00
Ephram Hardy	293–259–5395	235 Carlton Lane, Joliet, IL 73858	8/12/20	56700.00
James Ikeda	834–938–8376	23445 Aster Ave., Allentown, NJ 83745	12/1/38	45000.00
Fred Fardbarkle	674–843–1385	20 Park Lane, Deluth, MN 23850	4/12/23	78900.00
Lesley Kerstin	408–456–1234	4 Harvard Square, Boston, MA 02133	4/22/62	52600.00
Barbara Kerz	385–573–8326	832 Ponce Drive, Gary, IN 83756	12/1/46	268500.00
Wilhelm Kopf	846–836–2837	6937 Ware Road, Milton, PA 93756	9/21/46	43500.00
Sir Lancelot	837–835–8259	474 Camelot Boulevard, Bath, WY 28356	5/13/69	24500.00

The number living in California is 2.
The average salary is $116653.33

A.7.2   SED to Perl Example

(The Text File):

Betty Boop:245–836–8357:635 Cutesy Lane, Hollywood, CA 91464:6/23/23:14500
Igor Chevsky:385–375–8395:3567 Populus Place, Caldwell, NJ 23875:6/18/68:23400
Norma Corder:397–857–2735:74 Pine Street, Dearborn, MI 23874:3/28/45:245700
Jennifer Cowan:548–834–2348:583 Laurel Ave., Kingsville, TX 83745:10/1/35:58900
John DeLoach:345–124–5678:12 Dodo Lande, Pleasonton, CA 96547:5/12/55:600000
Fred Fardbarkle:674–843–1385:20 Park Lane, Deluth, MN 23850:4/12/23:78900
Lori Gortz:327–832–5728:3465 Mirlo Street, Peabody, MA 34756:10/2/65:35200
Paco Gutierrez:835–365–1284:454 Easy Street, Decatur, IL 75732:2/28/53:123500
Ephram Hardy:293–259–5395:235 Carlton Lane, Joliet, IL 73858:8/12/20:56700
James Ikeda:834–938–8376:23445 Aster Ave., Allentown, NJ 83745:12/1/38:45000
Fred Fardbarkle:674–843–1385:20 Park Lane, Deluth, MN 23850:4/12/23:78900
Lesley Kerstin:408–456–1234:4 Harvard Square, Boston, MA 02133:4/22/62:52600
Barbara Kerz:385–573–8326:832 Ponce Drive, Gary, IN 83756:12/1/46:268500
Wilhelm Kopf:846–836–2837:6937 Ware Road, Milton, PA 93756:9/21/46:43500
Sir Lancelot:837–835–8259:474 Camelot Boulevard, Bath, WY 28356:5/13/69:24500

(The Sed Script):
$ cat sed.sc
This sed script will edit a text file

```
1i\
        TITLE\

        _____


/^Fred Fardbarkle/c\
     ABSENT FOR THIS QUARTER


s/^Ephram/Ebeneezer/
# Make a substitution


$d
#delete last line
```

(The Sed Output):
$ sed –f sed.sc datebook
TITLE

_____

Betty Boop:245–836–8357:635 Cutesy Lane, Hollywood, CA 91464:6/23/23:14500
Igor Chevsky:385–375–8395:3567 Populus Place, Caldwell, NJ 23875:6/18/68:23400
Norma Corder:397–857–2735:74 Pine Street, Dearborn, MI 23874:3/28/45:245700
Jennifer Cowan:548–834–2348:583 Laurel Ave., Kingsville, TX 83745:10/1/35:58900
John DeLoach:345–124–5678:12 Dodo Lande, Pleasonton, CA 96547:5/12/55:600000
ABSENT FOR THIS QUARTER
Lori Gortz:327–832–5728:3465 Mirlo Street, Peabody, MA 34756:10/2/65:35200

Paco Gutierrez:835–365–1284:454 Easy Street, Decatur, IL 75732:2/28/53:123500
Ebeneezer Hardy:293–259–5395:235 Carlton Lane, Joliet, IL 73858:8/12/20:56700
James Ikeda:834–938–8376:23445 Aster Ave., Allentown, NJ 83745:12/1/38:45000
ABSENT FOR THIS QUARTER
Lesley Kerstin:408–456–1234:4 Harvard Square, Boston, MA 02133:4/22/62:52600
Barbara Kerz:385–573–8326:832 Ponce Drive, Gary, IN 83756:12/1/46:268500
Wilhelm Kopf:846–836–2837:6937 Ware Road, Milton, PA 93756:9/21/46:43500

(Running s2p Translator):
$ s2p sed.sc > perl.sc
(The Perl Translation):

```
    #!/usr/local/bin/perl
eval 'exec /usr/local/bin/perl –S $0 ${1+"$@"}'
    if $running_under_some_shell;

while ($ARGV[0] =~ /^–/) {
  $_ = shift;
 last if /^—/;
  if (/^–n/) {
   $nflag++;
   next;
  }
  die "I don't recognize this switch: $_\\n";
}
$printit++ unless $nflag;

$\ = "\n";                    # automatically add newline on print

LINE:
while (<>) {
  chop;
  # This sed script will edit a text file
  if ($iter = ($. == 1)) {
       if ($iter == 1) { print <<'End_Of_Text'; }
TITLE
_____
End_Of_Text
  }
  if ($iter = (/^Fred Fardbarkle/)) {
       if ($iter == 1) { print <<'End_Of_Text'; }
ABSENT FOR THIS QUARTER
End_Of_Text
     $printit = 0;
     next LINE;
  }
  s/^Ephram/Ebeneezer/;
  # Make a substitution
```

```
   if (eof()) {
      $printit = 0;
      next LINE;
   }
   #delete last line
}
continue {
   if ($printit)
   { print; }
   else
   { $printit++ unless $nflag; }
}
```

(The Perl Translation Output
$ perl.sc datebook
TITLE

Betty Boop:245–836–8357:635 Cutesy Lane, Hollywood, CA 91464:6/23/23:14500
Igor Chevsky:385–375–8395:3567 Populus Place, Caldwell, NJ 23875:6/18/68:23400
Norma Corder:397–857–2735:74 Plne Street, Dearborn, MI 23074:3/28/45:245700
Jennifer Cowan:548–834–2348:583 Laurel Ave., Kingsville, TX 83745:10/1/35:58900
John DeLoach:345–124–5678:12 Dodo Lande, Pleasonton, CA 96547:5/12/55:600000
ABSENT FOR THIS QUARTER
Lori Gortz:327–832–5728:3465 Mirlo Street, Peabody, MA 34756:10/2/65:35200
Paco Gutierrez:835–365–1284:454 Easy Street, Decatur, IL 75732:2/28/53:123500
Ebeneezer Hardy:293–259–5395:235 Carlton Lane, Joliet, IL 73858:8/12/20:56700
James Ikeda:834–938–8376:23445 Aster Ave., Allentown, NJ 83745:12/1/38:45000
ABSENT FOR THIS QUARTER
Lesley Kerstin:408–456–1234:4 Harvard Square, Boston, MA 02133:4/22/62:52600
Barbara Kerz:385–573–8326:832 Ponce Drive, Gary, IN 83756:12/1/46:268500
Wilhelm Kopf:846–836–2837:6937 Ware Road, Milton, PA 93756:9/21/46:43500

A.8   Plain Old Documentation—POD

This Is a Way to Embed Documentation into Your Program

A pod file is just an ASCII text file embedded with special commands that can be translated by one of Perl's special interpreters, *pod2html*, *pod2latex*, or *pod2man*. The purpose is to create formatted documents that can be represented in a number of ways. The UNIX man pages are an example of documentation that has been formatted with *nroff* instructions. It is now easy to embed one set of formatting instructions called *pod* in your scripts to provide documentation in any of the three formats, *html*, *latex*, or *nroff*.

It's quite easy to embed pod instructions in a text file. All commands start with an equal sign and end with =cut. Everything after the first =pod instruction to the =cut instruction will be ignored by the compiler, just as comments are ignored. The nice thing about using the commands is that they allow you to create bold, italic, plain text, to indent, to create headings, etc. The chart below contains a list of instructions.

Paragraph Command	**What It Does**
=head1 heading	Creates a level1 heading
=head2 heading	Creates a level2 heading
=item *	Starts a bullet list
=over N	Moves over N number of spaces, usually set to 4
=back	Returns indent back to default
=cut	Marks the end of pod
=pod	Starts documentation with pod instruction

Formatting Command	**What It Does**
I<text>	Italicizes text
B<text>	Emboldens text
S<text>	Contains text non-breaking spaces
C<code>	Contains literal code
L<name>	Creates a link (cross reference) to name
L<name>manpage	Creates a link to a manpage
L<name/ident>	Links to an item in manpage
L<name/"sec">	Links to section in another manpage
L<"sec">	Links to section in this manpage L</"sec">ditto
F<file>	Used for listing filenames
X<index>	An index entry
Z<>	A zero-width character

Example of a pod File:
(The following is a segment of the *perpod.pod* man page embedded with *pod* commands)
=head1 NAME
perlpod - plain old documentation
=head1 DESCRIPTION
A pod-to-whatever translator reads a pod file paragraph by paragraph and translates it to the appropriate output format. There are three kinds of paragraphs:
=over 4
=item *
A verbatim paragraph, distinguished by being indented (that is,it starts with space or tab). It should be reproduced exactly, with tabs assumed to be on 8-column boundaries. There are no special formatting escapes, so you can't italicize or anything like that. A \ means \, and nothing else.
=item *
A command. All command paragraphs start with "=", followed by an identifier, followed by arbitrary text that the command can use however it pleases. Currently recognized commands are
    =head1 heading

```
=head2 heading
=item text
=over N
=back
=cut
=pod
```

The "=pod" directive does nothing beyond telling the compiler to lay off through the next "=cut". It's useful for adding another paragraph to the doc if you're mixing up code and pod a lot.

Head1 and head2 produce first and second level headings, with the text on the same paragraph as "=headn" forming the heading description.

And don't forget, when using any command, that that command lasts up until the end of the B<paragraph>, not the line. Hence in the examples below, you can see the blank lines after each command to end it's paragraph.

Some examples of lists include:

```
=over 4
=item *
First item
=item *
Second item
=back
=over 4
=item Foo()
Description of Foo function
=item Bar()
Description of Bar function
=back
=item *
```

An ordinary block of text. It will be filled, and maybe even justified. Certain interior sequences are recognized both here and in commands:

```
I<text>    italicize text, used for emphasis or variables
B<text>    embolden text, used for switches and programs
S<text>    text contains non-breaking spaces
C<code>    literal code
L<name>    A link (cross reference) to name
      L<name>          manpage
      L<name/ident>    item in manpage
      L<name/"sec">    section in other manpage
      L<"sec">         section in this manpage
                       (the quotes are optional)
      L</"sec">        ditto
F<file>    Used for filenames
```

X<index> An index entry
Z<>   A zero-width character

                              ...

That's it. The intent is simplicity, not power. I wanted paragraphs to look like paragraphs (block format), so that they stand out visually, and so that I could run them
through fmt easily to reformat them (that's F7 in my version of B<vi>). I wanted the
translator (and not me) to worry about whether " or ' is a left quote or a right quote
within filled text, and I wanted it to leave the quotes alone in verbatim mode, so I
could slurp in a working program, shift it over 4 spaces, and have it print out, er,
verbatim. And presumably in a constant width font.

                              ...

    L<pod2man> and L<perlsyn/"PODs: Embedded Documentation">
=head1 AUTHOR
Larry Wall
You can embed pod documentation in your Perl scripts. Start your documentation
with a =head1 com-
mand at the beg, and end it with an =cut command. Perl will ignore the pod text.
See any of the supplied
library modules for examples. If you're going to put your pods at the end of the file,
and you're using an
__END__or __DATA__ cut mark, make sure to put a blank line there before the first
pod directive.
    __END__

Example of How to Use the pod Interpreter:
The pod interpreters come with the Perl distibution, by default stored in the Perl5/bin directory (UNIX). Make sure the directory is in your path or use a full pathname.

(At the command line)
  $ pod2html perlpod.pod
  Creating perlpod.html from perlpod.pod
  $ ls
  perlpod.pod perlpod.html

NAME

perlpod – plain old documentation

DESCRIPTION

A pod-to-whatever translator reads a pod file paragraph by paragraph, and translates it to the appropriate output format. There are three kinds of paragraphs:

- A verbatim paragraph, distinguished by being indented (that is, it starts with space or tab). It should be reproduced exactly, with tabs assumed to be on 8-column boundaries. There are no special formatting escapes, so you can't italicize or anything like that. A \ means \, and nothing else.

- A command. All command paragraphs start with "=", followed by an identifier, followed by arbitrary text that the command can use however it pleases. Currently recognized commands are

```
=head1 heading
=head2 heading
=item text
=over N
=back
=cut
=pod
```

The "=pod" directive does nothing beyond telling the compiler to lay off of through the next "=cut". It's useful for adding another paragraph to the doc if you're mixing up code and pod a lot.

Head1 and head2 produce first and second level headings, with the text on the same paragraph as "=headn" forming the heading description.

Item, over, and back require a little more explanation: Over starts a section specifically for the generation of a list using =item commands. At the end of your list, use =back to end it. You will probably want to give "4" as the number to =over, as some formatters will use this for indention. This should probably be a default. Note also that there are some basic rules to using =item: don't use them outside of an =over/=back block, use at least one inside an =over/=back block, you don't _have_ to include the =back if the list just runs off the document, and perhaps most importantly, keep the items consistent: either use "=item *" for all of them, to produce bullets, or use "=item 1.", "=item 2.", etc., to produce numbered lists, or use "=item foo", "=item bar", etc., i.e., things that looks nothing like bullets or numbers. If you start with bullets or numbers, stick with them, as many formatters you the first =item type to decide how to format the list.

And don't forget, when using any command, that that command lasts up until the end of the paragraph, not the line. Hence in the examples below, you can see the blank lines after each command to end it's paragraph.

Some examples of lists include:

```
=over 4
=item *
First item
=item *
Second item
=back
=over 4
=item Foo()
Description of Foo function
=item Bar()
Description of Bar function
=back
```

Example of the Perlpod.html File Seen from the Netscape Browser

Appendix B

B.1　taintperl script

Before I joined them, the group I work with had become accustomed to having their upcoming schedules charted, but this was a time-consuming task that the manager was doing manually. All of the information had to be transferred from the central database to a text file by hand. I took on the task to automate the task with a shell script.

The original program was a C shell script to access the database and create the text file containing the charted schedule. For security reasons I wanted the programs displaying the chart to have a different user identity than my own, but the program to access the database had to run as an authorized user. These requirements led to the use of a shell script that was set user-id.

The original C shell script was about one thousand lines and took around ten minutes to execute. Then I found perl and thought I would convert the program and see if this new scripting language was any good. Admittedly, I didn't translate all of the error checking from the C shell script to the perl program (most of it was redundant or unnecessary), but the size difference was remarkable—the first fully functioning perl program was around five hundred lines of code. The difference in size was not nearly as exciting as the reduction in execution time. The script that took ten minutes with the C shell took ten *seconds* as a perl program! And it isn't even pre-interpreted object code.

Since the original security requirements for user identity were still in place, running the perl script with set user-id was needed. But since standard perl will not work with set user-id, taintperl was required. A couple of features from the original script had to be altered so that taintperl would accept the script. For instance, the PATH environment variable had to be set within the perl script rather than externally. Taintperl seems to require that command paths or program names used with system calls all be defined within the program to prevent any trojan horses from being referenced.

With few exceptions (usually programmer error or database problems), this perl script to build the schedule chart has been working maintenance free for almost three years. This may not be the most efficient program for performing the desired task, but I was learning perl while I was writing this program, and for a reasonably complex goal as a first attempt at writing a perl program, I think it came out pretty good.

B.1.1   Program by Mark Houser

```
#! /usr/local/bin/taintperl
#
# This program will generate an input list of the form:
#
#  Loc  Course Start    #    Instructor    Lab      Room      Class#    First
#  MPTS SA-135 Apr 11    12   Lastname      MPLAB-4  MPLAB-5   12345     First
#
# as generated by an ISQL database query, sorted by Start date,
# Location, and Course number, then convert the information to
# a chart similar to the following:
#
#                                          Created:  9:07am, April 11, 1994
#
#          1994
#          April                    May                                   J
#          | 11    | 18    | 25    | 2     | 9     | 16    | 23    | 30    |
#=============================================================================
#First     | SA-135|       |       | Course| Course|       | Course|       |
#Lastname   | 5/4  |       |       | Rm/Lab| Rm/Lab|       | Rm/Lab|       |
#          |       |       |       |       |       |       |       |       |
#---------+-------+-------+-------+-------+-------+-------+-------+-------+
#
# NOTES:
#
# The original input list was based on a query used by management, in order
# reduce the amount of ISQL design necessary.  The ISQL queries for the
# list already existed.
#
# For simplicity, the program is itself run from a shell script which
# checks the validity of certain arguments (like month names), although
# many of these checks have been incorporated here as well.
#
# taintperl is used since the program was designed to run as a set-uid
# program, and regular perl will not run as a set-uid program.
#
#
#
# taintperl does not like any external or environment variables,
# therefore all needed environment variables are defined internally.
#
# Make sure command paths for necessary commands are defined
$ENV{'PATH'} = '/usr/ucb:/usr/bin';
#
# Set up the database access environment variables
#
$ENV{'SYBASE'} = '/usr/sybase';
$ENV{'DSQUERY'} = 'YALE';
#
# Check for arguments
#
if ( $#ARGV > 1 )
```

```
    {
    print STDERR "Usage: maker [ month [ date ] ]\n";
    exit (3);
    }
#
# Define array of last names
#
@instr_last_name = ( "Lastname", "LastnameA", "LastnameB", "LastnameC",
          "LastnameD", "LastnameE", "LastnameF" );
#
# Define associative array of first names, indexed by last names
#
%instr_first_name =
    (
    "Lastname", "First",
    "LastnameA", "FirstA",
    "LastnameB", "FirstB",
    "LastnameC", "FirstC",
    "LastnameD", "FirstD",
    "LastnameE", "FirstE",
    "LastnameF", "FirstF",
    "Others", ""
    );
#
# Define month names
#
@monthnames = ( "January", "February", "March", "April", "May", "June",
    "July", "August", "September", "October", "November", "December");
#
# Define month lengths
#
@monthlen = ( 31, 28, 31, 30, 31, 30, 31, 31, 30, 31, 30, 31 );
#
# Define associative array to determine month number (0-11) from
# abbreviated month name.
#
%monthabrs =
    (
    "Jan", 0,
    "Feb", 1,
    "Mar", 2,
    "Apr", 3,
    "May", 4,
    "Jun", 5,
    "Jul", 6,
    "Aug", 7,
    "Sep", 8,
    "Oct", 9,
    "Nov", 10,
    "Dec", 11
    );
#
# Define Location expansions based on location code using associative array
#
```

```
%locations =
    (
    'ANDV', 'Andover',
    'ATLN', 'Atlanta',
    'BALT', 'Balitmo',
    'CHIG', 'Chicago',
    'DALL', 'Dallas',
    'DENV', 'Denver',
    'DETR', 'Detroit',
    'HOUS', 'Houston',
    'LOSA', 'LosAngl',
    'MILW', 'Milwalk',
    'MPTS', 'Milpita',
    'NYNY', 'NewYork',
    'OFFA', 'OffSite',
    'OFFB', 'OffSite',
    'OFFM', 'OffSite',
    'OHIO', 'Columbu',
    'ORCO', 'OrangCo',
    'ORLA', 'Orlando',
    'SEAL', 'Seattle',
    'STLO', 'StLouis',
    'UNKN', 'Unknown'
    );
#
# Define correction values to add/subtract to date to determine the
# date of the next/previous Monday from a certain day of the week.
#
@adj2monday = ( 1, 0, -1, -2, -3, 3, 2);
#
# Retreive the current time from the system
#
@localtime = localtime(time);
#
# Break out the wanted pieces from the current system time
#
($lmin,$lhour,$lmday,$lmonth,$lyear,$lwday) = @localtime[1..6];

#
# Subroutine mondays is used to find the mondays for the particular
# month and year passed as arguments
#
sub mondays
    {
    # define the local variables
    local ($month, $year) = @_;
    local (@mondays);
    # increment month for use with the cal command
    $month ++;
    # use the cal command to get the dates for the given month and year
    open (CALIN, "/usr/bin/cal $month $year |");
    # count is used to count the number of input lines seen
    $count = 0;
    # while the cal command provides input ...
```

```
while ( <CALIN> )
    {
    $count ++;
            # chop off the return at the end of the line
    chop;
            # break up the line
    @y = split;
            # remove the first empty entry, if one exists, created by
            # leading spaces
    shift (@y) if ("$y[0]" == "");
    if (($#y > 4) && ($count  == 3))
                # the first week of the month (the 3rd line of output from
                # the cal command) may not have a Monday, but if it does
                # there are at least 4 other dates, too, and we'll have to
                # count backwards to find the Monday to add to the list.
        {
        push (@mondays,$y[$#y-5]);
        }
    elsif ($#y > 0 && $count > 3)
                # every other week of the month, the monday is always the
                # second date of the week.
        {
        push (@mondays,$y[1]);
        }
    }
return (@mondays);
}


#
# A quick subroutine to determine if the passed year is a leap year
#
sub leapyear
    {
    local ($year) = @_;
    ((!($year % 4)) && (!(!(($year % 100) || (!($year % 400))))));
    }


#
# subroutine leapmonth returns true in the month is February and
# it is also a leap year
#
sub leapmonth
    {
    local ($month, $year) = @_;
    (($month == 1) && (&leapyear($year)));
    }

if ( $#ARGV >= 0 )
    {
    # get the month from the command line (if given)
    $month = shift (@ARGV);
    # starting year is the current year
    $syear = $lyear;
    # convert month and check
```

```perl
if ( $month =~ /^[0-9]+$/ && ($month < 1 || $month > 12))
        # handle invalid month numbers first
    {
    print STDERR "I only understand month numbers between 1 and 12.\n";
    exit 3;
    }
if ( $month =~ /^[1-9]$|^1[0-2]$/ )
        # valid month numbers may be 1 to 12, but will be used as 0 to 11
    {
    $smonth = $month - 1;
    }
else
        # determine the month from the month name
    {
        # only the first three letters of the month name are significant
    $tmp_month = substr($month,0,3);
        # and those will be made all lowercase ...
    $tmp_month =~ tr/A-Za-z/a-za-z/;
        # ... except for the first letter
    substr ($tmp_month,0,1) =~ tr/a-z/A-Z/;
        # look up the name number in the associative array
    $smonth = $monthabrs{$tmp_month};
    if ( "$smonth" eq "" )
            # the month name given can't be found in the associative array
        {
        print STDERR "I don't understand the month of $month.\n";
        exit 3;
        }
    }
# if the starting month is more than 5 months in the past, let's make
# it next year instead ...
$syear ++ if (($lmonth - $smonth) > 5);
# ... or it could be last year
$syear -- if (($lmonth - $smonth) < -5);
# get them mondays for the staring month and year
@mondays = &mondays ($smonth, "19$syear");
# if there are still more arguments, it has to be a date
if ( $#ARGV >= 0 )
    {
    $date = shift (@ARGV);
    if ($date =~ /^[0-9]+$/)
        {
        if ($date > $monthlen[$smonth] +
                &leapmonth($smonth,$syear))
                # date too high for specified month, such as April 31
                # or February 30 (Feb. 29 is valid some years).
            {
            print STDERR "Error: $monthnames[$smonth] only has ";
            print STDERR $monthlen[$smonth] +
                &leapmonth($smonth,$syear);
            print STDERR " days";
            print STDERR " in 19$syear" if ($smonth == 1 );
            print STDERR ".\n";
            exit 4;
```

```
            }
        $is_a_monday = 0;
                # compare the date provided with the mondays of the
                # starting month
        foreach $tmp_ (@mondays)
            {
            $is_a_monday = 1 if ($date == $tmp_);
            }
        if ( ! $is_a_monday )
                        # only deal with mondays
            {
            print STDERR "Date provided is not a Monday.\n";
            exit 4;
            }
        $sdate = $date;
        }
    else
            # date provided was not a number
        {
        print STDERR "I don't understand the date of $date.\n";
        exit 4;
        }
    }
else
        # if date is not provided on command line, take first monday of
        # the provided month
    {
    $sdate = $mondays[0];
    }
}
else
    # otherwise starting point is "nearest" Monday to today
    {
    $syear = $lyear;
    $smonth = $lmonth;
    # use Monday of this week until Friday, then use next Monday
    # (see adj2monday array definition)
    $sdate = $lmday + $adj2monday[$lwday];
    if ( $sdate <= 0 )
            # adjustment could move us back to last month ...
        {
        $smonth --;
        if ( $smonth < 0 )
                # ... and that could move us back to last year ...
            {
            $syear --;
            $smonth = 11;
            }
            # ... correct the start date accordingly
        $sdate += ($monthlen[$smonth] + &leapmonth($smonth, "19$syear"));
        }
    elsif ( $sdate > ($monthlen[$smonth] + &leapmonth($smonth, "19$syear")) )
            # adjustment could move us into next month ...
        {
```

```
                # ... correct the date ...
        $sdate -= ($monthlen[$smonth] + &leapmonth($smonth, "19$syear"));
        $smonth ++;
        if ( $smonth > 11 )
                    # ... adjustment could move us into next year
            {
            $syear ++;
            $smonth = 0;
            }
        }
    }

# perl indexes starting at 0, isql (and most everything else outside perl)
# tends to index starting with 1, so we'll adjust when needed to have the
# right values for the outside world
$tmp_month = $smonth+1;

# isql uses leading zeros, so they're added when needed
$imonth = ($tmp_month < 10) ? 0.${tmp_month} : $tmp_month;
$idate = ($sdate < 10) ? 0.${sdate} : $sdate;
$iyear = $syear;

$isql_date = "${imonth}/${idate}/${iyear}";

# run the isql query, saving to output in a temporary file
# Note: the isql query is actually being performed by another user-id, and
#        this is the reason the program is run as a set-uid program and that
#        taintperl is needed
open (QUERY, "| /usr/sybase/bin/isql -Uisqluser -P password > /tmp/query$$");

# all standard output will go to the isql query we just opened
select (QUERY);
print "print ''\n";
print "select\n";
print "  Loc=convert(char(4),clstloc),\n";
print "  Course=convert(char(8),counumb),\n";
print "  Date=convert(char(7),(convert(char(3),datename(month,clstart))+' '+\n";
print "  convert(char(2),datename(day,clstart)))),\n";
print "  Enr=convert(char(3),clsenro),\n";
print "  Instr=convert(char(12),inslnam),\n";
print "  labcode,\n";
print "  crmcode,\n";
print "  Class#=convert(char(6),clsnumb),\n";
print "  FName=convert(char(8),insfnam)\n";
print "\n";
print "from class, course, instructor, laboratory, classroom\n";
print "\n";
print "where clscour = counumb and\n";
print "  crmcode = clsclrm and\n";
print "  clsinst = insnumb and\n";
print "  clslabr = labcode and\n";
print "  clstart between '$isql_date' and dateadd(week, 8, '$isql_date') and\n";
print "  clsstat != 'CANC' and\n";
print "  (counumb like 'SG%' or\n";
```

```
print "    counumb like 'SI%' or\n";
print "    counumb like 'SP%' or\n";
print "    counumb like 'SL%' or\n";
print "    counumb like 'SM%' or\n";
print "    counumb like 'PM%' or\n";
print "    counumb like 'SA%' or\n";
print "    counumb like 'IN%' or\n";
print "    counumb like 'SC%' or\n";
print "    counumb like 'FR%' or\n";
print "    counumb like 'OA%' or\n";
print "    counumb like 'EU%')\n";
print " \n";
print "order by clstart, clstloc, clscour\n";
print "go\n";
select (STDOUT);

# isql query is closed and standard output is back where it belongs
close(QUERY);

# open the query file generated by the isql
# Note: given an input file of appropriate form (see above), all of the
#       isql query could be replaced by just an open statement like this
open (QUERY, "/tmp/query$$");
while (<QUERY>)
    # foreach entry in the list generated by the isql query ...
    {
    # ... get rid of the carriage return
    chop;
    # break up the line into an array
    @class_entry = split;
    if ( ( "$instr_first_name{$class_entry[6]}" ne "" ) &&
         ( "$instr_first_name{$class_entry[6]}" eq "$class_entry[10]" ) )
            # check that the instructor name is known in the associative array
            # and that the first names (in the associative array and the isql
            # query) match [check of the first names was added in a late
            # revision when more than one instructor had the same last name];
            # if so ...
        {
            # ... put the relevant information for that instructor into
            # colon (:) separated lists
        $name = $class_entry[6];
        $class_instr{$name} .= ":$name";
        $class_site{$name} .= ":$class_entry[1]";
        $class_title{$name} .= ":$class_entry[2]";
        $class_month{$name} .= ":$class_entry[3]";
        $class_date{$name} .= ":$class_entry[4]";
        $class_lect{$name} .= ":$class_entry[8]";
        $class_lab{$name} .= ":$class_entry[7]";
        $class_number{$name} .= ":$class_entry[9]";
        }
    elsif ("$class_entry[1]" eq "MPTS" || "$class_entry[1]" eq "OFFM")
            # otherwise this may be a contract instructor, in which case ...
        {
        if ( "$class_entry[2]" =~ /^EU|^SA/ &&
```

```
        ! ("$class_entry[2]" =~ /^EU-10[123]/ ))
                # ... we're only interested in certain classes, but we still
                # need to save the relavant information ...
        {
                # ... and we'll put that information in the lists for Others
        $class_instr{'Others'} .= ":$class_entry[6]";
        $class_site{'Others'} .= ":$class_entry[1]";
        $class_title{'Others'} .= ":$class_entry[2]";
        $class_month{'Others'} .= ":$class_entry[3]";
        $class_date{'Others'} .= ":$class_entry[4]";
        $class_lect{'Others'} .= ":$class_entry[8]";
        $class_lab{'Others'} .= ":$class_entry[7]";
        $class_number{'Others'} .= ":$class_entry[9]";
        }
    }
}

# query file created with isql is no longer needed
system ("rm -f /tmp/query$$");

foreach $name (@instr_last_name, 'Others')
    # for every known instructor and any other instructor
    {
    # delete the initial colon (:) from the lists
    # print statemennts are for debugging (note that they're commented)
    #print "${name}:\n";
    substr ($class_instr{$name},0,1) = "";
    #print "\t$class_instr{$name}\n";
    substr ($class_site{$name},0,1) = "";
    #print "\t$class_site{$name}\n";
    substr ($class_title{$name},0,1) = "";
    #print "\t$class_title{$name}\n";
    substr ($class_month{$name},0,1) = "";
    #print "\t$class_month{$name}\n";
    substr ($class_date{$name},0,1) = "";
    #print "\t$class_date{$name}\n";
    substr ($class_lect{$name},0,1) = "";
    #print "\t$class_lect{$name}\n";
    substr ($class_lab{$name},0,1) = "";
    #print "\t$class_lab{$name}\n";
    substr ($class_number{$name},0,1) = "";
    #print "\t$class_number{$name}\n";
    }

# open another file for output of the chart ...
open (CHART, "> /tmp/chart_$$" );
# ... and make standard output go to that file
select (CHART);
# output file creation time ...
print " " x 40, "Created: ";
# ... and the time shoule be on a 12 hour clock with am and pm
if ($lhour == 0)
    # midnight is 12am
    {
```

```
    $lhour = 12;
    $ampm = "am";
    }
elsif ($lhour < 12)
    {
    $ampm = "am";
    }
elsif ($lhour == 12)
    # noon is 12pm
    {
    $ampm = "pm";
    }
else
    {
    $lhour -= 12;
    $ampm = "pm";
    }
# display the adjusted time ...
printf ("%2d:%02d%s", $lhour, $lmin, $ampm);
# ... and date
print ", $monthnames[$lmonth] $lmday, 19$lyear\n";
# display the headers, including the year(s) covered
$year_line = " " x 11 . "19$syear      ";;
# and prepare for the months headings line
$month_line = " " x 76;
substr ($month_line, 11, 0) = "$monthnames[$smonth]";
# and prepare the Monday of the week heading line
$date_line = " " x 10 . "|";
$count = 0;
$tmp_year = $syear;
$tmp_month = $smonth;
$tmp_date = $sdate;
#
# the chart will cover 8 weeks, so we'll alter the heading lines to contain
# the appropriate info ...
#
while ( $count < 8 )
    {
    $count ++;
    push (@weeks, "${tmp_year}:${tmp_month}:${tmp_date}");
    $date_line .= sprintf (" %2d    |", $tmp_date);
    $tmp_date += 7;
    $year_line .= "          ";
    if ( $tmp_date > $monthlen[$tmp_month] + &leapmonth($tmp_month,
"19$tmp_year") )
        {
        $tmp_date -= ($monthlen[$tmp_month] +
&leapmonth($tmp_month,"19$tmp_year"));
        $tmp_month ++;
        if ( $tmp_month > 11 )
            {
            $tmp_year ++;
            $tmp_month = 0;
            substr ($year_line, -8, 4) = "19$tmp_year";
```

```perl
            }
        $real_pos = 11 + ($count * 8);
        if ( substr($month_line, $real_pos, 1) ne " " )
            {
            $real_pos ++;
            while ( (substr($month_line, $real_pos, 1) ne " ") &&
                ($real_pos < 80) )
                {
                $real_pos ++;
                }
            }
        substr ($month_line, $real_pos, 0) = $monthnames[$tmp_month];
        }
    }
print "\n";
# cut off any extra stuff that may have been added to the line
$month_line = substr($month_line, 0, 76);
substr($month_line, -1, 1) =
    (substr($month_line, -1, 1) eq " ") ? "" : substr($month_line, -1, 1);
# cut off the last 8 chars of the year header
substr($year_line, -8, 8) = "";
# finally display the heading lines
print "$year_line\n";
print "$month_line\n";
print "$date_line\n";
# end of the headers, display a separator
print "=" x 75, "\n";;


foreach $instructor ( @instr_last_name, "Others" )
    {
    #
    # prepare for the posibility that the instructor may be assigned
    # more than once in the same week -- especially true of Others
    #
    $pass = 0;
    # debugging print statement ...
    #print "Before loop:  $class_instr{$instructor} $pass\n";
    $more_instr = "";
    while ( ("$more_instr" ne "") || ($pass < 1) )
            {
    # ... commented prints to STDERR are also used for debugging
    # [early versions of the program did not use STDERR for debugging
    #  print statements; debugging print statements in later revisions
    #  added the STDERR due to standard output being directed to a file.]
    #print STDERR "TEST:  Inside loop:  $class_instr{$instructor} $pass\n";
            $pass ++;
            #
            # reset the display variables
            #
        $instr_display = "";
        $title_display = "";
        $site_display = "";
        $number_display = "";
        $more_instr = "";
```

```
$more_sites = "";
$more_title = "";
$more_month = "";
$more_date = "";
$more_lect = "";
$more_lab = "";
$more_number = "";
        #
        # make arrays of information for this instructor
        #
@instr_list = split (/:/, $class_instr{$instructor});
@site_list = split (/:/, $class_site{$instructor});
@title_list = split (/:/, $class_title{$instructor});
@month_list = split (/:/, $class_month{$instructor});
@date_list = split (/:/, $class_date{$instructor});
@lect_list = split (/:/, $class_lect{$instructor});
@lab_list = split (/:/, $class_lab{$instructor});
@number_list = split (/:/, $class_number{$instructor});
foreach $week ( @weeks )
    {
        # get the "current" time for display
    ($curr_year, $curr_month, $curr_date) = split (/:/,$week);
    #print "Checking week for $monthnames[$curr_month] ",
    #    "$curr_date, 19$curr_year\n";
    $test_range = -1;
        # determine if the instructor is assigned during "current"
        # week
    if ($curr_month == $monthabrs{$month_list[0]})
        {
        $test_range = $date_list[0] - $curr_date;
        }
    elsif (($curr_month - $monthabrs{$month_list[0]}) == -1 ||
        ($curr_month - $monthabrs{$month_list[0]}) == 11 )
        {
        $test_range = (($monthlen[$curr_month] +
                &leapmonth($curr_month,"19$curryear")) -
                $curr_date) + $date_list[0];
        }
        #
        # if the class start date is within 4 days of the beginning
        # of the week, the instructor is assigned to that class
        #
    if ( $test_range >= 0 && $test_range < 5 )
        {
        #print STDERR "TEST:  $instructor teaches this week!\n";
                #
                # get the information from the array, and remove
                # from the array for the next pass through the loop
                # use sprintf for formatting
                #
        $instr = shift @instr_list;
        $title_display .= sprintf ("%7.7s|", shift @title_list);
        $site = shift @site_list;
        $number_display .= sprintf ("%7.7s|", shift @number_list);
```

```
                   #
                   # lecture and lab locations retreived with the isql
                   # query have something in front of the room number,
                   # the following will get only the desired numbers
                   #
$lect = shift @lect_list;
$lect =~ s/\D+0*(\d+)$/\1/;
$lab = shift @lab_list;
$lab =~ s/\D+0*(\d+)$/\1/;
                   # get the class/lab combination ready
$clslab = "$lect/$lab";
                   # center the information
$fill = (7 - length ($clslab)) / 2;
$clslab .= " " x $fill;
if ( "$site" eq "MPTS" )
                   # if the location is in Milpitas (CA) than we'll
                   # display the classroom/lab location
     {
     $site_display .= sprintf ("%7.7s|", $clslab);
     }
else
                         # otherwise the city location...
     {
                         # ... if known ...
     $site = "UNKN"
         if ("$locations{$site}" eq "");
                         # ... is displayed
     $site_display .= sprintf ("%7.7s|",
         $locations{$site});
     }
                   # make an class with no instructor assigned
                   # look better
$instr = "N/A" if (("$instr" eq "Not_assigned") ||
         ("$instr" eq "Assigned_Not"));
                   # fill it for centering
$fill = (7 - length ($instr)) / 2;
                   # add to display
$instr_display .= ( $instr ne $instructor ) ?
     sprintf ("%7.7s|", $instr . " " x $fill) :
     " " x 7 . "|" ;
shift @month_list;
shift @date_list;
                   #
                   # double check to see if the next class is
                   # assigned to the same week -- test code from
                   # above repeats ...
                   #
                   #print STDERR "TEST:  Entering test loop...\n";
#print STDERR "TEST:  month_list = @month_list\n";
#print STDERR "TEST:  date_list = @date_list\n";
#print STDERR "TEST:  dates left = $#date_list\n";
while ( (($test_range >= 0) && ($test_range < 5)) &&
         ( $#date_list >= 0) )
     {
```

```perl
            $test_range = -1;
#print STDERR "TEST:  Range reset to $test_range\n";
#print STDERR "TEST:  Current Month = $curr_month\n";
#print STDERR "TEST:  Checking Month
# $monthabrs{$month_list[0]}\n";
        if ($curr_month == $monthabrs{$month_list[0]})
            {
            $test_range = $date_list[0] - $curr_date;
            }
        elsif (($curr_month - $monthabrs{$month_list[0]}) == -1 ||
            ($curr_month - $monthabrs{$month_list[0]}) == 11 )
            {
            $test_range = (($monthlen[$curr_month] +
                    &leapmonth($curr_month,"19$curryear")) -
                    $curr_date) + $date_list[0];
            }
                #print STDERR "TEST:  New Range = $test_range\n";
                #
                # this instructor is assigned to more than one class
                # "this" week ...
        if ( $test_range >= 0 && $test_range < 5 )
            {
                #print STDERR "TEST·  Range - $test_range\n";
            if ( "$instructor" eq "Others" )
                # ... which is OK if the instructor is Other ...
                {
                $more_instr .= ":$instr_list[0]";
                $more_sites .= ":$site_list[0]";
                $more_title .= ":$title_list[0]";
                $more_month .= ":$month_list[0]";
                $more_date .= ":$date_list[0]";
                $more_lect .= ":$lect_list[0]";
                $more_lab .= ":$lab_list[0]";
                $more_number .= ":$number_list[0]";
                }
                else
                    # ... but otherwise it means something is wrong,
                    # so flag it in the display
                    {
                    substr ( $title_display,
                        length($title_display)-8,
                        length($title_display)) = "Multi- |";
                    substr ( $site_display,
                        length($site_display)-8,
                        length($site_display)) = " Assign|";
                    substr ( $instr_display,
                        length($instr_display)-8,
                        length($instr_display)) = "^^^^^^^|";
                    }
                #
                # shift the list for the next pass through the loop
                #
            shift @instr_list;
            shift @site_list;
```

```
                    shift @title_list;
                    shift @month_list;
                    shift @date_list;
                    shift @lect_list;
                    shift @lab_list;
                    shift @number_list;
                    }
                                    #print STDERR "TEST:  End of test loop...\n";
                                    #print STDERR "TEST:  month_list = @month_list\n";
                                    #print STDERR "TEST:  date_list = @date_list\n";
                    #print STDERR "TEST:  dates left = $#date_list\n";
                    }
            }
        else
                    # otherwise the instructor is not assigned to that week
                    # so we'll just fill the display
            {
            $instr_display .= (" " x 7 . "|");
            $title_display .= (" " x 7 . "|");
            $site_display .= (" " x 7 . "|");
            $number_display .= (" " x 7 . "|");
            }
        }
        #
        # finally display the lines for this instructor
        #
printf "%-10s|", substr($instr_first_name{$instructor},0,10);
print "$title_display\n";
printf "%-10s|", substr($instructor,0,10);
print "$site_display\n";
printf "%10s|", "";
print "$instr_display\n";

        # Extra stuff for display of class number, which is not needed
        # for common use

        # For Management Use:
#print " " x 10, "|", "$number_display\n";

print "-" x 10, "+", "-------+" x 8, "\n";

if ( "$more_instr" ne "" )
        # another pass needs to be done for this instructor (Others)
    {
        #
        # strip off the initial colon (:) from each list
        #
    substr ($more_instr,0,1) = "";
    substr ($more_sites,0,1) = "";
    substr ($more_title,0,1) = "";
    substr ($more_month,0,1) = "";
    substr ($more_date,0,1) = "";
    substr ($more_lect,0,1) = "";
    substr ($more_lab,0,1) = "";
```

```
            substr ($more_number,0,1) = "";
                    #
                    # reset the lists for the instructor for the next pass
                    #
            $class_instr{$instructor} = $more_instr;
            $class_sites{$instructor} = $more_sites;
            $class_title{$instructor} = $more_title;
            $class_month{$instructor} = $more_month;
            $class_date{$instructor} = $more_date;
            $class_lect{$instructor} = $more_lect;
            $class_lab{$instructor} = $more_lab;
            $class_number{$instructor} = $more_number;
            }
        }
    }

# close the output file
close (CHART);

# reset the location of standard output to normal
select (STDOUT);

# open the previously created output file
open (CHART, "/tmp/chart_$$" );

# display the file
# this was done so that we don't see the program think -- it just shows
# the final chart all at once
print <CHART>;

# output file is no longer needed -- clean up
system ("rm -f /tmp/chart_$$");
```

B.2   maxpstat

B.2.1   Program by John J. Nouveaux

```
#!/usr/bin/perl
#
# maxpstat
#
# Usage:
#   maxpstat   [interval [ count ]]
#
# Where:
#   interval = Interval, in seconds, between "pstat" checks (default = 60).
#   count = Number of reports before quitting (default = infinite ).
#
#
# Description:
#   This script runs the "pstat" system command every interval seconds,
#   comparing the output from previous "pstat" runs, and
#   saves the maximum values for the "process", "files", and "inodes"
```

```
#    output fields.
#
#    When a new maximum value for any field is discovered it is immediately
#    reported, and when the script has finished a summary report is printed.
#    If the script is interrupted via a control-c, or a TERM signal ( see
#    signal (3V)), the summary report is immediately printed.  Other signals
#    are ignored by the script.
#
#    See the pstat(8) man page for details of that command.
#
# Written by:
#    John J. Nouveaux
#    Copyright, 1992
#
# History:
#        May 13th, 1992          1.0 - initial release.
#
# Version:
#    1.0


# Define external references.

require 'ctime.pl';    # Displays time in readable format

# Set up signal processing, currently catching only interrupt and terminate
# signals.

$SIG{'HUP'}    = 'IGNORE';     #1
$SIG{'INT'}    = 'sighandler';#2
$SIG{'QUIT'}   = 'IGNORE';     #3
$SIG{'ILL'}    = 'IGNORE';     #4
$SIG{'TRAP'}   = 'IGNORE';     #5
$SIG{'ABRT'}   = 'IGNORE';     #6
$SIG{'EMT'}    = 'IGNORE';     #7
$SIG{'FPE'}    = 'IGNORE';     #8
$SIG{'KILL'}   = 'IGNORE';     #9
$SIG{'BUS'}    = 'IGNORE';     #10
$SIG{'SEGV'}   = 'IGNORE';     #11
$SIG{'SYS'}    = 'IGNORE';     #12
$SIG{'PIPE'}   = 'IGNORE';     #13
$SIG{'ALRM'}   = 'IGNORE';     #14
$SIG{'TERM'}   = 'sighandler';#15
$SIG{'URG'}    = 'IGNORE';     #16
$SIG{'STOP'}   = 'IGNORE';     #17
$SIG{'TSTP'}   = 'IGNORE';     #18
$SIG{'CONT'}   = 'IGNORE';     #19
$SIG{'CHLD'}   = 'IGNORE';     #20
$SIG{'TTIN'}   = 'IGNORE';     #21
$SIG{'TTOU'}   = 'IGNORE';     #22
$SIG{'IO'}     = 'IGNORE';     #23
$SIG{'XCPU'}   = 'IGNORE';     #24
$SIG{'XFSZ'}   = 'IGNORE';     #25
$SIG{'VTALRM'} = 'IGNORE';     #26
$SIG{'PROF'}   = 'IGNORE';     #27
```

```
$SIG{'WINCH'}  = 'IGNORE';      #28
$SIG{'LOST'}   = 'IGNORE';      #29
$SIG{'USR1'}   = 'IGNORE';      #30
$SIG{'USR2'}   = 'IGNORE';      #31

# Define local variables.

$counterr = "count";           # for error processing
$intervalerr = "interval";# for error processing
$pstat = "/usr/etc/pstat -T";# path to "pstat" command
@DoW = ( 'Sun', 'Mon', 'Tue', 'Wed', 'Thu', 'Fri', 'Sat' );
@MoY = ( 'Jan', 'Feb', 'Mar', 'Apr', 'May', 'Jun',
                'Jul', 'Aug', 'Sep', 'Oct', 'Nov', 'Dec' );

# Set defaults.

$interval = 60;
$count = 9999999999;           # infinity (actually 316+ years)

# Process input parameters (if any).

if (@ARGV) {

# Set the interval parameter.

            $interval = shift (@ARGV);

# If the interval is non-numeric, print a usage error and exit.

    if ($interval =~ /\D+/) {
            &usage ($intervalerr, $interval);
    }

# Set the count parameter.

    if (@ARGV){
            $count = shift (@ARGV);

# If the count is non-numeric, print a usage error and exit.

    if ($count =~ /\D+/) {
        &usage ($counter, $count);
    }
  }
 }
}

# Initialize starting date/time (used in final report).

 $starttime = time;
 ($startsec, $startmin, $starthour, $startmday, $startmon, $startyear, $startwday,
  $startyday, $startisdst) = localtime ($starttime);

# Add leading zeros as appropriate.
```

```perl
if ($starthour < 10) {
  $starthour = "0" . "$starthour";
}

if ($startmin < 10) {
  $startmin = "0" . "$startmin";
}

if ($startsec < 10) {
  $startsec = "0" . "$startsec";
}

# Get "pstat" system table sizes (this is configured into the kernel).

open (PSTAT, "$pstat |");
$currentfiles       = <PSTAT>;                  # Raw input lines
$currentinodes      =<PSTAT>;
$currentprocesses   = <PSTAT>;

if ($currentfiles =~ m".*/(\d*)") {
   $filetabsize = $1;                           # Size of files table
}


if ($currentinodes =~ m".*/(\d*)") {
   $inodetabsize = $1;                          # Size of inode cache
}

if ($currentprocesses =~ m".*/(\d*)") {
   $proctabsize = $1;                           # Size of process table
}

close (PSTAT);

# Check parameters as specified in command arguments.

for ($loopindex = $count; $loopindex != 0; $loopindex--){

# Get "pstat" input via a named-pipe filehandle.

   open (PSTAT, "$pstat |");
   $currentfiles       = <PSTAT>;# Raw input lines
   $currentinodes      = <PSTAT>;
   $currentprocesses   = <PSTAT>;
   close(PSTAT);

# Extract current count for each category.

  if ($currentfiles =~ m"\s*(\d*)/") {
     $currentfiles = $1;        # current number of opened files
  }

  if ($currentinodes =~ m"\s*(\d*)/") {
```

```perl
    $currentinodes = $1;        # current number of cached inodes
  }

  if ($currentprocesses =~ m"\s*(\d*)/") {
    $currentprocesses = $1;  # current number of active processes
  }

# If the current counter for any of the categories exceeds
# the stored maximum replace the stored maximum with the current
# value and print a message.

  if ($currentfiles > $maxfiles) {
    $maxfiles = $currentfiles;
    $filepercent = int (((100*$maxfiles)/$filetabsize) + .5);

    print ("$maxfiles files out of $filetabsize or $filepercent percent.\n");
  }

  if ($currentinodes > $maxinodes) {
    $maxinodes = $currentinodes;
    $inodepercent = int (((100*$maxinodes)/$inodetabsize) + .5);
    print ("$maxinodes inodes out of $inodetabsize or $inodepercent percent.\n");
  }

  if ($currentprocesses > $maxprocesses) {
    $maxprocesses = $currentprocesses;
    $procpercent = int (((100*$maxprocesses)/$proctabsize) + .5);
    print ("$maxprocesses processes out of $proctabsize or $procpercent percent.\n");
  }

# Sleep until next interval.

  sleep ($interval);

} # end while


# Final output processing (presuming we've fallen through the above loop.
# Note: Control-c's and kill's are caught in the signal handler.

&finalreport;

exit;

# Subroutine.

sub finalreport{

# This routine generates the final report giving summary
# information about the maximum values observed.

# Set ending date/time.

  $endtime = time;
```

```perl
# Duration is initially set to the number of seconds this report ran.

  $duration = $endtime - $starttime;

# Divide duration by number of seconds in a day to get
# the number of days.

  $enddays = int ($duration / (60 * 60 * 24 ));

# Divide remainder of duration by number of seconds in an hour to get
# number of hours.

  $duration = $duration - ($enddays * 60 * 60 * 24);
  $endhours = int ($duration / (60 * 60));

# Divide remainder of duration by number of seconds in a minute to get
# number of minutes.

  $duration = $duration - ($endhours * 60 * 60 * 24);
  $endmins = int ($duration / (60 * 60));


# Write the final report.

  write;

}

sub sighandler {

# This routien is used to process ALL signals received by this script
# and is called internally by perl whenever a signal is received.
#
# Called:
#    sighandler = (signal);
#
# Where:
#   signal = signal received (see signal(3V))

 local ($signal) = @_;

# print "Signal $signal received\n";   # for debug purposes

# Process signals of interest.

  if ("$signal" eq "INT" || "$signal" eq "TERM" ) {
    &finalreport;
    exit;
  }
}


# Usage processing.
```

```
sub usage {

# Called:
#   usage (msgtext, value)
#
# Where:
#   msgtext = parameter name to be inserted into the error message
#   value = illegal value for that parameter name

# Assign input parameters.

  ($msgtext, $value) = $@;
  local ($usage);

# Print error message, based upon input parameters.

  $usage =
   "The $msgtext parameter you specified, contained a non-numeric value:
    $value\n",
   "Please try again.\n",
   "\n",
   "Usage: maxpstat [interval [count]]\n" ,
   "  Where: interval = the number of seconds between checks\n",
   "                   count = the number of times to check the pstat values\n",
   "  interval has a default value of 60 (seconds)\n",
   "  count has a default value of infinity (you must type ctl-c to\n",
   "     stop the checking\n";

  die $usage;

}

# Output report file format specification.

format STDOUT =

This script started on @<< @<< @<, @<<< at @<:@<:@<
$DoW[$startwday], $MoY[$startmon], $startmday, $startyear+1900, $starthour,
$startmin, $startsec
and ran for @>> days, @> hours, and @> minutes.
            $enddays, $endhours,      $endmins
During that time the following maximum usage was observed:

@>>> out of @>>> files   or @>> percent of the file table
$maxfiles, $filetabsize, $filepercent
@>>> out of @>>> inodes    or @>> percent of the inode table
$maxinodes,  $inodetabsize,  $inodepercent
@>>> out of @>>> processes or @>> percent of the process table
$maxprocesses,  $proctabsize,  $procpercent.
```

B.3 randomize

B.3.1 Program by John J. Nouveaux

```perl
#!/usr/bin/perl
#
# randomize
#
# This script randomizes the order of lines in an input file.
#
#
# Usage:
#   randomize
#
# Written by: John J. Nouveaux
#
# History:    V1.0 (3/19/92) - initial release.

# Set local variables.

$INPUTFILE = "$ENV{'HOME'}/education/ASA/rev.d/ta.sorted";
# Input file

$OUTPUTFILE = "$ENV{'HOME'}/education/ASA/rev.d/ta.random";
#  customers report file

# Set window header.

print "Reading input file\n";

# Open input file.

open ( INPUTFILE, "<$INPUTFILE" );

# Copy input file to internal array.

$numinlines = 1;
while ( <INPUTFILE> ){
  $inarray [$numinlines] = $_;
  $numinlines++;
} # end while

close ( INPUTFILE );
$numinlines--;

# Generate random number sequence.

print "Generating random numbers\n";

srand (time);
$outindex = 2 * $numinlines;
while ( $outindex != 0 ){
```

```
# Generate pairs of random numbers, and switch those array entries.

  $ran1 = int ( rand ($numinlines)) + 1;
  $ran2 = $ran1;
  while ( $ran2 == $ran1 ) {
    $ran2 = int ( rand ($numinlines)) + 1;
  } # end while

  $tmp = $inarray [$ran1];
  $inarray [$ran1] = $inarray [$ran2];
  $inarray [$ran2] = $tmp;
  $outindex--;
} # end while

# Generate randomized output file.

print "Writing output file\n";

open ( OUTPUTFILE, ">$OUTPUTFILE" )|| die "Can't open $!\n";
$index = $numinlines;
while ( $index != 0 ) {
  print  OUTPUTFILE "$inarray[$index]";
  print "$inarray[$index]";
  $index--;
} # end while

# Done.

print "Finished\n";
exit;
```

Index

About the CD

This CD-ROM has much code and information about PERL and is divided into four main sections:

FAQ	Frequently Ask Questions about Perl related subjects
Ported OS	Source code and binaries for different OS and version of PERL
Scripts	Examples of source code, notes and documentation
TOOLS	Some binaries to aid in unzipping, packing, compressing files

A web browser can be use to navigate around this CD-ROM but it is not required. Descriptions of all programs can be found in the "htm" files for each section and sub-section.

Please read the toplevel.htm file related to code found on this CD-ROM for usage.

There is no installation required for this CD-ROM. Most of the information can be viewed with a web browser. Source code and such may required a C complier, not included on the CD-ROM.

The book comes with a CD-ROM that has source for examples plus a section of free-ware, shareware, and pointers to other code and scripts that can be found on the Internet. Some files and packages were compressed not to save disk space but to allow for the file-name to be intact on the designated OS when they are uncompressed. Be aware that some filenames will exceed the standard ISO9660 filename syntax when compressed onto the hard disk. In some cases, pointers to the actual web site was left intact to allow for the latest and greatest information.

LICENSE AGREEMENT AND LIMITED WARRANTY

READ THE FOLLOWING TERMS AND CONDITIONS CAREFULLY BEFORE OPENING THIS DISK PACKAGE. THIS LEGAL DOCUMENT IS AN AGREEMENT BETWEEN YOU AND PRENTICE-HALL, INC. (THE "COMPANY"). BY OPENING THIS SEALED DISK PACKAGE, YOU ARE AGREEING TO BE BOUND BY THESE TERMS AND CONDITIONS. IF YOU DO NOT AGREE WITH THESE TERMS AND CONDITIONS, DO NOT OPEN THE DISK PACKAGE. PROMPTLY RETURN THE UNOPENED DISK PACKAGE AND ALL ACCOMPANYING ITEMS TO THE PLACE YOU OBTAINED THEM FOR A FULL REFUND OF ANY SUMS YOU HAVE PAID.

1.   **GRANT OF LICENSE:** In consideration of your payment of the license fee, which is part of the price you paid for this product, and your agreement to abide by the terms and conditions of this Agreement, the Company grants to you a nonexclusive right to use and display the copy of the enclosed software program (hereinafter the "SOFTWARE") on a single computer (i.e., with a single CPU) at a single location so long as you comply with the terms of this Agreement. The Company reserves all rights not expressly granted to you under this Agreement.

2.   **OWNERSHIP OF SOFTWARE:** You own only the magnetic or physical media (the enclosed disks) on which the SOFTWARE is recorded or fixed, but the Company retains all the rights, title, and ownership to the SOFTWARE recorded on the original disk copy(ies) and all subsequent copies of the SOFTWARE, regardless of the form or media on which the original or other copies may exist. This license is not a sale of the original SOFTWARE or any copy to you.

3.   **COPY RESTRICTIONS:** This SOFTWARE and the accompanying printed materials and user manual (the "Documentation") are the subject of copyright. You may not copy the Documentation or the SOFTWARE, except that you may make a single copy of the SOFTWARE for backup or archival purposes only. You may be held legally responsible for any copying or copyright infringement which is caused or encouraged by your failure to abide by the terms of this restriction.

4.   **USE RESTRICTIONS:** You may not network the SOFTWARE or otherwise use it on more than one computer or computer terminal at the same time. You may physically transfer the SOFTWARE from one computer to another provided that the SOFTWARE is used on only one computer at a time. You may not distribute copies of the SOFTWARE or Documentation to others. You may not reverse engineer, disassemble, decompile, modify, adapt, translate, or create derivative works based on the SOFTWARE or the Documentation without the prior written consent of the Company.

5.   **TRANSFER RESTRICTIONS:** The enclosed SOFTWARE is licensed only to you and may not be transferred to any one else without the prior written consent of the Company. Any unauthorized transfer of the SOFTWARE shall result in the immediate termination of this Agreement.

6.   **TERMINATION:** This license is effective until terminated. This license will terminate automatically without notice from the Company and become null and void if you fail to comply with any provisions or limitations of this license. Upon termination, you shall destroy the Documentation and all copies of the SOFTWARE. All provisions of this Agreement as to warranties, limitation of liability, remedies or damages, and our ownership rights shall survive termination.

7.   **MISCELLANEOUS:** This Agreement shall be construed in accordance with the laws of the United States of America and the State of New York and shall benefit the Company, its affiliates, and assignees.

8.   **LIMITED WARRANTY AND DISCLAIMER OF WARRANTY:** The Company warrants that the SOFTWARE, when properly used in accordance with the Documentation, will operate in substantial conformity with the description of the SOFTWARE set forth in the Documentation. The Company does not warrant that the SOFTWARE will meet your requirements or that the operation of the SOFTWARE will be

uninterrupted or error-free. The Company warrants that the media on which the SOFTWARE is delivered shall be free from defects in materials and workmanship under normal use for a period of thirty (30) days from the date of your purchase. Your only remedy and the Company's only obligation under these limited warranties is, at the Company's option, return of the warranted item for a refund of any amounts paid by you or replacement of the item. Any replacement of SOFTWARE or media under the warranties shall not extend the original warranty period. The limited warranty set forth above shall not apply to any SOFTWARE which the Company determines in good faith has been subject to misuse, neglect, improper installation, repair, alteration, or damage by you. EXCEPT FOR THE EXPRESSED WARRANTIES SET FORTH ABOVE, THE COMPANY DISCLAIMS ALL WARRANTIES, EXPRESS OR IMPLIED, INCLUDING WITHOUT LIMITATION, THE IMPLIED WARRANTIES OF MERCHANTABILITY AND FITNESS FOR A PARTICULAR PURPOSE. EXCEPT FOR THE EXPRESS WARRANTY SET FORTH ABOVE, THE COMPANY DOES NOT WARRANT, GUARANTEE, OR MAKE ANY REPRESENTATION REGARDING THE USE OR THE RESULTS OF THE USE OF THE SOFTWARE IN TERMS OF ITS CORRECTNESS, ACCURACY, RELIABILITY, CURRENTNESS, OR OTHERWISE.

IN NO EVENT, SHALL THE COMPANY OR ITS EMPLOYEES, AGENTS, SUPPLIERS, OR CONTRACTORS BE LIABLE FOR ANY INCIDENTAL, INDIRECT, SPECIAL, OR CONSEQUENTIAL DAMAGES ARISING OUT OF OR IN CONNECTION WITH THE LICENSE GRANTED UNDER THIS AGREEMENT, OR FOR LOSS OF USE, LOSS OF DATA, LOSS OF INCOME OR PROFIT, OR OTHER LOSSES, SUSTAINED AS A RESULT OF INJURY TO ANY PERSON, OR LOSS OF OR DAMAGE TO PROPERTY, OR CLAIMS OF THIRD PARTIES, EVEN IF THE COMPANY OR AN AUTHORIZED REPRESENTATIVE OF THE COMPANY HAS BEEN ADVISED OF THE POSSIBILITY OF SUCH DAMAGES. IN NO EVENT SHALL LIABILITY OF THE COMPANY FOR DAMAGES WITH RESPECT TO THE SOFTWARE EXCEED THE AMOUNTS ACTUALLY PAID BY YOU, IF ANY, FOR THE SOFTWARE.

SOME JURISDICTIONS DO NOT ALLOW THE LIMITATION OF IMPLIED WARRANTIES OR LIABILITY FOR INCIDENTAL, INDIRECT, SPECIAL, OR CONSEQUENTIAL DAMAGES, SO THE ABOVE LIMITATIONS MAY NOT ALWAYS APPLY. THE WARRANTIES IN THIS AGREEMENT GIVE YOU SPECIFIC LEGAL RIGHTS AND YOU MAY ALSO HAVE OTHER RIGHTS WHICH VARY IN ACCORDANCE WITH LOCAL LAW.

ACKNOWLEDGMENT

YOU ACKNOWLEDGE THAT YOU HAVE READ THIS AGREEMENT, UNDERSTAND IT, AND AGREE TO BE BOUND BY ITS TERMS AND CONDITIONS. YOU ALSO AGREE THAT THIS AGREEMENT IS THE COMPLETE AND EXCLUSIVE STATEMENT OF THE AGREEMENT BETWEEN YOU AND THE COMPANY AND SUPERSEDES ALL PROPOSALS OR PRIOR AGREEMENTS, ORAL, OR WRITTEN, AND ANY OTHER COMMUNICATIONS BETWEEN YOU AND THE COMPANY OR ANY REPRESENTATIVE OF THE COMPANY RELATING TO THE SUBJECT MATTER OF THIS AGREEMENT.

Should you have any questions concerning this Agreement or if you wish to contact the Company for any reason, please contact in writing at the address below.

Robin Short
Prentice Hall PTR
One Lake Street
Upper Saddle River, New Jersey 07458

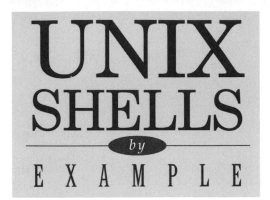
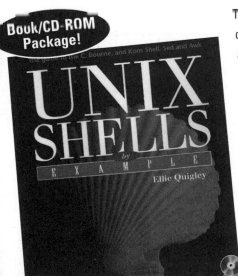

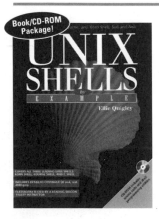